D1177105

BLESSED ARE THE BARREN

BLESSED ARE THE BARREN

The Social Policy of Planned Parenthood

By
Robert G. Marshall
and
Charles A. Donovan

IGNATIUS PRESS   SAN FRANCISCO

Cover by Kelly Connelly

© 1991 Ignatius Press, San Francisco
All rights reserved
ISBN 0–89870–385–9 (HB)
ISBN 0–89870–353–0 (PB)
Library of Congress catalogue number 90–84812
Printed in the United States of America

Contents

A large crowd of people followed Jesus,
including many women who mourned and lamented
him. Jesus turned to them and said,
"Daughters of Jerusalem, do not weep for me,
weep instead for yourselves and your children,
for indeed, the days are coming when people will say,
'Blessed are the barren, the wombs that never bore
and the breasts that never nursed.'
At that time, people will say to the mountains,
'Fall upon us!' and to the hills, 'Cover us!'
for if these things are done when the wood is green
what will happen when it is dry?"

The Way of the Cross
Luke 23:27–31
New American Bible

Foreword

It seems providential that in the same week in which I composed the preface to this exciting, truly encyclopedic, monumental work, it was announced that "Another Sanger heads Planned Parenthood". Alexander Sanger, the grandson of Margaret Sanger, a wealthy Wall Streeter and long-time member of the Board of Planned Parenthood of New York City, was elected president and chief executive officer of that organization. One week after he assumed office he had already committed himself to a firm support of New York City Schools Chancellor Joseph Fernandez's plan to distribute condoms to high school students, and promised to expand the family business from a paltry three clinics in New York City to thirteen, adding: "There are so many areas that are underserved. We currently have a small storefront office in central Harlem, and it is my first priority to see if we can transform that into a clinic."

The French had it right: *plus ça change, plus c'est la même chose* (the more things change, the more they remain the same).

I never had the dubious pleasure of meeting Margaret Sanger, but her adoring biographer Lawrence Lader (with whom I founded NARAL in 1969) assured me repeatedly that she was a charming, brilliant, seductive, and benignly Machiavellian character with a determination quotient off the charts. Indeed. Only an utterly ruthless, steely-nerved manipulator such as Sanger could have parlayed a daring, New Age-style immorality into a massive, multibillion-dollar enterprise so immensely powerful that in many countries (the U.S. included) it is—like its political counterpart, the C.I.A.—a government within a government.

Some years ago, in an excess of curiosity—and through the good offices of the Freedom of Information Act—we obtained the tax returns of Planned Parenthood of New York City for the years 1974–1976. U.S. government grants to PPNYC in 1976 came to just over one million dollars, and total contributions that year came to $3.5 million. Fees earned from abortion services and allied enterprises came to a little over $3 million, hence the total spendable funds for this one operation in New York City added up to approximately $6 million. Glitzy names such as Mrs. Theodore Sorensen, Peter Tufo, Rev. Donald Harrington (long-time head of the Liberal Party here in New York State) turned up serving on the Executive Committee and Board of Directors. Squeaky-clean corporations such as American Airlines,

vii

American Express, Bank of New York, Bristol-Myers, the Celanese Corporation, Drydock Savings Bank, the Squibb Corporation, and Exxon checked in regularly as devoted and dependable contributors and patrons. The New York Times Foundation, the *New Yorker* magazine, the *New York Post,* and the Paley family (CBS) headed the media contingent of donors; the theatrical brigade was spearheaded by Mr. Joseph Papp and Mr. and Mrs. Richard Rodgers. The Rockefeller Foundation kicked in $200,000 in 1974 and $250,000 in 1976; not to be outdone, the Rockefeller Brothers Fund (those Rockefellers are insatiable in their appetite for good works) was in for $300,000 in 1974 and a measly $100,000 in 1976. I pass over in charity the lengthy list of individual contributors from the Rockefeller family; it reads like a list of boxholders for opening night at the Met. Truly, a herd of independent minds.

In 1971, at a major conference on abortion in New York City, I publicly castigated Dr. Alan Guttmacher for his timidity in the abortion arena (Planned Parenthood did not yet have a functioning abortion clinic at a time in which my own clinic had already done 25,000 abortions). He was deeply hurt by my accusation and responded with a slashing counterattack, pointing out that while I was still in medical school he was already devising an end-run around restrictive abortion laws with the invention of the therapeutic abortion committee. I rose and publicly apologized for my intemperate remarks. A week later I received the following letter from him, on Planned Parenthood stationery:

"Dear Bernie:
I apologize for exploding at Saturday morning's meeting but I believe your remarks gave me good reason to do so.
I am very grateful for your retraction and trust that our brief exchange will not interfere with our friendship. I admire very much what you are doing [sic].
With warm personal regards,
Alan

That was a millennium ago scientifically: no ultrasound, no electronic fetal heart monitoring, no concept of the unborn as our second patient.

Alan, Alan, ye hardly knew me.

Bernard Nathanson

Preface

French physician Joseph-Ignace Guillotin was a marvelously democratic fellow. He was distressed that Scotland, England, and various other countries too often restricted decapitation—neat, swift, "painless"—to the execution of criminals of noble birth. Determined that the democratic France of the Revolution would not deprive the poor of that enjoyed by the wealthy, he brought about passage of a law that *all* sentences of death be carried out by "means of a machine".

Hence, the name "guillotine", first used during the French Revolution not on a noble, but on a highwayman. Madame Defarge and her associates could tend to their knitting with clear conscience, then, knowing that the poor had the same access to decapitation as the rich.

The analogy with the argument that abortion must be as available to the poor as to the rich—if not, indeed, made more available—limps badly, of course. Everyone decapitated by the guillotine was at least *alleged* to be a criminal, rich or poor, noble or of low estate. While I *have* heard unborn babies called "aggressors", I am unaware of their ever being labelled criminals. Hence, they should not be compared to the guillotined, I realize, except that the end result is the same: the violent death of human beings, decapitated, crushed, ripped apart, scraped, suffocated, or whatever. And all the while, the world knits, satisfied that the whole business is thoroughly democratic, because no one is deprived of a "right" available to others.

This is a sickening book, terribly difficult for any reader who wants to believe in the integrity of the political system, the judiciary, the legal and medical professions, the decency and reasonableness of people in a whole variety of influential positions. The story of deceit the book relates is devastating. One can recover balance only by setting the book aside after every ten or twelve pages, and reminding oneself of all the good and decent and honest politicians and judges and lawyers and doctors and nurses and social workers and others one knows.

I can pray about this book. I can hope it will distract a "knitter" here or there. But if so few have paid attention to Dr. Bernard Nathanson's published confessions about the way he and his colleagues lied and manipulated and justified their abortion practices "conniving in this twilight zone of surgery", as he puts it, will this book get a serious reading? Dr. Nathanson, now one of the most committed pro-life advocates in the country, has described the whole sordid story of duplicity. The *Washington Post* called his *Aborting America* a "reasoned call to the whole country to rethink what we have sanctioned". Has the whole country listened to that call? Has any Congress since *Roe v. Wade*? Have State legislators far and wide, or educators, or the media? Have physicians or lawyers? Have the organized and powerful forces described in *Blessed are the Barren*?

What can we do but hope and pray and learn. To read this book is to risk disenchantment with much of the most "respectable" elements of the establishment. Not to read is to remain serene, with all the serenity of Madame Defarge.

+ John Cardinal O'Connor

Introduction

Planned Parenthood:
The Organization and Its Founder

At a March 1925 international birth control gathering held in New York City, a speaker warned of the menace posed by the "black" and "yellow" peril.[1] The man was not a National Socialist (Nazi) or a leader of the Ku Klux Klan. The speaker was Dr. S. Adolphus Knopf, a member of Margaret Sanger's American Birth Control League (ABCL), which along with other groups eventually became known as Planned Parenthood. Another doctor at this conference lamented that preventive medicine was saving the lives of "worthless unfits", and he seriously suggested that euthanasia be used to "dispose of some of our utterly hopeless dependents", but noted that this could not happen until the public changed its "prejudices" on the subject.[2]

Not to be outdone by her followers, Planned Parenthood founder Margaret Sanger wired President Coolidge urging him to establish a "Federal Birth Rate Control Commission", which was to have "free access to all facts and statistics as to all customs and conditions now menacing the racial health of our country".[3] This suggestion was in line with her opening address in which she suggested to the delegates a system of bonuses "to decrease or to restrict the incessant and uninterrupted advent of the hoards of the unfit".[4]

Elsewhere Sanger spoke of her plan for sterilizing those she designated as "unfit" as the "salvation of American civilization".[5] And she also spoke of those who were "irresponsible and reckless", among whom she included those "whose religious scruples prevent their exercising control over their numbers".[6] She further contended that "there is no doubt in the minds of all thinking people that the procreation of this group should be stopped".[7] Whether this

[1] S. Adolphus Knopf, M.D., "The Survival of the Unfit", vol. 3, in *Proceedings—Sixth International Neo-Malthus and Birth Control Conference,* published and copyright by the American Birth Control League (ABCL), 1926, 197.

[2] Ibid., Dr. Max Schloff, 149.

[3] Ibid., vol. 1, 243–44.

[4] Margaret Sanger, "Welcome Address", ibid., vol. 1, 7

[5] Margaret Sanger, *Birth Control Review* (October 1926): 229. References to *Birth Control Review* were found in a reprint edition (New York: Da Capo Press, 1970).

[6] Margaret Sanger, First American Birth Control Conference, November 11–12, 1921, *Proceedings,* 172.

[7] Ibid.

1

was to be accomplished "voluntarily" does not appear to have been a serious policy impediment.

That many Americans of African origin constituted a segment the Sangerites considered as "unfit" can be denied only with great difficulty and in the face of policies that affirm this assumption. At one point Sanger expressed a fear that Negroes might think birth control a clever extermination project, but that selected black ministers could dispose of that idea.[8]

Sanger's other colleagues included avowed and sophisticated racists.[9] One, Lothrop Stoddard, was a Harvard graduate and the author of *The Rising Tide of Color against White Supremacy*.[10] Stoddard was something of a Nazi enthusiast who described the eugenic practices of the Third Reich as "scientific" and "humanitarian".[11] And Dr. Harry Laughlin, another Sanger associate and board member of her group, described Slavic and Italian immigrants as "even inferior to our native Negro population not long released from slavery".[12] Laughlin also spoke of purifying America's human "breeding stock" and purging America's "bad strains".[13] These "strains" included the "shiftless, ignorant, and worthless class of antisocial whites of the South".[14]

Laughlin apparently was the inspiration for the NAZI compulsory sterilization law passed in 1933. Under its provisions, nearly two million people were forcibly sterilized from 1933 to 1945.[15]

These eugenic and racial origins are hardly what most people associate with the modern Planned Parenthood Federation of America (PPFA), which gave its Margaret Sanger award to the late Dr. Martin Luther King in 1966,[16] and whose current president, Faye Wattleton, is black, a former nurse, and very appealing.

Though once a social pariah group routinely castigated by religious and government leaders, the PPFA is now an established, high-profile, well-funded organization with ample organizational and ideological support in

[8] See Clarence Gamble, M.D., "Suggestions for a Negro Project", November 1939; and Margaret Sanger letter to Gamble, December 10, 1939, Sophie Smith Collection, Smith College (hereafter referred to as SSCSC).

[9] Allan Chase, *The Legacy of Malthus: The Social Costs of the New Scientific Racism* (New York: Alfred A. Knopf, 1975), 54.

[10] Cited in Havelock Ellis, "The World's Racial Problems", *Birth Control Review* (October 1920): 16.

[11] Lothrop Stoddard, *Into the Darkness* (New York: Duell, Sloan, and Pierce, 1940), 196.

[12] Guy Irving Burch, news article about the U.S. House of Representatives Immigration Hearings, citing testimony of Harry Laughlin, *Birth Control Review* (November 1926): 345.

[13] Harry H. Laughlin, "Calculations on the Working out of a Proposed Program of Sterilization", *Proceedings of the First National Conference on Race Betterment, January 8–12, 1914*, Race Betterment Association, Battle Creek, Michigan, 478–84.

[14] Chase, *Legacy of Malthus*, 313.

[15] Ibid., 135.

[16] See *Congressional Record*, May 23, 1966, S-11194.

high places of American society and government. Its statistics are accepted by major media and public health figures as "gospel"; its full page ads appear in major newspapers; its spokesmen are called upon to give authoritative analyses of what America's family policies should be and to prescribe official answers that congressmen, state legislators, and Supreme Court justices all accept as "social orthodoxy".

How this transformation happened is the subject of this study.

Chapter One

Margaret Sanger:
The Founding Mother of Birth Control

Emerson's dictum that institutions are lengthened shadows of their founders applies to Margaret Sanger as it applies to few others. Margaret Higgins Sanger, the sixth of eleven children, was born in 1879 to a Catholic mother and an agnostic father in Corning, New York. Though baptized a Catholic she abandoned the Church early in her youth. She had wanted to study medicine at Cornell, but later went to a practical nursing school in White Plains, New York.

In 1911 she began a long career of radical activism working with such leftist stalwarts as Emma Goldman, Eugene Debs, Bill Heywood, and later with John Reed, the author of the Red Revolutionary tract, *Ten Days That Shook the World.* Reed is the only American whose remains are interred inside the Kremlin. (Sanger helped finance his trip to Russia.)[1] During this period, she addressed her letters to "Comrades and Friends". She also supported the International Workers of the World, the United World Federalists, the Euthanasia Society of America, the American Civil Liberties Union, and the Federal Council of Churches.[2]

It was during this time in her life that Sanger "learned the propaganda techniques that were later to stand her in such good stead".[3] As Sanger tells it, the turning point in her life came in 1913, when she vowed to spread the knowledge of birth control ostensibly to prevent recurrences of deaths like that of Sadie Sachs, a poor mother who died from a second, self-induced abortion.[4] Biographers have disputed the complete accuracy of this account and note that Sanger was, at times, dishonest about her own life. She falsified her birth date on passports and even in the family Bible.[5]

The woman who would become the Carrie Nation of contraception claims

[1] Letter of J. A. K. of Milbank Memorial Fund to K. A. Umansky, Foreign Office, Moscow, U.S.S.R., June 25, 1934, Margaret Sanger Collection, Library of Congress, (hereinafter referred to as MSCLC).

[2] Memos of contributions and notes for 1947, 1948, 1950, MSCLC.

[3] Madeline Gray, *Margaret Sanger: A Biography of the Champion of Birth Control* (New York: Marek, 1979), 37.

[4] Margaret Sanger and John Connolly, Jr., "Does the Public Want Birth Control?" *True Confessions,* April 1936, 78.

[5] Gray, *Margaret Sanger,* 13, 37.

she spent the next year after Sadie Sachs' death hunting for information on birth control in such places as the Library of Congress. She apparently came up empty handed. Biographer David Kennedy points out, however, that she could not have looked very hard because the Library of Congress contained a two-page list of books and articles on birth control compiled by the U.S. Army Surgeon General's Office in 1878.[6]

In any case after further research overseas, some of Sanger's early "contraceptive" concoctions included bizarre antifertility nostrums such as psychic "magnatation methods".[7] Others were useless or capable of causing immediate or long range physical damage. She suggested Beecham's Pills, a laxative, or castor oil; quinine with water; one teaspoon of lysol with 2 quarts water; bichloride and water; potassium permanganate and water; boric acid, alum, citric acid, hydrochlorate of quinine.[8] Little wonder that the doctors of her day called some of her methods "filthy, untested, and unsafe".[9] Moreover, some of her laxative "remedies" were clearly abortifacient in their intent, notwithstanding their ineffectiveness.[10]

Margaret's first marriage was to architect William Sanger. She was unfaithful to him, even suggesting that he take a mistress.[11] Alleging that her "necessities were thwarting or dwarfing his progress", she would later leave him.[12]

Sanger was something of a sexual adventurer and high society camp follower who, in today's vernacular, liked to party. Mildred Dodge wrote of her that "she was the first person I ever knew who was openly an ardent propagandist for the joys of the flesh. This in those days was radical indeed."[13]

One of Sanger's lovers was English sexologist Havelock Ellis. Other paramours included English writers Hugh de Selincourt, Harold Child, and H. G. Wells, who once called her the "greatest woman in the world".[14] She had what is now called a "trial marriage" with Corey Alberson and liaisons with her lawyer J. G. Goldstein, American architect Angus S. MacDonald, and several more. She had "crushes" on two female class-

---

[6] David Kennedy, *Birth Control in America: The Career of Margaret Sanger* (New Haven: Yale University Press, 1970), 19.

[7] Magnatation Methods of Birth Control, n.d., MSCLC.

[8] Margaret Sanger, *Family Limitation,* 1st ed., 1914, 8–9, MSCLC.

[9] Gray, *Margaret Sanger,* 280–81.

[10] Margaret Sanger, *Family Limitation,* 1st ed., 1914, 15–16, MSCLC.

[11] Gray, *Margaret Sanger,* 65.

[12] Margaret Sanger, *Margaret Sanger, an Autobiography* (Long Island, N.Y.: Dover Publishers, 1971), 148.

[13] Quoted in Gray, *Margaret Sanger,* 59.

[14] Quoted in Emily Taft Douglas, *Margaret Sanger: Pioneer of the Future* (New York: Holt, Rinehart, and Winston, 1970), 1.

mates, which drew comments.[15] In 1922 she would marry Three-in-One oil magnate J. Noah Slee of South Africa. They agreed to have what would be called in modern terms "an open marriage".[16] Slee's wealth would later enable her to pursue her cause in ways she could only dream of during her overtly radical phase.

In her early activist days Sanger took it upon herself to found a feminist magazine, at a time when female publishers of any sort were rare. Not one for nuance in serious matters, she called her magazine the *Woman Rebel,* and she appended the words, "No Gods, No Masters" below the masthead. The brawling publication saw as its mission "to look the whole world in the face with a go-to-hell-look in the eyes . . . to speak and act in defiance of convention".[17] The *Woman Rebel* claimed the right to "be lazy . . . an unmarried mother . . . to create . . . to destroy . . . to love".[18]

Other issues of the *Woman Rebel* supported birth control and abortion; denounced capitalism; railed against St. Paul; claimed "the marriage bed is the most degenerating influence of the social order . . . a decadent institution, a reactionary development of the sex instinct"; the remedy was to give women total "control of their reproductive functions".[19]

Perhaps seeking to ensure that she would be indicted, Sanger included an article in the July 1914 issue endorsing political assassination.[20] Her timing could not have been worse: World War I would start later that month as the result of the July 28 assassination of Austrian Archduke Francis Ferdinand. In the September–October 1914 *Woman Rebel* she published the August 24, 1914, federal indictment citing her for publishing articles in violation of the federal anticontraception/abortion/obscenity "Comstock" law and for the assassination article.[21] Besides attracting prosecution, her efforts also galvanized her followers.

In November 1914 Sanger fled to England via Canada, leaving her family behind. She wired friends to distribute her birth control pamphlet, *Family Limitation.*[22] William Sanger was arrested by Anthony Comstock himself for possession of the offending birth control pamphlet.[23] She returned

---

[15] Gray, *Margaret Sanger,* 22.

[16] Kennedy, *Birth Control in America,* 99; Gray, *Margaret Sanger,* 192.

[17] Margaret Sanger, *The Woman Rebel and the Rise of the Birth Control Movement in the United States* (Stony Brook, N.Y.: State University of New York at Stoneybrook, 1976), vol. 1, no. 1, 1.

[18] Ibid., vol. 1, no. 1, 3.

[19] Ibid., vol. 1, no. 2, 10; vol. 1, no. 3, 20; vol. 1, no. 5, 33.

[20] Ibid., vol. 1, no. 5, 33.

[21] Ibid., vol. 1, no. 7, 49.

[22] Sanger, *Autobiography,* 121–22.

[23] Letter of Margaret Sanger to "Comrades and Friends", February 4, 1915, MSCLC.

home in October 1915 with the indictments still pending, though the federal charges were dropped in February 1916.[24]

In October 1916 she opened the first American birth control clinic in the Brownsville section of Brooklyn, New York. As a result she was arrested for violating the state of New York's "Comstock" law, which prohibited the dissemination of birth control information. She was later convicted of violating the New York anti–birth control law.

Sanger appealed her conviction to the New York State Supreme Court, which on January 8, 1918, upheld one section of the penal code against her that forbade the distribution, sale, or advertizing of contraceptives. But the court provided a wedge for Sanger by interpreting section 145 of the penal code to exempt physicians who prescribed or distributed contraceptives "for the cure of disease".[25] This tiny crack in New York State's "Comstock" law "moved the American birth control movement decades ahead".[26]

But Sanger had lost no time waiting for the outcome of her case. In February 1917 she founded the *Birth Control Review*, serving as its editor until 1929. In 1921 the *Birth Control Review* was taken over by the American Birth Control League, which Sanger had also founded. The ABCL was the parent organization of Planned Parenthood, and it was legally established as a corporation on April 22, 1922, though its officials had come together first at the establishment of Sanger's 1916 birth control clinic.[27]

Under Sanger's editorship, three themes were constant: (1) the value of birth control in promoting social goods such as personal health, family life, economic stability, liberation from biological slavery, and world peace; (2) opposition to birth control came from militarists and Catholics—primarily the bishops and, of course, their servile Protestant supporters, and (3) birth control would eliminate disease, crime, and the burden of the socially and/or eugenically unfit having children.

While Planned Parenthood's current apologists try to place some distance between the eugenics and birth control movements, history definitively says otherwise. The eugenic theme figured prominently in the *Birth Control Review*'s table of contents. Sanger published such articles as "Some Moral Aspects

[24] Letter of Margaret Sanger to "Comrades and Friends", January 5, 1916, MSCLC; also see Sanger, *Autobiography*, 185, 189.

[25] Copy of judgment, *The People of the State of New York v. Margaret Sanger*, January 8, 1918, MSCLC.

[26] Dr. Alan F. Guttmacher, "Margaret Sanger's New Look", *Family Planning Perspectives*, vol. 2, no. 3 (June 1970), 50.

[27] Restated Certificate of Incorporation of Planned Parenthood Federation of America, Inc., approved by the New York State Supreme Court, Justice Birdie Amsterdam, March, 1972; see Planned Parenthood Federation, Inc., *Annual Report*, 1980; prepared testimony of Faye Wattleton, March 31, 1981, before U.S. Senate Labor and Human Resources Subcommittee, chairman, Sen. Jeremiah Denton (R–Ala.).

of Eugenics" (June 1920), "The Eugenic Conscience" (February 1921), "The Purpose of Eugenics" (December 1924), "Birth Control and Positive Eugenics" (July 1925), "Birth Control: The True Eugenics" (August 1928), and many others.

Her own views on this topic were quite clear, even if crudely expressed as on the masthead of the December 1921 *Birth Control Review* where she emblazoned "Birth Control: To Create a Race of Thoroughbreds". She explained how birth control fit in with the barnyard "approach" to human generation:

> Birth Control is thus the entering wedge for the Eugenic educator . . . the unbalance between the birth rate of the 'unfit' and the 'fit' admittedly the greatest present menace to civilization . . . The most urgent problem today is how to limit and discourage the overfertility of the mentally and physically defective.[28]

The problems Sanger faced in trying to translate her views into public policy in the 1920s are difficult to appreciate if one's only reference point is the sexual and social atmosphere of the post-Pill era. Birth control paraphernalia are now on grocery store shelves. Cable TV viewers see birth control commercials. Public service spots advertize items that would have earned an indictment thirty years ago. In 1988 a little over 107 million American households received a congressionally mandated mailing from the U.S. Surgeon General urging condom use in heterosexual and homosexual liaisons as a means of AIDS (acquired immunodeficiency syndrome) prevention.

But in the 1920s, the entire social order—religion, law, politics, medicine, the media—was arrayed against the idea and practice of birth control. The proximate origin of this opposition began in 1873 when an overwhelmingly Protestant Congress passed, and a Protestant president signed into law, a bill that became known as the Comstock Law, named after its main proponent, Anthony Comstock. The U.S. Congress classified obscene writing, along with drugs, devices, and articles that prevented conception or caused abortion, under the same net of criminality and forbade their importation or mailing.[29] By 1926 at least twenty-three of the forty-eight states and Puerto Rico made it illegal to publish or advertise birth control information. Other state restrictions included prohibitions on possessing, making, and disseminating information on, or directing someone to secure, birth control drugs or devices.[30]

Sanger set out to have such legislation abolished or amended by the Congress or the state legislatures or declared invalid by the courts. Although she would eventually win her point in the federal judiciary, her initial efforts

---

[28] Margaret Sanger, *Birth Control Review* (October 1921): 5.

[29] U. S. Statutes at Large, 42d Congress, 1873.

[30] Marie Stopes, *Contraception* (London: Putnam's and Sons, 1932), 372–73; U.S. Senate Judiciary Subcommittee Hearings on S. 4582, Birth Control Hearings, 71st Congress, 3rd Session, February 13–14, 1931, testimony of William F. Montovan.

were directed at the Congress with the opening of a Washington, D.C. office of her American Birth Control League in 1926.[31] Sanger wanted to amend section 211 of the U.S. criminal code to allow the interstate shipment and mailing of contraceptives among physicians, druggists, and drug manufacturers.[32]

During January and February of 1926, Sanger and her co-workers personally interviewed forty senators and fourteen representatives. None agreed to introduce a bill to amend the Comstock Act.[33] Fresh from this unanimous rejection, Sanger issued an update to her followers:

> Everywhere there is general acceptance of the idea, except in religious circles.... The National Catholic Welfare Council [sic] [NCWC] has a special legislative committee organized to block and defeat our legislation. They frankly state that they intend to legislate for non-Catholics according to the dictates of the church.[34]

There was no such committee.[35] But twenty non-Catholic lay or religious organizations joined the NCWC in opposition to amending the Comstock Act.[36] This was not the first time, nor was it to be the last, that Sanger sought to stir up sectarian strife by blaming Catholics for her legislative failures. Catholic-baiting was a standard tactic (one that Planned Parenthood still finds useful to this day), although other Christian groups now also come in for criticism.

Sanger published the views of a select list of congressmen and senators in the May 1926 *Birth Control Review,* telling her readers, in effect, to become single-issue voters: "Make your political interest this year a vote for the man who will support Birth Control Legislation".[37] Sanger found that the tactics of the ABCL Congressional Committee were not aggressive enough, as they consistently failed to convince even one congressional sponsor to support amending the Comstock Act.

Once again she formed another front group, the National Committee on Federal Legislation for Birth Control, which operated under her direction from 1929 through 1936. Although four senators and five representatives quietly introduced Comstock repeal measures and several hearings were held,

---

[31] "Notice", *Birth Control Review,* vol. 10, no. 1 (January 1926): 5.

[32] Ibid.

[33] Sanger, Report to the Congressional Committee of the American Birth Control League, March 1926, MSCLC, 7. Mimeo.

[34] American Birth Control League, *Newsletter,* March 1926, Margaret Sanger, president, MSCLC.

[35] Rev. John Burke, General Secretary, NCWC, letter to Margaret Sanger, April 21, 1926, MSCLC.

[36] Kennedy of the ABCL to Sanger's congressional committee supporters, undated memo, MSCLC.

[37] Margaret Sanger, *Birth Control Review* (May 1926): 163.

none of the bills became law. She was opposed by the American Federation of Labor, and the American Medical Association (AMA) also refused to support her.[38] Congressman John W. McCormack, who later became Speaker of the House, said of Sanger's proposal, "I can conceive of no more dangerous piece of legislation to the future of America than this pending bill."[39]

She did receive support, however, from a majority of the Committee on Marriage and the Home of the Federal Council of Churches (later the National Council of Churches). This committee was composed largely of prominent Protestants.[40] This prompted an editorial reply from the *Washington Post* on March 22, 1931, which, from today's perspective, seems somewhat prophetic:

> It is impossible to reconcile the doctrine of the divine institution of marriage with any modernistic plan for the mechanical regulation of birth. The church must either reject the plain teachings of the Bible or reject schemes for the "scientific" production of souls.... The committee's report... would sound the death knell of marriage as a holy institution ... [and] would encourage indiscriminate immorality. The suggestion that the use of legalized contraceptives would be "careful and restrained" [by married couples only] is preposterous.[41]

Also a number of Protestant church bodies publicly repudiated the committee's endorsement.[42]

But Sanger and her liberal religious allies let the impression remain that the contest for and against preserving the Comstock Act was a Catholic versus Protestant one. And it must be remembered that it was only in 1930 that the first Christian body, the Anglican Bishops of England, issued a nonbinding directive to members that allowed the use of artificial contraceptives in certain cases.

But Sanger eventually drove a wedge into the Comstock Act in a court case she contrived with a Japanese friend who sent Dr. Hannah Stone a package of 120 birth control devices for experimental use at Sanger's clinic. On December 7, 1936, a three-judge panel of the Federal Court of Appeals overturned part of the Comstock Act, stating:

> [W]e are satisfied that this statute ... embraced only such articles as Congress would have denounced as immoral if it had understood all the conditions under which they were to be used. Its design ... was not to prevent the importation, sale, or carriage of things which might be employed by

---

[38] Senate Judiciary Subcommittee, *Birth Control Hearings*, 71st Congress, 3d sess., February 13–14, 1931, S. 4582, 70–71, testimony of Edward F. McGrady and letter of Mr. Woodward to Sen. Norris, 31.

[39] Ibid., testimony of Rep. John McCormack, 50.

[40] David Goldstein, *Suicide Bent: Sangerizing Mankind* (St. Paul, Mn.: Radio Replies Press, 1945), 88–90.

[41] Editorial, *Washington Post*, March 22, 1931.

[42] Goldstein, *Suicide Bent*, 90.

conscientious and competent physicians for the purpose of saving life or promoting the well-being of their patients.[43]

"Well-being" in this context took on the same broad meaning that "health" did nearly half a century later in the U.S. Supreme Court's abortion decisions. If a legislature had devised it, the Court would no doubt have voided it for vagueness. At Dr. Stone's trial, Dr. Frederick C. Holden appeared as a witness and specified that the cases where it was medically proper to prescribe a contraceptive included: where a mother had TB, heart or kidney disease, diabetes or goiter; if either parent had epilepsy or mental deficiency; if children were "improperly" spaced; or if the family lacked sufficient food, clothing, and shelter for health and welfare.[44]

Since available contraceptives did not prevent or cure diseases, the result in the Stone case represented an important turning point in the medicalization of birth control: The mental sufficiency, family size, and relative poverty of generally healthy people all instantly became the province of the physician and the property of his clinical judgment. The physician was beginning a transition to social architect. As a consequence, the reinterpretation of child-bearing also began, with the logically certain result that children—particularly "unwanted" children—could be reclassified as either a disease or its most dysgenic symptom.

Having achieved this court-created crack in the national Comstock law, Sanger abandoned her federal committee in 1937. Planned Parenthood continued to use the path of judicial legislation, with great success as the years went on.

From this time on, human sexuality would increasingly fall under the sphere of medicine rather than morals, although it would soon be clear that the criterion of health was often little more than a convenient cover for hedonism.

The ABCL was able to expand its operations quickly in states that did not have operative Comstock laws of their own. By June 1937 the ABCL had affiliates in the following states: Arkansas, Connecticut, Delaware, Florida, Illinois, Iowa, Indiana, Maine, Massachusetts, Michigan, Missouri, Minnesota, Nebraska, New Jersey, New York, North Dakota, Pennsylvania, Rhode Island, Virginia, and Washington.[45] The Arkansas affiliate was called the "Arkansas Eugenic Association", while in Missouri the affiliate was known

---

[43] *U.S. v. One Package* 86 F.2d 737 (C.C.A. 2d 1936), affirming 13 F. Supp. 334 (S.D., N.Y. 1936).

[44] Morris L. Ernst and Alexander Lindsay, *The Censor Marches On* (New York: Doubleday, Doran, and Co., Inc., 1940) 162–63.

[45] *Birth Control Review* (January 1934): 7; ibid. (June 1937): 1.

as the "Maternal Health League". In a few states where Comstock laws regarding the provision of birth control services remained in effect, some affiliates had to be satisfied with letter writing or lectures.

Sanger's "One Package" decision also left the official medical organizations free to take their first cautious steps toward approving birth control. Thus in 1937, the American Medical Association House of Delegates gave limited, formal approval to birth control. The AMA resolution provided for: clarification of doctors' legal rights in advising or providing birth control, testing of birth control devices, providing medical students with birth control instruction, and urging that all such dispensaries, clinics, etc., be under medical supervision.[46]

With birth control attaining legality under limited conditions, the federal Internal Revenue Service issued a ruling granting the ABCL tax-exempt status on March 2, 1938.[47]

But as Sanger would find out, legality was one thing, and state and federal promotion of birth control was another. One project Sanger had initiated around this time to remedy this problem was carried out by the "Committee on Public Progress", which had been engaged in a letter-writing campaign to key federal officials, such as Miss Katherine F. Lenroot, chief of the Children's Bureau, U.S. Department of Labor. Lenroot would be especially sensitive to pressure for the inclusion of birth control in Children's Bureau programs for several reasons.

First, the Children's Bureau administered the Maternal and Child Health title of the Social Security program. Second, the Children's Bureau had conducted a widely publicized study that Planned Parenthood had been using as justification for birth control.[48]

Adding to the indignation that fueled the Committee on Public Progress (CPP) campaign were Lenroot's first responses to Sanger's epistolary associates. Sanger associate Dr. Clarence Gamble was told, "It has been the consistent policy of the Children's Bureau to take no positions with reference to birth control."[49] Lenroot also told another CPP member:

> I am greatly concerned about the problems confronting children in America today, but I am much more concerned about policies that will increase family income and provide health and social services for children than I am

[46] Ibid. (June 1937): 1.

[47] Letter from J. F. Wortley, chief, Exempt Organizations, Internal Revenue Service, Treasury Department, January 26, 1962 to PPFA.

[48] Information sheet, U.S. Children's Bureau, BCFA, MSCLC.

[49] Letter from Katherine F. Lenroot, chief of the Children's Bureau, U.S. Department of Labor, to Dr. Clarence Gamble, March 31, 1938, MSCLC; other March 1938 letters also in files.

about policies which will restrict still more the number of children born in this country.[50]

Members of the CPP were given a "fact" sheet with which to bombard Lenroot. The sheet suggested that if the U.S. Children's Bureau included birth control as part of its efforts to improve maternal and infant health, the number of induced abortions would decrease and all children could be wanted children.[51]

Mary Irene Adkinson, director of the Bureau's Child Welfare Division, responded to a CPP member in July 1938 that birth control was "in the first place controversial, and in the second place, is primarily a matter of public health" (i.e., it was not a welfare issue).[52] Furthermore, the inclusion of birth control in a welfare program would threaten its very existence by opening it to selective political attack.[53]

When the CPP targeted other federal health officials for letters, they received similar replies. Assistant U.S. Surgeon General Robert Oleson wrote a CPP member in October 1938 that no legal authority existed for either the Children's Bureau or the U.S. Public Health Service to engage in birth control activities. He also wrote:

> You state in your communication to the President, "Religion should be adjusted to serve mankind." However, the achievement of this would appear to require a dictatorship. It so happens that a considerable portion of our population objects to the public teaching of birth control measures and this opposition is neither to be lightly regarded nor ignored. It is quite likely that the giving of offense to this group might very readily jeopardize some of the Congressional appropriations now made to the Public Health Service for other purposes.
>
> I feel too that there is no such unanimity of opinion among physicians as would enable birth control measures to be applied on a scale satisfactory to its proponents.[54]

One CPP letter writer urged Harry Hopkins, administrator of the Works Progress Administration (WPA), to spend relief money on birth control, or

---

[50] Letter from Katherine F. Lenroot, chief of the Children's Bureau, U.S. Department of Labor, to Mrs. Emeth Tuttle Cochran, member CPP, West Park Avenue, Tallahassee, Florida, March 14, 1938, MSCLC.

[51] ABCL information sheet, U.S. Children's Bureau, MSCLC.

[52] Letter of Mary Irene Adkinson, director, Child Welfare Division of the Labor Department's Children's Bureau, to Mrs. Tom Ragland, 981 Frances St., Knoxville, Tennessee, July 16, 1938, MSCLC.

[53] Ibid.

[54] Reply of Assistant U.S. Surgeon General Robert Oleson to an October 11, 1938, letter from Professor John L. Buys, St. Laurence University, Department of Biology, Canton, N.Y. October 18, 1938, MSCLC.

the country would be populated primarily by offspring of mentally deficient parents.[55] The letter also pointed out that a set of black women using birth control had just as many children as their non-contracepting neighbors.[56] Was this a hint, perhaps, that more drastic measures were needed to curb these ineffective contraceptors from an "overproduction" of births?

In any case, it appears that a small amount of WPA money may have indirectly helped Planned Parenthood through maternal health referrals, since at the peak of WPA activities, there were four thousand nurses and seven thousand doctors employed in the field of postnatal care nationwide.[57] However, no money was earmarked in Washington for birth control purposes.

By June 1, 1939, a tally of CPP efforts showed that over 48,000 letters had been sent soliciting participation in the CPP. This produced a net membership of 2,803 letter writers. A total of 1,341 wrote the Children's Bureau; 717 wrote the U.S. Public Health Service; and 1,766 wrote Harry Hopkins' WPA.[58] This seemingly small number of letters eventually paid off, if only because the campaign alerted sympathetic bureaucrats who then "silently" campaigned for the birth control cause with superiors and collaborated with outside help as well.

The CPP campaign continued for some time after the ABCL and Sanger's Clinical Bureau had been renamed the Birth Control Federation of America (BCFA). This second change in Planned Parenthood's name was necessitated by the January 1939 merger of the Margaret Sanger Clinical Research Bureau with the ABCL and its state leagues.[59] Sanger emerged as honorary chairman of the BCFA and other "old hands" were given positions on newly formed committees. But policy initiatives, with the notable exception of the development of the birth control pill, would come more and more from the organization she had spawned, and less and less from specialized units like the CPP or Sanger herself.

By March 1939 the BCFA had added individual state representatives in New Hampshire, Oklahoma, Kentucky, North Carolina, West Virginia, Vermont, and the District of Columbia. They also added affiliated organizations in the states of North Carolina, Texas, and Vermont; in the cities of Milwaukee, Wisconsin, and Kansas City; and in Alameda County (Oakland), California.[60]

But increased support still left private money as the mainstay for birth control services, with only two states—North and South Carolina—permitting

[55] Letter of R. E. Newell, M.D., 17 West 11th St., N.Y., N.Y., to Harry Hopkins, administrator of the Works Progress Administration, November 21, 1938, MSCLC.

[56] Ibid.

[57] ABCL information sheet: *WPA and Public Health,* MSCLC.

[58] Public Progress Report, totals to June 1, 1939, MSCLC. Mimeo.

[59] *Birth Control Review,* vol. 23, nos. 5–6 (February–March 1939): 159; ibid., 162.

[60] Ibid., 182–83.

birth control services to be offered as a part of its public health program by April 1939.[61] But even these efforts were quite modest. In North Carolina, which inaugurated its program in mid-1937, a report on the program's first eighteen months of operation showed that birth control advice had been given to 1,140 wives.[62] In South Carolina, officials had sought no newspaper publicity for the project.[63]

In other states the BCFA's efforts would not fare as well. Maryland Public Health director Dr. R. H. Riley responded in three days to a CPP solicitation, saying: "I feel we have no place in our program for the establishment of contraceptive center [sic] for the under-privileged."[64] In Florida, Sanger herself received a same-day reply letter from Edward M. L'Engle, M.D., the director of the Florida State Board of Health, who wrote that: "... I do not feel that the State Board of Health should take official action in what is still a controversial question without the approval of organized medicine in Florida."[65] In Tennessee, the State Department of Public Welfare had only a tenuous connection with a birth control program for "maternity hygiene", and that was financed by private funds. State welfare commissioner Paul Savage reported that: "No appropriation was set up by the last legislature for birth control work in this or any other Department ... it is my belief that if the state is to sponsor a birth control movement, such sponsorship should be under the Department of Public Health."[66]

Given the resistance of state welfare officials to the inclusion of birth control programs in their services, the birth control program could expand only if it had a conservative, medical basis. For example, in 1939 the Georgia State Medical Society endorsed a resolution supporting the distribution of birth control information by licensed physicians, public health officials, or county health officers, but only for child-spacing and "for the protection of the life of the expectant mother".[67]

But again, mere legality and more affiliates did not translate into social

[61] Article, "South Carolina Adds Birth Control to its Public Health Program", *Birth Control Review* (December 1939): 27–28.

[62] Unsigned article, "North Carolina Leads the Way", *Birth Control Review* (December 1938): 143.

[63] See n. 61.

[64] Reply of Dr. R. H. Riley, Maryland Public Health director, to November 1, 1938, letter of Miss Alice E. Frame, Woodlawn Road, Baltimore, Maryland, November 4, 1938, MSCLC.

[65] Letter of Edward M. L'Engle, M.D., director, Florida State Board of Health, December 20, 1938, responding to letter of Margaret Sanger, December 17, 1938 MSCLC.

[66] Reply of Mr. Paul Savage, commissioner, Tennessee Department of Public Welfare, to March 28, 1939, letter of Mr. C. Arthur Bruce, E. L. Bruce Company, Memphis, Tennessee, April 4, 1939, MSCLC.

[67] News from the States, *Birth Control Review* (May 1939): 209.

acceptability, or absence of controversy. The tenor of the times is clear in an article writer and radio news commentator Fulton Oursler of the Blue Network of the National Broadcasting Company (NBC) wrote for *Liberty* magazine

> Mahatma Gandhi and Margaret Sanger were to debate the question of birth control. I was not allowed to mention even these words on the air. I was told that only an expert could discuss birth control or be mentioned in connection with it. I asked if Margaret Sanger were not an expert on birth control. I was told that only a doctor was an expert.[68]

While NBC might not have recognized Margaret Sanger as an expert of any sort in 1939, her manipulative talents displayed themselves most impressively that year in setting a permanent foundation for her birth control goals for minorities. In 1930 her fervor had resulted in an offer of $5,000 from the Julius Rosenwald Fund in Chicago for the establishment of a birth control clinic in Harlem's black section.[69] Busy with other aspects of her movement, her first outreach to the black community was largely limited to her Harlem clinic and speaking at black churches.[70]

It was only in 1939 that Sanger's larger vision for dealing with the reproductive practices of black Americans emerged. After the January 1939 merger of her Clinical Research Bureau and the ABCL to form the Birth Control Federation of America, Dr. Clarence J. Gamble was selected to become the BCFA regional director for the South.[71] Dr. Gamble, of the soap-manufacturing Proctor and Gamble company, was no newcomer to Sanger's organization. He had previously served as director at large to the predecessor ABCL.[72]

Gamble lost no time and drew up a memorandum in November 1939 entitled "Suggestions for Negro Project". Acknowledging that black leaders might regard birth control as an extermination plot, he suggested that black leaders be placed in positions where it would appear that they were in charge—as had been done previously at a birth control conference in Atlanta.[73]

It is evident from the rest of the memo that Gamble conceived the project almost as a traveling road show. A charismatic black minister was to start a revival, with "contributions" to come from other local cooperating ministers. A black nurse would follow, supported by a subsidized black doctor.

---

[68] Fulton Oursler, "They Wouldn't Let Me Tell It on the Air", *Liberty,* September 23, 1939, copy in MSCLC.

[69] Letter from Edwin B. Embre, president, Julius Rosenwald Fund, Chicago, to Margaret Sanger, April 29, 1930, MSCLC.

[70] Gray, *Margaret Sanger,* 337, 343.

[71] *Birth Control Review,* vol. 23, nos. 5–6 (February–March 1939): 162, 172.

[72] *Birth Control Review,* vol. 22, no. 6 (March 1938): 71.

[73] Gamble memo, "Suggestions for Negro Project" memorandum, November 1939, SSCSC.

Gamble even suggested that music might be a useful lure to bring the prospects to a meeting.[74]

Sanger answered Gamble on December 10, 1939, agreeing with the assessment. She wrote that while the "colored Negroes" do respect white doctors, more trust would ensue with black physicians. She wrote that: "We do not want the word to go out that we want to exterminate the Negro population and the minister is the man who can straighten that idea out if it ever occurs to any of their more rebellious members."[75]

Sanger had received some coaching here from W. E. B. DuBois, a black sociology teacher at Atlanta University. In an article in the *Birth Control Review,* he had traced out the importance of religious opposition to birth control among the emancipated African slaves:

> After emancipation, there arose the inevitable clash of ideals between those Negroes who were striving to improve their economic position and those whose religious faith made the limitation of children a sin.
> ... the mass of Negroes knew almost nothing about the birth control movement.... Like most people with middle-class standards of morality, they think that birth control is inherently immoral.[76]

The southern states finally received money in 1940 for two "Negro Project" demonstration programs funded by advertizing magnate Albert D. Lasker and his wife, Mary.[77] One project undertaken at Nashville, Tennessee, in February 1940 was very important because it was near Meharry Medical School which trained more than half of all black doctors in the United States.[78] The other black-oriented project began May 1, 1940, and was headed by Dr. Robert E. Seibels, who chaired the maternal welfare committee of the South Carolina Medical Association.[79] Dr. Seibels had earlier cautioned the BCFA officials that limiting their funding to just birth control would decrease black participation and also would not set well with Berkeley County doctors.[80]

The Christmas 1941 newsletter of the BCFA's Division of Negro Services referred to Dr. Seibels' work in Berkeley County, South Carolina,

---

[74] Ibid.

[75] Letter from Margaret Sanger (MS/MH) to Dr. Clarence J. Gamble, 255 Adams St., Milton, Mass., December 10, 1939, SSCSC.

[76] W. E. B. DuBois, Ph.D., "Black Folk and Birth Control", *Birth Control Review,* vol. 22, no. 8 (May 1938): 90.

[77] Dorothy Boulding Ferebee, M.D., "Negro Project" report, BCFA Annual Meeting, January 29, 1942, 1, MSCLC.

[78] Ibid., 3.

[79] Ibid.

[80] Letter from Dr. Clarence Gamble to Margaret Sanger, January 25, 1940, SSCSC.

emphasizing that eighty percent of low intelligence blacks introduced to birth control would use a method after receiving proper instructions.[81]

During this period, organizational outreach efforts were undertaken by Sanger's followers within the BCFA to secure increasing influence within the leadership of the black community. The BCFA sought to entice influential blacks to serve on the National Negro Advisory Council of the BCFA. This project was extremely successful. An impressive list of black leaders did join the council. To mention only a few:[82]

- Arthur Spingarn, president, National Association for the Advancement of Colored People (NAACP)
- Claude A. Barnett, Associated Negro Press
- Mary MacLeod Bethune, president, National Council of Negro Women, and special advisor to President Roosevelt on minority groups
- Eugene K. Jones, executive secretary, National Urban League
- John W. Davis, president, West Virginia State College
- Max Yergan, president, National Negro Congress
- L. Hollingsworth Wood, president, National Urban League
- Frederick D. Patterson, president, Tuskegee Institute
- Charles D. Hebert, president, Morehouse College
- Charles S. Johnson (later first black president of Fisk University)
- Rev. Adam Clayton Powell (later chairman, House Education and Labor Committee)

At the 1942 BCFA annual meeting, BCFA Negro Council board member Dr. Dorothy B. Ferebee—a cum laude graduate of Tufts and also president of Alpha Kappa Alpha, the nation's largest black sorority—addressed the delegates regarding Planned Parenthood's minority outreach efforts. As with whites, birth control was presented both as an economic betterment vehicle and as a health measure that could reduce the incidence of infant mortality.[83] Ferebee said:

> With the Negro group some of the most difficult obstacles ... to overcome are: (1) the concept that when birth control is proposed to them, it is motivated by a clever bit of machination to persuade them to commit race suicide; (2) the so-called "husband objection" ... ; (3) the fact that birth control is confused with abortion; and (4) the belief that it is inherently immoral. However, as formidable as these objections may seem, when thrown against the total picture of the awareness on the part of the Negro leaders of the improved conditions under Planned Parenthood, or the

[81] Meetings We've Attended, News, from the Division of Negro Services, Birth Control Federation of America, 501 Madison Ave, N.Y., N.Y., 3, MSCLC.

[82] BCFA, Division of Negro Services, stationery, MSCLC.

[83] Dr. Dorothy B. Ferebee, "Planned Parenthood as a Health Measure for the Negro Race", for release after 9:30 AM, January 29, 1942, MSCLC.

genuine interest and eagerness of the families themselves to secure the services which will give them a fair chance for health and happiness, the obstacles to the program are greatly outweighed.[84]

Ferebee suggested a very practical way around these problems:

> I cannot overemphasize the importance of utilizing Negro professionals, fully integrated into the staff of this organization. This key professional worker could interpret the program and the objectives to them in the normal course of day to day contacts; could break down fallacious attitudes and beliefs and elements of distrust; could inspire the confidence of the group; and would not be suspected of the intent to eliminate the race.
>
> . . . the Negro professional can be utilized to help create a community demand in areas where health departments are reluctant to accept it.[85]

Birth control as an economic improvement measure had some appeal to those lowest on the income ladder. In the black *Chicago Defender* for January 10, 1942, a long three-column women's interest article discussed the endorsement of the Sanger program by prominent black women. There were at least six express references, such as the following example, to birth control as a remedy for economic woes: " . . . it raises the standard of living by enabling parents to adjust the family size to the family income." Readers were also told that birth control " . . . is no operation. It is no abortion. Abortion kills life after it has begun. . . . Birth Control is neither harmful nor immoral."

But the moral stumbling block could only be surmounted by Afro-American religious leaders, so black ministers were solicited. Florence Rose, long-time Sanger secretary, prepared an activities report during March 1942 detailing the progress of the "Negro Project". She recounted a recent meeting with a Planned Parenthood Negro Division board member, Bishop David H. Sims (African Methodist Episcopal Church), who appreciated Planned Parenthood's recognition of the extent of black opposition to birth control and its efforts to build up support among black leaders. He offered whatever assistance he could give.[86]

Bishop Sims offered to: (1) identify the most influential ministers and target the meetings they were attending; (2) bring up birth control at the yearly meetings of bishops; (3) let his name be used for additional PPFA Negro Board membership solicitations; (4) assemble a list of liberals in other groups and of the Social Service Committee through which the PPFA program could be furthered; (5) begin the "softening process" among the representatives of different Negro denominations attending the monthly meetings of the Federal

---

[84] Ibid., 3–4.

[85] Ibid., 4–5.

[86] Florence Rose, "Activities Report, from the Special Projects Department", etc., March 23–24, 1942, 3, MSCLC.

Council of Churches and its Division of Race Relations. Bishop Sims told Rose that he was pleased to see the pamphlet on "Moral Values" issued by the Committee on Marriage and the Home, and that he would aid in preparing a question-and-answer pamphlet based on the Bible to help meet objections.[87]

An interesting exchange of letters took place between Sanger and the prominent black minister J. T. Braun, editor-in-chief of the National Baptist Convention's Sunday School Publishing Board in Nashville, Tennessee. Sanger had written to Braun in late 1941, enclosing some birth control literature and asking that he join the nationwide movement for black endorsement of birth control. Braun told Sanger that, "I confess, the very idea of such a thing has always held the greatest hatred and contempt in my mind. . . . I am hesitant to give my fullest endorsement of this idea, until you send me, perhaps, some more convincing literature on the subject."[88]

Sanger wrote back on December 22, 1941, giving Braun the Federal Council of Churches' Marriage and Home Committee pamphlet praised by Bishop Sims. Sanger assured Rev. Braun that: "There are some people who believe that birth control is an attempt to dictate to families how many children to have. Nothing could be further from the truth."[89]

Sanger's assistants gave Braun more pro-birth control literature and, later, a copy of Sanger's autobiography, which Braun gave to his wife to read. Mrs. Braun was moved by Sanger's hypothesis that the deaths of mothers and children could be prevented by birth control. Rev. Braun eventually let his chapel be used by a group of women for a birth control talk, and in May 1943, moved by the number of prominent Christians backing the proposition, he wrote Sanger a letter stating: "At first glance I had a horrible shock to the proposition because it seemed to me to be allied to abortion, but after thought, and prayer, I have concluded that especially among many women it is necessary both to save the lives of mothers and children."[90]

These and other efforts paid off handsomely after World War II. By 1949, virtually the entire black leadership network of social, professional, and academic organizations had endorsed Planned Parenthood's program (see footnote for listing).[91]

[87] Ibid.

[88] Letter of J. T. Braun, Nashville, Tennessee, to Margaret Sanger, 501 Madison Ave. N.Y., N.Y., December 8, 1941, MSCLC.

[89] December 22, 1941 (MS/FM) to J. T. Braun, MSCLC.

[90] Letter of J. T. Braun to Margaret Sanger, May 18, 1943, MSCLC.

[91] March 18, 1949, memo to: "State Leagues and Local Committees for Field Service Department, PPFA, Subject Directory of National Negro Organizations with which PPFA has developed working relationships". The list included the National Association for the Advancement of Colored People, National Urban League, National Medical Association, National Association of Colored Graduate Nurses, National Council of Negro Women, and virtually every major African-American religious, social, economic, educational, and parental organization.

And just as Rev. Braun would be favorably impressed by influential black American clergy, America's Protestant middle classes would also be given their "contraceptive" role models by Margaret Sanger. One exceptionally valuable endorsement for Sanger's birth control program came from First Lady Eleanor Roosevelt. The endorsement was a prototypical product of Planned Parenthood's behind-the-scenes maneuvering.

In late 1938 Sanger's CPP had considered targeting Mrs. Roosevelt, but hesitated until they were a little more certain of what she might say.[92] Sanger associate Hazel Moore had related that:

> One of the White House "press buddies" took up the subject with her, planning to ask her about her position on birth control in a press conference, but at that time Mrs. Roosevelt gave the impression that she would refuse to answer the question, which we felt might not be good as the newspapers would probably turn that refusal to answer as "opposition".[93]

Mrs. Roosevelt had also declined to answer when this question was given in written form at a conference. Moore however, knew that the President's wife favored birth control and was anxious to secure a clear statement of support.[94]

Mrs. Roosevelt publicly disclosed her views a year later, on January 16, 1940, during her weekly press conference: "No, I am not opposed to the planning of children."[95] "Mrs. Roosevelt revealed that she had once been a subscriber to an organization which conducted birth control clinics in New York City, but she could not recall its name. This was the first time, she admitted, that she had commented on the subject since her views had been 'of any interest to any one.'"[96] The clinic was, of course, Margaret Sanger's.[97]

Sanger wallowed in this endorsement. She told her CPP followers:

> As your letter this month, we suggest that you write the "First Lady" expressing appreciation of her fine, democratic statement. Her refusal to impose her views upon others is in striking contrast to the attitude of the small but well-organized religious minority in this country which seeks to prevent both Catholics and non-Catholics from obtaining this essential health service.[98]

---

[92] Letter of Hazel Moore to Mrs. Mary Woodard Reinhardt, January 12, 1939, MSCLC.

[93] Ibid.

[94] Ibid.

[95] Press clippings: *New York Herald Tribune,* January 16, 1940; Easton, *Pennsylvania Express* for January 17, 1940; others; MSCLC.

[96] *New York Herald Tribune,* undated clipping, MSCLC.

[97] Gray, *Margaret Sanger,* 386.

[98] January 1940, "Dear Friend" letter of Margaret Sanger and Richard Pierson to Committee on Public Progress members, MSCLC.

Mrs. Roosevelt had said of this that "she never felt honest about her silence" on birth control "but it was necessary".[99]

A total of 564 CPP members reported sending a "thank-you" letter to Mrs. Roosevelt. Sanger's letter writers at this time numbered 1,312 active members, and 759 "reserve corps".[100] One additional outreach effort of the CPP consisted of copying names from *Who's Who* and sending unsolicited birth control material through the mail.[101]

Mrs. Roosevelt's endorsement of birth control, so self-conscious and diffident at first, quickly went above and beyond the call of duty. She called pro-contraception proponents and government officials to two White House meetings on the subject during 1941.[102] Showing that birth control had truly "arrived", Mrs. Roosevelt hosted a White House luncheon for pro-contraception notables, who directed their pleadings to federal officials from the Children's Bureau, the Public Health Service, the Works Progress Administration, the U.S. Navy, and the Farm Security Administration. Minutes of the meeting make it clear that Miss Lenroot of the Children's Bureau was singled out for special pressure to include birth control in her agency's programs. She offered resistance on several fronts, but suggested that if strategic members of Congress on the appropriations committees and several authorizing committees, including Rep. John McCormack [D–Mass.], chairman of the House Rules Committee, approved, then she would include birth control. It was considered unwise to take up her offer.[103]

Dr. Prentiss Willson, a Planned Parenthood supporter who attended the White House meeting, considered the gathering the most important event in the history of birth control since the birth of Margaret Sanger. Both the fact of the meeting and its timing, which even Mr. Rose of the BCFA had tried to delay or postpone, argue for this interpretation, as Mrs. Roosevelt had refused to delay the meeting even though the Japanese had employed some rather brutal population reduction techniques only the day before (December 7, 1941) at Guam, the Northern Marianas, and Pearl Harbor, killing some 2,500 Americans.

With birth control coming more and more to the fore in public policy, the BCFA was emboldened to take out full page ads in major newspapers. It was undertaken as a special project of the National Committee for Planned

[99] Letter of Hazel Moore to Dr. Clarence Gamble, January 22, 1940, MSCLC.

[100] Public Progress Committee, Report of Special Mailings during 1940, CPP, 3, 1, MSCLC.

[101] CPP, Weekly Report, October 10–November 2, 1940, MSCLC.

[102] David Kennedy, citing report on Washington, D.C., meeting, March 5, 1941, 263, SSCSC.

[103] Report of the luncheon meeting held at the White House at the invitation of Mrs. Franklin D. Roosevelt, December 8, 1941, 9, SSCSC.

Parenthood. Full-page or near-full-page ads appeared in the March 18, 1941, *New York Times;* March 19, 1941, *New York Herald Tribune;* and the March 21, 1941, *World Telegram.* [104] The ad read: "The First Key to Strong National Health—BIRTH CONTROL—Through Planned Parenthood. To Make America Strong, We Must First Make Americans Strong." It pictured a pretty, Caucasian mother and one smiling baby. Readers were told that by 1956 a full 37% of children born in 1941 would be wasted: 9% dead, 1% crippled, 3% tubercular, 15% mentally deficient, .75% delinquent, and 8% maladjusted. The ad narrative read: "A part of everyone's income goes for relief and care of the under-privileged . . . "; it also suggested that there were 700,000 abortions ("over-whelmingly married women") for every 2,000,000 births.

While Planned Parenthood sought to sell the general public on the health and welfare-reduction benefits of birth control, its approach to the medical profession was more direct. Instructions were given to BCFA affiliates on how to approach doctors.

For example, BCFA affiliates were discouraged from promoting birth control as a panacea for all problems, or telling doctors about the long-range economic and social goals of the birth control movement. Affiliates were encouraged to tell physicians that by providing birth control they could reduce their case load of free obstetrics, increase the number of other patients, and reduce deaths to mothers. [105]

By the end of 1941, the BCFA had thirty-four state league affiliates that would seek to implement the BCFA's medical advice. Some affiliates had the name "Planned Parenthood" as part of their title. Finally, at a special membership meeting of the BCFA on January 29, 1942, with eighty members present, it was decided by unanimous vote to change the name of the BCFA to the "Planned Parenthood Federation of America, Inc.". [106] Sanger once again emerged as honorary chairman of the PPFA. But Sanger biographer David Kennedy writes that by 1942, with Sanger's "dreams well on the way to full realization, she had 'left the front'. She went home to Arizona and nursed her failing husband, who died in 1943. . . . By the end of the war, she was little more than a figurehead in the American birth control movement. Her doggedly militant style now seemed more a liability than an asset." [107]

State leagues shortly followed suit in changing their name and bylaws. The New York State Federation for Planned Parenthood is a case in point. The

---

[104] Copy of ad slick, SSCSC.

[105] Medical Standards Practice, "To Promote More Effective Working Relationships with the Medical and Health Professions", prepared by the Medical Department, BCFA, 1941, MSCLC.

[106] BCFA, Minutes of Special Membership Meeting, Tuesday, January 29, 1942, 2:15 P.M., Hotel Waldorf Astoria, N.Y., N.Y., MSCLC.

[107] David Kennedy, citing Washington, D.C., meeting report, 270, SSCSC.

affiliate's old bylaws stipulated that the object was: "To develop and organize on sound *eugenic,* social and medical principles, interest in and knowledge of *birth control* throughout the State of New York as permitted by law" [emphasis added]. The new bylaws replaced "birth control" with "planned parenthood". The word "eugenics" was dropped because in 1943 it had unpopular connotations.[108] With the United States at war with a German government founded in large part on race-improving eugenic theories that were implemented through forced sterilization and segregation of the "unfit"—in short, measures Planned Parenthood leaders had advocated for many years—it indeed was prudent for the organization to drop mention of eugenic goals from its bylaws, if not from its policies, at least for the duration of World War II.

World War II presented both obstacles to and opportunities for Planned Parenthood's program.[109] The key document is an October 2, 1942 memorandum from PPFA official Kenneth Rose to state and local Planned Parenthood leaders. It recognized that, in the minds of some people, curbing the birth rate when American fighting men were being killed was not emotionally palatable, and the rise in the birth rate partially reflected that. One U.S. Public Health Service officer who believed in birth control nevertheless said that having fewer babies was like a suggestion for making fewer and fewer bullets. Rose pointed out that when casualty lists grew heavy, this type of objection would increase and would be difficult to handle with the Catholics as well. Rose suggested a theme of "Strengthening Parenthood in Wartime" and argued that Planned Parenthood must hammer home to the American people that it was "concerned with the health of mothers and babies".[110]

Rose and others believed that about six million women, many under forty-five, would eventually be drawn into war industries, creating problems for the care of the children of working mothers whose husbands were in the military [page 4]. The Rose memorandum suggested that medical birth control would help national security by preserving the health of mothers and children [page 5]. The Planned Parenthood target group had historically been the poor, but as unemployment decreased, the poor were less susceptible, which Rose said was a problem [page 5]. He noted that more and more medical care was being offered to the public, and Planned Parenthood should

---

[108] Planned Parenthood Committee of New York, Executive Secretary Report for July 1 to October 1, 1943, 3–5 year plan, Revision of Constitution and By-Laws of the New York State Federation for Planned Parenthood, Article II: Objectives, MSCLC.

[109] Memorandum to state leagues and local committees from Mr. D. Kenneth Rose, national director, PPFA, October 2, 1942, "Planned Parenthood in Relation to the War", page 1: One measure of America's sagging orientation toward family life is that, even at the height of World War II, the U.S. birth rate was some 25–33% higher than it is today, despite the deployment of millions of young American men overseas.

[110] Ibid., 2.

take advantage of it. Trade unions and management were offering health care [page 5], and the Lanham Act provided $300 million for health care in areas affected by the war; additionally, industrial hygiene was being provided by the U.S. Public Health Service (USPHS).

There were, however, strong critics of declining or low American birth rates in wartime, such as Congressman Louis Rabat, who, at a congressional hearing, had attributed the amazing six-week military collapse of France in the summer of 1940 to a low birth rate. The French themselves had recognized the disastrous national security and economic effect of their low birth rate, their high proportion of elderly people, and consequent reliance on imported labor to sustain their economy.[111] But Congressman Rabat's remarks only prompted PPFA president Dr. J. H. J. Upham to suggest that if a high birth rate would have saved France, Poland should have defeated Germany in 1939 because it had one of the highest birth rates in Europe.[112] Dr. Upham apparently forgot that Poland had had to fight Russia as well; that it only had horse cavalry and no mechanized armor against the world's most advanced tanks; that Germany had rearmed during the previous ten years, while Poland largely had World War I equipment; and that Poland lacked easily defensible natural frontiers.

Dr. Upham also claimed that "unplanned births and overly large families" contributed to the 30% to 50% draft rejection rate. While Upham was making his ideological statement, American families like the "overly large" Sullivans were paying the high price of liberty. In 1942, during a naval battle in the Solomon Islands, the five Sullivan sons were lost in the destruction of the cruiser *U.S.S. Juneau,* and all of America wept with the family at what Lincoln had once called so "costly a sacrifice on the altar of freedom".

Perhaps the most successful vehicle during World War II for Planned Parenthood propaganda was the unproven public health claim that birth control would preserve the health of mothers and children and thus keep the nation strong. With the influx of female workers in war production plants, an area ripe for exploitation presented itself. The U.S. Public Health Service's Division of Industrial Hygiene published an "Outline of Industrial Hygiene Program", which included a section on child-spacing suggesting that at war plants the personnel "counselor should refer married women workers with special problems to the medical service or a private physician for advice on the proper spacing of children as a means of protecting the health of the mother

[111] William L. Shirer, *The Collapse of the Third Republic* (Simon and Schuster, 1969), 79–80, 142–43, 166, 174, 732.

[112] Public Information Department, PPFA, "Draft Rejections Laid to Unfit Babies", July 3 and 9, 1943?, news release sent to women editors of daily newspapers, SSCSC.

and her children".[113] The PPFA's brochures claimed birth control would prevent married women from taking "sick leave" away from the assembly lines because of exploitation from abortionists. But the real though hidden message was that keeping married women on war production assembly lines meant keeping them free from pregnancy and ready for work. Sanger biographer David Kennedy states that the U.S. Public Health Service "recognized that vital war industries required women workers who would not be disabled by unwanted pregnancies".[114] In May 1942 the USPHS's passive policy of approving state requests for birth control gave way to a more aggressive approach. The head of the USPHS's Division of Industrial Hygiene told the PPFA that his physicians would initiate discussions with state health officers about keeping women in war industries healthy by promoting medically approved child-spacing.[115] That this situation never might have developed if America's population had been larger did not occur to these population solons. That the U.S. Public Health Service took upon itself a mission for birth control in wartime—a state of national emergency—is truly ironic.

Within two months after the attack on Pearl Harbor, Planned Parenthood would also achieve its long-standing goal of securing the direct monetary support of the U.S. Public Health Service for its efforts. In response to a question, Surgeon General Thomas Parran told a meeting of public health officers:

> If any State Health Department desires to include planned parenthood programs as a part of their regular State Health Department work, and for this purpose wishes to utilize any of the Title VI and V.D. Control funds that are allotted to the State, a budget setting forth the program, which comes to my attention through the District Directors, will receive my approval.[116]

This was an advance on a policy initiated just three months prior in October 1941 whereby the U.S. Public Health Service would treat any legal state proposals for child-spacing on a par with other programs.[117] Though offi-

---

[113] "Outline of Industrial Hygiene Program", prepared by Division of Industrial Hygiene, National Institute of Health, U.S. Public Health Service, Bethesda, Maryland, February 8, 1943; memo from Dr. C. C. Pierce, PPFA medical director; and page 12 from "outline", MSCLC.

[114] David Kennedy, *Birth Control in America,* 266.

[115] David Kennedy, citing a letter from J. G. Townsend to C. C. Pierce, May 1, 1942, Population Council.

[116] Letter from C. C. Pierce, M.D., U.S. Public Health Service, district director, Dist. 1, to Mr. D. Kenneth Rose, national director, Birth Control Federation of America, February 2, 1942, MSCLC.

[117] Report of the luncheon meeting held at the White House at the invitation of Mrs. Franklin D. Roosevelt, December 8, 1941, 6, SSCSC.

cially accepting birth control, Dr. Parran privately believed that "the Federation is trying to ride in on the coat-tails of the U.S. Public Health [Service]."[118] PPFA national director Rose cautioned against any publicity being given to this newly found success with the U.S. Public Health Service.[119]

Planned Parenthood moved quickly and shrewdly to maximize the benefits of "inside assistance" by hiring as their new medical director a former U.S. Public Health Service official, Dr. C. C. Pierce.[120] Dr. Pierce offered some helpful suggestions to birth control workers. For example, "If a state health officer says it is impossible to put in a new service, the answer is that the program can be included in an already existing service such as infant and maternal health, or venereal disease. When he asks for the allotment, he can label it 'extension of maternal health service' "; and: "Dr. Pierce stressed the importance of going to the health officer and doctors for their advice rather than going to tell them what you have already decided to do about the situation."[121]

By June 1942 the PPFA officials had completed a thirteen-state survey of state health officers, state boards of health, state medical societies, and governors regarding support for birth control. The political affiliation and religious denomination (including Masonic membership) were tallied for all governors. The results were mixed, with no clear patterns emerging. For example, in West Virginia the state health officer opposed the idea, while Governor Neely, a Mason, favored it.[122]

The second most important of Planned Parenthood's institutional targets were the nation's social welfare organizations. At the 1942 annual meeting of the National Conference of Social Work, Kenneth Rose gave a talk entitled, "How Community Support for Planned Parenthood Has Developed". Rose told social workers that birth control was a health matter "whether physiological or mental, or as a factor in the economics of the family".[123] Yet, in spite of these glowing claims for birth control before professional groups, the fact of

[118] Letter from D. Kenneth Rose to Mrs. Albert D. Lasker, February 28, 1942, MSCLC.

[119] PPFA Meeting, Introductory Session, "Evidence of Progress in Recent Years", June 15, 1942, MSCLC.

[120] Letter from C. C. Pierce to D. Kenneth Rose, February 2, 1942, MSCLC; letter from D. Kenneth Rose to Mrs. Albert D. Lasker, February 28, 1942, MSCLC; Minutes of PPFA Meeting, Dr. C. C. Pierce, presiding director, Medical Department, PPFA, "Procedures for Gaining Acceptance by Public Health Officials", June 7, 1942, MSCLC.

[121] Minutes of PPFA Meeting, Dr. C. C. Pierce, presiding director, Medical Department, PPFA, "Procedures for Gaining Acceptance by Public Health Officials", June 7, 1942, MSCLC.

[122] PPFA, Summary: Public Health Monthly Progress Report[s] for April 16, 1942, June 15, 1942, MSCLC.

[123] "PPFA Represented at New Orleans National Social Work Conference", PPFA, Inc., News Letter, vol. 1, no. 4, June, 1942, 2, MSCLC.

the matter was different. At an April 1943 PPFA executive committee meeting, it was noted that "getting birth control information to those who need to defer having children is still our greatest responsibility, because it is here that we have the greatest opposition".[124]

With social workers eventually in league with birth control providers, such resistance would undoubtedly lessen, as the poor family would have to consider whether shoes or dental care for their children were somehow tied to acceptance of birth control by the mother. Charity workers from religious denominations exacted no such price when attending to the parish poor or misfortunate. Contributing to Planned Parenthood's eventual success in this field was a development in the social work field to amalgamate denominational family and children's welfare programs into nonsectarian programs that made relief work independent of religious influence.[125] With social workers trying to free themselves from religious strictures, and birth control pictured as leading to the fulfillment of social work goals, poor families were in no position to refuse "suggestions" from social superiors who recommended birth control to alleviate their situation.

But before social workers would accept the pro-contraception message as their own, Planned Parenthood had to remove certain stumbling blocks. Thus, a formal program for enlisting the support of social work agencies for birth control programs was drawn up during 1943. The program sought to address two problem areas. First, Planned Parenthood would have to be viewed as a health agency employing educational techniques "rather than as a militant promotional agency".[126] Second, "Any implication that those on relief, by virtue of that fact alone, should not have children would antagonize the social worker. That implication has been in some of our literature of the past."[127]

Planned Parenthood's own efforts at persuasion consisted initially of a handbook cast in terms of social work interests, *The Case Worker and Family Planning*, which was sent unsolicited along with a PPFA clinic directory to thirteen thousand social workers.[128] By 1945 such outreach efforts had produced requests from more than four thousand social workers for copies of the "Outline for a Course in Planned Parenthood", which was prepared for the

---

[124] "Suggested Policy on Our Responsibility for the Positive Aspects of Planned Parenthood and Suggestions for Action", as approved at Executive Committee meeting on April 6, 1943, for referral to the Board, 1, SSCSC.

[125] "Program to Enlist Cooperation in the Social Work Field", November 1943, PPFA, 1, SSCSC.

[126] Ibid., 2.

[127] Ibid.

[128] Ibid., 3.

PPFA by Mary A. Cannon, professor of social work at Columbia University.[129] This and other mailings of professional interest to social workers paid off. By May 1946 the PPFA Social Work Advisory Committee reported that twenty-three of twenty-six schools of social work in the United States included some instruction in birth control in their curriculum.[130]

A third method of increasing the social acceptability of birth control was through direct-mail mass marketing targeted at various pivotal groups. These mailings were begun in a systematic way during September 1942 with a postcard mailing to 136,000 general practitioners offering a booklet on birth control, which produced a response via a business reply card from 36,000 doctors.[131] In June 1943 the Federation had hoped to mass mail offers of free publications and other materials, each highlighting aspects of birth control that would be of particular interest to the professional needs and concerns of the targeted group. For example, the Federation targeted 200,000 Protestant and Jewish clergy at a mailing cost of $17,000 and offered them its religious statement, a list of prominent clergy endorsing birth control, a Gallup poll showing 77% support for birth control, a clinic directory, a one-page statement explaining the legal situation of birth control, sermon material, and marriage counseling information. A response of 30% was expected.[132]

Ten thousand heads of industry were sent information from the Industrial Hygiene Division of the U.S. Public Health Service favorable to birth control, including a leaflet for married women in industry, a pamphlet outlining the importance of general health programs for employees, and data on population trends. A response of 10% was expected.[133]

The outreach mailing project proposed to solicit the following over a three-year period: college presidents; sociology teachers; public health, hospital, and private nurses; editors or columnists on papers with circulation of 25,000 or more; women's club presidents and parent-teacher association heads; federal officials; radio owners and commentators; presidents of hospital boards; authors of medical, economic, or sociology texts; screen and motion picture writers; heads of farm bureaus; labor leaders; and others.[134]

By and large the most receptive response came from the doctors, as noted above. A partial evaluation of the mailing efforts conducted during the summer of 1944 produced the following results: of 4,250 newspaper editors,

[129] "A Statement on Behalf of the Planned Parenthood Program for 1945", presented by PPFA, Inc., 50 Madison Ave, N.Y., N.Y., 15.

[130] PPFA, Digest of Minutes of Operating Committees, April and May 1946, 3, SSCSC.

[131] Statement on Mass Educational Program to Pivotal Groups Whose Support Can Implement the Planned Parenthood Program, DKR, June 25, 1943, 1, SSCSC.

[132] Ibid.

[133] Ibid., 2–3.

[134] Ibid., 2–5.

104 or 2.4% responded; of 1,600 magazine editors, 54 or 3.4% responded; of 3,150 radio science editors and commentators, 116 or 3.7% responded; of 8,500 authors and screen writers, 128 or 1.5% responded.[135] PPFA officials were at a loss to explain the low response from authors and screen writers, but attributed the slightly higher, though still disappointing, response from other media people to a low interest in background information and a need for information of ready use by their respective audiences.

By December 1945 the Federation had mailed to almost 500,000 members of professional groups, with a heavy concentration on physicians, nurses, clergy, social workers, and educators.[136] An evaluation sent to state affiliates in that month asked if the mailings had increased acceptance of birth control. The Ohio League answered "yes" to the question, pointing to increased referrals from clergy, health and social workers, educators, and private physicians.[137] The Ohio League identified clergy as most helpful, with public health nurses and social workers following.

By far the worst results came from labor union mailings. The lowest response rate was among the labor-management committees, with only seven responses out of a mailing of 3,300, or .2% response.[138] Of 4,991 leaders of local labor unions, fifty-eight, or just 1.2%, responded. The responses that were received came from unions that already had health plans in operation.[139] The paucity of labor union responses did not cause the PPFA to change its tactical goal of gaining labor union support; it simply adapted itself to the fact that acceptance by labor would take longer. Mark Starr, educational director of the International Ladies Garment Workers Union, attributed the hesitation of unions to accept birth control to two factors: the widespread presence of Catholics in labor unions, and the fact that the birth control movement had overlooked labor's influence on public opinion and had not previously tried to gain the support of labor for its cause.[140] Of course, the latter reason might simply have been the flip side of the Catholic issue.

After the war, the PPFA moved ahead with further union contacts, hosting a meeting in February 1947 with Rose Schneidermann, president of the Women's Trade Union League; Leo Perlis, national director of the Congress of Industrial Organizations (CIO) Community Services Committee; and others.

[135] JHS–Public Information Department memo to D. Kenneth Rose from James H. Scull, Analysis of Mailings, September 21, 1944, 3–6, SSCSC.
[136] Memo to state leagues from PPFA, Educational Mailings, Ohio League, December 3, 1945, SSCSC.
[137] Ibid.
[138] JHS–Public Information Department memo to D. Kenneth Rose from James H. Scull, Analysis of Mailings, September 21, 1944, 1, SSCSC.
[139] Ibid., 2.
[140] Mark Starr, educational director of International Ladies Garment Workers Union, "Labor Looks at Birth Control", reprinted by the PPFA, n.d., SSCSC.

Plans were set for placing publicly identifiable, elected labor union representatives on Planned Parenthood local boards; hiring married women with grown children to help PPFA affiliates work with labor councils; obtaining select voter lists from primary elections to identify labor voters (management had been reluctant to give out names); and preparing a short feature article about Planned Parenthood by Mrs. Roosevelt or Frances Perkins, who was secretary of labor from 1933 to 1945 and the first woman appointed to a cabinet post. Labor representatives also thought that medical men rather than clergy would be more effective in reaching their membership.[141] A doctor endorsing birth control could appear neutral to union members, but a Protestant clergyman might appear biased to Catholic union members.

With World War II over, Planned Parenthood prepared a long-range planning document in September 1949 that reflected the consensus of its state leagues, local affiliates, and the Federation. The immediate and ultimate aims were envisioned as using the local birth control clinic as a vehicle for securing "universal acceptance of family planning as an essential element of 'responsible parenthood and stable family life' ".

Further goals included: gaining acceptance of birth control clinics; bringing family planning services into public and private health care; generating birth control courses in schools of social work and in seminaries; and finding the ideal birth control method. It was resolved not to include marriage counseling in its programs.[142]

Securing the "holy grail" of birth control, a failsafe, easily obtained and used device or medication, was precisely the reason why Margaret Sanger stepped back into her role of pro-contraception activist once again. She ultimately employed not just one, but all three avenues of research suggested by the PPFA long-range planning committee to produce the first commercially available birth control pill. By 1946 Sanger was despondent over the inability of the diaphragm to meet the antifertility desires of millions of women and lamented that a simple "birth control pill was not available".[143] It took her until 1951 to find the right researchers for the Pill to start what would be a nine-year project.[144]

While an easier method of birth control would facilitate greater acceptance, additional policy initiatives were necessary in four areas to achieve universal

[141] Conference on Labor and Planned Parenthood, held at PPFA offices, 501 Madison Ave., N.Y., N.Y., February 24, 1947.

[142] PPFA, Inc., Report of the Long Range Planning Committee on Program, September 1949, 1–4, MSCLC 143.

[143] Gray, *Margaret Sanger,* 396, citing an undated letter of Margaret Sanger to Hobson Pitman, SSCSC.

[144] Gregory Pincus, *The Control of Fertility* (New York & London: Academic Press, 1965), 6.

acceptance of birth control. These areas were: creating the "need" for expanded use of birth control because of the "threat" of population growth; expanding legal access of birth control to the unmarried and to minors; securing government support for birth control in social welfare programs and in public health programs and hospitals; developing additional antifertility drugs and devices, including the liberalization of sterilization laws and practices and legal access to abortion on demand.

Only one of Sanger's tactical goals was unrealized when she died in 1966, and that was legal abortion on demand. But here again her efforts were instrumental in securing that result. Just the year before she died, the U.S. Supreme Court issued a decision in a Connecticut anticontraception controversy that established a constitutional right to "privacy". The justices would use this precedent to strike down all state antiabortion laws in January 1973. But the groundwork she had laid for birth control would help to subvert the nation's and the world's notions of sexuality, marriage, commitment, motherhood, and human life itself, besides having many other family- and faith-destroying consequences as well.

Chapter Two

The Institutionalization of Birth Control

Securing acceptance of the *idea* of birth control as a *personal "good"* would be followed by a campaign to secure the public acceptance of the *practice* of birth control as both an *individual* and *social necessity.* And birth control as a social factor could not be achieved without widespread institutional changes in American society. The lessons Sanger and her followers learned in securing the legality and moral acceptability of birth control would have to be recast to meet the goals, circumstances, needs, and modes of operation of individuals and groups targeted for birth control "acceptance".

This entailed some tactical changes on the part of Planned Parenthood coupled with greater social outreach, not just through direct advertising, but subtle propagandizing as well. Thus, the so-called "population explosion" was made to be everybody's concern, and no problem (education, crime, housing, the good life, etc.) could be solved until this one was sufficiently addressed.

And then there were those, notably the poor, who would have to be helped along a little to "accept" birth control for their own good by short-sighted social workers and politicians eager to do something "practical" to cut welfare dependency.

But birth control would have to become more efficient and easier to use before a wider clientele could be lured to Sanger's vision. This meant research to expand antifertility options beyond diaphragm, condom, and messy gels, and a medical buffer or "damage control" system capable of deflecting, watering down, or obscuring the adverse health consequences of new birth control techniques.

And finally, the question of who would have access to birth control would have to be addressed. There were two aspects to this problem: personal freedom and using birth control to address the social problems caused by single parenting.

Thus, the paths that Planned Parenthood leaders used to turn America into a contracepting society were: personalizing the "need" for population control, securing the development of new birth control drugs or devices, implementing and expanding birth control services for the unmarried, and making birth control a means of addressing community welfare and health problems. These four areas became the carefully crafted causeway that Sanger's disciples trod after World War II to transform an America where birth control was a matter of private discussion and practice limited to select middle- and upper-class matrons, to its present status as an indispensable social given of the American ethos. These policies were also responsible for creating the social infrastructure by which Planned Parenthood was no longer a loose association of birth control propagandists headed by skillful and determined women. At the present time it is not just an organization, it has become a way of life with institutional support in every major aspect of modern American society.

1. THE "THREAT" OF POPULATION GROWTH

Gregory Pincus, who helped develop the Pill, has said that the growing appreciation of the population explosion in the 1950s was a major factor driving the development of oral contraceptives.[1] The *Milwaukee Journal,* in light of the supposed population threat, editorialized on July 23, 1955, in support of the PPFA's efforts to develop an antifertility pill. "The conviction that people in population-pressed areas would accept such a pill is supported by the overwhelming response of Japanese women to the more dangerous reliance on abortion as a means of birth control when abortions were legalized after the war."[2]

In policy discussions in the United States, the population question was usually discussed in terms of the ability of underdeveloped nations to produce enough food for their citizens. U.S. assistant secretary of commerce for international affairs, Samuel W. Anderson, honorary fund raising chairman for the PPFA, said in November 1955 that:

> [T]he struggle for economic development in underdeveloped countries was seriously impeded by rapid growth in their population. At the same time there has been a resurgent awareness in America of the need to help stabilize and strengthen family life—in order to help curb juvenile delinquency, to increase the emotional and economic health of the family.
>
> Family planning is an essential part both of solving the population problem and of stabilizing and enriching family life.[3]

Dr. Brock Chisholm, former director general of the United Nations World Health Organization, added the weight of his voice to the chorus pointing to population growth as underlying literally every social problem. At the thirty-

---

[1] Gregory Pincus, *The Control of Fertility* (New York and London: Academic Press, 1965), 6.

[2] "Exploding World Population", reprinted from the *Milwaukee Journal* for July 23, 1955, *Planned Parenthood News,* no. 13, Fall 1955, 4. (In 1990 the Pill was still not legal in Japan for birth control.)

[3] Samuel W. Anderson, excerpts from a November 22, 1955, statement, "Family Planning and America's Future", *Planned Parenthood News,* Winter 1956, 2.

sixth annual PPFA luncheon held May 3, 1956, he held that unless the population problem was adequately addressed, he doubted the other great problems facing mankind could be solved.[4]

Underscoring the insistence that every problem was amenable to solution only if the "population problem were solved" were the observations of PPFA national director (1958–68) William Vogt on the Suez Canal crisis of 1956. The crisis developed after two events: the withdrawal of Western and, in particular, American help from the proposed Aswan Dam project and the seizure of the Canal by the Egyptian government on July 26 from the mostly French- and British-owned Suez Canal Company.

Writing just prior to the October 29, 1956, invasion of Egypt by Israel, and then by England and France ostensibly to regain control of the Suez Canal, Vogt claimed:

> Perhaps [the crisis] will be worth the high price if it finally makes the world, including the Vatican, face up to the realities of the population problem. . . . For this is, fundamentally, what the Suez crisis is about. Were the population-resource ratio in Europe and Egypt as favorable as it is in America, the conflict could scarcely have developed.
>
> And this is one of the most important things that Planned Parenthood is about. Unless such population pressures can be avoided we must expect more incidents like Suez.
>
> A mere 1% or 2% of what an oil lift bypassing Suez would cost the first year would probably give us the means of breaking the Malthusian juggernaut with an oral contraceptive. Col. Nasser should now have made it clear that such an investment in future peace would be well justified.[5]

But Vogt's simplistic theory could not, of course, explain why Egypt, which had finished the Aswan Dam in 1967 and presumably was increasing its economic output, attacked Israel in 1973. Nor could it explain, retrospectively, why many ancient animosities that had brought neighboring countries to blows, from Thermopylae to Hastings to Lepanto, occurred in eras when so-called population "pressures" were minimal—that is, unless all matters of greed are perforce "resource questions" and all wars are "population" wars by virtue of their participants' being, generally speaking, people.

But Planned Parenthood, despite a strong overlay of "national security" rationalizations and a growing roster of supporters, failed in its attempts to budge the Eisenhower administration off dead center. Ike's administration maintained its hands-off posture toward foreign assistance programs designed

[4] Dr. Brock Chisholm, "The World's Most Pressing Problem", text of May 3, 1956, remarks, 1, MSCLC.

[5] Dr. William Vogt, "Dr. Malthus, I Presume . . . ?", *Planned Parenthood News*, no. 16, Fall 1956, 4.

to solve the world population "problem". On December 2, 1959, Eisenhower personally ruled out the promotion of birth control with U.S. foreign aid "as long as I am here", adding that it was a religious question.[6]

Simultaneously with Eisenhower's comments, the State Department released a study showing that global food production had increased at a higher rate than population and would probably continue to do so for the next fifteen years.[7]

Six years later the facts were little changed, but not so the nation's political leadership. In his 1965 State of the Union address, President Lyndon B. Johnson told the country that he would "seek new ways to use our knowledge to help deal with the explosion in world population and the growing scarcity of world resources". This confident assertion was the result of Planned Parenthood–World Population (PPWP, a world population thrust of PPFA) efforts to lobby Johnson's staff after the 1964 election.[8] Not only did the American government kowtow to Planned Parenthood, but the United Nations General Assembly gave wide berth to PPWP policy experts as well.[9]

Population control orthodoxy would exact its own price, however, and that was conformity. With Johnson's insistence upon seeking "new ways" to curb global population, the administrator of the U.S. government's Food for Peace program announced at a Planned Parenthood conference that the United States would insist that foreign governments give "evidence of policies that will assure balance between food production and population growth" and "that governments . . . carry through their food production program and family planning efforts to make sure that in the long run their own people do not go hungry or malnourished".[10] In India, the Johnson administration even applied this policy during a food shortage, in effect requiring India, if it wanted food, to set up a national birth control program.[11]

But to attain universal acceptance of birth control would entail pressure directed not just at governments but at individuals as well, affecting the most basic cell of society, the family. Thus, at this same conference, famed anthropologist Margaret Mead told a luncheon audience that American women, who are considered "style setters" for the world, should opt for "a new chic of small families as a first step towards a new ethic of individual responsibility".

[6] John D. Morris, "President Bars U.S. Help for Birth Control Abroad: Asserts Issue Is Religious and Should Not Enter Realm of Politics", *New York Times,* December 3, 1959, 1.

[7] E. W. Kenworthy, "President Bars U.S. Help for Birth Control Abroad: State Department Says Food Output Exceeds Population Growth", *New York Times,* December 3, 1959.

[8] Alan Guttmacher, *Presidential Letter,* no. 2, January 26, 1965, 1.

[9] Ibid.

[10] News release (embargoed copy), PPWP, New York City, October 18, 1966, at the PPWP 50th Anniversary Conference, Hotel Roosevelt, 2, SSCSC.

[11] Joseph Califano, *Governing America* (New York: Simon and Schuster, 1981), 52.

Birth control, she said, was "a social necessity"; and that "there can now be active support for . . . no children at all".[12]

Additional steps toward this new ethic of "individual responsibility" were suggested by Vogt to Guttmacher, now president of Planned Parenthood. In a July 7, 1968, letter, Vogt took PPWP to task for its hands-off population policy and belief that only parents, "should determine the number and spacing of children".[13]

Guttmacher's own views differed, but only on tactical grounds. He thought that as long as the birth rate continued to fall or remained at a low level, Planned Parenthood should "advocate voluntarism and non-coercion in family size" while teaching the implications of continued population growth; and further, he said, "Abortion and sterilization on request should certainly be introduced *before family size by coercion is attempted*" [emphasis added].[14]

Yet, Guttmacher praised Dr. Gordon Perkin, former PPWP medical director, who had co-authored a population control document for Ghana that contained "mild incentives and coercives toward family limitation", noting to readers of his periodic insider's newsletter that Perkin had "been transferred to Accra for several months to implement the new policy".[15]

Guttmacher was, at least, egalitarian in his views on population. He suggested at the 1969 annual PPWP meeting that it would improve family well-being and promote the common good if all American parents limited their family size.[16] Donald Strauss, former chairman of Planned Parenthood's Executive Committee, added that there was no question that America must reach zero population growth, asking only: "How fast can we get there . . . ?" Guttmacher asked rhetorically, "Can anyone seriously challenge his position?"[17]

Reaching this goal, he thought, would best be accomplished by having groups other than the PPFA preach the doctrine of a normative 2.1-child family, as doing this would offend Planned Parenthood's minority clients. He suggested that family size would decrease if abortion were liberalized nationwide and received government support.[18] In this prediction he was right on target.

The last year the U.S. birth rate exceeded the replacement level was 1971, the year Guttmacher wrote the above statement. From 1972 through 1988 (the

---

[12] PPWP, News, Press Release, New York City, October 19, 1966, 50th Anniversary Conference, SSCSC.

[13] Guttmacher, *Presidential Letter,* no. 34, July 17, 1968.

[14] Ibid., no. 35, October 4, 1968, 3.

[15] Ibid., no. 41, July 25, 1969, 2.

[16] Ibid., no. 45, February 14, 1970.

[17] Ibid., 4.

[18] Guttmacher letter to Mr. Del Neal, Tacoma, Washington, July 8, 1971, Countway Library, Harvard Medical School (hereinafter referred to as CLHMS).

last year for which the USPHS has complete figures) the U.S. fertility rate averaged 1.83 births per childbearing woman. Ben Wattenberg of the American Enterprise Institute has highlighted preliminary data from the National Center for Health Statistics (NC S) for 1989 that show the birth rate climbing above 2.0—still below replacement level but a significant rise that, if true, reverses a two-decade old trend. But the NCHS will not confirm the data until 1991 and, of course, it is far too early to say that it represents the emergence of a new or even long-lasting trend.

The central fact is that the U.S. birth rate remains very low by historical standards, especially when viewed in the context of near decade-long economic growth nationwide. It should be noted that the total "fertility rate" is the "number of children that would be born to a woman if she were to survive her childbearing years and were to experience those age specific birth rates throughout her child bearing years".

This unprecedented drop in American birth rates resulted from the acceptance, or imposition, in respect to *Roe v. Wade,* of Planned Parenthood's program of the Pill, sterilization, and abortion on demand. All three of these fertility depressants have received direct and indirect taxpayer subsidy at the federal and state level, with the direct funding of birth control and abortion, and preferential tax treatment of many abortion and birth control providers as exempt entities.

As in pre-World War II France, there are two major areas of national interest directly and adversely impacted by this rapid and severe population decline.

First, present and future military manpower needs may escalate pressure to reinstate the draft or expand the number of females in combat-support positions. The number of Americans seventeen to twenty years old is shrinking. By late 1991, there will be around 13 million in this age group, where as there were 17.5 million in 1980. Thus, the military services will have to draw a higher percentage from the available pool.[19] Many dedicated defenders of the right to life are troubled at using this line of argument regarding the impact of depopulation, but its real significance is that it should, in fact, neutralize what has been one of the most influential behind-the-scenes factors in the success of Planned Parenthood and other antipopulation organizations in adversely influencing the course of U.S. foreign policy.

Sharon Camp of the Population Crisis Committee, a Planned Parenthood ally, sent a strongly worded letter to the Agency for International Development (AID) in 1986 challenging the Reagan administration's "Mexico City" policy, which denied U.S. birth control funding to agencies overseas that

---

[19] Tim Carrington, "Some Democrats Weigh Reviving Draft to Bolster Armed Services and to Make Their Mark on Defense", *Wall Street Journal,* November 17, 1986, 70.

promoted abortion or provided it with their own funds. The letter was based solely on national security concerns, charging that worldwide destabilization and damage to U.S. interests would occur if the nation did not reverse the Mexico City policy and pursue more aggressive population control overseas. It was signed by a long list of prominent military figures, from William Westmoreland and Maxwell Taylor to former U.S. defense secretary Robert McNamara.[20] The role of these defense and military advisers in U.S. population policy is not well known. But the fact is that if any national security justifications exist for a domestic U.S. population policy, they are basically a wash.

Interestingly, the number of female military personnel who served in the U.S. Armed Forces in Operation Desert Storm against Iraq was roughly 11,000. Had the 1.65 million legal abortions occuring in the U.S. between 1968 and 1972 not taken place, approximaely 11,000 males, according to Defense Department manpower needs estimates, would have been available to the all-volunteer army.

Second, the Social Security system is supporting more and more beneficiaries with fewer and fewer people. The 1975 report of the advisors to the Social Security system noted that:

> Fertility rates are the most important factor in the trustees' determination of future costs of the system, with changes in such rates accounting for some two-thirds of the prospective long term deficit. The trustees have assumed a gradual increase in the fertility rate from the present very low rate of 1.9 to 2.1 by 1985 and stabilizing at that rate thereafter.
>
> The persons who will draw retirement benefits between the years 2005 and 2035 are already born. We already know that the number of beneficiaries in that period will be relatively large and that the total benefits, therefore, will be relatively high. . . . If the fertility rate does hold at 2.1 . . . the number of workers will be relatively small and the tax rate will be high.
>
> It must be remembered that the average person cannot be expected to pay Social Security taxes until some 18 to 20 years after he is born. This means that, in a certain sense, time is already starting to run out. The fertility rate will have to start moving well above the projected rates within the next 15 years, and remain at a relatively high level for three decades, in order to produce any meaningful reduction in the high taxes that will otherwise be payable. Working against this possibility are . . . advances in the technology of controlling conception and the wider use of abortion . . . [and] . . . many more married women who work.[21]

When the current Social Security trustees projected fertility rates in 1987, their

---

[20] Letter from Sharon Camp, Population Crisis Committee, to Peter McPherson, administrator, Agency for International Development, U.S. State Department, September, 1986.

[21] Report of the Quadrennial Advisory Council on Social Security, 1975, House Document no. 94-75, 94th Cong., 1st sess., appendix A, Report of Subcommittee on Finance of the 1974 Advisory Council on Social Security, February 3, 1975, sec. III, "Testing Trustees' Conclusions", 101.

optimistic figures were *lower* than the pessimistic projections of the 1974 Social Security trustees. The present trustees hope for a replacement level birth rate of 2.1 births (assuming net immigration were zero and infant mortality rates were constant) in 2000—a full fifteen years later than the 1974 projections! They also hope that higher fertility rates will

> ultimately exceed the level of the past decade because such a low level has never been experienced in the United States over a long period ... it is not believed that the total fertility rate will return to the high levels of the 1940's, 1950's and early 1960's. Several changes in our society have occurred during the past 20 years that have contributed to reducing the number of children being born. Some of these changes are increased availability and use of birth control methods, increased female participation in the labor force, increased prevalence of divorce, increased postponement of marriage and childbearing among young women, and the shift in the perception of the status of children within their families from economic assets to economic liabilities. No significant reversal of these changes is anticipated.[22]

The increased availability of privately and publicly subsidized birth control is the linchpin behind every one of the above factors. Birth control, including abortion, helps to keep a woman in the labor market or keeps her there longer; birth control was supposed to reduce the pressures of children on marriages and thereby decrease divorce, but has not—in fact, it may have made the situation worse, as divorce occurs more often among couples who have fewer children or are completely childless.

Government, it seems, has now done for population what it did for commodities from agricultural goods and energy to housing, namely, turn an abundance into a shortage. Even Planned Parenthood's own forecasters have sensed such a future. As demographer Charles Westoff noted in 1978:

> Although it seems ironic, if not ludicrous ... there are reasons to believe that some subsidization of reproduction may eventually become necessary. The problem has already arisen in more than one European country, and the social trends apparent in the United States today all seem to point in that direction.[23]

2. BIRTH CONTROL FOR THE UNMARRIED

Dr. Alan Guttmacher, at a 1951 conference on "World Population Problems and Birth Control", disclosed the results of a survey he had conducted on

[22] Alice H. Wade, "Social Security Area Population Projections: 1987", *Social Security Bulletin,* vol. 51, no. 2, February 1988, 3–30.

[23] Charles Westoff, Ph.D., "Some Speculations on the Future of Marriage and Fertility", *Family Planning Perspectives,* vol. 10, no. 2 (March–April 1978): 79–83.

physician attitudes toward giving birth control to married women. Of the 3,400 doctors polled, 68% would give married women birth control; 29% would not.[24] Guttmacher said that he had no answer to the "very complex" question of giving birth control to the unmarried. He told the conference that further investigation and knowledge were needed to replace taboo and prejudice on this topic.[25] Describing opposition to giving unmarried women birth control as a "taboo" and "prejudice" surely was a hint that a "rational" solution was on the horizon.

Although the question of accepting obviously single women as clients constantly came up, the national Planned Parenthood office had not issued policy guidelines. Instead, each local Planned Parenthood affiliate was left to its own devices when it came to accepting unmarried women as clients.[26] In January 1952, one affiliate's medical advisory committee had suggested that patients with irregular marital status be accepted if they were referred by a social agency or a doctor. There was a circular aspect to this policy. For example, if an acquaintance of a prospective client had referred a woman, the woman was referred in turn to a "private doctor of the Medical Advisory Committee", who obviously could then refer her back to Planned Parenthood.[27]

By 1956 this policy had generated considerable discussion, and although the legal and religious aspects were recognized, it was thought best to leave it a medical matter. It was in 1956 that the PPFA National Medical Advisory Committee first agreed to accept as clients "unmarried women who are referred to Affiliates by recognized social or medical agencies".[28] It apparently was understood that unmarried women who had not given birth could be included in any policy that applied to serving unmarried mothers.[29]

In January 1957 the PPFA National Medical Committee adopted a policy under which any woman who claimed to be married would have her statement accepted.[30]

By June 1957 it had become official PPFA policy to serve unmarried mothers who were referred from a social or health agency.[31] By 1961 "quite a few affiliates" were giving birth control to unmarried women and unmarried mothers.[32]

The "wedge" that Planned Parenthood found useful in gaining public

[24] "Doctors Queried on Birth Control", *New York Times,* October 21, 1951, 74; 2% opposed birth control in any medical setting; 1% had no opinion; and 2% ignored the question.

[25] Ibid.

[26] Minutes, PPFA Medical Committee, October 3, 1956, 3.

[27] Ibid.

[28] Ibid.

[29] Ibid.

[30] Ibid., January 17, 1957.

[31] Ibid., June 5, 1957.

[32] Ibid., February 5, 1961, 4.

support, or at least nonopposition, to birth control for the unmarried was the familiar Sanger theme that birth control would reduce welfare caseloads. In 1962, Guttmacher, then president-elect of the PPFA, said that the failure of state and local governments to curb caseloads and welfare costs "borders on a national scandal".[33] Legislators in Sanger's day rejected this appeal, but this time some policy makers accepted the "solution". The difference was the Pill. Guttmacher told his San Francisco audience that health and welfare officials in Mecklenburg County, North Carolina, were using the Pill to see if welfare caseloads were reduced. Without mentioning how many women dropped out of the program and how accurate official estimates of pregnancies were, Guttmacher claimed that none of the ninety-nine women who had a total of 533 pregnancies had become pregnant in the seventeen months they were on the Pill. The cost was ten cents a day versus the dollar a day a "relief" child would cost the taxpayers, and the Pill would soon cost only ten dollars a year.[34]

But no sooner had New York and other states implemented this policy than Guttmacher and others denounced it as naive and unrealistic because eligibility was restricted to married women living with their husbands.[35] The clear implication was that even more money could be saved if sexually indulgent, poor, single women were given the Pill.

Finally, in 1969 the PPFA recommended that adolescents be accorded legal access to birth control without parental consent. Guttmacher suggested that such a policy would reduce illegal abortion and out-of-wedlock, adolescent motherhood.[36] At a 1970 speech to students at Smith College (where Margaret Sanger had deposited many of her papers), Guttmacher elaborated on the "new morality" of birth control. He told the young ladies that they were the first generation of young women to have nearly complete legal and medical control over fertility; that premarital sexual involvement could be responsible; and that, regardless of marital status, sexual intercourse without the most effective birth control was immoral save when both partners wanted a child.[37]

By the time of Guttmacher's address, the sexual revolution spawned by the Pill and other cultural factors was already in evidence and poised to take off. The Planned Parenthood message of "contraception plus premarital sexual activity equals responsibility" was a carefully crafted marketing appeal to what the organization hoped would be a lifelong clientele.

Between 1940 and 1968 the incidence of nonmarital births and pregnancies

[33] PPWP Press Release, May 15, 1962, Winfield Best, 3, SSCSC.

[34] Ibid., 2.

[35] PPWP, "Thoughts on Our Program for the Mid-Sixties", remarks at Affiliate and Board Meeting, January 24–25, 1964, 1, CLHMS.

[36] 1969 testimony of Dr. Alan Guttmacher, New York State Senate Committee on Health, September 23, 1971, CLHMS.

[37] Alan Guttmacher, speech at Smith College, 1970, CLHMS.

had increased. Planned Parenthood writers had some creative explanations for this rise, among them that the age at onset of menstruation had decreased over the three previous decades. However, even Guttmacher had disputed this claim, stating that a one-year decline in the age of menarche from 1940 to 1968 "had little to do with the fertility of 18 and 19 year olds. . . . What other factor than greater sexual activity could explain a change of such magnitude?"

The magnitude of the change was indeed great. In 1940 nonwhite women aged eighteen to nineteen experienced 61 births/1,000 unmarried women. In 1968 the corresponding figure was 112/1,000. In 1940 white women aged eighteen to nineteen experienced 5 births/1,000 unmarried women; in 1968 the rate was 17 births/1,000.[38] And what other factor could account for the increased rate of sexual activity than wider access to birth control, with its promise of sex without tears and consequences?

Planned Parenthood's spirit of erotic license, or at least its pragmatic "damage control" exigencies, steadily permeated the medical community after Guttmacher's 1951 poll. Thirty-three years later pro-birth control writers would lament that "only 73 percent" of private physicians would provide prescriptive birth control to minors without parental consent.[39]

What has been the effect of over twenty years of publicly telling all American adolescents and young adults that sexual intercourse has nothing to do with marriage and that responsible sex always means birth control? We examine some of the more harrowing data in a subsequent chapter. But a few observations are worthwhile here.

To the surprise only of pro-birth control writers who profess complete pessimism about changing the present situation save by more birth control, the link between having and rearing children has been weakened whether the births take place in marriage or not.[40] Almost 25% of all children under eighteen are living with only one parent.[41] Many authors now estimate that close to half of all children living today will live in a single-parent household before they reach the age of eighteen. In the District of Columbia, that dubious demographic distinction has already been attained.

Although claiming that no one knows how to change the present family malaise, a pro-birth control writer suggests that narrowing people's choices about "family life" would overly burden "individual autonomy", and further-more, that any policy that tried to make marriage more attractive, but which

---

[38] Guttmacher, *Presidential Letter*, no. 61, June 15, 1972.

[39] Elise F. Jones et al., *Pregnancy, Contraception, and Family Planning Services in Industrialized Countries* (New Haven and London: Yale University Press, 1989), 91.

[40] Andrew J. Cherlin, "The Weakening Link between Marriage and the Care of Children", *Family Planning Perspectives*, vol. 20, no. 6 (November–December 1988), 302.

[41] Ibid.

limited women's work opportunities, would fail.[42] If he is correct, then sexual freedom and "family planning" produce complete cultural inertia when it comes to initiatives that would protect the family.

3. HEALTH AND WELFARE

Obtaining the support of public federal, state, and local hospitals and social assistance programs for the direct delivery of birth control services was a two-step process. The hospital battle was fought in the 1950s, and the welfare issue was largely settled in the 1960s.

Securing birth control distribution in public hospitals was a high priority for Planned Parenthood, as it would expose both poor and middle-class women to offers of birth control even where welfare programs and private physicians did not.

The perfect opportunity surfaced in New York City during 1958, with a little assistance from Planned Parenthood officials. The principal actor was Dr. Louis M. Hellman, the director of obstetrics at the Kings County Hospital in Brooklyn, who previously was chairman (and then member) of Planned Parenthood's National Medical Committee.[43,44] Apparently there had been an unwritten rule not to prescribe birth control at city-run hospitals.[45] In July 1958 Dr. Hellman intended to challenge this policy by prescribing a diaphragm for a diabetic woman and attempting to fit it at the Kings County Hospital. Hellman alleged that the woman's life or that of her child would have been endangered by another pregnancy.[46] However, when he attempted to fit the diabetic woman, Hellman was told that he was under orders from Dr. Morris A. Jacobs, New York City hospitals commissioner, not to proceed. The controversy became public.[47]

This battle was a major news story in New York City for two months, with the Catholic Archdiocese of New York and the Diocese of Brooklyn defending the policy and virtually everyone else attacking it. That it was a completely unnecessary conflict was pointed out by a letter writer to the *New York Times* who said that, "As a Protestant New Yorker I should like to ask

[42] Ibid., 305.

[43] *Planned Parenthood News,* no. 21, Spring 1958, listing of officers; *Planned Parenthood News,* no. 15, Summer 1956, 7.

[44] Robert Alden, "City Stops Doctor on Birth Control", *New York Times,* July 17, 1958, K-29.

[45] Ibid.

[46] Ibid.

[47] Ibid.

why a diabetic patient in one of our city hospitals is attracting so much attention. We have well-run clinics for birth control. They are private and voluntary. A patient therefore need not depend on a busy city hospital, which is tax supported, for this service."[48] After an acrimonious public battle in which Protestant and Jewish groups traded charges with their Catholic counterparts, the New York City Board of Hospitals voted seven to two on September 17, 1958, to lift its prior ban on artificial birth control.[49] The Board's statement limited itself to "[c]learly defined medical conditions in which the life or health of a woman may be jeopardized by pregnancy". It further provided that, "Physicians, nurses, and other hospital personnel who have religious or moral objections should be excused from participation in contraceptive procedures".

The Archdiocese of New York and the Diocese of Brooklyn issued a joint statement declaring that the Board's decision "introduces an immoral practice in our hospitals that perverts the nature and the dignity of man".[50]

The PPFA praised the decision as a great victory for New Yorkers, "which has nationwide significance and consequences". This was no hazardous guess: The "national significance" of using tax-supported facilities for the provision of birth control was precisely the reason the Kings County policy was challenged in the first place.

While the hospital fight concentrated on the alleged health aspect of birth control, securing the inclusion of birth control in social welfare programs necessarily focused attention on the social make-up of Planned Parenthood itself. Planned Parenthood's own social profile was distinctly different from the groups it targeted for birth control "assistance". Its membership in the 1960s was decidedly upper class, financially and socially. With isolated exceptions gleaned from direct mail solicitations, there was virtually no grass-roots leadership or support for its program.[51] Alan Guttmacher said that Planned Parenthood had to correct the image that it wanted to preserve "white Protestant supremacy", and he insisted that it had no interest in increasing or decreasing the birth rate of "any particular ethnic or social group".[52] Rather curiously, though, Guttmacher characterized the social situation in America, under which the upper-income and educated stratum would demand equal treatment for the "less sophisticated and less privileged", as a "people's movement".[53]

---

[48] Letters to the Editor, *New York Times,* August 9, 1958.
[49] Edith E. Asbury, "Birth Control Ban Ended by City's Hospital Board", *New York Times,* September 18, 1958, 1, 12.
[50] Ibid., 12.
[51] PPFA–PPWP Program 1963–1970, SSCSC.
[52] Ibid., 6.
[53] Guttmacher, *Presidential Letter,* no. 22, May 17, 1967, 3.

He did recognize that to achieve an expansion of birth control promotion in public facilities would require constant political pressure at the federal, state, and local levels, which could only come from a public clamor for liberalization.[54]

In spite of the many public claims made on behalf of birth control as a cure for poverty, welfare, family instability, etc., Guttmacher privately recognized that many Planned Parenthood arguments were based on logical hypotheses and not proven facts. He wanted to prove that birth control would not only rehabilitate mothers on public assistance, but would also reduce "welfare rolls and taxes". He also wanted to show policy makers that birth control would produce a situation whereby "minority groups who constantly outbreed the majority will no longer persist in doing so . . . ".[55]

Despite claims that racial or ethnic groups were not being "targeted", American blacks, among whose ranks a greater proportion of the poor were numbered, received a high priority in Planned Parenthood's nationwide efforts. Donald B. Strauss, chairman of Planned Parenthood–World Population, urged the 1964 Democratic National Convention to liberalize the party's stated policies on birth control and to adopt domestic and foreign policy platform resolutions to conform with long-sought Sangerite goals. The Democratic Platform Committee delegates were told that:

> [W]hile almost one-fourth of non-white parents have 4 or more children under 18 living with them, only 8% of the white couples have that many children living at home. For the Negro parent in particular, the denial of access to family planning professional guidance forecloses one more avenue to family advancement and well-being.
>
> Unwanted children would not get the job training and educational skills they needed to compete in a shrinking labor market; moreover, unwanted children are a product and a cause of poverty.

Strauss urged the delegates to end restrictions which hinder the free provision of birth control in health programs; create a Presidential Commission to study population problem; support more research for birth control and give foreign aid for birth control to developing nations as an essential concomitant of national economic development efforts.[56]

Planned Parenthood's effort to get states to make birth control part of public health and welfare programs experienced phenomenal success during 1965 to 1967. In seventeen states, either general access to birth control

---

[54] PPWP, "Thoughts on Our Program for the Mid-Sixties", 2, SSCSC.

[55] Ibid., 3.

[56] PPWP press release, statement of Donald B. Strauss, chairman, PPWP, to the 1964 Democratic Convention Committee on Resolutions and Platform, August 18, 1964, SSCSC.

was provided or health and welfare laws or policies were liberalized to accommodate the provision of birth control in such programs.[57]

But with state governments pursuing Planned Parenthood's agenda, was Planned Parenthood as an organization still needed? Yes, Guttmacher observed that increased government involvement was caused by the pressure which the organization was continually making and the continuous educational campaign being carried out.[58]

The "educational" campaign Guttmacher referred to was frankly more of an appeal to the prejudices and unproved assumptions of legislators, health and welfare program administrators, and the general public. A grant made by the Social Science Committee of the PPFA to Edward Pohlman, for the purpose of surveying the social science literature to document the supposedly undesirable outcome of unwanted conceptions, is instructive. Professor Pohlman found that direct evidence of such a relationship

> [i]s almost completely lacking, except for a few fragments of retrospective evidence. . . . It was the hope of this article to find more convincing research evidence and to give some idea of the amount of relationship between unwanted conception and undesirable effects. This hope has been disappointed.
>
> This reviewer originally thought that if the undesirability of unwanted conceptions could be demonstrated with research, this would provide a powerful additional argument for the importance of birth planning. He now feels that such research is not so important. Alarm over population pressures provides a major impetus to public action concerning birth planning. Also, many individuals perceive unwanted conceptions as having undesirable effects . . . these perceptions probably influence their actions as effectively as views based on additional research.[59]

Pohlman noted that further research along these lines would have only academic interest, and be of no practical help in achieving population goals. Thus, he concluded, resources could be better directed elsewhere.

And they were, especially at Americans of African descent. Surveying the "successes" of tax-subsidized birth control programs, Guttmacher noted in 1970 that "[B]irth control services are proliferating in areas adjacent to concen-

---

[57] In 1965: Kansas, Colorado, Iowa, Nevada, California, Illinois, New York, Michigan, Ohio, and Connecticut; the U.S. Supreme Court struck down a state anti–birth control law. In 1966: Massachusetts, Alaska, Georgia, and West Virginia; 1967: Missouri, Oklahoma, and Oregon. PPWP "Ending Comstockery in America", V [2.7] September 1966, D-884 memo to presidents and executive directors of Planned Parenthood affiliates, from Department of Program Planning and Development; ibid., VI 333/667, undated, apparently 1967; ibid., VII, 408/867, 2.7, undated, apparently 1967; ibid., VIII, [2.7] 74/168, undated, apparently 1967.

[58] Guttmacher, *Presidential Letter*, no. 18, December 28, 1966, 3.

[59] Edward Pohlman, Ph.D., "Unwanted Conceptions: Research on Undesirable Consequences", *Eugenics Quarterly*, vol. 14, no. 2, (c. 1967): 143–54; reprinted in *Child and Family Quarterly*, vol. 8, no. 3 (Summer 1969): 249–50.

trations of black population".[60] In spite of this "success", Planned Parenthood suffered internal difficulties over the intensity of its domestic efforts with "people of color". Dr. Alan Sweezy, a colleague of Guttmacher, had taken issue with an Ad Council campaign supported by Planned Parenthood that "blamed" the domestic population increases on white Americans. Sweezy argued that 90% of whites were already on birth control and, taken as a whole, had below replacement-level fertility.[61] Guttmacher acknowledged that PPWP had taken a false posture in blaming whites while absolving blacks for the increase in population, pointing to birth figures as proof. He added that the PPFA leadership was intimidated by minorities and that he suspected that the PPFA minority board members might deliver an unacceptable policy proposal in response to this posture.[62]

Whatever the nature of Planned Parenthood's internal minority problems, it has managed to present the image of toleration and minority participation through the vehicle of its divorced, telegenic, African American president, Ms. Faye Wattleton, appointed titular head of the PPFA in 1978, a post she still holds. Though paid in the six-figure range, she has impeccable minority credentials that would have fit the public relations criteria of both Margaret Sanger and Dr. Clarence Gamble.

Wattleton's PPFA biography touts her as a friend of the "Poor and the young"; a nurse at Harlem Hospital; and the recipient of the 1989 Congressional Black Caucus Foundation Humanitarian Award and the World Institute of Black Communicators' 1986 Excellence in Black Communications Award. It further states she was featured in a national photography exhibit, "I Dream a World: Portraits of Black Women Who Changed America"; interviewed in *Ebony*; and was the cover story in *Black Enterprise* magazine.[63]

Her ideological orientation has received certification in the form of the Better World Society's 1989 Population Medal, the 1986 American Humanist Award, and others.[64] But surely, the spectacle of the Congressional Black Caucus awarding its humanitarian award to the black woman who presides over the organization that has hastened and justified the death of almost eight million black children since 1973 and facilitated the demise of the black family is ironic in the extreme.

---

[60] Guttmacher, *Presidential Letter*, no. 50, November 4, 1970, 3.

[61] Letter of Dr. Alan Sweezy to Robin Eliot of Planned Parenthood–World Population, October 30, 1971, CLHMS.

[62] Alan Guttmacher letter to Dr. Alan Sweezy, California Institute of Technology, November 5, 1971, CLHMS.

[63] "Faye Wattleton, President, Planned Parenthood Federation of America", biographical sketch, PPFA news release, April 17, 1990.

[64] Ibid.

4. BIRTH CONTROL METHODS

For birth control to become universally accepted, abstinence from sexual intercourse must be universally rejected. Thus, Planned Parenthood's Medical Committee, in preparation for a 1960 challenge to Connecticut's anticontraception law, denied that abstinence was an "alternative, reasonable or otherwise" to contracepted marital intercourse.[65] The formal PPFA policy, propounded by then-medical director Dr. Mary Calderone, was that: "*Any* method is better than *no* method"; and "The most effective method for a couple is the one that the couple will use consistently."[66]

To what extent this bias caused researchers or clinicians to gloss over the problems with various forms of artificial birth control is difficult to say. It is, however, easy to point to the public statements of PPFA or its spokesmen that exonerate the Pill, the many varieties of the intrauterine device (IUD), Depo-Provera, and other methods, when other researchers were finding problems with these methods. For example, when reports first surfaced in 1962 with respect to Pill-associated blood clots, Planned Parenthood issued a statement that at nine affiliates, with eleven thousand women on the Pill, there was no incidence of this complication.[67]

A report by the PPFA National Medical Committee issued July 29, 1964, gave preliminary endorsement to the IUD. It was heralded as in no way impeding any desired births, and the reported incidence of pelvic infection was alleged to be low.[68] In December 1964 the PPFA took satisfaction in the development of the IUD and noted that PPFA centers constituted the "largest single group of patients using this method and hence form[ed] the most important source of information which will be used in its final assessment . . . ".[69] The data, which were supposedly derived from this pool of information, were used to continue the IUD safety theme, with the renewed claim that even if the IUD fails, the "pregnancy progresses normally and the child is unaffected".[70] Moreover, there was no "significant increase in pelvic infection".[71]

There was, however, a curious dual tack taken when problems could not be denied. When foreign research data showed, as they did in Britain, that the Pill was associated with blood clots, Guttmacher claimed that: "Disease inci-

[65] PPFA Medical Committee Minutes, June 15, 1960, 1, 2.

[66] Ibid., September 21, 1960, 6.

[67] PPWP press release, by Mary Calderone, medical director, PPFA, August 8, 1962, SSCSC.

[68] PPWP press release, July 29, 1964, Winfield Best, 3.

[69] Guttmacher, *Presidential Letter,* no. 1, December 31, 1964, 2.

[70] Ibid., Supplement, no. 4, April 1, 1965, 2.

[71] Ibid.

dence figures for Britain may not hold for America."[72] But when foreign data exonerated the Pill, the findings were hailed and unhesitatingly applied to American women. "[S]erious side-effects including clots . . . are likely to be reduced by at least 50 per cent as a result of new medical findings reported from Britain, Denmark and Sweden."[73]

The demand for the Pill and IUD was powerfully driven by the high claims of ease, effectiveness, and reversibility. When Guttmacher was challenged by Dr. Eugene L. Saenger of Cincinnati to conduct a prospective study measuring these characteristics in a group of women randomly assigned different birth control methods, he balked.[74]

Guttmacher had previously gone to the head of the Food and Drug Administration (FDA) and secured permission to continue patients on the Pill beyond the FDA-recommended two-year time limit, and to keep women on the Pill for four to five years, conducting liver, chemical, and blood tests. In response to Dr. Saenger's proposal he related that the low number of women still on the Pill made it meaningless to continue. He also asserted that the mobility of the clinic population made medical follow-up difficult.[75] One wonders how many women slipped through the follow-up loop back in 1962 when Planned Parenthood was ostensibly looking for blood clot complications.

Another Planned Parenthood colleague also counseled against a large prospective Pill/IUD study, telling PPWP medical director Dr. George Langmyhr that: as a luteolytic agent[76] might be available within a few years as well as an orally administered abortifacient within five years, he thought research in these areas would be a better investment.[77]

Not all of the PPFA research efforts produced commercially marketable antifertility drugs or devices. One case in point is Depo-Provera, an injectable steroid administered to women. From 1965 to 1972, the Margaret Sanger Research Bureau had been studying Depo-Provera on 3% of its patients; i.e.,

---

[72] Ibid., no. 32, May 20, 1968, 1.

[73] Ibid., no. 47, May 22, 1970. (But Guttmacher did acknowledge objections to the Pill such as the "burdensome necessity" of taking it daily.)

[74] Letter from Dr. Eugene L. Saenger, professor of Radiology, Univ. of Cincinnati, to Dr. Alan Guttmacher, May 11, 1970, CLHMS.

[75] Letter from Alan Guttmacher to Mrs. Ann Mitchell, Cincinnati Planned Parenthood, March 18, 1970, CLHMS.

[76] Leuteolytic refers to an agent that works against the normal physiologic function of the corpus leutum and that is indispensable for the maintenance of early pregnancy, thus a leuteolytic agent would cause abortion at or around the time of implantation.

[77] Letter from Dr. Alan Barnes of Johns Hopkins University to George Langmyhr, medical director, PP–WP, June 15, 1970, CLHMS.

adolescents in foster care, girls who had had abortions.[78] The FDA had notified doctors that women receiving Depo-Provera should sign an informed consent form. Dr. Aquiles J. Sobrero, director of the Margaret Sanger Research Bureau, objected, contending among other things that the requirement was an insult to doctors.[79] The FDA consent form stated in its first paragraph that beagle dogs given Depo-Provera had "developed tumors in their breasts. Some of these tumors may be cancer or may develop into cancer."[80] Other problems cited were similar to those for the Pill.

Sobrero's concerns were well placed, as he believed that no woman in her right mind would sign the consent form; in fact she would probably hate her doctor before she finished reading it.[81] Sobrero also claimed that the proposed consent form worked at cross purposes with efforts to slow population growth and decrease unwanted pregnancies. His arguments notwithstanding, Depo-Provera to this day has not been approved by the FDA for use as a contraceptive.

About the same time as the Depo-Provera controversy, Guttmacher was stirring up his troops to write the White House in support of the recommendations of the Presidential Commission on Population Growth and the American Future. Chaired by John D. Rockefeller, the Commission had yielded an influential report recommending that teens be given legal access to birth control and that laws prohibiting abortion or placing restrictions on voluntary sterilization be repealed.[82]

These latter efforts were successful, as can be seen by the prevalence of the following birth control practices among both married and unmarried women for 1987: 51% of married women used the Pill, and 22% were sterilized; 48% of unmarried women used the Pill, and 13% were sterilized.[83]

However sterilization, though widely practiced, has been criticized on grounds of its biased application against the poor. Dr. John L. S. Holloman, an African American physician and former head of the New York City Health and Hospitals Corporation, said in 1977 that doctors learn their trade by practicing on the poor, and also that sterilization of the poor is being used as a social tool to control "undesirables".

[78] Letter from Dr. Aquiles J. Sobrero, director, Margaret Sanger Research Bureau, to Dr. Alan Barnes, chairman, FDA Obstetrical and Gynecological Committee, April 6, 1972, CLHMS.

[79] Ibid.

[80] FDA form 95-1945, Government Printing Office, January 1972.

[81] Letter from Aquiles J. Sobrero, Director, Margaret Sanger Research Bureau, to Dr. George J. Langmyhr, medical director, PPWP, March 20, 1972, CLHMS.

[82] Guttmacher, *Presidential Letter* [alert to "Dear Friends of PP"], March 14, 1972.

[83] Jacqueline D. Forrest and Richard R. Fordyce, "U.S. Women's Contraceptive Attitudes and Practice—How Have They Changed in the 1980s?" *Family Planning Perspectives*, vol. 20, no. 3 (May–June 1988).

Dr. Donald Sloan, of Metropolitan Hospital, a large city hospital in New York, confirmed this statement. "We're a city hospital, so most of our patients are poor", he said. "They are considered chattel by the physicians here. We practice on the poor so we can operate on the rich. Hysterectomies and simple tubal ligations are performed all the time just for that practice."

Several studies [of federally subsidized clinics] add fuel to the racial debate surrounding sterilization. One study by Dr. Carl W. Tyler, Jr., of the Family Planning and Evaluation branch of the Center for Disease Control in Atlanta, deals specifically with the sterilization of minors. Dr. Tyler found that black women under 21 years of age were sterilized with greater frequency than white women in the same age group. More important, he found that welfare recipients under 21, regardless of race, were more likely to be sterilized than those not on welfare.[84]

Another criticism stated:

> ... Family planning professionals ... do not weigh the special needs or wishes of this one person; rather, their credo is that in all situations effective contraception is the answer to the plight of the poor. . . .
>
> For many social workers the clinics' major function is to reduce the welfare rolls. For others it is to relieve the poor of the economic and emotional burdens of numbers of unwanted children. But under the aggressive superintendence of both groups, voluntary consent evaporates. So the poor become pawns in the welfare game. . . . Their zeal often results in experimentation with dangerous techniques (for example, Depo-Provera).
>
> The messianic zeal of family planners to reduce the birth rate among the poor will not be stifled or inhibited by formal requirements. . . . The planners are ultimately convinced that . . . they are saving us from ecological disaster and rescuing the poor from a lifetime of poverty. Procedural requirements are a flimsy protection against this sense of mission.[85]

---

[84] John Elliot, "Sterilization: No Color Line, but a Poverty Line", *Medical Tribune,* September 21, 1977, 16, 28.

[85] Sheila M. Rothman, "Sterilizing the Poor", *Society,* January/February 1977.

Chapter Three

A New Code or No Code?
Planned Parenthood's Philosophy of Sex

Thank you for the world so sweet.
Thank you for the food we eat.
Thank you for the birds that sing.
Thank you, God, for everything.

—A Children's Prayer

Myth 11. *Young women who have more than one sexual partner are easy.* Some people, both men and women, prefer to relate sexually to more than one person at a time. This is an individual preference.

—(Adolescent Curriculum Planned Parenthood
of Alameda–San Francisco)

Only a generation ago, there would have been very little controversy in America, at least among American parents, about which of the above statements would be out of place in one of the nation's classrooms. It is a tribute to the scale of the seemingly sudden and radical changes of the past twenty-five years that it is the latter assertion that now rests comfortably within the educational mainstream, and the former that is not only considered questionable, but constitutionally prohibited—at least insofar as what we as a society determine will be the orthodoxy of childhood.

For the only common value permitted to reign in American schools at the end of the twentieth century is a doctrine of absolute choice. But it is not even choice in the classic sense, for, as the typical Planned Parenthood curriculum quoted above suggests, the new regime holds that nothing changes once the chooser has chosen. Values, this philosophy insists, do not have consequences. "Choices" are mere "preferences", as one would prefer chocolate over cherry flavoring, nor is there even the minimal sense of choice mattering as it would for one taking Frost's road "less travelled by".

A quarter century ago the Supreme Court of the United States refused to hear an appeal in a case (*Stein v. Oshinsky*) involving the popular children's prayer reprinted at the beginning of this chapter. The Court let stand a Second Circuit Court of Appeals' decision upholding the authority of a public school official to ban its recitation before a midmorning snack.[1] Three years later, the Seventh Circuit reached a similar conclusion about the same prayer, altered only by omission of the word "God".[2]

As a result of judicial decree, organized prayer and voluntary religious practice disappeared from America's public schools virtually overnight. In literal (perhaps optimistic) terms, this meant only that activities conceived of as distinctly religious in character were now constitutionally suspect. But the abolition of public school religion quickly became the abolition of a public school morality, and Planned Parenthood's forces, geared for a nationwide battle from the very beginning, rushed to fill the void. They fought with special effectiveness where they have always fought, in the least representative institutions of our society: the courts and the administrative bureaucracies.

By 1980, Planned Parenthood lawyers had worked a revolution in "minor's rights" in the federal courts. In 1977, in *Carey v. Population Services International,* the Supreme Court struck down as unconstitutional a New York law banning the sale of nonprescription contraceptive devices to children under the age of sixteen. In 1979, in the heyday of the Carter administration's unflinching support of the Planned Parenthood agenda, the U.S. Department of Health, Education and Welfare (HEW, now the Department of Health and Human Services) published a curriculum guide for a "model program" for sex education.

The quotation at the beginning of this chapter appears in the guide. In addition to debunking "myths" like monogamy and fidelity, the HEW–Planned Parenthood guide advocated distribution of birth control drugs and devices to adolescents, promoted what it termed a "sexual simulation game" called Plan-a-Fam (teenage players use dominoes marked "abortion" and "contraception" to advance around the game board), and encouraged schools to develop directories for teenagers seeking birth control devices and abortions.[3]

---

[1] *Stein v. Oshinsky,* 348 F2d. 999 (2 Cir. 1965), cert. den. 382 U.S. 957, 86 S. Ct. 435, 15 L.Ed.2d 361 (1965). The major school prayer case, *Engel v. Vitale,* was decided several years earlier. *Stein* involved a prohibition on voluntary recitation of school prayer led by the children themselves, a question left unresolved by *Engle,* and still in some doubt today. *Stein* reached the Supreme Court the same year it handed down the *Griswold* decision, described at some length in chapter 5. As Robert Bork has noted (see Bork, *The Tempting of America: The Political Seduction of the Law*), *Griswold* created a "constitutional time bomb" in the form of a generalized "right to privacy". 1965 was not, judicially speaking, a very good year.

[2] *DeSpain v. DeKalb County Community School District,* 384 F2d. 836 (7 Cir. 1967), cert. den. 390 U.S. 906, 88 S. Ct. 815, 19 L.Ed.2d 873 (1968).

[3] *A Decision-Making Approach to Sex Education: A Curriculum Guide and Implementation Manual for a Model Program with Adolescents and Family Planning Services,* Bureau of Community Health Services, U.S. Department of Health, Education and Welfare (1979). Contrast C. S. Lewis, "The Law of Sexual Justice", in *The Abolition of Man.* Lewis makes clear that no religious code respects a view that multiple sexual liaisons are merely a matter of individual preference, and that one is extremely hard-pressed to find any cultural codes (save nihilism and anarchism) that do, either. Lewis finds the "Law of Fidelity" fundamental to the notion

How did it come to pass, in so brief a time, that the child who cannot offer thanks for "birds that sing" can be taught that fidelity in love is a myth? The answer, of course, is that it did not happen in so brief a period. Such a profound inversion in public attitude and public policy was the result of decades of concerted programs for institutional change. Today this agenda for change is embraced by a large number of American institutions: legal and medical societies, teachers' unions, environmental groups, foundations, and pharmaceutical companies. There can be little argument, however, that the catalyst for change is found in the person and philosophy of Margaret Sanger and in her progeny, the American Birth Control League and Planned Parenthood.

Margaret Sanger and Sex Education

Margaret Higgins Sanger's views on sex education, and the effect of these views on the formation of the birth control movement, cannot be described without contradiction and counterpoint. The first published account of Sanger's childhood years, the autobiographical *My Fight for Birth Control,* revealed her almost matter-of-fact ambivalence toward family life. Although "there was an atmosphere in the home which reflected the love of our parents" and the eleven Sanger children "were all healthy and strong, vigorous and active", Sanger could write, "I can never look back on my childhood with joy."[4] The courage and comity of her own parents did not offset what she called the "determining influence" of a large family and the hardships of survival in the industrial city of Corning, New York.

"Very early in my childhood", she wrote, "I associated poverty, toil, unemployment, drunkenness, cruelty, quarreling, fighting, debts, jails with large families."[5] Just as important was the impression in her childhood of an inferior family status, exacerbated by the iconoclastic, "free-thinking" views of her father, whose "anti-Catholic attitudes did not make for his popularity"[6] in a predominantly Irish community. "We, the children of poorer parents, knew not where we belonged. Everything that we desired most was forbidden ... we were made to feel inferior to teachers, to elders, to all. We were burdens, and dependent on others for our existence. Every poor family was burdened with many children."[7]

---

of civilization, a common ethic. To the Carter administration HEW and Planned Parenthood, a model sex education program would first make this law a "myth", then topple it.

[4] Margaret Sanger, *My Fight for Birth Control* (New York: Farrar and Rinehart, Inc., 1931), 10–11.

[5] Ibid., 5.

[6] Ibid., 6–7.

[7] Ibid., 9.

The fact that the wealthy families of Corning had relatively few children Sanger took as prima facie evidence of the impoverishing effect of larger families. The personal impact of this belief was heightened by the death of her mother, Anne, on March 31, 1899, at the age of forty-eight. Sanger was convinced that the "ordeals of motherhood" had caused the death of her mother. The lingering consumption (tuberculosis) that took her mother's life visited Sanger at the birth of her own first child on November 18, 1905. The diagnosis forced her to seek refuge in the Adirondacks to strengthen her for the impending birth. Despite the precautions, the birth of baby Grant was "agonizing", the mere memory of which Sanger described as "mental torture" over twenty-five years later.[8] She once described the experience as a factor "to be reckoned with" in her zealous campaign for birth control.

From the beginning, Sanger's presentation of the need for sex education was imbued with the mindset of population control and her creed of birth prevention among the "unfit". The object of sex education was never merely informational—although that alone was a lightning rod in the era of the Comstock laws—but strictly and thoroughly ideological. This despite the fact that, as even *My Fight for Birth Control* acknowledged, understanding of sexual and reproductive matters could be imparted without overt communication. "Sex knowledge was a natural part of life", Sanger wrote, "I had always known where babies came from. My mother never discussed sex with us."[9]

The typical sex information pamphlet of Sanger's day was of the "social hygiene" variety, an admonitory tract concentrating on the dangers of venereal disease and sexual mischief.[10] The content of Sanger's first venture in the field, a handbook for adolescents published in 1915 and entitled *What Every Boy and Girl Should Know,* is hardly provocative. However, a jarring afterword to the book reveals her Malthusian obsession with "breeding" as the key to solving the problem of poverty:

> It is a vicious cycle, ignorance breeds poverty and poverty breeds ignorance. There is only one cure for both, and that is to stop breeding those things. Stop bringing to birth children whose inheritance cannot be one of health or intelligence. Stop bringing into the world children whose parents cannot provide for them.[11]

---

[8] Ibid., 37.

[9] Ibid., 14.

[10] See, for example, R. C. Bull's *Notes on Personal and Social Hygiene.*

[11] Margaret Sanger, *What Every Boy and Girl Should Know* (Fairview Park, Elmsford, N.Y.: Maxwell Reprint Co., 1969), 140; reprint of the 1927 edition; originally published in 1915.

The introduction to the book includes another theme familiar to twentieth century sexologists: praise for the new openness about sexuality among youth coupled with an announcement (clearly not regretted) that social and religious constraints on sexual behavior and attitudes are losing their power. Sanger's refrain that "young people are creating their own standards to suit their own generation" and that they want "neither advice nor moralizing"[12] has a curiously modern ring. This openness and discarding of convention, she argues, had produced a whole array of social benefits:

> Social factors have been thrust aside. Moral and religious codes have been weak and helpless in determining an influence over sexual conduct, but there has been less illegitimacy, less prostitution, more individual responsibility, a higher regard for those about to be born, less whining and crying on the part of those involved.[13]

Knowledge about sexuality, "courage and honesty", would produce the stronger characters and better relationships that conventional and religious morality could not.

Among her contemporaries, Sanger argued, the view prevailed that "the aim of life . . . is to free all inhibitions . . . to direct one's controls [sic] from logic and reason—not from fear and morality. . . . These ideas have become the guide to conduct."[14] To Sanger, the ebbing away of moral and religious codes over sexual conduct was neither a temporary nor a lamentable phenomenon, but a natural consequence of the worthlessness of such codes in the individual's search for self-fulfillment. "Instead of laying down hard and fast rules of sexual conduct", Sanger wrote in her 1922 book *Pivot of Civilization,* "sex can be rendered effective and valuable only as it meets and satisfies the interests and demands of the pupil himself."[15]

Her attitude is appropriately described as libertinism, but sex knowledge was not identical with individual liberty, as her writings on procreation emphasized. This theme of Sanger's thought is pervasive in Planned Parenthood's history: liberality in all things sexual save procreation. The second edition of Sanger's life story, *An Autobiography,* appeared in 1938. There Sanger described her first cross-country lecture tour in 1916, a journey spawned by publicity surrounding the dismissal of several indictments against her stemming from articles published in the *Woman Rebel.* Sanger's standard speech on this tour asserted seven conditions of life that "mandated" the use of birth control: the third was "when parents, though normal, had subnormal children"; the fourth, "when husband or wife were adolescent"; the fifth, "when the earning capac-

---

[12] Ibid., 7.
[13] Ibid., 13.
[14] Ibid., 12.
[15] Margaret Sanger, *Pivot of Civilization* (New York: Brentano's, 1922), 253.

ity of the father was inadequate".[16] No right existed to exercise sex knowledge to advance procreation. Sanger decried the fact that "anyone, no matter how ignorant, how diseased mentally or physically, how lacking in all knowledge of children, seemed to consider he or she had the right to become a parent."[17]

It was during this period of evangelization that Sanger wrote a letter to her husband of fourteen years, the artist William Sanger, and demanded a divorce. The previous years had seen her take extended trips overseas, during which she collected much of the material and made many of the contacts that led to the formation of the American Birth Control League. These periods of separation from her family and three children were also the occasion of several extramarital affairs, including, as already noted, a notorious liaison with sexologist Havelock Ellis, the author of *The Psychology of Sex*. Ellis' theories of sexual experimentation and response had a profound impact on the development of Sanger's belief in the power of birth control. "Her own specialty, birth control, merged with Ellis' studies on the art of love",[18] one of Sanger's biographers remarked.

Ellis shared Sanger's belief in the total Birth Control League agenda. His devotion to eugenics, Malthusianism, and euthanasia had credentials: In 1911 he had written a book entitled *The Problem of Race Regeneration*, which advocated a policy of "voluntary" sterilization of the poor as a precondition for receiving benefits under England's Poor Laws.[19]

Once more, Sanger's personal morality—a morality of eugenic birth control and libertinism—meshed deftly with the public creed she was in the process of articulating. This meshing, as we shall see, has remained a fixed star of pro-birth control philosophy to this day.

[16] Margaret Sanger, *An Autobiography* (W. W. Norton and Co., 1938), 193. See, generally, the chapter "Hear Me for My Cause".

[17] Ibid., 195.

[18] Emily Taft Douglas, *Margaret Sanger: Pioneer of the Future* (Garrett Park, Md.: Garrett Park Press, 1975), 145.

[19] Havelock Ellis, *The Problem of Race Regeneration* (New York: Moffat, Yard, 1911), 65. The American Birth Control League statement of purpose reflected the Malthusian heritage in full, labeling birth control "an imperative necessity . . . for national and racial progress" and lamenting the expenditure of funds to support the offspring of those "least fit to carry on the race" ("Statement of Purpose and Principles", American Birth Control League; text in *Women Together,* Judith Papachristou [A *Ms.* Book, New York: Alfred Knopf, 1976]). Planned Parenthood took a great leap forward toward this goal in the United States in 1967 when Congress, adopting the Aid to Families with Dependent Children (AFDC) program, required that any woman applying for AFDC benefits be informed on the spot of the availability of birth control devices and offered a referral to a birth control provider. The legislation specifies that birth control acceptance be "voluntary", but the impact of such an offer upon an impoverished mother, especially when coupled with her dependency on government and its prescribed solutions, hardly requires any overt coercion. Put another way, how would we expect a typical non-poor woman to react to an unsolicited, government-sponsored offer of birth control?

Planned Parenthood's Nordic Romance: Sex Education in Sweden

The cultural and legal changes Planned Parenthood achieved in the 1960s and 1970s in the United States occurred a generation earlier in Sweden. There in 1933, long before the American equivalent pursued an overt national sex education strategy, a National League for Sex Education was formed. Its first head was Elise Ottesen-Jensen, who later served as president of the International Committee on Planned Parenthood, established in 1950 after a series of meetings in London.

Despite its title, the National League for Sex Education was concerned from its inception with a full panoply of "programmes": "compulsory sex education . . . at all public schools", establishment of the "right to legal abortion on social grounds"; and governmental steps for the "promotion of . . . research in the field of sex" and "social reforms" to "utilize this research".[20] The Swedish League, which moved intact into affiliation with the International Committee on Planned Parenthood in 1950, traced almost exactly the course that Planned Parenthood Federation of America would follow twenty years later. The founding report of the International Committee cited the National League for establishing in 1940 "the first institution for social case work for women wishing to terminate pregnancy". This action was followed in 1941 by establishment of a summer institute for "sex education" for "teachers, child welfare workers, social workers and nurses".[21]

Planned Parenthood Federation of America officials were in close contact with the Swedish League during the 1930s and 1940s, and several figures emerged in the Federation as the foremost advocates for an expanded role in sex education, therapy, and counseling. The most notable of these were Drs. Abraham and Hannah Stone and Dr. Lena Levine. On August 23–26, 1946, Abraham Stone, Levine, and Sanger attended the Conference on Sex Education, Family Planning and Marriage Counseling held in Stockholm, Sweden.

Among the resolutions adopted by the Stockholm conference was a brief, unelaborated statement on sex education: "It is the right of all children to receive scientific sex information as part of their general education and of youth to receive adequate marriage preparation."[22] Note that the focus of the resolution remained, ostensibly, on marriage. This was to be a very temporary situation. The resolution was unanimously approved by the Executive Committee of Planned Parenthood at its September 1946 meeting. It represented

---

[20] "Report August 1948–August 1950", The Provisional International Committee on Planned Parenthood, September 1950; see especially organizational summary, *Riksforbundet For Sexuell Upplysning* (National League for Sex Education), 15–16.

[21] Ibid., 16.

[22] Minutes of Executive Committee Meeting, Planned Parenthood Federation of America, September 10, 1946.

the first significant formal statement by domestic Planned Parenthood on sex education. Prompted by this action, the Federation took its first steps beyond the provision of birth control to married women by initiating a counseling service for a group of six to ten couples about to be married. According to the report of the International Committee, these sessions involved discussion of the "physiological, psychological and social aspects of marriage and family life".[23]

In May 1953 the Planned Parenthood Federation's Margaret Sanger Research Bureau conducted a full-fledged seminar on its marriage counseling and preparation program. It was at this seminar that Dr. Levine, a member of the Federation's Medical Advisory Committee and co-founder of its group-therapy marriage counseling program, read a prophetic paper entitled, "Psychosexual Development". The unpublished paper is worth quoting at length:

> We are faced with two possible alternatives in sex education. Since heterosexual sex involves another person, and since sex with love gives much greater satisfaction than sex purely as a biological function, can we not teach sex with love as a desired goal of sex education? And since sex with love functions most effectively within the framework of the marital relationship, can we not teach sex with love in marriage?
>
> [O]ur alternate solution, is to be ready, as educators and parents to help young people obtain sex satisfaction before marriage. By sanctioning sex before marriage, we will prevent fear and guilt. We must also relieve those who have them of their fears and guilt feelings, and we must be ready to provide young boys and girls with the best contraceptive measures available, so they will have the necessary means to achieve sexual satisfaction without having to risk possible pregnancy. We owe this to them.[24]

Dr. Levine hereby acknowledged the basic dilemma of the Planned Parenthood sex educator. She did not choose between the alternatives in the conclusion of her paper. The remainder of her remarks were devoted to a rather dry account of patient services at the Sanger Bureau. History, however, was to make clear under which banner the Planned Parenthood crusade would be fought.

Only four years after Dr. Levine's paper was delivered in New York, a European nation mandated sex education countrywide by legislative fiat. The twenty-five-year headstart of the National League for Sex Education had paid

---

[23] "Report August 1948–August 1950", International Committee on Planned Parenthood, 9.

[24] Dr. Lena Levine, "Psychosexual Development", unpublished paper, In-Service Training Seminar on Education for Marriage and Parenthood, May 2–4, 1953, MSCLC; speech noted in *Planned Parenthood News,* Summer 1953, 10.

dividends.[25] The "right to scientific sex education" had become an "unavoidable duty" for schoolchildren.

To this day, pro-birth control authors and leaders cite the Swedish social and sexual model as ideal for American culture: It is important to recognize that it is a system that has sharply devalued marriage and religious influence, that it is generally approving of abortion and premarital sex, that out-of-wedlock childbearing is prevalent (reaching nearly half of all births in 1986), and childbearing itself is subreplacement level. James Trussell, discussing teenage pregnancy in the November–December 1988 issue of the Alan Guttmacher Institute journal *Family Planning Perspectives,* wrote, "[B]ecause my goal is to improve the quality, not decrease the quantity, of sexual relationships, I would cheerfully choose the Swedish over the American status quo."[26]

To understand how the Swedish model was transferred to the United States, the work of a new figure must be discussed. Just as the fundamental themes of the American Birth Control League represented the synthetic genius of the implacable Margaret Sanger, so too did the new future of sex education for birth control possess its symbol and its pioneer: Mary Steichen Calderone.

Calderone: Planned Parenthood and SIECUS

The major public force for sex education in the United States after 1965 was the Sex Information and Education Council of the United States (SIECUS). Chartered in May 1964, SIECUS shared many things with Planned Parenthood: philosophy, public policy agenda, and personnel. Its first executive director, the guiding light for all its programs and initiatives, most of which were designed to remold public opinion, was Dr. Mary S. Calderone.

Calderone had been medical director of the Planned Parenthood Fed-

[25] Edmund H. Kellog and Jan Stepan, "Legal Aspects of Sex Education", *The American Journal of Comparative Law,* vol. 26, no. 4 (Fall 1978): 573. Sweden was the first nation to mandate "comprehensive sex education" nationwide. The merits of the law aside, its adoption in 1957 was at least the result of an indigenous movement. Fifteen years later, international organizations and movements began systematic efforts to pressure nations to change their laws in this regard. The United Nations Fund for Population Activities and the International Planned Parenthood Federation combined to facilitate a survey of "possibly significant legal impediments to family planning programs, including sex education". The study was conducted by the Tufts University Law and Population Programme, and the fact that it treated sex education as an appendage of family planning and population control programs, a not altogether necessary concomitant, was a tribute to the goals of its benefactors.

[26] James Trussell, "Teenage Pregnancy in the United States", *Family Planning Perspectives,* vol. 20, no. 6 (November–December 1988): 271.

eration of America from 1953 to 1964. As described by her colleagues, the position of medical director in the Federation involved the implementation, subject to the approval of the National Board of Planned Parenthood, of decisions made by the National Medical Committee.[27] In an article entitled "The National Medical Committee in the Decade 1954 to 1964", Calderone stated that during her tenure "the Planned Parenthood Federation of America (PPFA) National Medical Committee finally succeeded in firmly establishing the medical foundations for birth control in the United States".[28]

The article makes clear that Calderone played a key role within Planned Parenthood on both social and medical issues (although this distinction is an artificial one), and that the organization was moving inexorably away from its focus on the married couple. It appeared in a collection of essays on birth control and population, edited by Calderone and entitled *Manual of Family Planning and Contraceptive Practice,* and it provides an interesting history of deliberations within Planned Parenthood on the controversial subject of birth control services for the unwed. These deliberations, although occurring in a context where legal issues would seem to be paramount, were held by the National Medical Committee (NMC).

In January 1952, Calderone reported, the NMC debated a policy regarding the unwed that had been adopted by one local Planned Parenthood affiliate. Under this policy, an unwed contraceptive patient would be accepted only when referred by a physician or by another social agency. Any unwed girl or woman seeking services directly was to be referred to a physician member of the local affiliate's medical advisory committee.

At the time of this discussion, a large proportion of Planned Parenthood affiliates refused to distribute birth control to the unwed under any circumstances. Indeed, this remained the organization's public image for many years after the policy actually changed. In October 1956 the topic was reviewed once more by the NMC and, according to Calderone, "the legal and religious aspects were brought up, but it was decided . . . to keep this on a medical basis".[29] The following month, the NMC recommended formally that the policy established by the single affiliate in 1952 be extended to all Planned Parenthood centers. The implicit factor in this debate, the provision of birth control to unwed minors, was rendered explicit by the NMC in an October 1967 "Policy Statement on Birth Control Services to Minors". The statement said, in part: "[T]he Committee feels that from a physician's point of view, minors

[27] S. L. Romney and G. L. Langmyhr, "The Rules of Voluntary Organizations—The Medical Program: Current Status", *Manual of Family Planning and Contraceptive Practice,* (Huntington, N.Y.: Robert Krieger Publ. Co., 1977), 106.

[28] Ibid., 96.

[29] Ibid., 104.

with a history of sexual activity who have been exposed to the risk of pregnancy should be considered for contraceptive advice."[30]

By this time, Calderone had left Planned Parenthood and begun her work with SIECUS. It was a move from medical missionary to sexual evangelist, a natural development for a woman devoted to changing the traditional values that stood in the way of Planned Parenthood's aggressive merchandising of contraceptives and abortion to children.

Like many other public policy operations, SIECUS started small, in July 1964, with Calderone as executive director and a lone secretary. Official announcement of the organization's existence did not take place until the following year. At the inaugural press conference on January 8, 1965, Calderone stated that SIECUS would not function as "an action group", but that it would "perhaps take positions on problems of sexuality in America".[31] The *New York Herald Tribune* for January 9 reported that Calderone had resigned her post as medical director of Planned Parenthood in July 1964 as SIECUS began functional operation.

The structure of SIECUS included a set of four elected officers, an executive director, and a 30-member board of directors. Officers and board members of SIECUS represented a diverse range of fields and a somewhat less-diversified range of beliefs concerning sexuality and ethics. The founding group of the organization, described as being composed of five persons in a 1971 address by Calderone at a SIECUS symposium,[32] was even more homogeneous. Most prominent among this inner circle were Calderone herself, Dr. Lester Kirkendall (an author, lecturer, and professor of family life at Oregon State University), William Genne (Commissioner on Marriage and Family Life of the National Council of Churches), Wallace Fulton (the first president of SIECUS, associated with the Equitable Life Assurance Company), and David Mace (executive director of the American Association of Marriage Counselors).[33]

---

[30] Ibid., 105.

[31] Earl Ubell, " 'Recognition' for Sexuality: A New Agency", *New York Herald Tribune,* January 9, 1965; reprinted in the *SIECUS Newsletter,* vol. 1, no. 1, February 1965. The attraction of reporters to their subject matter provides an interesting aside. Ubell, the *Herald Tribune*'s science editor, joined the SIECUS Board of Directors in 1967 (*SIECUS Newsletter,* vol. 3, no. 2, Summer). By that time, he was science editor of WCBS–TV, New York, sitting on the SIECUS board in an individual capacity.

[32] Mary S. Calderone, M.D., M.P.H., "First Isadore Rubin Memorial Lecture: Love, Sex, Intimacy and Aging as a Life Style", in *Proceedings of the Second Annual SIECUS Symposium: Sex, Love and Intimacy—Whose Life Styles?,* 1972 SIECUS, New York, N.Y., 32. The address was given on November 5, 1971.

[33] *SIECUS Newsletter,* vol. 1, no. 1, February 1965. See particularly Sol Gordon and Roger Libby, *Sexuality Today and Tomorrow: Contemporary Issues in Human Sexuality* (Belmont, Cal.: Duxbury Press, 1976). The authors, whose works are discussed in the following

None of these individuals was a practicing lawyer, an omission that was quickly corrected. Isadore Rubin and Harriet Pilpel—the latter, a senior law partner with the New York firm of Greenbaum, Wolff, and Ernst, was legal counsel to Planned Parenthood of New York City, the Planned Parenthood Federation of America, and Planned Parenthood–World Population—were the first two persons elected to the SIECUS board by the five original co-founders.[34] A key figure in the American Civil Liberties Union as well, Pilpel was described in the first SIECUS newsletter simply as "senior partner, law firm, New York". Despite Calderone's intimation at the SIECUS-launching press conference that the organization would steer clear of public policy agitation, Pilpel identified the role of SIECUS as essentially one of confronting "antiquated laws". In a statement that appeared in the first SIECUS newsletter in February 1965, Pilpel wrote:

> [W]e continue to maintain on the books antiquated and unreasonable laws that exert an arbitrary impact not only on normal human sexual behavior but also on related fields such as birth control and medically-indicated abortion. Because I believe SIECUS can help to clarify some of this confusion . . . I am happy to be on its board.[35]

The remainder of the original SIECUS board was composed of authors, physicians, sociologists, theologians, and psychologists; their writings in the area of sexuality and sex education would define the SIECUS mission over the subsequent decade. Among the most prolific and outspoken of these were Wardell Pomeroy, Dr. John Rock, Clark Vincent, and Dr. Harold Lief.

From the beginning, the SIECUS approach to sex education and sexual values emphasized "choices among an array of competing alternatives",[36] as President Fulton phrased it in his introductory article to newsletter readers. The original statement of "The SIECUS Purpose" had as its slogan, "To establish man's sexuality as a health entity". The initial justification statement in SIECUS committed the organization to "expand the scope of sex education to all age levels and groups", and to provide, among other things, "indications as to how constructive attitudes can be developed about such problem areas as sex in the aging, premarital sex [and] homosexuality".[37]

The careful wording of initial SIECUS goals and philosophy was com-

---

chapter, were associates of the Institute for Family Research and Education at Syracuse University. They dedicated their volume to the "founders and early board members" of SIECUS and to Margaret Sanger.

[34] Calderone, "Love, Sex, Intimacy and Aging", 32.

[35] *SIECUS Newsletter,* vol. 1, no. 1 (1965): 3.

[36] Ibid., W. C. Fulton, M.P.H., "Why the Need for a Sex Information and Education Council of the United States as a New, Separate Organization".

[37] Ibid., "Justification" and "Selected Initial Programs", 2.

bined with a program emphasis on achieving "comprehensiveness" and a "scientific" sense of openness. SIECUS newsletters from 1965 to 1973 generally avoided direct criticisms of social policy regarding sex education, abortion, and related issues. In fact, it was not until July 1973 that a SIECUS newsletter promulgated a "Statement of Belief", which expressed its commitment "to identify and publicize social policies which perpetuate unhealthy attitudes about sexuality".[38] The same issue featured a column by SIECUS board member Dr. E. James Lieberman hailing the recent U.S. Supreme Court decision legalizing abortion (*Roe v. Wade*) as an "uncelebrated milestone in public health".[39]

There was, however, at least one aspect of moral and sexual values about which SIECUS was firmly decided from the very first. A volume of SIECUS-selected and edited papers that appeared in 1970, entitled *Sexuality and Man*, recounted an exchange that occurred in 1965 between Calderone and a well-known medical author, Goodrich C. Schauffler. At the time SIECUS was formed, Schauffler "urged it to take on the task of defending traditional morality against 'the false prophets' and the 'prosexual propagandists'."[40] Responding in the April 21, 1965, *Medical Tribune*, Calderone stated that SIECUS did not view its role as that of trying "to impose conformity in or to a set of standards of human behavior, but rather to stimulate questioning about old, and questing for new, basic knowledge in a given field and to open up that knowledge for exchange, discussion and individual decision".[41]

Sexuality and Man, which was edited and formally approved by the entire SIECUS board of directors, was a compilation of a series of study guides written by board members on a variety of topics, including premarital sexual standards, sexual encounters between adults and children, and "the sex educator and moral values". The aim of the guides, wrote Dr. Harold Lief in the preface, was to replace "misconceptions with facts". Each guide, he said, "had found its own audiences among professionals and parents involved in initiating, administering, or supporting school or community programs of sex education".[42] Lief was the president of SIECUS in 1970; in addition, he was a member of the National Medical Committee of Planned Parenthood.

The persistent theme of *Sexuality and Man* was completely consistent with the tenets of the original SIECUS statement of purpose. The chapter on "Sex

[38] *SIECUS Report*, vol. 1, no. 6, (1973): 1. The *Report* was the successor to the *SIECUS Newsletter*, the final edition of which appeared in April 1972.

[39] Ibid., 2.

[40] SIECUS, comp. and ed., *Sexuality and Man* (New York: Charles Scribner's Sons, 1970), 173. The introduction to this volume was written by Mary Calderone; the preface to this edition was written by Dr. Harold Lief.

[41] Mary S. Calderone, "Responsible Sexuality and SIECUS", *Medical Tribune*, April 21, 1965; response to Goodrich C. Schauffler, "Caution for SIECUS", letter appearing in *Medical Tribune*, March 21, 1965.

[42] *Sexuality and Man*, viii.

Education", credited to Dr. Lester Kirkendall, who joined the Oregon State Planned Parenthood Board of Directors in December 1970,[43] admonished prospective sex educators that they "must take into account the current freedom of choice and personal decision-making that now exists".[44] The subsequent chapter on "Sex, Science, and Values" described the range of choices as running from moral absolutism to hedonism, a "morality of indulgence" that recognizes "pleasure [as] its own justification". SIECUS warned that "one must be careful not to equate hedonism with irresponsibility", and claimed that the "hedonistic position is a legitimate alternative for those who accept its premises".[45]

"Sex, Science, and Values" concludes with an argument that "in the classification of value positions", the concept of freedom of choice, or "responsible choice", is most compatible with a moral position between absolutism and hedonism, a "relativistic one". Kirkendall and Joseph Fletcher, the Episcopal theologian who wrote *Situation Ethics,* are cited as leading authorities on this new approach that would allow premarital sex. The next, and final, chapter of *Sexuality and Man,* "The Sex Educator and Moral Values", brings the SIECUS position into clearer focus.

Echoing the theme of the original SIECUS newsletter, this essay argued that "most of our sex values have left the core of our culture and entered the arena of competing alternatives". The new "universal values", SIECUS stated, "suggest the right of the individual to engage in any form of sex behavior"[46] within the limits of social obligation so long as exploitation, cruelty, or "personality violation" are not involved. Within the ambit of these alternatives, social agreement should come through "operating permissively".[47] For the first time, SIECUS observed, "the monopoly once held by an absolutistic, religiously based sex ethic has now been destroyed".[48] The ultimate effect of sex education, the book concludes, "cannot be judged on its character-building results, but rather on the knowledge, insight, and clarity it conveys".[49]

These relatively early writings by the founders and partisans of SIECUS provide a mere glimmer of the extensive philosophy being developed within the organization. The application of the "freedom of choice" perspective to particular fact situations and to the literal content of sex education materials

[43] *SIECUS Newsletter,* vol. 6, no. 2, December 1970, 11.
[44] *Sexuality and Man,* 132.
[45] Ibid., 141.
[46] Ibid., 161.
[47] Ibid., 160.
[48] Ibid., 161. Compare Margaret Sanger's introduction to the 1915 edition of *What Every Boy and Girl Should Know.* Throughout the century-long history of the Planned Parenthood movement, its leaders and spokesmen were constantly declaring religious codes dead, seldom mindful of their unseemly haste to bury the still-warm corpse.
[49] Ibid., 173.

and curricula remained to be elaborated. As individuals writing in more specialized publications, the leaders of SIECUS expressed themselves less ambiguously on questions of values and behavior, a phenomenon encouraged by the explosive growth of sex periodicals of all kinds in the 1960s and 1970s and the rash of national policy initiatives SIECUS and Planned Parenthood spawned.

Despite the apparent differences in the perspectives of the two organizations, they were unified about their overriding raison d'être: government-sponsored population control. In a 1974 address to the Association of Planned Parenthood Physicians, former SIECUS president Dr. Lief and Planned Parenthood medical director Dr. George Langmyhr drew attention to the words of one of Margaret Sanger's modern biographers:

> Mrs. Sanger intended birth control not simply to reduce the suffering of the poor and the number of the unfit, but also to increase the quantity and the quality of sexual relationships. The birth control movement, she said, freed the mind from "sexual prejudice and taboo", by demanding the frankest and most unflinching re-examination of sex in its relation to human nature and the basis of human society. This function of the movement she pointed out was the "most important of all".[50]

Today, said Langmyhr and Lief, the "denial of the relationship between birth control and human sexual functioning is no longer useful or helpful".[51]

Calderone herself believed that the sex-education mission of SIECUS was merely a portion of the larger concern for population control. She considered national population planning by the U.S. government essential to the goals of SIECUS. She summarized these themes in her preface to the 1970 edition of the *Manual of Family Planning and Contraceptive Practice.*

> Population and demography only lightly touched on herein comprise the third area which is needed to complete the population control whole. In other words, family planning practice and contraceptive practice as they are being developed, can now only be applied with total effectiveness in the service of population practice.[52]

Family planning, in this sense, was to be understood as a broader policy

[50] David M. Kennedy, *Birth Control in America: The Career of Margaret Sanger* (New Haven: Yale University Press, 1970); quoted in Langmyhr and Lief, "Human Sexuality Training for Family Planning Personnel", address given to the 12th Annual Meeting of the Association of Planned Parenthood Physicians, April 17, 1974.

[51] Dr. George Langmyhr and Dr. Harold Lief, "Human Sexuality Training for Family Planning Personnel", paper presented to the 12th Annual Meeting of the Association of Planned Parenthood Physicians, April 17, 1974, 1.

[52] Mary S. Calderone, preface, *Manual of Family Planning and Contraceptive Practice,* 1970 ed., vii.

devised and supported by government and adhered to by the populace. Calderone concluded:

> No matter how great the expertise of the dedicated contributors of this volume and their thousands of colleagues throughout the world, these will avail little in the absence of official population policy well integrated to and understood by all of the people of that population.[53]

To sell this package—"religion is dead" morality, absolute "freedom of choice" among sexual behaviors, and government control of the nation's fertility— Planned Parenthood and SIECUS needed new allies. They also needed to work from within the walls of the federal city. And so they did, lobbying furiously in professional groups and in the halls of Congress and the executive branch in Washington, D.C., and making the decade 1965 to 1975 a nearly unbroken string of remarkable successes for the antilife agenda.

SIECUS started, however, with a remarkable base of support, including a number of academic, religious, and political figures who rose to its defense in the public press. In October 1969, the formation of a National Committee for Responsible Family Life and Sex Education was announced in an advertisement in the *New York Times*. The ad supported SIECUS and lambasted the benighted opposition to sex education. Prominent signatories included Ralph Bunche, the Rev. Charles Curran, Peggy Guggenheim, University of Notre Dame President Theodore M. Hesburgh, Jonas Salk, and Robert S. McNamara.[54]

Calderone and the American Medical Association

One of the most important coups achieved by the Planned Parenthood movement in the 1960s was the incorporation of the American medical establishment into its ranks. The development of the Pill (a powerful drug whose contraindications required that it become something of an anomaly: a medication prescribed for perfectly healthy people) fueled a rapid expansion of the field of contraception as medical practice. But the mere distribution of contraceptives is a far cry short of a political judgment to participate in a campaign for population control—a decision, based on manifold social and demographic assumptions and guesses, that has as an immediate effect the subjection of the individual seeking medical care to the physician's world view of the putative needs of others.

---

[53] Ibid., viii.

[54] *New York Times,* October 16, 1969. Among others who signed: Julia Child, Lammot DuPont Copeland, Arthur J. Goldberg, Philip M. Klutznick, Ann Landers, Lewis Mumford, the Rev. Reinhold Niebuhr, Joseph Papp, Chuck and Lynda Robb, Rep. James Scheuer of New York, Gore Vidal, and Andrew Young. The National Committee for Responsible Family Life and Sex Education was hailed in the *SIECUS Newsletter,* vol. 5, no. 2, March 1970, 5.

Recruiting the AMA to the birth control crusade became Mary Calderone's responsibility. For almost a decade, while Calderone was still director of Planned Parenthood's National Medical Committee, the AMA resisted the organization's efforts to reopen for discussion its position of neutrality on the issue of population control. In December 1962, after years of inquiry, Calderone approached the AMA Board of Trustees directly and convinced them, in a decision implemented in April 1963, to appoint a new committee to study the entire question. A Committee on Human Reproduction was ultimately established by the AMA at its November 1963 meeting. Calderone and one other Planned Parenthood physician were members of the eight-person group.

On December 1, 1964, the AMA House of Delegates, meeting at its eighteenth Clinical Convention, approved the Committee's report. The policy stated that "the need for population control" was "a matter of responsible medical practice",[55] and that the AMA would take the responsibility for disseminating information on sexual behavior to all physicians. The *New York Times* interpreted this development accurately, reporting the next day that the AMA Board of Trustees had urged their colleagues to cooperate with birth control groups. The first issue of the SIECUS newsletter reprinted the *Times* article in its entirety alongside the article announcing SIECUS's formation.

The magnitude of this philosophical watershed in the medical community has yet to be fully measured. In literal terms, it meant that physicians—at least the branch of the profession represented by the AMA—were willing to identify childbearing itself as a menace to public health. Pregnancy beyond the narrow boundaries established by the national birth planners was necessarily reinterpreted as a disease process. It was no surprise that little more than a decade later a federal official at the Centers for Disease Control, Dr. Willard Cates, would describe "unwanted pregnancy" as a "venereal disease".

SIECUS, the NEA, and Federal Sex Education

Other major national organizations began to move into the Planned Parenthood population control/sex education orbit during roughly this time period. In 1959, the American Public Health Association adopted a strongly worded population control policy. In 1966, the National Education Association (NEA), the nation's largest teachers' union, approved a resolution calling for "comprehensive sex education".[56] That same year, the U.S. Department of Health,

---

[55] Calderone, *Manual of Family Planning and Contraceptive Practice*, 98.

[56] J. Likoudis and P. Beach, "Sex Education: The New Manicheanism", *Triumph,* October 1969, 11–19. The NEA endorsement of sex education evolved over the years: In 1971, the NEA journal *Today's Education* published a poll showing that nearly 60% of teachers favored sex education before the sixth grade, with one quarter favoring it at the kindergarten or prekindergarten level; in 1977, the NEA endorsed inclusion of birth control in sex education

Education, and Welfare released a document initiating a policy with respect to sex education, identifying it as part of the family planning/population control crusade. The Summer 1966 SIECUS *Newsletter* reported on this development, hailing the HEW publication *Family Planning: One Aspect of Freedom to Choose,* issued by Undersecretary Wilbur J. Cohen. Describing in some detail a model program developed by the District of Columbia, HEW concluded that there existed a "need for sex education as an integral part of the school curriculum beginning in the earliest grades".[57]

Although HEW remained nominally deferential to state and local prerogatives in education, the 1966 publication represented a major step forward for advocates of a strong federal role in sex education. Cohen wrote that the curriculum employed in particular programs should be determined by those who control individual schools, but that federal funds should be used to stimulate "research in curriculum development and for demonstration teaching projects". The clear assumption was made that birth control and the understanding by the young of their sexual development were somehow synonymous:

> As another aspect of the nation's growing concern for family planning, we are becoming increasingly aware of the need for sex education in the schools. There is a small but hopeful awakening in some public and private schools to the responsibility of formal education for helping young people understand their own sexual development. We have a long way to go in this respect, but there are encouraging signs that Victorian inhibitions are giving way to open, direct, and constructive public attitudes.[58]

Implementation of this policy was overseen by the Office of Education within HEW (a cabinet-level Department of Education was not created until 1979). U.S. commissioner of education Harold Howe announced on August 30, 1966, that his office would "support family life education as an integral part of the curriculum from pre-school to college and adult levels". Howe also committed his agency to develop programs in teacher training, as well as in research. One of the first actions taken in the "family life" field by the Office of Education was to finance a SIECUS working conference in

---

programs; in July 1978, the association went further and adopted its first resolution favoring "reproductive freedom" (i.e., abortion). America's schoolrooms have begun to empty, but in Kansas City, July 1990, the NEA refused to modify or repeal the pro-abortion plank.

[57] Wilbur J. Cohen, *Family Planning: One Aspect of Freedom to Choose,* HEW, June 1966 (noted in *SIECUS Newsletter,* vol. 2, no. 2, Summer 1966, 1).

[58] Ibid., 1.

Washington, D.C., from November 30 to December 2, 1966. The conference provided the basis for the preparation by SIECUS of a manual on sex education for teachers-in-training. The resulting volume, *Sex, the Individual and Society: Implications for Education,* became the centerpiece of SIECUS' library of materials for teacher training in schools across the nation.

"Sub Rosa": A New Planned Parenthood–SIECUS Collaboration

Convincing the "E" in HEW to finance curriculum development and a SIECUS conference helped to bolster SIECUS' legitimacy, but the real action on sex education remained not with the federal government or even with visionary teachers' guides, but with the hard fact of local school boards and individual instructors. SIECUS realized it needed more muscle behind its efforts to promote a sex revolution in the nation's schools. It needed an entity with a national presence and a network of facilities with access to community leaders and to young people. No more ideal candidate could be found than its godfather and soulmate, Planned Parenthood. The joint project SIECUS and Planned Parenthood pursued in 1970 is worth examining in some detail.

Despite its inaugural denial, SIECUS had, in fact, turned out to be an "action group", willing to push an initially unpopular agenda of early sex education. Planned Parenthood, by contrast, was more plodding, concerned primarily about the building of its clinical empire and willing to pass countless resolutions without measurably raising its public profile. In 1968 Planned Parenthood had received a report by yet another of its internal committees, this one called the Advisory Group on Population and Family Planning Education in Schools. Debate continued as well among the members of the National Medical Committee.[59]

Apparently frustrated with the pace of developments in sex education and determined to take advantage of every opportunity to insert its philosophy into the American school system, SIECUS officials sought a meeting with the national Planned Parenthood office in April 1970. The request was spawned by a constituent letter written to the SIECUS Executive Committee that suggested that Planned Parenthood and SIECUS work together to develop a sex education program and "methods of teaching it".[60] SIECUS and Planned Parenthood cooperation had apparently been strong primarily at the community level,[61] through each organization's affiliates, but not at the level of

---

[59] Langmyhr and Lief, "Human Sexuality Training".

[60] Memorandum from Gerald Sanctuary, SIECUS executive director, to Dr. Alan F. Guttmacher, president of PPWP, April 8, 1970, 1,, CLHMS.

[61] Memorandum from Dr. George Langmyhr to John Robbins and Alan F. Guttmacher, October 28, 1970, 1, CLHMS.

national leadership. In April 1970 SIECUS executive director Gerald Sanctuary wrote to Alan Guttmacher and sent him a memorandum outlining an agenda for their meeting on April 16.

"I have no doubt at all of the need to link sex education and family planning education", Sanctuary wrote. Neither human sexuality nor population education were "tools of the other", but "complementary and indeed inseparable in the 1970's". To carry the project through, Sanctuary said, it had been proposed that Planned Parenthood–World Population staff member Dorothy Millstone work at SIECUS offices to draft a plan for presentation to Planned Parenthood's October 1970 meeting.

Millstone was enthusiastic. In an April 13 memo to Guttmacher, she endorsed the introduction of family planning and population dynamics into U.S. schools as a "feasible project to reinforce efforts to meet PPWP's two major aims: making birth control universally available and fostering limitation of the U.S. population".[62] Millstone recommended that SIECUS/PPWP develop a national strategy based on finding key points of entry into the schools. Health, not population control, would be the justification. "Cooperation with SIECUS offers significant advantages", Millstone wrote, "If SIECUS did not exist, it would be necessary to invent it." She offered ideas for extending the cooperation to include teacher training, curriculum development, establishment of graduate and postgraduate programs in schools of education, and an approach to the U.S. commissioner of education to stimulate federal funding.

That summer the Planned Parenthood National Medical Committee, under pressure from Planned Parenthood affiliates, debated the relationship of sex education to in-clinic birth control programs. After what Langmyhr and Lief described as a "spirited discussion",[63] the NMC recommended that sex education programs be incorporated into the overall Planned Parenthood program. The sticking point appears to have been primarily financial, not philosophical. The organization had, in Langmyhr and Lief's words, "severe financial problems" in 1970.

A major interstaff meeting took place on October 1, 1970. A memorandum of the meeting reveals the political role the two organizations hoped sex education would play. Dr. Lief expressed concern that any comprehensive national family planning program including "abortion and sterilization" could be reversed in whole or in part because of political concerns, e.g., a declining fertility rate. "This political action", as the memorandum summarizes his remarks, "makes sex education programs much more imperative".[64] Lief was well aware of the implication of this political and propagandistic use of

---

[62] Memorandum from Dorothy Millstone to Alan F. Guttmacher and Alfredo Perez, April 13, 1970, 1. CLHMS.

[63] Langmyhr and Lief, "Human Sexuality Training".

[64] Langmyhr memorandum, October 28, 1970, 3, CLHMS.

education. Planned Parenthood did not want to be drawn into a public fray. Thus, he argued, SIECUS could take the lead and the two organizations could find "ways to work sub rosa".[65]

Expanding the Federal Role in Sex Education

Implementing the nationwide program SIECUS and Planned Parenthood envisioned and solving the financial crisis Lief identified suggested a common solution: opening the federal treasury. The organizations moved quickly on both the executive and legislative fronts. The major legislative vehicle was the Family Planning and Reproductive Health Services Act of 1970. SIECUS and Planned Parenthood were equally successful in shaking the federal grants money tree, particularly in the area of sex education.

Planned Parenthood's initial emphasis was on the expansion of sex education as a component of its in-clinic programs for adolescents, in line with its inclination to let SIECUS fight the public fight for sex education. In June 1970 the National Medical Committee, responding to requests from affiliates, "recommended that sex education be incorporated into the general program of Planned Parenthood".[66] Following a meeting with affiliates keenly interested in sex education, Lief prepared a grant application to the National Institute of Mental Health (NIMH) seeking funds to train twenty Planned Parenthood staff members from ten affiliates. NIMH awarded the grant to Lief's Marriage Council of Philadelphia,[67] with the Commonwealth of Pennsylvania supplying funding for thirty additional trainees.

One aspect of the training program is worth mentioning, if for no other reason than to point out that current controversies like the National Endowment for Arts' funding of sexually explicit work are not altogether new. The highlight of the training program was a seminar and social gathering held in Philadelphia later that year. In Langmyhr and Lief's own words, the trainees participated for a "day and a half" in "a mini-marathon of sexually explicit films and small group discussions".[68] The point of these screenings was "to lead to desensitization of anxieties surrounding sexual behavior ... with a resultant development of understanding and tolerance of the range of sexual behavior". Six months later a second seminar was held to conduct "a review of agency experience in attitude modification". This seminar was supported with state money as well as with grants from the Scaife and Rockefeller Foundations.

The need to "desensitize" Planned Parenthood's own personnel suggested

---

[65] Ibid., 4.

[66] Langmyhr and Lief, "Human Sexuality Training".

[67] "Training of Family Planning Workers in Sex Education", Grant no. T21MH 13085-01, Experimental and Special Training Division of Manpower and Training Programs, NIMH.

[68] Langmyhr and Lief, "Human Sexuality Training", 4.

that at least a few of the organization's staff members retained moral scruples that required "attitude adjustment". When the question is raised whether Planned Parenthood programs merely reflected societal change or helped to instigate and reinforce the movement to sexual liberalization, such training programs provide a partial answer. That same year, Alan Guttmacher testified before a House subcommittee that Planned Parenthood had begun to prescribe contraceptives to adolescents in certain target communities before they were sexually active. The *SIECUS Report* for March 1973 summarized the view of Mary Calderone in a series of tapes prepared for the Center for the Study of Democratic Institutions: "Dr. Calderone postulates that society is changing individual sexual behavior rather than the opposite, and that the by-elements in effecting this change are the major professional groups. . . . "[69]

The 1970s, as has been discussed, were the heyday of Planned Parenthood cooperation with the federal government. The Office of Economic Opportunity (OEO), an early cog in the Johnson administration antipoverty war machine, made a major contribution as the decade began. Dr. George Contis, of OEO's Family Planning Program, published a report, *A National Five-Year Plan for Family Planning.* The report urged a federal role in sex education, urged cautious progress toward federal promotion of abortion as a method of family planning, and insisted that "the continued involvement of Planned Parenthood–World Population is essential to the success of any national birth control program".[70]

OEO proved to be a fine opportunity indeed for Planned Parenthood. A number of affiliates submitted grants to the agency. In May 1971 the Virginia League for Planned Parenthood applied to OEO's Community Action Program for funds to conduct a "basic sex information" program targeted partially to teenagers. The project application included justifying language strongly reminiscent of Margaret Sanger's race purification ardor, pledging to attack "the grim list of social ills that the too-large family fosters—from inferior physical and mental health to criminal behavior".[71] C. M. G. Battery, director of public health for the state of Virginia, wrote a letter to Virginia Planned Parenthood officials praising the project. The letter, included by the League in its application packet, urged federal efforts to convince citizens that control of family size was no longer an option:

> We would hope, however, that you will, in future educational programs for
> the public . . . point out that parenthood of unlimited numbers of children is

[69] *SIECUS Report,* vol. 1, no. 4 (March 1973): 4. The tapes, entitled "There Are No Monsters" and "How Good Is Gay?" were prepared for the Center in 1972.

[70] George Contis, *A National Five-Year Plan for Family Planning,* U.S. Office of Economic Opportunity, January 28, 1970, 15–16, 63.

[71] Virginia League for Planned Parenthood Grant Application, Office of Economic Opportunity, Community Action Program, May 1, 1971 (CG 3802 A10), 5.

no longer a right, but that responsible parenthood and citizenship demands [sic] control of family size by all peoples without respect to income, creed or color.[72]

While Dr. Contis was recommending close collaboration with Planned Parenthood at OEO, the U.S. Department of Health, Education and Welfare had established a unique publishing venture with the same entity. Entitled *Family Planning Digest,* this bimonthly publication was launched in 1971 and distributed via the government's postage-free franking privilege by HEW's National Center for Family Planning Services (NCFPS). The content of the *Digest* was produced, under contract, by the Center for Family Planning Program Development at Planned Parenthood-World Population. The *Digest* published a regular column advertising job opportunities in public- and private-sector family planning agencies and included a wide variety of professional and propagandizing articles on contraception, population control, and sex education.

A May 1973 article gives the flavor of the *Digest* and neatly summarizes its "chummy" character. Entitled "NCFPS Director Calls for 'Second Generation' Services", the article pictured NCFPS director Marjorie Costa over a caption that read, "Miss Costa raps with teens at Planned Parenthood clinic in Pasadena, California". The article described her view that sex education must be included as a "priority objective" in health education programs from "preschool on through high school and college". It also described her vision that NCFPS take a lead role in instituting sex education programs, including contraception, in U.S. schools and quoted her as saying, "Where provision of services to minors is legal without parental consent these services will receive priority support from NCFPS". The aim, she concluded, was to convince young people that sex and contraceptives were as natural and wholesome for them as learning "how to brush their teeth or wash their ears".[73]

Given its pedigree, the next step in the *Digest's* history was anticlimactic. When the magazine met its demise in 1975, the deputy assistant secretary for population affairs at HEW, Dr. Louis Hellman, announced that it would continue in the private sector as *Family Planning Perspectives,* becoming (as it remains today) the flagship publication of Planned Parenthood and its Alan Guttmacher Institute. Dr. Hellman had been chairman of the National Medical Committee of Planned Parenthood in 1956.[74]

While Planned Parenthood continued its penetration of the executive agencies and pursued congressional legislation, SIECUS followed a higher profile of

[72] Ibid., "Operation Plan", Charles R. L. Pratt, 1.
[73] "NCFPS Director Calls for 'Second Generation' Services: Involve Hospitals, Serve Teenagers, Improve Sex Education", *Family Planning Digest,* vol. 2, no. 3 (May 1973): 3–4.
[74] *Family Planning Digest,* vol. 3, no. 7 (January 1975): 3.

agitation for sex education. In May 1974 SIECUS published an updated "State-ment of Belief" that highlighted its permissive or libertarian viewpoint in a much more specific way than heretofore. A few specifics are worth quoting in full:

Sexual Orientation
It is the right of all persons to enter into relationships with others regardless of their gender, and to engage in such sexual behaviors as are satisfying and non-exploitive.

Contraceptive Care for Minors
Contraceptive services should be available to all—including minors who should enjoy the same rights of free and independent access to medical contraceptive care as do others.

Explicit Sexual Materials
The use of explicit sexual materials (sometimes referred to as pornography) can serve a variety of important needs in the lives of countless individuals and should be available to adults who wish to have them.[75]

This latter statement reflected the permissive, even "therapeutic", attitude of the Nixon administration's Commission on Pornography. Even with a philosophy parallel to that of an official government report (all but overturned fifteen years later by the report of the attorney general's Task Force on Pornography), the SIECUS position statements are significantly more liberal than the extremely liberal era in which they were born, if only because they contain absolutely no hint of hesitation or qualification, no suggestion that parental consultation with minors is advisable, no glimmer of harm from the morbid and violent pornography that, though more prevalent today, was surely available when the statements were ratified.

Once youth were targeted for medical services, the nature of American politics immediately suggested to Planned Parenthood and its allies a variety of ways to utilize teenagers for the ends of sex education and population control. In short, young people were recruited into lobbying and staff positions. In the early 1970s, Planned Parenthood of Los Angeles hired a full-time staff member to organize high school students into a lobbying organization. The resulting group, Youth for Education in Sexuality (YES), launched a statewide campaign for legislation to authorize distribution of birth control drugs and devices to youths and to maintain the mandate for "health education" in California secondary schools. The governor of California, Ronald Reagan, vetoed the birth control bills, but YES remained as a continuing force for legal change.[76]

---

[75] "SIECUS Position Statements", *SIECUS Report*, vol. 2, no. 5 (May 1974): 2. It should be noted that the repeated phrase "It is the position of SIECUS that" has been edited from each selected quotation.

[76] The story of YES is told in *The Population Activist's Handbook*, the Population Institute,

The making of federal grants for sex education curricula and promotion continued to expand. In 1973 the Health Services Administration (HEW) awarded a contract to the Westinghouse Population Center in Maryland to produce *A Guidebook for Family Planning Education*. The guidebook's sole focus was on building acceptance of birth control and sexual activity among the young. "Education's major goal, then," the guidebook said, "is to go beyond providing facts to developing sound birth control practices".[77] It recommended as most likely to succeed the creation of "referral mechanisms with school nurses and counselors" to move teenagers from the school setting to birth control clinics.[78] The guidebook closed with a recommended bibliography of sex education materials, including Sol Gordon's Ed-U Press, Multi-Media Resource of California, five Planned Parenthood affiliates, SIECUS, and a smattering of drug companies, including Upjohn.

HEW's Bureau of Community Health Services (BCHS) made a similar grant in 1973 that led to the publication of a resource guide specifically for birth control programs for teenagers, *Practical Suggestions for Family Planning Education*. This resource guide also featured Sol Gordon and a host of Planned Parenthood educators and publications. HEW was actively building the Planned Parenthood clinical and education network. And the network was growing fast. By 1975 the number of teenagers enrolled in organized birth control programs had grown to 1.2 million from only 214,000 in 1969.[79] In approximately half of the nation's Planned Parenthood affiliates, teenagers were required to attend a "rap session" featuring SIECUS-inspired themes before receiving birth control.[80] Despite the rapid expansion, Planned Parenthood

---

Foreword by Stephanie Mills (Collier Books: MacMillan, 1974), 134. The *Handbook* has no single author; an acknowledgement on the reverse of the title page lists a number of coauthors: Helaine Hammelstein, Youth and Student Affairs Division of Planned Parenthood; Roy Lucas, activist attorney, associated with the National Abortion Rights Action League; Mills herself, a former employee of Planned Parenthood–Alameda and a board member of national Planned Parenthood.

[77] *A Guidebook for Family Planning Education*, HEW Publication no. (HSA) 74-16002: Westinghouse Population Center, Columbia, MD, for the Bureau of Community Health Services, Health Services Administration, U.S. Public Health Service, HEW, December 1973, 4.

[78] Ibid., 7.

[79] *Contraceptive Services for Adolescents: United States, Each State and County, 1975* (New York: Alan Guttmacher Institute, 1978), 22. It should be noted that this AGI study estimated that half of all teenagers receiving birth control services (0.6 million) were obtaining them from private physicians; this estimate may be high, but Planned Parenthood by no means stood alone in providing such services.

[80] House and Goldsmith, *Family Planning Perspectives*, vol. 4, no. 2 (April 1972).

officials established an additional target of 1.6 million teenagers to recruit to organized programs.[81]

Once high school students were recruited, the next target was obvious, and the failure of these programs to reduce teenage sexual activity, pregnancy, venereal disease, and abortion provided a rationale. A 1975 article in Planned Parenthood's *Family Planning Perspectives* argued that "sex education offered in high school comes rather late and may be inappropriate to this group's [male adolescents] needs. Birth control programs should reach out to younger male (as well as female) adolescents in the junior high schools."[82]

For a number of years, HEW's Bureau of Community Health Services remained the focal point of the birth control education effort. Many other sex education guides published by BCHS were similar to those already described. For a time HEW followed the course laid down by Undersecretary Cohen in 1966, that HEW should not attempt to establish the precise course content for birth control and sex education programs, but should limit itself to collecting and publishing information on books, films, and pamphlets.

In 1977 HEW went a step further, awarding a contract to officials of Planned Parenthood of Alameda to produce a *model* school program for sex education. The quotation that appears at the head of this chapter is taken from this guide. Oddly enough, the guide was published by HEW without the routine disclaimer that the views it contained did not necessarily represent the views of the U.S. government. The model program noted, accurately, that despite the tripling of adolescent enrollment in birth control programs from 1971 to 1976, the rate of teen pregnancy had "continue[d] to climb".[83] The guide quoted as "appropriate" the words of Elizabeth Canfield that the schools and the home were to blame for this phenomenon: "The school joins the home in depriving young people of a forum for values clarification. Young people remain the victims of moralizing."[84] (For Canfield's views on "sexual adventuring" and adultery, see the next chapter.)

The guide advocated classroom demonstrations of contraceptive devices.

Teens . . . like to see the "real" thing. They like to touch and play with the birth control methods. The leader needs to be comfortable demonstrating

[81] *Contraceptive Services for Adolescents: United States, Each State and County, 1975* (New York: Alan Guttmacher Institute, 1978), 50.

[82] D. J. and M. Finkel, "Sexual and Contraceptive Knowledge, Attitudes and Behavior of Male Adolescents", *Family Planning Perspectives*, vol. 7, no. 6 (November–December 1975): 256ff.

[83] *A Decision-Making Approach to Sex Education: A Curriculum Guide and Implementation Manual for a Model Program with Adolescents and Parents*, HEW, Bureau of Community Health Services, 1979.

[84] Ibid., quotation from Elizabeth Canfield, "Am I Normal?", the *Humanist*, March–April 1978.

the methods and needs a sense of humor when discussing this material. The rubber usually attracts a lot of giggles and the teens like to experiment with the [contraceptive] foam.

Another demonstration involved a game, called "Plan-a-Fam", played with dominoes and dice. The game rules informed teenagers that "induced abortion can be chosen immediately after a pregnancy confirmation". Players are told simply: "Turn a domino on its side and use an abortion marker."

Another HEW grant, in 1979, produced *Family Life Education: Curriculum Guide,* prepared by the educational staff of Planned Parenthood of Santa Cruz.[85] The guide urged that sex educators be aware of and inform teenagers of laws regarding access to birth control; noted that some children "may have received strong parental or religious training to oppose abortion", and urged that these children be dealt with by emphasizing "listening and respecting other people's feelings and opinions". Its model answer to a question about abortion complications was categorical and categorically false: "Studies show that there are no increased risks with future pregnancies." Finally, the guide reprinted and recommended Plan-a-Fam.

Planned Parenthood of Memphis also received a HEW grant and produced *A Problem Solving Curriculum* for family life education. Similar to the other guides, it included an additional section on genetic diseases and a classroom exercise where students are tasked to enumerate all of the problems handicapped children face: "adult misunderstanding, other children teasing, difficulty in participating in games with other children, the child or adult's . . . repeated illnesses, hospitalization, embarrassment". The students are told that, in these circumstances, doctors and geneticists can help and each student "should watch for diseases which may apply to them".[86]

In addition to curriculum guides, federal officials disseminated the Planned Parenthood message during the Carter administration via funding of regional conferences. In March 1977 HEW awarded a contract to the Youth and Student Affairs Division of the Planned Parenthood Federation to conduct four regional conferences on "Teenagers and Family Planning". The conferences were held in 1977 and 1978 and featured, naturally, largely Planned Parenthood materials and speakers. Al Moran, executive vice president of Planned Parenthood of New York City gave the keynote address to the Kansas City regional conference. Moran once summarized his expectations for

---

[85] *Family Life Education: Curriculum Guide,* Family Life Education Program Development Project, developed under contract with the Department of Health, Education and Welfare: Grant #09–H–00260–08–0 FT H70, Summer 1979.

[86] *Family Life Education: A Problem Solving Curriculum* (ages 15–19), prepared under grant for the Department of Health, Education and Welfare, Public Health Service, Health Services Administration, Bureau of Community Health Services.

teenagers by saying that changes in U.S. laws could yield "700,000 induced abortions in teenagers each year". He told the *Toledo* [Ohio] *Blade:*

> If I were 14 today, I'd be sexually active. And if you were 14 you would be too. It is vital that there be a kindergarten through 12th grade curriculum that helps young people understand the joys, responsibilities, and consequences of sex and sexuality . . . those adolescents who are sexually active need help in preventing pregnancy whether politicians, educators or parents like it or not.[87]

The HEW conferences helped to spread such assertions nationwide under a blanket of federal authority. Unfortunately, they were not true. While sexual activity rates among teenagers climbed steadily in the 1970s and 1980s, an authoritative study of sexual behavior among youths reported in 1986 by researchers at Ohio State University showed that "by their 15th birthday only 6.6 percent of American teenage girls had had sex".[88]

The basic goal of the conferences was made quite clear in the final report submitted to HEW. Planned Parenthood lawyer Harriet Pilpel had presented the conference workshop on legal issues; Rep. James Scheuer of New York, co-author of the federal legislation creating the Title X family planning mechanism for Planned Parenthood, gave another of the keynote addresses; the Population Institute presented its federally subsidized advertising spots featuring rock stars and athletes promoting birth control. To make their combined message work, the states must mandate sex education throughout the nation's public school system. The final report noted that only six states had such mandates as of 1978, and happily reported that the conference delegations from three states left with the resolve to seek mandatory programs back home.[89]

Toward the latter half of the Carter administration, Planned Parenthood

---

[87] *Toledo Blade,* October 25, 1976.

[88] William Marsiglio and Frank Mott (1986). The study was confirmed by rival data sets published in the journal *Demography,* (vol. 25, no. 2 (May 1988): 189–204). Reported by Dr. William Coulson, Ph.D., Research Council on Ethnopsychology, unpublished paper in the possession of the authors. Coulson, a leading associate of psychotherapist and educational theorist Carl Rogers, has written and spoken extensively about the misapplication of Rogers' theories of nondirective psychotherapy to educational settings, particularly through values clarification and other nondirective educational models. Coulson was junior editor of Rogers' seventeen-volume series on humanistic education for Charles E. Merrill Publishing Company. His critique of the defects of this educational approach, as applied to issues from tobacco, alcohol, and drug abuse to sexual behavior, is devastating.

[89] "Teenagers and Family Planning", a series of four regional conferences funded under HEW Contract no. 240–77–0052 to the Youth and Student Affairs Division, Planned Parenthood Federation of America, Office of Family Planning, Bureau of Community Health Services, Health Services Administration, U.S. Department of Health, Education and Welfare (1977). All conferences were funded under a single grant, and all references in the text are taken from the conference reports filed with the Bureau of Community Health Services.

officials joined forces with the burgeoning teenage pregnancy industry to promote a major new adolescent pregnancy initiative. Having largely had their way with the grant-making bureaucracy and with Congress, and having a close ally in President Carter (who from his days as governor of Georgia had worked closely with Dr. Robert Hatcher of the Grady Memorial Family Planning Program and Dr. Peter Bourne, his personal physician and an instigator of the 1973 *Doe v. Bolton* abortion case), they may not have been prepared for the political and philosophical battle the initiative became.

One phase of the battle involved abortion, where the Carter administration offered right to life forces an ally, HEW secretary Joseph Califano. Another phase was the Planned Parenthood demand for primary focus on birth control and sex education, rather than Califano's preference for "comprehensive services" that, while excluding abortion payments and permitting promotion of birth control, added such costly but effective services as prenatal care, nutrition education, and social and psychological counseling.

In March 1978 Rep. Scheuer's Select Committee on Population held a hearing on the proposed initiative and the differences between the two approaches. Speaking on behalf of the Carter administration's proposal, which reflected Califano's policy preferences, Sargent Shriver, chairman of the International Advisory Board of the Kennedy Foundation at Georgetown University, acknowledged his support for the availability of contraception and sex education to promote it, but urged the Committee to support the "comprehensive" approach and to pay more attention to abstinence as an alternative.[90]

Frederick S. Jaffe, president of the Guttmacher Institute at the time and prime author of the original national birth control needs assessment for OEO in 1968, attacked the initiative vociferously. He quoted with derision a statement by a HEW official that "you can't just give contraceptives to teenagers", and argued that the federal government should take the lead in efforts to enroll two million more teenagers in birth control programs like that of Planned Parenthood. He called on HEW and the Carter administration to lead a new drive to insert "realistic sex education" programs in American schools and neighborhoods.[91]

In retrospect, this public split among presumed allies in a liberal Democratic administration was the first sign of the weakening of Planned Parenthood's federal strategy for sex education and birth control. Congress, in inimitable fashion, responded to the dispute by adopting something for each side in the debate. First, it reauthorized the Title X birth control program, Planned Parenthood's primary funding source, at $135 million for fiscal year 1979.

[90] Testimony of Sargent Shriver, *Hearings Before the Select Committee on Population,* 95th Cong., 2d sess., February 28, March 1–2, 1978, vol. 2, no. 31, 635.

[91] Testimony of Frederick S. Jaffe, president of AGI, ibid., March 2, 1978, 545.

More importantly, though the program had funded services and in-clinic sex education for teenagers from the beginning, Congress granted Planned Parenthood a major victory in 1978 and specifically authorized "services for adolescents". This language added impetus, an "insurance" program really, to Planned Parenthood's effort to protect the adolescent programs from charges that they either violated various state laws or constitutional prerogatives of parents.

Congress responded as well to the Califano proposal by adopting a modest ($7.5 million in the first year) Adolescent Health Services and Pregnancy Prevention and Care Act. Planned Parenthood rejoiced when President Carter's clean sweep of his cabinet resulted in Secretary Califano's replacement by the ardent abortion advocate Patricia Roberts Harris. Her presence helped for a time to ensure that the comprehensive programs went no further. But the new cabinet proved, to the American people at least, no substitute for a new president, and Planned Parenthood faced its greatest test when Ronald Reagan was sworn in as the nation's fortieth president.

Sex Education for the 1980s

There were two immediate effects of the Reagan victory and the election of a strong class of freshman pro-life senators in 1980. First, the growth of Planned Parenthood's federal funding sources was stymied, if not altogether reversed. As part of this effect, Senator Jeremiah Denton, famed Vietnamese War POW, succeeded in winning congressional approval of the Adolescent Family Life Act (AFLA), an almost exact mirror alternative to Planned Parenthood's Title X that replaced the Carter-era adolescent program and emphasized adoption, parental involvement, abstinence from sexual intercourse, and pro-family education for teenagers. The second effect was to drive Planned Parenthood's public policy architects to seek new influence through the private sector and through state and local governments, using such avenues as school-based clinics, family life education programs, and spin-off organizations.

The AFLA program provided the first alternative to the Title X program that represented distinctly different program objectives. It was adopted in 1981, partially as a compromise package including reauthorization of Title X. The intent of the abstinence component of the AFLA program was to support educational initiatives and projects stressing the value of postponing sexual activity until marriage. That it has done, providing support for family-oriented curricula like the *Teen Aid* and *Sex Respect* programs. But Planned Parenthood worked hard in the 1980s to limit the AFLA program's impact. It did this in several ways.

First, it sought to limit funding for the program, relying on its allies in Congress. It largely succeeded in this, for while AFLA funding averaged $9.6

million annually from 1981 to 1989, the program peaked in fiscal year 1984 at $12.1 million in expenditures and declined to $6.5 million in fiscal year 1990, a drop of nearly 50% without accounting for inflation.[92] The decline was abetted by flagging commitment to the program in the Reagan Office of Management and Budget, which slated the program for zero funding on at least one occasion. At the same time, in 1981 and 1984 the Reagan administration made major efforts, thwarted by Planned Parenthood, to convert Title X into a block grant program. This would have transferred program design and control to the states, without necessarily decreasing the dollar flow to Planned Parenthood.

Planned Parenthood opposed this idea, arguing instead for increased Title X funding and centralized program design. Title X had been extremely useful in sweeping aside state policies on medical treatment for minor children, and allowing the program to become a block grant risked restoring some measure of parental participation. Despite Planned Parenthood's efforts, Reagan administration nonsupport and deficit politics stultified the Title X program: In real dollars, program spending fell from 1981 to 1989, and the fiscal year 1989 budget was below the decade's average.

Overall, Planned Parenthood continued to benefit handsomely from federal subsidies during the decade. One key to this support was the fact that, by the beginning of the decade, over one hundred different laws authorized expenditures for birth control, in programs ranging from Aid to Families with Dependent Children and the Maternal and Child Health Block Grant to the Indian Health Service. Even with a stand-off over AFLA and Title X, the U.S. government supported the Planned Parenthood approach to sexuality over abstinence-based programs by a ratio of at least 75:1.

Planned Parenthood attacked the AFLA program in other ways, including direct and indirect assaults on the abstinence-based curricula and more subtle attempts to undermine the program and similar state programs by redefining the meaning of the term "abstinence". With regard to the former tactic, a March 1987 report written by Marie Haviland-James for the Planned Parenthood Federation regarding the *Sex Respect* program provides a fascinating glimpse of the agency's sex education politics. *Sex Respect* is a program developed under grants from the Office of Adolescent Pregnancy at the Department of Health and Human Services (HHS), using AFLA funds. It fulfills the authorizing statute's criteria to devise educational programs that promote the value of premarital virginity in preventing emotional heartbreak, venereal diseases, pregnancy, and abortion.

[92] For a fuller discussion of the relationship between the AFLA and Title X programs, see "Teenage Pregnancy: National Policies at the Crossroads", Charles A. Donovan, *Family Policy*, publication of the Family Research Council, Washington, D.C., November–December 1989.

The Haviland-James report provided guidance to Planned Parenthood sex educators opposing *Sex Respect* or seeking its removal from the schools. The memo urged opponents of *Sex Respect* to argue that it "violates the separation of church and state" and risks litigation from the American Civil Liberties Union. It charged that the program is faulty because it: contained "many references . . . to a 'spiritual' dimension of sexuality"; contained "use of the word 'baby' for fetus"; expressed "bias . . . against people who are sexually active and unmarried"; "compared stealing of money continually with contin-ued sexual activity"; contained "a description of a woman haunted by guilt"; omitted "pro-choice material"; and, of greatest interest, included "unsub-stantiated claims" such as "abstinence has future benefits for teens" and "because of the special nature of human sexuality, there's no way to have premarital sex without hurting someone".[93] The memo concluded that *Sex Respect* "appeals . . . to the lowest common denominator of mentality".

A cover letter from the Planned Parenthood Federation enclosing the Haviland-James report urged local Planned Parenthood officials to use the report to attack *Sex Respect* before local school boards. The letter recommended an alternative AFLA-funded curriculum, *Human Sexuality: Values and Choices,* that school boards could be urged to adopt if they continue to resist "comprehensive" Planned Parenthood-style programs. The letter praised this curriculum because "its tone says that while sexual abstinence is best for young teenagers (junior high age), everyone has a *right* to know about contraception. It provides that information." Note the interpolation apparently limiting the appropriateness of abstinence education to *junior-high-age children.* The letter went on to say that the curriculum was "designed by some of the same people who developed the first school-based clinic in the United States".

By alleging that *Sex Respect* violated the separation of church and state by advocating abstinence, Planned Parenthood was merely echoing the federal Court strategy of the American Civil Liberties Union against the AFLA. In *Bowen v. Kendrick,* the Supreme Court by a five to four margin laid to rest at least one part of that strategy by upholding the anti-sexual activity message of the AFLA as a constitutional expression of public policy preferences. The Court remanded the case to the federal district court to determine whether particular AFLA grantees may have violated statutory or constitutional guide-lines by including specifically religious practices in their programs; for now, however, the Planned Parenthood thesis that premarital abstinence itself consti-tutes a religious practice has been rejected by the Court.

The other means of undermining AFLA suggested by the Haviland-James

[93] Marie Haviland-James, "A Report on 'Sex Respect' ", Planned Parenthood Federation of America, subhead Michigan Planned Parenthood for the Forest Hills, Michigan Board of Education, March 1987. Cover letter, Planned Parenthood Federation of America, "Interested Educators", 2 (n.d.).

report is, however, still viable: that of turning the meaning of the term *abstinence* into outright advocacy of sexual indulgences other than normal intercourse, or limiting abstinence only to the first few years of adolescence. Mainstream AFLA grantees define abstinence as waiting until marriage, including "body respect", "training for fidelity", " 'no' to premarital sex", and "non-conformity to media and peer pressure".[94] Debra Haffner, executive director of SIECUS, wrote that abstinence for teenagers can and should be redefined to include any and all sexual behaviors that do not result in normal intercourse. A passage from her article "Safe Sex and Teens" in the September–October 1989 *SIECUS Report* is worth quoting at length:

> Colleagues and I have fantasized about a national "petting project" for teenagers. The object would not be to increase petting among teenagers, but to help them learn courting behaviors. . . . We need to tell teens that the safest sex doesn't necessarily mean no sex, but rather behaviors that have no possibility of causing a pregnancy or a sexually transmitted disease. A partial list of safe sex practices for teens could include: Talking, Flirting, Dancing, Hugging, Kissing, Necking, Massaging, Caressing, Undressing each other, Masturbation alone, Masturbation in front of a partner, Mutual masturbation. Teens could surely come up with their own list of activities. By helping teens explore the full range of safe sexual behavior, we may help to raise a generation of adults that do not equate sex with intercourse, or intercourse with vaginal orgasm, as the goal of sex.[95]

This is one of the most remarkable passages in a very remarkable history of revealing statements by SIECUS spokesmen. For an organization that over the years has portrayed itself as an advocate of realism to expect young people to forgo sexual intercourse at this level of experimentation seems delusional. But note where the conundrum of sexual activity, venereal disease, HIV infection, unwed pregnancy, and abortion have left the champions of the new morality: as offering teenagers a path to everything but normal intercourse! On its own terms, the Planned Parenthood/SIECUS philosophy defeats the fullness of sexuality between man and woman. But despite this delusion, the threat of such redefinitions to the future of abstinence-based sex education programs is very real.

The final method of subverting the AFLA is via an all-out frontal assault on the legislative foundations of the program. That is what Senator Edward Kennedy (D–Mass.) sought to do in the 101st Congress via two bills, S. 110 and S. 120. S. 110 was designed to reauthorize and expand the Title X birth

[94] "ABSTINENCE", information sheet detailing ten principles of sexual behavior using the acronym "A–B–S–T–I–N–E–N–C–E", distributed by Sex Respect, Project Respect, Golf, Ill.

[95] Debra W. Haffner, executive director, SIECUS, "Safe Sex and Teens", *SIECUS Report* (September–October 1989), 9.

control program and S. 120 to completely subvert the AFLA program, making it the ideological twin of Title X, repealing its adoption and abstinence focus, requiring abortion counseling, and repealing the mandate for parental involvement currently in the program. The *Planned Parenthood–Washington Memo* for March 28, 1989, warmly praised the Kennedy bills, describing the parental involvement and abstinence aspects as "controversial" and applauding Senator Kennedy's attempt to make AFLA another population control program that is designed to "prevent teenage pregnancy rather than teenage sex".

School-Based Clinics

Over the years Planned Parenthood has devised several projects in an attempt to get around the general problem of parental and academic opposition to birth control and sex education programs for teenagers. Installing birth control clinics directly on the campuses of America's junior and senior high schools was not merely a stratagem to overcome flagging federal support; it was also the natural culmination of several other projects Planned Parenthood initiated to weaken other institutions (family, church, and community) it saw as preventing teenagers from accepting their own sexual activity and practicing birth control and abortion.

In our view, the historical roots of school-based clinics (SBC—an acronym that will do as well for "school birth control" centers) are to be found in the Planned Parenthood–devised in-clinic "rap session" and the "peer counselor" concept. The idea is also modeled on the "outreach efforts" of federal health grantees, the free or self-help clinic movement that spread across America in the 1970s, community health centers, and the experience of a very small number of school birth control clinics here in the United States and, to a larger extent, in Sweden.

Planned Parenthood initiated teen "rap sessions" as early as 1967. One memorandum from an official of New York City's Margaret Sanger Research Bureau, dated May 12, 1971, discussed the need for separate teen clinics because of the uncomfortable interaction that occurred when adult women clientele observed teenaged girls visiting Planned Parenthood for birth control. The memo noted that some of the "teenagers" were all of twelve years old. Holding completely separate clinic sessions for teenagers provided a solution to this problem.

But other problems remained. How to get teenagers to the clinics? How to spread the word about the availability of birth control and abortion? How to keep parents out of the process and school administrators and reluctant school nurses at bay? Various methods were devised. One was to film the basic clinic rap session, as was done in the film *About Sex,* and promote showings in recreation centers, boys clubs, and other places where young people naturally gathered.

Another was to devise a program of "peer counselors", young people specifically recruited, and sometimes—if not always—paid, by Planned Parenthood to serve as a source of feedback and referrals to the out-of-school clinics. Some early examples of this type of arrangement are recorded in *The Population Activist's Handbook,*[96] a 1974 publication of the Population Institute. The *Handbook* describes in detail the school birth control initiative in Lebanon, New Hampshire, where students were permitted to remit tuitions by performing community service tasks or by "serving as in-school representatives of Planned Parenthood". The project eventually resulted in Planned Parenthood being granted a meeting room in all three of Lebanon's high schools to conduct weekly rap sessions during school hours.

Planned Parenthood also established its own full-fledged, school-based clinic in the 1970s, at Woodson High School in the District of Columbia. It was a one-of-a-kind operation. In 1978, before the House Select Committee on Population, three teenaged girls who worked as peer counselors in the school program and Joan Benesch, co-chair of the D.C. Sex Education Coalition, testified to what they regarded as the program's unique worth. The three girls were chosen because one had had a baby, one was currently sexually active and contracepting, and the third had been contracepting and was now expecting a child. The panel told the members of Congress, to peals of laughter, that they had also hoped to bring a virgin, but "couldn't find any".[97]

The Woodson experiment failed, however, and Planned Parenthood eventually abandoned it. But as the political horizon changed in the 1980s, the idea was resurrected with full force. Planned Parenthood recognized, however, that school birth control clinics alone would be too controversial to be saleable to most school systems, and the question of targeting the inner-city black community had become more sensitive than expected. The second incarnation of SBCs was to be as full-service medical centers, with the Planned Parenthood component advertised not at all or as a very low-profile part of the program. Moreover, a new SBC initiative would allow Planned Parenthood to maintain the offensive in the face of overwhelming evidence that its existing programs were not only not working, but actually helping to drive teenage sexual activity, pregnancy, and abortion through the roof.

Philosophically, SBCs were just what Dr. Guttmacher ordered. The PPFA president told attendees at the 1970 PPFA annual meeting that in order to achieve "the perfect contracepting society", Planned Parenthood, in addition

---

[96] See part 4, "Action for High School Students", esp. chap. 15, "Education", 119–27.

[97] Testimony of Joan Benesch, House Select Committee on Population, etc.

to offering contraception, sterilization, abortion, and genetic counseling, would have to establish "contraceptive education for all youth so that at the appropriate time in their lives contraception will be accepted as naturally as breathing".[98]

In March 1985, opening its drive for SBCs in earnest, the Alan Guttmacher Institute (AGI) published a study of teenage pregnancy in thirty-six other developed countries. The study concluded that the United States leads almost all other developed nations of the world in rates of teenage pregnancy, abortion, and childbirth.[99] The lessons "learned" were that: Lower teen pregnancy rates were not achieved by greater recourse to abortion; young teenagers overseas were not too immature to use birth control effectively; teen pregnancy rates were lower in these countries because of greater availability of birth control and sex education; teen pregnancy, and not adolescent sexual activity, was the main problem; and religiosity was associated with higher teen fertility rates.[100] A possible solution, AGI demurely suggested, was the SBC.[101] However, there were flaws in the AGI study.

First, the AGI studied only those countries that had similar adolescent birth control programs and/or legal regimes and then contrasted the "results" with America. Ignored were countries like Japan, Ireland, Hong Kong, and Singapore, all of which have lower marital and nonmarital teen pregnancy rates and rely upon social pressure to discourage premarital sexual experimentation.[102] Also ignored were countries like Portugal, Spain, and individual states in the United States that, by law, policy, or tradition, restricted access to birth control and abortion and that have or had lower out-of-wedlock adolescent pregnancy rates than the United States as a whole. To include these entities would have undermined the school clinic approach.

Second, the study contained a number of self-admitted caveats and subjective opinions:

> The results of the multivariate analysis ... have to be taken as suggestive rather than conclusive. ... There seems to be more tolerance of teenage sexual activity in the European countries visited. ... The United States does

[98] Alan F. Guttmacher, "Planned Parenthood: Profile and Prospectus", *Family Planning Perspectives*, vol. 3, no. 1 (January 1971): 57–58.

[99] Jeannie Rosoff et al., "Teenage Pregnancy in Developed Countries: Determinants and Policy Implications", *Family Planning Perspectives*, vol. 17, no. 2 (March–April 1985); 53–63. This is a study summary.

[100] Ibid.

[101] Jeannie Rosoff and Richard Lincoln, "Policy Implications for the U.S.", *Teenage Pregnancy in Developed Countries*, Elsie F. Jones, ed. (New Haven: Yale University Press, 1986), 230.

[102] Charles Westoff et al., "Teenage Fertility in Developing Nations", *Family Planning Perspectives*, vol. 15, no. 3 (May–June, 1983): 105.

not appear to be more restrictive than low-fertility countries in the provision of contraceptive services to teenagers. However, comparable data could not be obtained.[103]

Third, in all of the other countries studied, restrictions on abortion were more numerous than in the United States, where the blanket permission of abortion until birth has led to an extremely high abortion count. In addition, abortion data were "reasonably complete" for only eleven of the thirty-six countries covered; no accurate measurements of teen sexual activity were available; and no data were presented to verify the AGI claim that teens overseas were more effective birth control users than their U.S. counterparts.[104]

While school birth control proponents point to the AGI study as supportive of their efforts to establish contraceptive centers in public schools, the inevitability of such a conclusion requires more evidence.

School Sex Clinics in Operation

From a public policy standpoint, the school-based clinic represents a final transformation of the public school system from a training ground for the transmission of traditional academic skills and national values to an antiethical laboratory for sexual liberation and behavioral change. At least one person prominently associated with Planned Parenthood has suggested that such programs be federally funded and extended to elementary schools as well.[105] Although at present Planned Parenthood does not directly operate school birth control clinics, it is important to review a few of the well-known studies Planned Parenthood has marshaled that purport to show that these clinics reduce teen pregnancy rates and even delay the onset of teen intercourse. It is also important to review, in fact, how the clinics would operate in practice.

The Baltimore Study, conducted by Johns Hopkins University, is seriously flawed. First, girls at schools with birth control clinics had a 33% drop-out rate—almost three times the nonclinic schools—and none of the girls who left school were even surveyed to see if they were pregnant! No attempt was made to explain this large decline among females at schools with clinics. The claim of a seven-month delay in first sexual intercourse and a reduction in pregnancy rates was based on a follow-up survey of only 96 of 1,033 girls originally surveyed. Furthermore, responses were not included from twelfth grade

[103] Rosoff et al., "Teenage Pregnancy in Developed Countries", 53–54, 59.

[104] Ibid. For an authoritative comparison of U.S. and Western European abortion laws, see Glendon, *Abortion and Divorce in Western Law: American Failures, European Challenges* (Cambridge, Mass: Harvard University Press, 1987).

[105] Remarks of Rep. James Scheuer, *Hearings before the House Select Committee on Population*, vol. 2, February 28, 1978.

students, reportedly because they lacked motivation.[106] Abortion was not even mentioned as a possible depressant on the reported pregnancy rate, yet in Maryland almost 33% of abortions are performed on teens.[107]

The St. Paul, Minnesota SBC study claimed a reduction in live births because daily student contact by nurses ensured that adolescent girls regularly took their birth control pills. The study does not, however, explain how daily nurse/student "pill compliance contacts" were maintained on weekends or during school breaks and vacations. Also, officials thought it was "reasonable" to attribute the reported birth decline to the program, but they did not verify if the drop in birth rates occurred because of abortion, a decrease in sexual activity, or birth control use.[108] The uncertainty about the role of abortion was admitted by a St. Paul school clinic administrator.[109] The "no repeat pregnancy claim" for girls in the program who returned to school was contradicted elsewhere.[110]

These studies have been repeatedly advanced as the "public health" justification for SBCs. But just as often SBC advocates seek to divert public criticism with the claim that the clinics are there only to help identify and address student health needs, especially those of poorer students. Yet cleaning teeth or screening for heart murmurs is not the source of controversy, giving adolescents birth control is. In review articles discussing how SBCs will work in practice, advocates sometimes frankly admit this. "These clinics often provide full health services so a teen need not identify sexual concerns until in the privacy of the examining room. This 'cover' is important to teens not comfortable using family planning as their presenting complaint."[111]

In fact, as Planned Parenthood may have tacitly acknowledged in closing down the Woodson SBC in the nation's capital, pro-SBC studies have found that clinics offering only birth control, pregnancy, and venereal disease testing, etc., were used by fewer students.[112] A Planned Parenthood doctor has

[106] Laurie Zabin et al., "Evaluation of a Pregnancy Prevention Program for Urban Teenagers", *Family Planning Perspectives,* (May–June 1986): 119–26.

[107] Maryland Department of Health, Division of Vital Statistics, *Reports, Abortion Data, 1984–1986.*

[108] Laura Edwards et al., "Adolescent Pregnancy Prevention Program Services in High Schools", *Family Planning Perspectives,* vol. 12, no. 1 (January–February 1980): 6–14.

[109] Asta Kenny, "School Based Clinics: A National Conference", *Family Planning Perspectives,* vol. 18, no. 1 (January–February 1986): 44–46.

[110] Edward Brann et al., "Strategies for the Prevention of School Pregnancies", *Advances in Planned Parenthood,* no. 2 (1979): 68–79; M. Berg et al., "Prenatal Care for Pregnant Adolescents in Public School", *Journal of School Health,* vol. 49, no. 1 (January 1979): 143–53.

[111] Susan Proctor, "A Developmental Approach to Pregnancy Prevention with Early Adolescent Females", *Journal of School Health,* vol. 56, no. 8 (October 1986).

[112] Joy Dryfoos, "School Based Health Clinics: A New Approach to Preventing Ado-

suggested that providing comprehensive health care *"may be considered necessary to justify the granting of contraceptives"* [emphasis added].[113]

The SBC movement is certainly spreading; the number of such centers has grown from 12 in 1984 to 31 a year later to approximately 150 today. Planned Parenthood literature suggests how the clinics will deal with such sensitive issues as abortion and parental consent. The confusing and complicated Supreme Court jurisprudence around the latter issue was not significantly clarified by the Court's 1990 rulings in *Hodgson v. Minnesota* and *Ohio v. Akron Reproductive Health Services.* For the time being, in most states an unemancipated minor is free to obtain an abortion without even single-parent notice if she can convince a judge (and for some judges, as NBC's Connie Chung has reported, this is only a fifteen-minute decision) that she is "mature" enough to do so on her own.

Public schools, as we have noted, have traditionally been reluctant to prescribe or obtain medical care for minors, in or out of school hours, without parental approval. Many states continue to bar school nurses from administering so much as an aspirin without specific parental authority. SBCs will do much to obviate this safeguard of traditional parental prerogatives. At some clinic sites, "parents are asked to sign a blanket consent form unrelated to any specific clinic visit" that, in some areas, will suffice for the entire period of the child's enrollment. An article in *Family Planning Perspectives* described this arrangement as follows: "As a general rule, parental consent for a student's participation at the clinic is sought at the beginning of the school year, but is not required for any individual service."[114]

Another well-known Planned Parenthood author has written that "the issue of abortion is frequently finessed in these clinics".[115]

A final ominous aspect of the school birth control clinics involves new abortion drugs such as RU-486, the antiprogestin pill that has been approved for use in France, Red China, and Great Britain. Pro-abortion proponents have previously noted, "We think all family planning agencies should be prepared to provide postcoital contraception. . . . For clinics not prepared to perform abortions this policy would be extremely important,

---

lescent Pregnancy?", *Family Planning Perspectives,* vol. 17, no. 2 (March–April 1985): 70–75.

[113] Sadja Goldsmith, "Medicalized Sex—To the Editor", *The New England Journal of Medicine* (September 24, 1970): 709.

[114] Kenny, "School-Based Clinics", 44. A similar description of the parental consent arrangement is found in a brochure published by the Robert Wood Johnson Foundation, a major benefactor of school-based clinics: Philip Porter, "Information Exchange", *High School-Based Health Services* (Winter 1984): 2.

[115] Dryfoos, "School-Based Health Clinics".

whether for licensing, liability insurance, accounting, or community relations."[116]

"RU-486 is expected to be a boon . . . to women who cannot, or do not, take the pill—'especially,' says [French research physician Dr. Beatrice] Couzinet, 'young women and teenagers whose sexual activity is very irregular and infrequent.' "[117] Alfred Moran of Planned Parenthood of New York City has stated that "if RU-486 is ever approved here, Planned Parenthood plans to make it available free or 'at cost' at its family planning centers".[118]

It takes little imagination to realize how soon this may mean that adolescents need only get a "hall pass" or take a "lunch break" to have an abortion.

Sex Education in the 1990s

As the 1980s closed, Planned Parenthood's old partner, the Alan Guttmacher Institute, published a national study of sex education laws and practices entitled *Risk and Responsibility: Teaching Sex Education in America's Schools Today*. From the opening caption, the report gives a clear idea of the "State of the Union" on sex education issues and where Planned Parenthood, SIECUS, and allies like the National Education Association are headed in the coming decade. The opening quotes a "nationally known expert" to the effect that students need "education about human sexuality . . . just as they need to know fractions . . . or grammar".[119]

The thrust of the study, not surprisingly, is toward more comprehensive (i.e., including "birth control methods, use of condoms . . . and homosexuality") sex education courses, which should be "taught earlier than they are", and which should be overseen by state education agencies that have a "clear statement of policy on sex education and *monitor enforcement*" [emphasis added]. The report deftly takes advantage of the HIV scourge to insist that sex education has been transformed "from an issue once only of local concern into a nationwide educational norm". Planned Parenthood had regularly insisted, of course, that this tranformation had taken place long before anyone suspected the existence of HIV.

Chapter Four examines in more detail the writings of the primary sex

[116] Eliot and McGreggor, "Postcoital Contraception by Endometrial Aspiration" (paper presented to the 1977 Association of Planned Parenthood Physicians, October 12–13), published by Excerpta Medica Foundation, 1978, 21–26.

[117] Jamie Murphy, "The Month After Pill", *Time,* December 29, 1986, 64.

[118] Matt Clark, "An Effective Abortion Pill", *Newsweek,* December 29, 1986, 47.

[119] *Risk and Responsibility: Teaching Sex Education in America's Schools Today,* Alan Guttmacher Institute, 1989. The report was funded by the Carnegie Corp. of New York, the New York Times Foundation, and the Brush Foundation. The following quotations, unless otherwise noted, are from this report.

educators promoted by Planned Parenthood. *Risk and Responsibility* measures how far the states have come in imposing sex education mandates on their public school systems. By 1989, seventeen states plus the District of Columbia required such courses, twenty-three encouraged local school districts to conduct them, and ten had no position on the subject. Within these general mandates, much to Planned Parenthood's chagrin, there is much diversity. Only two of the thirteen states that have devised statewide curricula include coverage of birth control methods and how they work, and none, the AGI says, suggest where the methods can be obtained.[120]

Among other major findings in the report is that sex education teachers regard "pressure from parents", community groups, and religious organizations as the primary problems they face in implementing programs. Other data in the report suggest why. While few sex education teachers expected opposition to teaching about "abstinence, STDs [sexually transmitted diseases] or HIV transmission", "higher percentages" of teachers encountered or expected to encounter "negative reactions from parents" and others if they taught about "condom use, sexual orientation, 'safer sex' practices and abortion". Despite this fact, AGI asserts that a majority of the sex education teachers surveyed desired to teach these subjects, excluding abortion, "by the end of seventh grade, if not earlier".

It is no doubt true, as Planned Parenthood asserts, that a large majority of American parents favor teaching something broadly described as "sex education". But AGI's data, if not its interpretation, suggest that parents have something different in mind when they respond to such surveys, that they believe in moral instruction, that sex educators are (depending on your point of view) way ahead of or out of synchronization with parental values, and that parents are making their views known to professional educators who desire to divorce sexuality from the moral life of the community. Moreover, in Planned Parenthood polls questions about sex education, the provision of birth control, etc., are assumed to correct and not worsen the problem of venereal disease, single parenting, etc. It is for this reason that ever more powerful state mandates, with detailed mandatory curriculum guidelines, are likely to be the continuing battleground on which the war for the hearts and minds of the nation's children will be fought in the coming decade.

Health 2000

Indeed, as this decade and century come to an end, the drive for sex education mandates in the style of Planned Parenthood is moving toward particular

---

[120] Ibid., 16. Despite the absence of such information in state curricula, a significant percentage of the nation's largest school districts provide either birth control instruction (75%) or referral information (41%).

targets, with a major boost from one of Planned Parenthood's strongest redoubts, the U.S. Public Health Service, Department of Health and Human Services. Despite the election of a third consecutive conservative administration in 1988, the HHS/USPHS bureaucrats appear to have succeeded in framing yet another executive document setting goals detrimental to the well-being of American teenagers. The report *Health 2000*, released in September 1990, calls for mandatory health (sex) education in twenty-five American states by the turn of the century; in draft form, it also called for such "health goals" as a doubling of condom sales nationwide, an increase in the percentage of sexually active teenagers using birth control methods, and nearly universal genetic screening of American pregnancies.

From a historical perspective, these goals seem likely to fail, for their premises are largely false. Supreme Court decisions and federal policies have basically made the United States a vast laboratory for Planned Parenthood's ideas these past twenty years. Abortion has been available on demand until term; with the exception of Utah, state laws or customs barring medical contraception and abortion for teenagers without parental knowledge have been swept away or invalidated virtually upon passage; 1.5 million teenagers per year, and maybe more since 1983, have been enrolled in birth control programs; 150 school-based clinics have opened; media of all kinds have glorified the pro-birth control sexual ethic. Major victories for traditional family values have been few and far between.

What has been the price? Between 1970 and 1987 the total number of births to women under the age of twenty has gone down, but only because the annual number of abortions has gone up by a much larger amount—250,000—and the number of female teenagers themselves—partly because of abortion—has declined by nearly 400,000. In 1970 nearly 70% of the births to teenagers were to married women, today the number is nearly reversed: 64% of all births to teenagers are nonmarital. The pregnancy rate for teenaged girls, despite increased exposure and access to contraceptives, rose by 10% from 1974 to 1985. Sexual activity rates for both sexes have soared. In 1987, 302,500 children were born out-of-wedlock to girls age fifteen to nineteen; a generation ago, fewer than 150,000 children were born out-of-wedlock to *all* American women.[121]

Planned Parenthood's grand experiment has truly proven, as George Grant has written, a grand illusion. What a tragedy it is that our nation has been forced to pay the price of so many broken lives, so many wounded families, to begin the process of recognition—and of healing.

---

[121] "Teenage Pregnancy: National Policies at the Crossroads", *Family Policy*, Family Research Council, 1989, 1.

Chapter Four

The Sex Educators

"We need to redefine the values of the family . . . "

— From *The Sexual Adolescent*

In 1981, the Planned Parenthood Federation of America developed and published its first guidebook for a national project in sex education. Prepared with the assistance of twenty-nine Planned Parenthood affiliates and a number of other private organizations, the guidebook provided a set of ideas and planning materials for National Family Sexuality Education Week, October 5–11, 1981. The guidebook opens with a series of acknowledgments; first and foremost among them is "a very special and warm appreciation" to Dr. Sol Gordon, the Syracuse University professor whose Institute for Family Research and Education founded National Family Sex Education Week as an annual event in 1975.

That Planned Parenthood should take a great leap forward in the field of sex education under the banner of Sol Gordon's national observance was a natural consequence of years of collaboration between the Federation and a group of sex educators, sexologists, and counselors whose essential leader was Gordon. In the years 1970 to 1980, when Planned Parenthood and organizations of similar philosophy moved aggressively into planning for national sex education curricula, the works of Gordon and his associates formed an avant-garde, a cutting edge in theme and content that actually represented the mainstream of Planned Parenthood's philosophy and ethics. An understanding of the practical goals of Planned Parenthood is impossible without an examination of those writers and educators whose literature and films dominate the organization's sex education programs from college to clinic to kindergarten.

The Institute for Family Research and Education

The Sexual Adolescent, a volume originally written by Sol Gordon (a second edition written in collaboration with Dr. Peter Scales and Dr. Kathleen Everly appeared in 1979) contains a comprehensive account of the development of the Institute for Family Research and Education (IFRE). Co-author Scales is listed on the title page of the later edition as a "Research Analyst and Consultant on Youth" from Washington, D.C. A prominent figure in the population control movement, Scales had been at various times an associate of the IFRE, director of the National Organization of Non-Parents (NON), and a research analyst for Mathtech, Inc., an organization based in Bethesda, Maryland. The National Organization for Non-Parents, headquartered in Baltimore, Maryland, seeks to promote a life-long commitment to childlessness among the young. The third co-author, Dr. Kathleen Everly, is listed as president of Ed-U Press, the publishing arm of the Institute for Family Research and Education.

The IFRE was founded by Gordon in 1970, according to *The Sexual Adolescent,* "for the purpose of strengthening the American family and reducing unwanted pregnancy and venereal disease".[1] A primary focus of all of the Institute's programming, which includes training of professional sex educators and preparation of educational materials, is in the field of adolescence. Throughout its brief history, the IFRE has followed the familiar path of influencing federal policy and acquiring federal funds for the conduct of its research and its programs. The IFRE testified before the Commission on Population Growth and the American Future in 1971 and before the Senate Committee on Labor and Human Resources in 1978 on a new role for the federal government in sex education. In 1974, the Institute received a grant from the National Institute of Mental Health in HEW to conduct a three-year research and training project for "family life education" programs for parents.

The IFRE also has taken an activist's role in organizing various birth and population control groups to focus on adolescent programs and on laws affecting delivery of medical services to youth. The IFRE initiated a national conference on "Adolescent Sexuality and Health Care" in 1974, which encouraged a variety of sex educators, counselors, foundation representatives, birth control providers, and population control advocates to form coalitions for pursuing change in the realm of adolescent sexuality. In addition to these efforts, the IFRE is one of the most prolific sources of sex education pamphlets, books, and films for teenagers and preteenagers, particularly those utilized by most Planned Parenthood centers across the nation. The most well known of these materials are a film, *About Sex,* and a series of comic books that includes such titles as *Ten Heavy Facts about Sex, Protect Yourself from Becoming an Unwanted Parent,* and *VD Claptrap.*

Most of these publications and the film *About Sex* have been effectively promoted through various federally funded curriculum guides and family planning programs. One of the more widely used HEW manuals, *Practical*

---

[1] Sol Gordon, Peter Scales, and Kathleen Everly, *The Sexual Adolescent,* 2d ed., "Communicating with Teenagers about Sex" (No. Scituate, Ma: Duxbury Press, 1979), 209.

Suggestions for Family Planning Education,[2] was actually prepared with the assistance of Gordon and a number of his colleagues. The comic book, *Protect Yourself from Becoming an Unwanted Parent*, was prepared at the request of a government agency that wanted a birth control comic for teens but ultimately found many of the cartoons objectionable.[3]

Ten Heavy Facts about Sex, originally produced in August 1971, was almost instantly immersed in controversy from the time of its introduction at the New York State Fair in Syracuse. The comic, which was written by Gordon and illustrated by Roger Conant, was described by an IFRE associate as "outrageously" drawn by intention and designed not for schools but "for such agencies as Planned Parenthood" and others that were "mature" enough to deal with its content.[4] Gordon himself termed the comic's illustrations "excellent" in a 1975 book entitled *Let's Make Sex a Household Word*.[5] Over three million copies of the comic books produced by Ed-U Press in this adolescent series had been distributed by 1979.

The text of *Ten Heavy Facts* was reprinted in the January 1972 edition of *Sexual Behavior*, a monthly magazine on a limitless range of topics whose board of editors included a number of the most prominent directors of SIECUS and Planned Parenthood.[6] In a brief introduction written for *Sexual Behavior*, Gordon described the intent of the comic to be the transmission of "facts", "concrete information" without "moralizing". The "facts" in the comic are themes in all of Gordon's subsequent material. The first "fact" states with regard to sexual fantasies that "all thoughts are normal". The second admonishes teens that "masturbation is a normal expression of sex for both males and females. Enjoy it." The third asserts that adolescents should "choose the sexual life you want", with heterosexuality, homosexuality, and bisexuality as equivalent alternatives. The fourth asserts that "there is nothing wrong with any kind of sex if both partners are mature and it doesn't hurt anyone". The sixth deals with venereal disease treatment. The eighth asserts that "pornography is harmless".

The ninth "fact" discusses pills, condoms, and other forms of birth control for "boys" and "girls". One of the "excellent" illustrations for this fact depicts a woman in a negligee, lying on her back, asking her male partner the purportedly

[2] *Practical Suggestions for Family Planning Education*, Bureau of Community Health Services, U.S. Department of Health, Education and Welfare (HEW publ. no. HSA 75–16007).

[3] Sol Gordon and Roger Libby, Contemporary Issues in Human Sexuality, *Sexuality Today and Tomorrow*: (No. Scituate, Ma.: Duxbury Press, 1976), 131–32.

[4] Ibid., 125.

[5] Sol Gordon, "A Guide for Parents and Children", *Let's Make Sex a Household Word* (New York: John Day, 1975), 105–6.

[6] *Sexual Behavior*, vol. 2, no. 1, 25–32. In 1972 the board of editors included Dr. Alan F. Guttmacher, then-president of Planned Parenthood, Drs. Harold Lief and Carlfred Broderick of SIECUS and a number of others.

humorous question, "Galoshes?" Fact ten is the necessary consequence of the previous material: "We think having an abortion is more moral than bringing an unwanted child into this world." Gordon advises the pregnant adolescent to visit Planned Parenthood to arrange for an abortion, and Conant's illustration depicts a girl ascending a stair to a building marked "Planned Parenthood of New York". The comic closes with the final thought that "sex is good when you are ready for it" and the admonition to "join Women's Liberation NOW!" This was the material the IFRE believed school systems too immature to utilize.

From 1971 to 1976 over two million copies of the comic were distributed. The Education for Parenthood program in HEW recommended *Ten Heavy Facts about Sex*, as it did *About Sex*, the more visibly controversial sex education film that appears to have been based on the structure of the 1971 comic.

Gordon noted in *The Sexual Adolescent* that *About Sex* had been awarded a blue ribbon at a New York film festival in 1973, a fact for which the Institute took credit. The film was produced with funds provided by the William Grant Foundation of New York. A prime distributor of *About Sex* was Texture Films of New York. In 1977, the National Center for Child Advocacy in HEW published a 160-page curriculum guide, *Education for Parenthood*, which listed Planned Parenthood as the appropriate source to procure copies of *About Sex*.[7]

In many ways, *About Sex* was a prototypical sex education film for the new breed of sex educator. Planned Parenthood and its allies were seeking to establish it as a model. The presentation was in the classic form of the Planned Parenthood adolescent clinic, the "rap session", wherein a group of young teenagers discuss any aspect of sexual behavior that occurs to them, with a decided emphasis on the physical preoccupations of the male. The filmed rap session in *About Sex* is directed by an adult "leader", a relatively young individual whose guidance consists of jokes and interpolations intended to illustrate similar preoccupations. As the film proceeds, the rap session concludes, and the session leader appears in a series of brief vignettes to state a few "facts" about sex. The form and content of these vignettes are the aspects of the film that follow most closely Sol Gordon's *Ten Heavy Facts* comic book.

The narrator of the film and rap session leader is listed in the credits as Angel Martinez. Although no affiliation or title is mentioned in the credits, Martinez was described in a federally funded study in 1976 as director of a "Specialized Service Program for Young People 18 and Younger", conducted by Planned Parenthood of New York City in two communities from November

---

[7] *Education for Parenthood*, National Center for Child Advocacy, Administration for Children, Youth, and Families, HEW (publ. no. OHDS 77–30125).

1969 to December 1971.[8] HEW said the guiding principle of the community program Martinez directed in 1969 involved "emphasis on nonjudgmental attitudes and acceptance of sexuality on the part of the staff". In 1975, Martinez was an administrative program specialist for Planned Parenthood–World Population in New York. In that capacity, Martinez and Sol Gordon assisted in preparation of a HEW/Bureau of Community Health Services manual entitled *Practical Suggestions for Family Planning Education,* which naturally listed *About Sex* as a suitable resource for adolescent education.

Opinions on the suitability of the film for audiences of various age levels varied widely. The advocates of population control treasured it. *The Population Activist's Handbook,* a how-to manual on population control projects for high school and college students, quoted one high school–aged activist, who dubbed the film "about perfect".[9] The North Carolina Division of Health Services made the film available for a time with a catalogue quoting Planned Parenthood's description of the film as "light-hearted", demonstrating a "delicate blend of the beauty, humor and earnestness that characterize young people. . . ." Planned Parenthood of the Miami Valley, Dayton, Ohio, termed *About Sex* "an excellent film for teen groups" with "some nudity . . . used when pertinent to the discussion". The brochure provided by Texture Films recommends use with junior and senior high school students. The March 1973 issue of *SIECUS Reports* reviewed *About Sex* warmly, proclaiming, "Finally we have a sex education film that is attempting to catch up with where youth is at today . . . a significant contribution to the evolution of sex education materials."[10]

Reaction in other quarters was somewhat different. The film was withdrawn from circulation in North Carolina in 1979, one day after a group of legislators from the General Assembly were permitted to view it in Raleigh.[11] The film was likewise condemned by the House Interim Committee on Obscenity in the Arizona legislature in 1975. Senator Orrin Hatch (R–Utah)

[8] *Improving Family Planning Services for Teenagers,* study by Urban and Rural Systems Associates (HEW contract no. HEW–US–74–304: June 1976).

[9] The name of the student activist was Harriet Surovell, a New York teenager who then headed the Coalition for Relevant Sex Education, a group established in the New York public school system to extend "rap and referral" programs for secondary students on venereal disease, birth control, and abortion. Surovell also testified in 1971 (as head of the New York High School Women's Coalition) before the Rockefeller Commission on Population Growth and the American Future. She recommended that schools establish referral programs in birth control and abortion for students. The Coalition for Relevant Sex Education also sought to establish "peer counseling" in the schools to conduct the rap sessions and arrange referrals. The group prescribed guidelines for abortion referral, as well, and sought academic credit for participation in the "counseling" program.

[10] *SIECUS Report,* vol. 1, no. 4 (March 1973): 12. Review by Dr. Derek Burleson, SIECUS education and research director.

[11] "Shocked Legislators Kill Sex Film", Ned Cline, from the *Charlotte Observer,* April 14, 1979 (quoted in the *Congressional Record,* April 30, 1979, S4874).

chaired a hearing of the U.S. Senate Labor and Human Resources Committee in 1981, which resulted in sharp criticism of the film from a number of the members of the Committee.

The nudity referred to in the Planned Parenthood of Dayton catalogue occurs in the film's opening sequence, a montage of the urban underside of bars and sex shows, and in a later vignette on sexual fantasies. The vignette, with Martinez' voiceover, shows a young male in thought and a brief scene of a couple having intercourse. Martinez simply repeats Gordon's phrase in *Ten Heavy Facts,* that "all thoughts are normal", and admonishes teenagers, "Don't worry about it". The vignette on birth control depicts a teenager entering a Planned Parenthood clinic and shows Martinez demonstrating the use of condoms. The sequence on homosexuality is a superficial gloss on the "to each his own" lifestyle; a similar ethic undergirds the film's final vignette on abortion.

This portion of the film features a New York abortionist, Dr. June Finer, who gives no description of the abortion procedure other than to say that it is "a safe, simple procedure", which can do "no damage" to any of the reproductive organs or to future childbearing. (Dr. Finer states that teenagers can continue to have a child in the future without "any difficulty or danger". Multiple abortions, which account for nearly one-third of all abortions among teenagers, are not discussed.) Dr. Finer, as it happens, had no residency training in obstetrics.[12]

"Sexuality, Today and Tomorrow"

In 1976, Sol Gordon collaborated with Roger Libby, an associate at the Institute for Family Research and Education, on a book entitled *Sexuality Today and Tomorrow.* More so than any other of Gordon's works, this volume clarifies the range of his personal views on sexuality and the way that those views should be translated into public policy and into cultural norms. Libby, at one time the research director of IFRE, previously published several works including a collaboration with Robert Whitehurst on *Marriage and Alternatives: Exploring Intimate Relationships.* Gordon and Libby dedicated their work to "the founders and early board members of SIECUS", particularly Mary Calderone, Lester Kirkendall, William Genne, Harriet Pilpel, and David Mace. This volume is also dedicated to Margaret Sanger. "All of these

---

[12] Bernard Nathanson, M.D. and Richard Ostling, *Aborting America* (Garden City, N.Y.: Doubleday, 1979), 131–32. Nathanson's account of Dr. Finer's history in the world's busiest abortion clinic centers on the controversy created by his handling of what, in the present context, is a rather ironic fact: Dr. Finer's suspension from the abortion clinic as an unwed mother carrying her pregnancy to term.

professionals", the authors state, "have helped pave the way for responsible sexuality".[13]

The preface to the book establishes the guiding principle of the modern sex educator, as Gordon and Libby envision such an individual:

> We do not expect people to fit a certain mold—to be heterosexual, homosexual or bisexual, or to practice any particular code of sexual morality, whether it includes multiple sexual relationships or complete abstinence from sexual behavior. Indeed, it would be *boring* [emphasis in original] if people were all similar![14]

The authors' starting point is at the level of "indifference to differences", a system that argues that no moral values exist save the moral value of tolerance of all sexual behaviors and values.

Gordon and Libby are, however, not personally indifferent to the lifestyles they find preferable. The collection of essays that appear in *Sexuality Today and Tomorrow* make this clear. One of the more interesting is Libby's brief article entitled, "Social Scripts for Sexual Relationships". Libby describes two alternative paths of psychosexual development for adolescents—the "Primrose Path of Dating (untouchables)" and "Branching Paths of Getting Together (touchables)". The first alternative is illustrated by a graphic showing an unhappy couple and two unhappy single individuals. The latter alternative features six happy individuals, all of whom are linked together. The "primrose path" is identified as "the traditional extreme".

In the fifth and sixth grades, the "primrose path of dating" (PPD) involves structured boy-girl activities; the "branching paths of getting together" (BPGT) involves unstructured activities with "no emphasis on marriage or relating to one member of the opposite sex". In the seventh to ninth grades, PPD includes group or chaperoned dates, BPGT includes no parental imposition of monogamous expectations. In high school, PPD is "going steady"; BPGT is "getting together". After high school, the dichotomies explode. PPD is monogamous with rigid code expectations: "living together" occurs but is sexually exclusive, marriage occurs and is sexually exclusive (nonadulterous), serial "monogamy" with cheating by both spouses occurs, as do divorce and disillusionment with marriage. BPGT, on the other hand, is "touching and sensuality encouraged": "love not seen as exclusive but as multiple", living together occurs but is sexually nonexclusive, marriage is a "renegotiated contract", there are various open marriages, "swinging—from recreational to utopian—group marriage", "communal living", "compartmentalized marriage—with 'night off' ", and, of course, "creative divorce". Libby gives some clue to

[13] Sol Gordon and Roger Libby, *Sexuality Today and Tomorrow* (No. Scituate, Mass.: Duxbury Press, 1976).

[14] Ibid., x.

his own preferences, placing his volume on alternatives to marriage in the middle of the final level of BPGT.[15]

The final section of *Sexuality Today and Tomorrow*, on "The Future of Sexuality", deals with probable consequences of extension of the divergent strain in contemporary beliefs about sex. The most specific of the essays in this section is by one of the individuals to whom the book is dedicated, Professor David Mace, a faculty member at Wake Forest University and a founding member of SIECUS. The Mace essay is entitled, "Sex in the Year 2000". In their introduction to this section of the book, Gordon and Libby describe "Sex in the Year 2000" with enthusiasm, describing tolerance of more prevalent "premarital and extramarital sex and sexuality" as "liberating trends".[16] The authors state, "Like Kirkendall and Libby . . . Professor Mace believes that the criteria for judging sexual behavior will be the 'health and happiness' of the individual, the quality of the relationship, the procreation of only wanted and cared-for children, and the 'greatest good' for society."

Mace proceeds with his analysis of future possibilities by phrasing them in dichotomies, analogous to those used by Libby, only Mace entitles them the "most liberal" and the "extreme conservative". Characteristics of the most liberal world are as follows: Children are encouraged to enjoy to the fullest all sensual libidinal experiences; the child would be exposed fully to adult sexual behavior, wherein it would be "commonplace for him to witness heterosexual and homosexual encounters" and other unspecified sexual experiences that, Mace says, cover the entire range of what is now considered normal and abnormal; no attempts would be made to restrain the "sexual play of children, including attempts to simulate intercourse"; at puberty, girls and boys would freely gratify any sexual urge, excluding only rape, as it arose; it would, he writes, "be entirely proper" to invite any person, of either sex or any age group, to participate in any kind of couple or group sex. Marriage would not exist; temporary or permanent relationships between any combination of two or more persons would be embarked upon and dissolved by mutual consent. Finally, and curiously in this catalogue of the "most liberal condition", Mace writes that "procreation would probably be controlled to some extent. Tests of health might be required of the intending parents."[17] Children would be raised at home or by "specially selected and trained 'up-bringers' at state expense".

The "extreme conservative" possibility is almost as interesting. Mace begins by saying that he need say little about this possibility, because it is already familiar. One characteristic: "Only after marriage could sexual experiences be permitted, and then in a serious, purposeful manner." In addition, "all sex acts

[15] Ibid., 172.
[16] Ibid., 368.
[17] David Mace, "Sex in the Year 2000", in *Sexuality Today and Tomorrow*, 402.

outside of marriage would be firmly discouraged, and young people would be under the exclusive supervision of their parents, who would assume full responsibility for them." "Concomitants" of these distinguishing marks of "extreme conservatism" are a prohibition of allusions to sex in plays or films and the frustration of a child's desire for knowledge about the subject.

Where does Mace stand on these posited dichotomies? He states:

> Even this brief description, viewed alongside the description of a sexually liberal society, is sufficient to demonstrate clearly that we have already come a long way since the sexual revolution began. Most of us, I expect, find our sympathies placing us somewhere between the two extremes, and probably nearer the extreme liberal than the extreme conservative position.[18]

The placement of controlled procreation, with the tests of "health" for prospective parents, in the category of "extreme liberalism" would seem wholly anomalous but for the fact that it is a near universal supposition among the eugenicists and writers like Mace and Gordon who earnestly desire the label of liberalism for themselves and their views. Gordon has stated his own views of sexual morality in terms that appear close to Mace's approximation of the year 2000. Pro-contraception advocates usually argue the case for abortion and eugenics in terms of the right of a child to be "wanted" or "well born". Gordon's formulation, announced in *Sexuality Today and Tomorrow* and elsewhere, focuses on the parents and a right, he says, they do not possess: "[T]here are some basic 'morals'. . . . No one has the right to bring unwanted children into the world."[19]

Libby and Gordon acknowledge their preferences in the epilogue to their work. "Our biases are obvious. We believe in making alternative sexual and marital lifestyles more visible through free media and educational systems, and we contend that individuals should receive social and legal support for their personal choices."[20] Opposition to the promulgation of these ethics amounts to political and economic repression, they assert. "Human needs for love and sexual pleasure will become more obvious as there are fewer reasons not to explore human erotic and emotional potential." *Sexuality Today and Tomorrow*, they conclude, "is intended as a partial basis for that exploration".

"The Sexual Adolescent"; or "Let's Make Sex a Household Word"

The *SIECUS Report* for May 1975 contained a review of Gordon's *The Sexual Adolescent*, published by Duxbury Press, the same company that printed

---

[18] Ibid., 403.

[19] Sol Gordon, "Freedom for Sex Education and Sexual Expression", *Sexuality Today and Tomorrow*, 336.

[20] Gordon and Libby, *Sexuality Today and Tomorrow*, 431.

Sexuality Today and Tomorrow in 1976. The former work focused on the specific task of sex education for adolescents. The SIECUS review described Gordon as "an advocate of youth" and his new collaboration as "a useful book".[21] The book was dedicated to Ann Landers, whom the authors described as an advocate of sex education and planned parenthood.

The authors utilized the pages of *The Sexual Adolescent* volume to press their advocacy of abortion on request and to emphasize their support of Planned Parenthood as an organization. The Supreme Court rulings in *Roe v. Wade*, legalizing abortion until term, and *Planned Parenthood v. Danforth*, invalidating state parental consent statutes, were described as having "the effect of allowing women to have control over their futures, thus enhancing their status".[22] The authors complained about conscience clauses for Catholic or other institutions that would refuse to perform or to provide abortions. Describing a bill adopted by the U.S. Senate in 1976 that ensured that an institution's refusal to provide abortions could not be used as a basis for a denial of federal funds, Gordon and Scales lamented that "such legislative action can only encourage hospitals' continued failure to offer abortion".[23]

Antipathy toward traditional, organized religion is a constant theme of Gordon and his colleagues, one employed in *The Sexual Adolescent* and reiterated in a 1975 sex education guide Gordon wrote, entitled *Let's Make Sex a Household Word.* In the latter book, Gordon gives his conception of the traditional Christian approach, which he states is "the less sex the better": Students who have been exposed to this putative Christian thought are said to be "victims". The chapter on social ethics and personal morals in *Sexuality Today and Tomorrow* includes an essay by Rustum and Della Roy that Gordon and Libby welcome as a "strong argument for 'humanistic' ethics and morals".

Describing one of their earlier volumes, *Honest Sex,* the Roys claim that emerging ethical patterns "will have to be found consistent with the highest Christian values, which lead to 'the expansion of the erotic community' beyond the married pair".[24] Proceeding from one unfounded statement to another, the authors link their sexual ethics with the activities of an unlikely ally: "We also predicted that where Martin Luther had failed to reform the Roman Catholic Church, the power of a blossoming sexual freedom would corrode it throughout its fabric." This is the essence of their humanistic Christian concept.

[21] *SIECUS Report,* vol. 3, no. 5 (May 1975).

[22] Ibid., 95.

[23] *The Sexual Adolescent,* 2d ed. (1979), 209.

[24] Rustum and Della Roy, "The Autonomy of Sensuality/The 'Final Solution' of Sex Ethics", in Sol Gordon and Roger Libby, *Sexuality Today and Tomorrow,* 317. The Roys refer to *Honest Sex* (New York: New American Library, 1968).

The Roys state that the "whole range of purely Venus (sex-sensual) acts have no dimension of right or wrong in themselves".[25] Such acts include "not only masturbation and erotic stimulation from girl-watching to pornographic movies", but also "physical contact, massage, even coitus, when performed by one person alone or between two consenting adults without personality contact". The Roys conclude that this viewpoint is in "radical consonance" with "the spirit of the New Testament and many church fathers". The objective of these values, to the Roys, is the "emerging of a healthy oligamous society".

Gordon's description of the postmarital "oligamous" (the word would literally mean "marriage to a few" but the authors do not have a limited polygamy in mind) utopia is almost reflexive. Writing for worried parents in *Let's Make Sex a Household Word*, Gordon endorses adultery. "Marriage", he writes, "has traditionally meant the union of two people for life to the exclusion of all others".[26] The only evils in the world that are truly unsurpassable are "compulsory pregnancy" and "the pain of being an unwanted and unloved child".[27] It should not be difficult to understand how the sexual ethics Gordon expounds necessitate the ethics of human life he advances.

The chief enemy of the sexual code Gordon espouses is "guilt". In the opening chapter on ethics and morals in *Sexuality Today and Tomorrow*, Gordon asserts that "social science cannot make moral decisions for us. Neither can religion." Gordon quotes the sexologist Wilhelm Reich, who stated that "compulsive morality and pathological sexuality go hand in hand".[28] Since none of the volumes Gordon has written provides even a sketchy definition of the term "guilt", one must assume Gordon means the reflective concern over the moral rightness or wrongness of an act, which is how most people understand guilt. *About Sex* and all of the books on sex education Gordon has written dismiss guilt out-of-hand as an obstacle to healthy sexual functioning. What becomes clear after a more thorough review of Gordon and his works is that the emotional and psychological components of guilt, fantasy, and premeditation are of no interest to him; his concern is simply the abolition of any cognitive judgment regarding the morality of sexual acts.[29]

The theme of equivalency among sexual acts is followed in nearly all of the

---

[25] Ibid., 326.

[26] Gordon. *Let's Make Sex a Household Word*, 29–30.

[27] Ibid., 12.

[28] Gordon and Libby, *Sexuality Today and Tomorrow*, 287.

[29] Although this narrative would be impeded by interpolation in the text, it bears mentioning that very little of interest in the world would exist without a continuous evaluation and reflection by human beings on the nature of moral actions, passion, and guilt. *Crime and Punishment, Anna Karenina, Ulysses, The Sound and the Fury*, and countless other works of literature are incomprehensible without interest in the nature of guilt. If Gordon had authored *Anna Karenina*, Tolstoy would read like Harold Robbins.

literature prepared by Planned Parenthood for consumption by the adolescent population, and Gordon is the least abashed of the theme's proponents. The Planned Parenthood Center of Syracuse, in the hometown of the Institute for Family Research and Education, published a pamphlet for teenagers entitled *Sex Facts*. Like Gordon's *Ten Heavy Facts*, the pamphlet's core was a set of opinions:

"Many people believe that sex relations are right only when they are married. Others decide to have sex outside of marriage. This is a personal choice."[30]

Elizabeth Canfield, a birth control counselor at the student health center at the University of Southern California, expressed a similar view in chapters contributed to Gordon's *Let's Make Sex a Household Word*. Engaged in a give-and-take session with participants at a summer workshop at Syracuse University, Canfield was asked whether a failure to masturbate frequently was a sign of abnormality. She responded:

> There are as many ways of being normal as there are of being abnormal; all these labels—who's to say? ... On the other hand, if you'd like to expand your horizon just to find out what the noise is all about, you might want to try masturbating more frequently, venture into some new relationships. ... [31]

A subsequent questioner sought guidance on the matter of adultery: "Before launching myself into an extramarital affair, what should I answer for myself to insure I don't destroy my marriage?" Canfield's response was exquisitely egalitarian: "There is no way to obtain marriage safety insurance, no way to know the outcome unless you try and see how it feels. Assess the risks first: Is your husband also willing to experiment with other relationships?"[32]

Both Canfield and Gordon proposed a "manifesto" of "rights and responsibilities" for adolescents. Canfield's treatise lists a group of words that she states are "undefinable with any consistency". The definitions are a parade of tautological dead ends: "perverted (is anything wrong with any kind of activity as long as the participants enjoy it and nobody gets hurt?); promiscuous (how frequent the partner change?); deviant (from what?); premarital (up to what age?)". Her final definition is a creed: "meaningful (can you decide what has meaning for me?)".[33] Gordon outlined his own "Bill of Sexual Rights and Responsibilities" at the conclusion of his book. "We have also been led to believe", Gordon wrote of this bill, composed with the assistance of Syracuse University students, "that heterosexual love is the only legitimate

---

[30] M. Lyman, *Sex Facts,* Planned Parenthood Center of Syracuse, illus. Helen Kahn, 1977.

[31] Gordon, *Let's Make Sex a Household Word,* 45–46.

[32] Ibid., 46.

[33] Ibid., 115.

and 'normal' kind of love. We must recognize that homosexuality, lesbianism, bi-sexuality, etc., are also valid sexual behaviors."[34] Other tenets of the bill of rights are the recognition of living together as a "healthy arrangement" equivalent to marriage, "the right to read pornography", abortion on demand, and access to contraceptives and abortion for minors without parental involvement. Canfield relies upon the same suppositions.

The framing of new sexual codes in terms of a "bill of rights" and responsibilities whose premise is little more than short-term volition is common to many of the Planned Parenthood sex educators. Lester Kirkendall, SIECUS founder and board member of Oregon Planned Parenthood, published his own "New Bill of Sexual Rights and Responsibilities" in *The Humanist* of January–February 1976 (reprinted in Gordon's *Sexuality Today and Tomorrow*). Kirkendall argues that the damning of the procreative purpose of sexuality, occasioned by the need to limit population growth and by developments in reproductive technology, will allow sexuality to "take its place among other natural functions". The elimination of "archaic taboos" will facilitate the increased acceptance of extramarital sex with mutual consent of husband and wife, premarital sexuality, homosexuality, and bisexuality. The final product of these developments, he writes, will be "the use of genital associations to express feelings of genuine intimacy, rather than as connections for physical pleasure or procreation alone, [to] transcend barriers of age, race or gender".[35] The availability of abortion is specifically enumerated as a right in this context.

The most frank statement of the values promulgated by these particular sex educators is found in the writings of Albert Ellis, psychotherapist-sexologist and author of the 1958 book *Sex without Guilt*. A prolific writer, Ellis contributed a chapter to Gordon's *Sexuality Today and Tomorrow* on "sexual adventuring". Introducing the chapter, Gordon noted that Ellis' "emphasis on choice" is consistent with a major theme of the former's volume. Elsewhere, Gordon termed Ellis' work "brilliant" and referred to him as one of "the most creative and action-oriented professionals currently working in the area of promoting mature and responsible sexual expression among teenagers".[36]

Ellis argues that almost all of the goals of mature personality growth can be better achieved by "sexual adventuring". He defines sexual adventuring as an individual engaging in "a good many sex-love relationships"[37] before marriage and continuing to engage in "further sex-love experimentation and

---

[34] Ibid., 186–87.

[35] Lester A. Kirkendall, "A New Bill of Sexual Rights and Responsibilities", in Gordon and Libby, *Sexuality Today and Tomorrow*, 424 et seq.

[36] Gordon et al., *Sexual Adolescent*, 224–25.

[37] Albert Ellis, "Sexual Adventuring and Personality Growth", in Gordon and Libby, *Sexuality Today and Tomorrow*, 268 et seq.

varietism" after some more or less monogamous pattern has been established. Acceptance of these principles, Ellis writes, allows the individual to become a "sexual adventurer", a person who accepts the point that "infidelity is the natural desire, if not the actual habit, of the average person" and that "giving in to this desire . . . is not horrible".[38] The objective for the sexual adventurer is the achievement of "flexibility" and "open-mindedness". These, Ellis says, are characteristics not found in the individual who believes that he or she must only go with one member of the opposite sex at a time, or that "he must remain absolutely faithful to his wife after marrying", or that "he must never contemplate divorce, remarriage, communal forms of marriage, or any other diversion from strict monogamous ways".

Ellis summarizes his views in a single sentence: "Sex-love varietism and pluralism obviously abet human flexibility."[39] He argues that more "honesty" between people and their "sex-love patterns" would produce fewer bonds between two particular individuals and "many more voluntary absorptions in various kinds of non-monogamous or quasimonogamous relations".[40] In Ellis' view, this would be a "considerably more emotionally satisfying and healthy" state of affairs. The sexual adventurer is the epitome of the mode that Gordon and many of his colleagues seek to engender: the individual "without any absolutes" who has full "self-acceptance". This is the individual who "ceaselessly experiments", particularly in the area of sexuality, and who, although unlikely "to experience sheer ecstasy for more than a few moments a day", is nevertheless "totally unashamed of his own hedonism".[41] Monogamous marriage, fidelity, and constancy, in Ellis' view, are the enemies of this self-acceptance.

In most of his works, particularly *Let's Make Sex a Household Word*, Gordon has espoused a similar "varietism", identifying in an almost reflexive manner the subjugation of moral and religious codes. Morals as a set of propositions categorizing certain behaviors as right or wrong in and of themselves, morals "based on codes of conduct religiously and socially expounded as 'the way' " are no more. "For most Americans", Gordon says, "those days are past." Gordon cites Lester Kirkendall in proposing the end of a period in which morality is accepted as an "edict from a deity". Having articulated this fundamentally simplistic view of morality, Gordon proceeds to a clear statement of the sexual ethics he believes must take hold: "[E]motional needs as defined by unmarried persons, separated couples, adulterers, communes, homosexuals, divorcees, teenagers and all non-traditional, non-family relationships, may appropriately involve sexual relations."[42] Couched in an

---

[38] Ibid., 272.
[39] Ibid., 373.
[40] Ibid., 276.
[41] Ibid., 278.

atmosphere of scientific and statistical research, the sex educators' thesis is one of sense in ascendancy—the value system espoused "is based on love and here the quality of feeling is all important".[43]

This is the value system Gordon believed had become an emblem of a new generation, indisposed to accept the traditional "extreme" of marriage and fidelity. In the course of *Let's Make Sex a Household Word,* however, the new value of love does not last a single page. Gordon rambles from the heraldic cry for a new generation to a paragraph extolling the "nationally renowned" Albert Ellis, whom Gordon cites as believing that "sex without love can be perfectly moral, providing neither partner is hurt . . . or expects more from the relationship than either is willing to give". Assessing this view of love, Gordon asserts that his "thinking is in the direction that sex with love is more fun and meaningful, but not necessarily more moral".[44] Separation of love from the new values Gordon proposes leaves only "quality of feeling", the most realistic common denominator of his ethics. It is not at all surprising that this ethic is grounded in an ultimate science of solipsism.

Under this cultivated form of self-acceptance, the paramount obstacle to the healthy human personality is anything that may impede the self in its closed journey to gratification. The tenets of many organized religions are clearly antithetical to this progress, and it is not surprising that Gordon and many of his associates display an unambiguous hostility to sects they believe to be rigid and moralistic. Canfield epitomizes the ancient heresy of gnosticism, an antipathy to the body, and a dualism that reserves positive qualities to the spirit alone: "[T]he traditional Christian approach", she says, "is the less sex the better." James W. Prescott, a member of the board of directors of the American Humanist Association and a developmental neuropsychologist with the National Institute of Child Health and Human Development, HEW, published an article in *The Humanist* in 1978 (also reprinted in Gordon's *The Sexual Adolescent*) that excoriated the Catholic Church as one of a group of "fundamentalist religious minorities" seeking to impose its views on abortion.

One of the most interesting statements of the new sexual ethic and its relation to a perceived religious heritage appeared in the Planned Parenthood bimonthly *Family Planning Perspectives.* Addressing the 1975 meeting of the Planned Parenthood Federation of America, the president of the Planned Parenthood Federation of Canada, Lise Fortier, spoke on the incomplete demise of the bogeymen of sexual freedom:

> Most of us, nowadays, would rather catch syphilis than tuberculosis. The ways of catching it are more enjoyable and we are assured of a cure. As for

---

[42] Gordon, *Let's Make Sex a Household Word,* 159–60.

[43] Ibid., 162.

[44] Ibid., 163.

pregnancy, we have efficient methods to avoid it, and if they fail, abortion can settle the problem. Why, then, is not sex considered as harmless as eating, listening to music or running in the woods? Why can we not do it with whomever and whenever it pleases us to do so? Is it because God spoke in very precise terms on this subject? Some people claim that sex creates emotional involvements which cannot be dealt with *a la legere*. But these are fears bred from our patriarchal society. In cultures like Samoa and Tahiti, sex is a game, no more, until people decide to have children. In reality, we are still undergoing the terrors of Pandora's box and Eve's punishment.[45]

The actuality of sexual freedom of which Fortier speaks, the sexual varietism of which Ellis writes, and the bills of sexual rights to which Canfield, Gordon, and Kirkendall pay homage, are of a piece: a game of infinite variety, a sexuality so blunt that only physical force is anathema to it. No possibilities are to be excluded, and only those interventions that shorten the game are to be scorned. In an address before the American Library Association, June 20, 1977, Sol Gordon reduced this theme to the absurd, without apparent irony:

All thoughts, all wishes, all dreams, all fantasies are normal! If you have a thought that you're quite guilty about, you'll have that thought over and over again until it becomes a self-fulfilling prophecy. If I walk down the street and I see a pretty girl that captures my fancy, I have sex with her. Now, the girl doesn't know about it, my wife doesn't know about it, and it enhances my walk. I don't want you to think that's my total repertoire, because it isn't. I have all kinds of thoughts about men and women—and animals. [Pronounced nervous laughter from the audience at this point.] Why is that funny? Who has never had a thought about an animal, stand up![46]

Sol Gordon is a man with a mission for youth. He regards the National Family Sex Education Week established by the IFRE and entrusted to the Planned Parenthood Federation of American as his "most successful project".[47] With colleague Peter Scales, Gordon has labored long and hard to expand and develop sex education programs that schools and birth control clinics can utilize to communicate a new set of sexual values. A master of political rhetoric, Gordon has succeeded often in making critics of his views appear as bigots, extremists, or individuals motivated by hatred or repression. With

[45] Lise Fortier, "Women, Sex and Patriarchy", *Family Planning Perspectives,* vol. 7, no. 6 (November–December 1975), 278–81.

[46] Sol Gordon, "It's Not OK to Be Antigay", address to the American Library Association, *The Sexual Adolescent,* 232. Originally appeared in *The Witness,* Episcopal Church Publishing, October 1977.

[47] Gordon, *Sexual Adolescent,* 214. SIECUS endorsed the National Family Sex Education Week project in the July 1975 *SIECUS Report,* vol. 3, no. 6, 6. The first year of the project was 1975.

considerable skill in grantsmanship, Gordon, Scales, and others have been instrumental in utilizing the powers of the federal government to trim the social and political obstacles in their path; Scales' 1978–79 study for the Center for Disease Control on barriers to sex education was one prominent example.

Curiously, as an analyst, Gordon has been unable to avoid recognition of the fact that the parent he often berates—the stereotyped opponent of sex education—is not his real antagonist. Like many before him, Gordon routinely reports that there is a high degree of support for sex education among young people and adults. Discussing the "politics of sociosexual issues", Gordon noted (in 1976) the research by his associate Roger Libby during 1969 to 1974, the peak years of Planned Parenthood adventurism in adolescent programming. Libby found considerable parental support for high school sex education, but discovered that many parents qualified their support and desired "a moralistic approach stressing premarital abstinence". A landmark study by General Mills in 1977, *Raising Children in a Changing Society,* reached similarly astonishing (to some) conclusions: 68% of those parents who consider themselves "New Breed" and 77% of traditional parents agreed with the statement that "strict, old-fashioned upbringing and discipline are still the best ways to raise children".[48]

These are the values that Scales, Gordon, and Everly assert need to be redefined. Those who hold them are, instinctively, families that are "strict and authoritarian", and therefore unable to communicate openly with their children. The fact of the matter is that almost all families desire and/or practice open communication with their children, but relatively few "openly communicate" the values, "rights", and responsibilities that educators like Ellis, Gordon, Kirkendall, and Canfield deem essential. To acknowledge this is to say no more than that the struggle over sex education is in essence one of content, a struggle that is not likely to end in silence on either side.

The Federal Curriculum: Clinic and Comic

Although the philosophical linchpin of the contemporary sex education movement is that a quasi-political "pluralism" requires the acceptance of most or all beliefs regarding sexual behavior, the movement has moved resolutely to standardize the field and to extend certain fundamental tenets to the national population. Just as Margaret Sanger believed in the inutility of a state-by-state strategy for legal change, the modern sex educator has emphasized the leveraging of federal power and the acquisition of federal funds.

The evidence is relatively clear that the production of many of the more controversial sex education materials occurred because funds were acquired

[48] General Mills, Inc., *Raising Children in a Changing Society,* Minneapolis, 1977.

by particular authors who were involved in passage of the legislation dictating materials of a particular quality or character. In fact, the distinguishing characteristic of these materials is that neither federal law nor the administrators responsible for directing the flow of funds possessed any substantive criteria for determining the acceptability of any point of view a sex educator might choose to espouse. The result was a curious series of experiments and exotic publications that reproduced the pro-contraception philosophy in the favorite formats of a generation of children: comic books and pulp magazines.

A prime source of federal funds for these enterprises, from 1970 to the present, has been Title X of the Public Health Service Act. In 1975, HEW published a national guidebook for birth control programs entitled *Practical Suggestions for Family Planning Education*. The guide was prepared with the assistance of Sol Gordon, Angel Martinez, and a number of other prominent sex educators. Among the smorgasbord of publications recommended for use were the film *About Sex*, a pamphlet entitled *Masturbation Techniques for Women*, and *Abortion Eve*. The latter was a comic book that depicted a group of women deliberating over their imminent abortions; amateurishly illustrated, the comic's antireligious tone was garishly consummated on its back cover. There a representation of Mary, the mother of Jesus Christ, appeared: Surrounded by a cluster of cherubs, her face was the grinning visage of Alfred E. Neuman, the idiot symbol of *Mad* magazine. Beneath her feet was printed the *Mad* slogan, "What, me worry?"[49] In October 1977, *Getting It Together*, newsletter of the Youth and Student Affairs Division of the Planned Parenthood Federation, recommended *Abortion Eve* as "a quality publication".

Another publication recommended by this HEW bibliography was *The Joy of Birth Control*, written by Stephanie Mills. Unlike the previously mentioned materials, *The Joy of Birth Control* was prepared under a federal grant.[50] The grant was made by HEW to the Emory University–Grady Memorial Hospital Family Planning Program through the Georgia Department of Human Resources. Dr. Robert Hatcher, director of the birth control program at the Atlanta, Georgia, university, is described on the title page as the "inspiration" for the booklet. Hatcher achieved some national attention during the 1976 presidential campaign when candidate Jimmy Carter was embroiled in controversy over his views on abortion. As governor of Georgia, Carter had written a foreword to a volume on birth control written by Hatcher and a Princeton University professor, James Trussell. The book *Women in Need* opened with Carter's statement, which appeared to urge the availability of abortion on

[49] *Practical Suggestions for Family Planning Education*, U.S. Department of Health, Education and Welfare (HEW: HSA 75–16007, 1975).

[50] *The Joy of Birth Control*, published by the Emory University-Grady Memorial Hospital Family Planning Program (HEW Grant #04–H–000311–04–0 to the Georgia Department of Human Resources, contract #900398). This booklet is undated, circa 1974, 2nd ed., 1977.

demand, a position taken by the text. It should be noted that Hatcher, in particular, was well-connected to the imposition of abortion on demand in the United States: He was one of the primary plaintiffs in *Doe v. Bolton,* the companion case to *Roe v. Wade.*

The Joy of Birth Control contained two sections on sexual behavior under the rubric "Human Beings Are Sexual by Nature". One section was an excerpt from *Our Bodies, Ourselves* by the Boston Women's Health Collective. The other was an interview with Dr. Harvey Caplan, a physician affiliated with Planned Parenthood of Alameda–San Francisco, specializing in sex counseling and therapy. The exchange between Mills, who described herself as having an "anti-maternal instinct", and Caplan brought forth many familiar themes:

MILLS: What are some common sexual problems of young people, things that people who are beginning to enjoy sex need to work on? Any brief bits of advice you can give?

CAPLAN: Can I start with a general statement? This is my own philosophy: Human beings are sexual by nature, not heterosexual or homosexual or bisexual—that means that we respond to many stimuli and our choice of partners or sex objects is determined not by our inborn sexual capabilities, but by our conditioning. If we could realize that, then we would permit young people to accept themselves in any way that was right for them....

MILLS: Recently I became aware of all the guilt that I was packing around about sex. It didn't affect my behavior any, but still, a part of me tends to believe that sex is for married people....

CAPLAN: ... the more messages we give young people that are validating, the better. There's a wide range of people; there's a wide range of practice and beliefs; you fit in there somewhere; you're normal and OK. Learning to say that to yourself would be very helpful.

MILLS: What about good old "promiscuity?" What's to watch out for in having numerous partners? (Assuming that if you start your sexual activity pretty young and don't have plans for marriage until some time in the future you'll wind up with numerous partners.) Can that affect your mind and your attitude towards sex?

CAPLAN: ... I think that it's the state of mind. If you're a young woman, and you have multiple sexual partners in quest of the ideal love relationship, and you're putting all your emphasis on the sex, then you may be hurt time and again and your ability to have intimate relationships may be minimal.

If, however, you have separated your sex and love needs and realize that a close relationship involves a lot more than just sex, and you're doing the sexual number for whatever reason—it interests you, it's fun, it's in keeping with your values, then you could have a hundred partners and still be a perfect candidate for a good close relationship later on. So having multiple sexual partners in itself doesn't mean anything.[51]

A companion to *The Joy of Birth Control,* written by Tom Zorabedian and entitled *The View from Our Side,* included a litany of familiar views dressed in particularly vivid prose. According to Zorabedian, abortion can be simply described "as safer than childbirth or having your tonsils out". Homosexuality is described, citing the Rev. Jim Snow of the Metropolitan Community Church of Atlanta, as follows: "Like apple pie, football and marriage, homosexuality has been, is now, and will continue to be, a part of the American culture—and should be accepted as such." The wide range of opinions expressed in these publications mask the basic premise that they are "family planning" materials.

The statutory authority under which they were created called for the funding of materials in birth control and population education. The objective of most of the materials, however, was to ensure that no semblance of family would ever be involved.

In 1976, for example, another publication, prepared under the same enabling grant as *The Joy of Birth Control,* was published by the Emory University–Grady Memorial Family Planning program. This was a magazine, *What's Happening,* with a cover story entitled "Things My Dad Never Told Me!". Most of the editorial support for *What's Happening* came from the same sources responsible for the content of the *The Joy of Birth Control:* Dr. Robert Hatcher, Dr. Harvey Caplan, Tom Zorabedian, and Felicia Guest. The 1976 edition of *What's Happening* was at least the third in a series: first published in 1971, it was "aimed at answering teenagers' questions on sex and sexuality".[52] Over 100,000 copies of this magazine had been sold by 1976 "for use in clinics, schools and youth clubs throughout the nation".

The opening article in *What's Happening* was called "Dr. Caplan Talks to Teens". Caplan counsels teens in a manner similar to his advice to fellow pro-contraception activist Mills. Referring solely to "boys" and "girls" in his exposition, Caplan says, "There are many ways to enjoy having sexual

---

[51] Ibid., 12–13. Dr. Caplan basically argues that the better preparation for a meaningful relationship is not to seek an ideal but to remain unmoved by the pursuit of multiple partners. This view is the only affirmation of an absolute separation between flesh and spirit that this author has found in the writings on sex education reviewed for this book. Nothing could be less Christian than Caplan's assessment of the impact of the "undefinable" term "promiscuity".

[52] *What's Happening,"* publication of the Emory University–Grady Memorial Hospital Family Planning Program (HEW Grant #04–H–00311–04–0 [sic] to the Georgia Department of Human Resources, contract #900398).

experiences, and climax is only one of them. What is really important is, did it feel good? Did the partners help each other feel good?" On saying "no" to sexual involvement, Caplan advises: "If we have sex for our reasons, and have carefully considered birth control, VD risks, and other consequences, and if we feel good about doing it, then there is nothing wrong with sexual activities."[53] A subsequent article, "Sex Is More than Getting Down", embodies Caplan's theme: Faye, a fictional teenager, explains a model relationship to a mixed group: "Yeah, well, to tell the truth, I like it when a boy tries, 'cause it makes me feel like I'm pretty and sexy, but I won't do it unless we're pretty close to each other and have some PROTECTION!" [emphasis in original].[54]

Another article in *What's Happening* describes masturbation techniques with crudely drawn cartoon illustrations; "Things My Dad Never Told Me" provides a variety of instructions on birth control and sexual technique; "Deciding about Birth Control" illustrates birth control methods for teenage girls and "boyfriends"; "It's Your Right to Decide" announces that "teenagers have a RIGHT to choose what to do if they get pregnant",[55] and states that "women wanting abortions in the later weeks of pregnancy (after 12 weeks) should contact their doctor or Planned Parenthood for information about a clinic or doctor doing late abortions"; "Homosexuality . . . Gay or Straight?" asserts that "Attraction to both sexes seems natural . . . but as we grow up, we are taught we are supposed to be turned on only by the opposite sex . . . many of us, when we stop and think about it, are 'bisexual.' " The magazine closes with a bibliography of comics and pamphlets by Planned Parenthood and Sol Gordon.

The Grady Memorial Hospital–Emory University birth control program has been the source of many of the most erotic "family planning" and sex education materials in use. In June 1970, three students in the Population Awareness Corps at Emory University were assigned to work with Grady Memorial birth control staff on production of a *True Confessions*-style magazine for patients of the program. The fruit of their work, described by Felicia Guest and her co-authors in the October 1972 *American Journal of Public Health,* was a thirty-two-page pulp magazine called *True to Life.* Medical consultant to the magazine was the ubiquitous Dr. Hatcher. According to the authors, the approach taken by *True to Life* "recognized the emotional compo-

[53] Ibid., 3.

[54] Ibid., 6.

[55] Ibid., 24. At the time *What's Happening* was published, it was not at all clear that teenagers possessed a legal "right" to choose abortion, at least without parental consent. In June 1976, the U.S. Supreme Court held in *Planned Parenthood v. Danforth* that a blanket requirement of parental consent for an abortion to be performed on a minor was unconstitutional. Fourteen years later, the Supreme Court upheld parental notice laws, if accompanied by a judicial bypass. See *Hodgson v. Minnesota* 110 S. Ct. 2926 (1990) and *Ohio v. Akron Center for Reproductive Health* 110 S. Ct. 2972 (1990).

nents of human behavior [using] appropriate advertising principles".[56] Funding for the magazine was provided by the U.S. Department of Health, Education, and Welfare.[57]

Three early printings of the magazine produced a total of 48,000 copies. The material in *True to Life* was written by students and staff of the Emory University Family Planning program. The magazine was distributed through public high schools, VISTA programs, Planned Parenthood clinics, adolescent pregnancy programs, and other outlets. In an evaluation performed by the authors, individuals who reported liking *True to Life* included respondents as young as twelve years old.

Stories in *True to Life* were similar in quality to material found in many of its pulp prototypes, with the addition of very explicit sexual material, contraception/abortion diatribes, and advertising material from Planned Parenthood, the National Organization for Women Legal Defense Fund, and other organizations. "Mama Made Me Do It—but She Wouldn't Tell Me Why!" and "Bedroom Games" were typical titles. The centerpiece of *True to Life* was an excerpt from a novel by Marjorie Ford entitled *Loving True, Living True,* a tale of the sexual experiences of various couples that promises to help the reader "discover how to enjoy freedom from sexual hang-ups" and "how to face menopause, abortion, adoption [and] insecurity".[58] The excerpt is a drifting story of depthless conflicts and incidents bridging sexually explicit passages whose only common characteristics are variety, anonymity, and an atmosphere of amorality.

Commentators in the sex education field were quickly intrigued by the approach of *True to Life*. The *SIECUS Newsletter* for February 1971 concluded that the pulp magazine could "prove to be a valuable teaching resource". The SIECUS review noted the original run of eight thousand copies and mentioned only one specific distributor, Planned Parenthood of Atlanta.[59] Resources in Review, the sex education column in *Family Planning Digest,* written by pro-contraception activist Dorothy Millstone, called *True to Life* an "unusual approach to family planning education".[60]

The fact of the matter is that this publication and others like it were not

[56] Crow, Bradshaw, and Guest, "True to Life: A Relevant Approach to Patient Education", *American Journal of Public Health,* vol. 62, no. 10 (October, 1972): 1328–30.

[57] HEW Grant #201 to Grady Memorial Hospital.

[58] Marjorie Ford, *Loving True, Living True,* no. 4a (New York: Warner Books, 1975); in *True to Life,* publication of Reproductive Health Resources, Inc., Sacramento, Calif., January 1977, 29.

[59] *SIECUS Newsletter,* vol. 6, no. 3, February 1971, 10.

[60] Dorothy Millstone, *Family Planning Digest,* vol. 2, no. 2 (March 1973), National Center for Family Planning Services, HSMHA, U.S. Department of Health, Education, and Welfare (contract No. HSM–110–71–176).

unusual at all. The availability of federal funds to support preparation and production of pamphlets like *What's Happening, The Joy of Birth Control,* and *True to Life* was a tremendous catalyst, and where the U.S. government was not assisting such material by direct subsidy, it was helping various agencies to procure it by grants or funds off-setting other costs. For example, Sol Gordon's Institute for Family Research and Education received $221,966 in federal funds during the time the film *About Sex* was produced, according to a statement in the *Congressional Record.*[61] Planned Parenthood of Syracuse, a recipient of federal funds under Title X of the Public Health Service Act, published a sex booklet for teenagers advising them that "abortion is a simple operation", that "masturbation can feel good at all ages and whether or not a partner is available", and that "there is no right way to have sex or place to have sex or time to have sex", all under the rubric of *Sex Facts.*[62]

Federal support of the sex educators has been in no way limited to the production of printed and audiovisual materials. The authors of *True to Life* professed their interest in developing sex education material based on the principles of advertising. With government assistance, the sex educators and population planners moved into direct advertising, particularly by means of radio spots targeted at hard-to-reach teenagers on rock music stations. In 1978 Syntex Laboratories, a California-based manufacturer of pharmaceuticals and contraceptives, devoted its bimonthly publication, *The Family Planner,* to the subject of "Teenage Sexuality and Family Planning". The focus of the magazine was the "particularly adept" use of "modern communications tools to reach teens—from radio to television spots, telephone hotlines to billboards".[63]

Making the marketing analogy and strategy clear, Steve Coles, information officer of the Virginia Bureau of Family Planning, stated his agency's policy of using "radio and television announcements, billboards and advertisements directed at the target audience—teenagers . . ."; this, he said, was "like a company introducing a new product". The opening article of *The Family Planner* described a specific project introduced in rural southern Ohio by Planned Parenthood of the Miami Valley. Project director Mary Beth Moore described her agency's rock radio spots as "our emphasis on reaching teens in a variety of ways to help guarantee confidentiality". One of these methods involved Planned Parenthood's sponsorship of a contest over an intramural high school radio station. The contest advertised the Planned Parenthood clinic and offered a $50 gift certificate donated by a local record store. Clinic ads were then placed in the school newspaper. According to Moore, teens' use

[61] Statement of Senator Jesse Helms, *Congressional Record,* April 10, 1979: S4874.

[62] *Sex Facts,* Planned Parenthood of Syracuse, 21–24.

[63] "Teenage Sexuality and Family Planning", *The Family Planner,* vol. 9, no. 213, Spring 1978, Syntex Laboratories, Palo Alto, CA.

of the clinic was established before commercial radio advertising was begun to forestall "negative feedback" from other quarters—presumably parents.

To close the school year, Planned Parenthood purchased an "every child a wanted child" ad in the school yearbook. Contraceptive supplier Syntex helped advertise the tapes produced by Planned Parenthood for use in other locales to reach teenagers. In many localities, the tapes used for similar projects have been those produced by the Population Institute under a grant from HEW. *The Family Planner* included a brief survey of a "rock stars" project funded in this manner, a series of brief messages by well-known musicians like Boz Scaggs, Bonnie Raitt, and Fleetwood Mac that urged teenagers to "be responsible" and to visit the "family planner". The language in some of these ads, as reported by Syntex, was in the vernacular: One rock musician reminded his teenage audience that "a few hits in the hay" could lead to "a twenty-five year gig".

Other articles in *The Family Planner* elaborated on these basic themes. Syntex published the results of one contest for teenagers called the "Condom Couplet" contest. This competition challenged adolescents to write a short rhyme on the subject of condoms. The project was similar to the "Love Carefully" campaign sponsored by Zero Population Growth, which encouraged teens to give one another valentines with bright red condoms enclosed. Syntex also reported on the national sojourns of Peter Scales, Sol Gordon's associate and head of the National Organization for Non-Parents.

Scales' project was inventive. Its target was to convince high school newspapers to print sex education articles and clinic information. The opener was a series of twelve press conferences in major cities across the country, solely for participation by high school journalists. A stipend/travel expense of $20 was offered to each teenaged reporter to attend. The objective of the project, in Scales' words, was to suggest to teenagers "that a child-free life is a normal option for anyone at any age". The Scales campaign against what Gordon called "unwanted parents" featured a number of ten-second radio spots with short sardonic messages; e.g., "Want to have a kid so you can watch something grow? Get a plant." The spots closed with a tag line for the local contraceptive-abortion provider. The intense interest of a drug company like Syntex in such projects is understandable.

Scales' efforts received an added impetus from the federal government, particularly in service of that ultimate goal of the pro-contraception sex educator—mandatory school programs. On March 1, 1978, Scales testified before the House Select Committee on Population in his capacity as director of the teen project "Are You Kidding Yourself?" for the National Organization of Non-Parents. Scales lamented to the committee that only six states and the District of Columbia mandated sex education by law, and that more such mandates for instruction should be provided. He recommended more national efforts to establish youth clinics for birth control and abortion, more Planned Parenthood and "street" clinics, repeal of parental consent laws for adolescent programs, publication of facts about contraceptive usage through the population press and youth groups, and production of films suited to adolescents "who", in his words, "are not intellectuals". In line with these recommendations, Scales urged that "free medical abortion . . . be available to any adolescent without parental consent".[64]

At roughly the same time as Scales' "non-parent" testimony was given, a Bethesda, Maryland research group named Mathtech was awarded a contract by the Centers for Disease Control to evaluate "successful" sex education programs and to identify barriers to sex education. The contract also called for Mathtech to compare the current U.S. sex education scheme with the mandatory policies of Sweden. Scales himself subsequently became associated with Mathtech as a research analyst and consultant on youth affairs. Part of the process of evaluation of sex education programs conducted by Mathtech included efforts to politically identify opponents to sex education and to evaluate the best methods for school districts to overcome such opposition. In a 1979 paper commissioned by the Family Impact Seminar of George Washington University, with funds provided by the Mott Foundation, Scales described how school districts might successfully "manage" the opposition. A highly important element, Scales found, was the avoidance of "public meetings" to initiate discussion of sex education curricula in favor of "forums less oriented to mass participation".[65] Sex education succeeds where community school systems adopt "decision making forums that nominally include elements of the community, while safely preserving the bureaucratic efficiency and predictability of the usual process, namely, that the 'professionals' make the decisions and that the emphasis is 'definitely on citizen cooperation rather than citizen participation' ".[66]

---

[64] Peter Scales, March 1, 1978; *Hearings before the House Select Committee on Population*, "Adolescent and Pre-Adolescent Pregnancy", vol. 2, 461ff.

[65] Peter Scales, "Sex Education and the Prevention of Teenage Pregnancy—An Overview of Policies and Programs in the United States", commissioned by the Family Impact Seminar, George Washington University Institute for Educational Leadership, for the study *Teenage Pregnancy and Family Impact: New Perspectives on Policy*, Spring 1979, 30.

[66] Ibid., 29. Scales is quoting Hottois and Milner's 1975 book, *The Sex Education Controversy* (Lexington, Mass.: D.C. Health, 1975). The technique is still in wide, and effective, use; Virginia, targeted for mandatory sex education by the Alan Guttmacher Institute, finally adopted a statewide mandate in 1987. The law called for the creation of Community Involvement Teams (CIT) to devise the sex education program; opponents in one local group, the Arlington Citizens' Council, have developed information showing that more than half of the members of the CIT in one county were public employees, and that another was the volunteer chair for the local Planned Parenthood.

Scales' 1979 paper argued the case for increased federal involvement in sex education efforts, suggesting a legislative scenario analogous to anti–sex discrimination initiatives under the Education Amendments of 1976. Under this scenario, the chief federal education officer could be charged with developing a sex education reporting system. State boards of education would be mandated to develop and to submit to the federal agency "five-year plans for progress in sex education", as well as required to develop more revised curricula. Scales recommended that the federal government fund more teacher training, more sex education for parents, and more programs to hire teenagers in sex education projects (e.g., programs such as CETA, the Comprehensive Employment and Training Act, repealed by the Congress in 1981, were used by Planned Parenthood and many other groups to acquire adolescent workers). Other recommended steps included funding of pro–sex education advertising campaigns, establishment of a Federal "advocacy unit for youth rights of access to information and services",[67] and support of "local coalition-building" to promote sex education.

Pornography, Exploitation, and the Sex Educators

The insistence of the pro-birth control sex educators on total freedom of sexual expression, not merely as a condition of law but as an affirmation of positive value, has led various elements of the movement into some apparently incongruous alliances. As has been noted, it is a tenet of the sex educators and such organizations as the American Civil Liberties Union that access to pornography of all kinds, including child pornography, should not be prohibited by law. The positions taken by these individuals and groups have attracted the support of an array of sex magazine publishers and film producers whose materials belie the supposed criterion of "non-exploitation" that motivates their sexual ethics. In the process, the sex educators have synthesized the difficult art of being antifeminist and antifamily at the same time.

The contacts, connections, and collaborations between some sex educators and pornographers have been monetary, consultative, and ad hoc political. For example, the British sex magazine *Penthouse,* founded by Bob Guccione, published a companion monthly called *Forum* in the 1970s, devoted to behavioral aspects of sex. Typical articles in one issue included "Cal & Joan: Totally Committed but Sexually Free", "What Makes a Sadomasochist", "The Illustrated Manual of Sex Therapy", and "Straight Meets Gay". The magazine makes use of a board of consultants for its "Adviser"; among the names of consultants appearing on the magazine's title page were several prominent present or past board members of SIECUS and the former director of the

[67] Ibid., 61.

medical advisory board of the International Planned Parenthood Federation (IPPF) based in London: Dr. Alan Bell, Dr. Robert Chilgren, Ted McIlvenna of SIECUS, and Dr. Malcolm Potts of the IPPF.[68]

McIlvenna, a Methodist minister from San Francisco, was a member of the SIECUS advisory board from 1974 to 1975. He was at that time the president of the San Francisco–based National Sex Forum. Leon Smith, a fellow SIECUS board member in 1975,[69] described the National Sex Forum as a producer of "explicit erotic films for education and research purposes".[70] Distributor of films for the National Sex Forum was Multi-Media, Inc., of San Francisco. According to Smith, erotic films from Multi-Media have been targeted by various church and professional groups for use in sexual attitude reassessment seminars. These seminars, in Smith's view, have been part of a "redefinition of pornography" toward "a joyful celebration of the erotic. Nudity is no longer considered pornographic, nor are certain explicit films depicting various kinds of sexual behavior."[71] Smith and his wife pioneered the use of such films in marriage communication labs in the pursuit of "sexual enrichment".

McIlvenna's Multi-Media, Inc., and National Sex Forum have offered various materials for use in school, church, and professional sex education programs. Films available from Multi-Media ran a gamut that cannot be distinguished from the standard pornography distributor's film list; in fact, the content of the Multi-Media collection was deemed objectionable enough that the chief counsel of the House Interstate and Foreign Commerce Subcommittee on Health and the Environment refused to publish even the catalogue in its hearing record. On March 15, 1977, counsel Stephen E. Lawton wrote one of the authors of this book and stated that the catalogue was "inappropriate for publication under the auspices of the subcommittee . . . ".[72] One of the innocuous films in the Multi-Media catalogue, *Orange,* has the following caption explaining its educational and research value: "[A] sensual macro-study of the hidden universes within a fruit . . . [it] can produce a peak of excitement when shown to a primed audience. It is one of the best erotic films made. . . . "[73]

---

[68] *Penthouse/Forum,* vol. 6, no. 4, January 1977.

[69] *SIECUS Report,* vol. 4 (November 1975): 2.

[70] Leon Smith, "Religion's Response to the New Sexuality", in Gordon and Libby, *Sexuality Today and Tomorrow.*

[71] Ibid., 160; Smith's brief article in Sol Gordon's collection of essays laments the action by "negative forces" to amend a statement by the 1972 United Methodist General Conference that would have been construed to condone homosexual marriage. Wrote Smith, "This action is a clear giveaway to the fact that an increasing number of ministers are presiding at a religious ceremony celebrating the commitment of persons of the same sex to a life of love and fidelity to one another." The "negative" amendment went no further than to "recommend" that homosexual marriages not take place.

[72] *Congressional Record,* October 11, 1978.

[73] Ibid.

Planned Parenthood of San Diego recommended this film for high school audiences, according to a *Congressional Record* speech by Congressman Robert K. Dornan of California.

Another Multi-Media film popular in Planned Parenthood settings is called *A Quickie.* This is a three-minute fast-frame film of a couple having intercourse, which is intended to have a humorous effect. A grim version of this anonymous sexuality appears in the Stanley Kubrick film, *A Clockwork Orange.* Multi-Media is the source of other materials as well, including a vulgar R. Crumb comic book entitled *Facts O'Life Funnies.* The center of this comic tale is the relationship between a quintessentially "hip" couple whose devotion to drugs, television, and pornography is interrupted by an "unwanted" pregnancy. The female of this duo departs the love nest after her paramour threatens to abort her with a coathanger. The lurid story concludes with the couple reunited after the procurement of a safe, legal abortion. SIECUS, of course, found the comic "hip, funny and factual. The comic is bound to seem crude and tasteless to some, but the information it conveys is solid."[74] The Youth and Student Affairs Division of the Planned Parenthood Federation, acknowledging that the comic represented "questionable taste", nevertheless included it in its *Guide to Sexuality Handbooks.*[75]

Sex magazine publishers have supplied the allies of Planned Parenthood with significant funds for conducting legislative campaigns and litigation. In addition to holding fund-raisers for the National Abortion Rights Action League, Hugh Hefner's *Playboy* (through the Playboy Foundation) funded the National Sexual Privacy Project of the American Civil Liberties Union. This project provided legal defense and trial expenses in cases "involving violations of sexual privacy". This description of the ACLU project is given in an article enumerating active participants in the movement to legalize prostitution; the article by Jennifer James, "Prostitution: Arguments for Change", appears in Sol Gordon's *Sexuality Today and Tomorrow.* According to James, the ACLU's arguments are "based on the constitutional rights to freedom of speech and privacy and the civil rights act prohibiting discrimination".

The collaboration between the sex industry's most polished marketeers and the leadership of the sex education movement occurred first on the level of principle: If to some feminists the objectification of women is offensive, to the harbingers of sexual freedom it is not. At the very least, to the sexologist who advocates experiments in sexuality or abortion on demand to sustain such experiments, mere monetary transactions to further the "celebration of the erotic" by either pornography or prostitution must seem *de minimis.* These are

---

[74] *SIECUS Newsletter,* vol. 2, no. 1, September 1973, 7.

[75] *A Guide to Sexuality Handbooks,* Youth and Student Affairs Division, Planned Parenthood Federation of America, 1974, 9.

practices that the sex educator must accept because he lacks a principled base from which to oppose them. In fact, he must become an advocate of such in the name of adventurism. As Roger Libby describes the goals of sex education, these attitudes can become the stuff of a "religious position". Describing the view of situation ethicist Joseph Fletcher, Libby concludes, "As religion becomes less dogmatic, there will be more support for a moral system which accepts and even advocates premarital intercourse in certain situations."[76]

Sexuality and Children

On September 7, 1981, an openly astonished *Time* magazine published an article on the new frontier of the sexologists: childhood sex. The article, aptly entitled "Cradle-to-Grave Intimacy", carried the tag line "Some researchers openly argue that 'anything goes' for children."[77] *Time* cited a number of arguments given by the sexologists to advance quietly what it called "a disturbing idea", that "very young children should be allowed, and perhaps encouraged, to conduct a full sex life without interference from the parents and the law". The arguments range from the physiological (the human body's sexual response systems begin to function at an early age) to the developmental ("children will grow up askew if they do not have early sex").

Time continued to outline the views of the most authoritative sexologists in the field, quoting Dr. Mary Calderone, sexologist John Money of Johns Hopkins, "family therapist" Larry Constantine, Norwegian psychologist Thor Longfeldt, Wardell Pomeroy, and a number of others. The most astonishing aspect of the *Time* article, besides its array of "disturbing" items, is the absence of any historical or legal perspective on the issue of childhood sex. The positions outlined in "Cradle-to-Grave Intimacy" are positions the leading sexologists have espoused for many years, albeit in many different forms and forums. Several of the quotations used in the *Time* article were from articles published in the 1970s, and the dislocation of these statements from context and source put the reader at a disadvantage.

"Cradle-to-Grave Intimacy" opened with the remark of SIECUS/Planned Parenthood leader Calderone that the child has a fundamental right "to know about sexuality and to be sexual". The Calderone statement actually appeared in the May 1977 *SIECUS Report*, in an article entitled "Sexual Rights". The

[76] Gordon and Libby, *Sexuality Today and Tomorrow*, 178.

[77] "Cradle-to-Grave Intimacy", *Time*, September 7, 1981, 69. Several letter writers to *Time* later complained about the article's characterizations of sexologists. Sol Gordon wrote, "You don't seem to understand the difference between sexuality and sexual intercourse." He argued that nearly no sex educator believed that children or teenagers should have intercourse, "nor do we believe that incest is ever a good idea" (*Time*, September 28, 1981, 13). Gordon was evidently not speaking for Pomeroy.

full Calderone quotation further details that children have a "right of access to educational and literary sexual materials, the necessary correlative right to produce and distribute these materials . . .".[78]

Calderone later elaborated on these views in other settings. In a June 1983 journal article, she outlined the case for acceptance of early childhood eroticism, deploring the fact that "during the so-called latency years, which in fact do not exist, children have learned that masturbation is a no-no as is self-other exploration."[79] She also wrote:

> I choose to believe that a truly divine purpose is served by the delay of capacity to reproduce until puberty, around age 12, while in contrast the sexual response system has been functioning since earliest days . . . [t]his timing makes it possible for the pleasure aspect of human sexuality, whether male or female, to be ours from the beginning of life to its end. . . .

Her article concluded with the thought, expressed as the goal of SIECUS, that society must produce a "basic change in attitude to recognize the ineluctability of childhood sexuality and the need to understand, accept, and cultivate it".

In a book written with Eric Johnson in 1981, Calderone was even more definitive, refraining from categorically condemning adult sexual contacts with children and, at one point, placing the blame for any negative effects of molestation not on the assault but on the response of legal authorities and parents. If this assertion seems ludicrous, consider the following passages:

> One thing is certain, in any cases of sexual contact between a child and an adult where there has been no force or violence, the greater the fuss and uproar the greater the possible damage to the minor.[80]
> The major effects of such incidents [molestation] are caused not by the event itself but by the outraged, angry, fearful, and shocked reactions of the adults who learn of it, whether they be parents, relatives, or police. It is these immoderate reactions which may cause whatever psychological damage occurs.[81]

Statements like these in Calderone's writing lend credence to critics who think the worst when they read another assertion like this in her work:

> It is important not to confuse incest with the healthy, pleasant physical expression of affection between members of a family. We have talked about the importance of body contact between young children and their parents

[78] Mary S. Calderone, M.D., M.P.H., "Sexual Rights", *SIECUS Report* (May 1977): 3.

[79] Mary S. Calderone, M.D., M.P.H., "On the Possible Prevention of Sexual Problems in Adolescence", *Hospital and Community Psychiatry*, vol. 34, no. 6 (June 1983): 528–30.

[80] Mary S. Calderone and Eric Johnson, *The Family Book about Sexuality* (New York: Harper and Row, 1981), 178.

[81] Ibid., 174.

and especially between mothers and infants. *The distinction between incest and healthy contact is found in the motivation for it* [emphasis added]. If the motive is simply to express love and fondness and to give a feeling of comfort and support, it is healthy and good; if the specific motivation of the adult is sexual arousal and gratification it is not.[82]

Larry Constantine of Tufts University cited the first Calderone statement quoted above in a 1977 paper, "The Sexual Rights of Children: Implications of a Radical Perspective", read at the International Conference on Love and Attraction held at Swansea, Wales. Described by *Time* as "one of the more intellectually disheveled of the new apostles of child sex", Constantine argued that "there may be cogent reasons for promoting free and sexual-erotic expression by children . . . ".[83] He also argued for a "rationalized legal framework" that would "recognize the right of the child to a free choice of sexual partners" so long as force was not employed by the adult involved and the child provided "informed consent". According to Constantine, "an extra burden is appropriately placed on the physically and intellectually more powerful adult to assure that the participation of the child is informed and voluntary".

Constantine also discussed child pornography in the examination of children's sexual rights. He argued that "too little of a healthy erotic nature is accessible to children, not too much". Constantine distinguished good quality "erotica" from "poorer pornography" and asserted that the problem can be alleviated if "healthy and affectionate . . . erotic portrayal" could be made "an integral part of children's literature and television". Acknowledging that some pornographers do engage in "abuse and exploitation", Constantine believed that childhood sex innovators like McBride and Fleischhauer-Hardt, authors of the controversial picturebook *Show Me!*, need to have their rights protected. Materials like this, he wrote, "are often experienced as sexually exciting by children and therefore should fall within the right of children to have access to sexual materials".[84] The source for this assertion is Constantine's own review of *Show Me!*, cited as a reference.[85]

"Few commentators have considered," Constantine wrote, "the role of erotica portraying minors, which may represent the only acceptable outlet for the sexual preferences of pedophiliacs and, as such, may be a substitute for actual child molestation. The experience in Denmark appears to support this

[82] Ibid., 177.

[83] Larry L. Constantine, "The Sexual Rights of Children: Implications of a Radical Perspective", in *Love and Attraction—An International Conference,* ed. Mark Cook and Glenn Wilson (London: Pergamon Press, 1979), 503–8.

[84] Ibid., 506.

[85] Larry L. Constantine, "Review of McBride and Fleischhauer-Hardt's *Show Me!*", *The Family Coordinator,* (1977): 26, 99–100.

hypothesis." He argued that people with "true concern" for children would prefer to have some children "participate willingly" in pornography under "monitorable conditions" than to have others exploited as runaways or "chattels" of their parents. Just how this set of alternatives constitutes a moral or even practical policy choice Constantine did not make clear.

The final topic on his agenda was "intrafamilial sex". The natural conclusion "from a radical persective", Constantine said, "is that children have the right to express themselves sexually even with members of their own families". In his view, "the only general conclusion warranted" by review of research data "is that not even prolonged incest is necessarily harmful". The remainder of his thesis was strewn with a litany of phrases from the sex educator's chapbook: "knowledgeable, positive attitudes", "openness of communication in the family", "favorable outcomes". Constantine closed by once again citing his own research, devaluing the "incest taboo" as "tied to assumptions about human relations and family structures that were once but no longer valid".

What are these "no longer valid" assumptions? "[T]hat roles (husband, sister, son, etc.) must be sharply delineated and that one can successfully maintain but one intimate sexual relationship within a family or living group." Constantine, it should be noted, was also a member of the board of consultants for *Penthouse/Forum* magazine.

Other experts cited in the *Time* article, like Dr. John Money, long maintained a close relationship with SIECUS. Dr. Money was one of the founding members of SIECUS with Calderone, having joined the organization's board in 1966.[86] Money argued in an article appearing in *The Sciences* that youngsters' sex play, or "rehearsal play", with adults "affects them beneficially". Money's assessment was based in part on scientific studies: "human beings, like the other primates," he argued, "require a period of early sexual rehearsal play". In the *Journal of Sex Research* in 1973, Money had advanced a theory of the sexual response of children, proposing a "threshhold for release of sexual response"[87] for children necessitating a higher level of stimulation than that for adults. In Constantine's blunt words, "rather than lacking 'drive', children may simply require more to become 'turned on' ".

Similar arguments were made by Wardell Pomeroy, founding member of SIECUS and president of the organization as recently as 1975.[88] *Time* identified Pomeroy as co-author of the original Kinsey reports, noting his view that incest "can sometimes be beneficial" to children. Sol Gordon and Peter Scales included Pomeroy on the *Sexual Adolescent* list of the "most creative and action-oriented professionals currently working in the area of promoting

---

[86] *SIECUS Newsletter,* vol. 1, no. 4, 1966.

[87] John Money, "Sexology: Behavioral, Cultural, Hormonal, Neurological, Genetic, etc.", *Journal of Sex Research,* no. 9 (1973): 3–10.

[88] Wardell Pomeroy, Board of Directors, *SIECUS Newsletter,* vol. 3, no. 3, January 1975.

mature and responsible sexual expression among teenagers". Another included in this list was Lester Kirkendall, the SIECUS co-founder and pro-contraception activist to whom Gordon and Libby dedicated *Sexuality Today and Tomorrow.* In that volume, Kirkendall set out his concurring thesis of a "new bill of rights" for sexual behavior. He, too, had children in mind:

> Individuals are able to respond positively and affirmatively to sexuality throughout life; this must be acknowledged and accepted. Childhood sexuality is expressed through genital awareness and exploration. This involves self-touching, caressing parts of the body, including the sexual organs. These are learning experiences that help the individual understand his or her body and incorporate sexuality as an integral part of his or her personality.... Just as repressive attitudes have prevented us from recognizing the value of childhood sexual response, so have they prevented us from seeing the value of sexuality in the middle and later years.... The joy of touching, of giving and receiving affection, and the satisfaction of intimate body responsiveness is the right of everyone throughout life.[89]

As *Time* noted, these rhetorical expositions on the "rights" of children to all kinds of sexual experience have created a field day for extremists. "Cradle-to-Grave Intimacy" suggested that "such views [as expressed by sexologists] fall just short of a manifesto for child molestors' lib", a fact "not lost on pedophiles". One such, Valida Davila of the Childhood Sensuality Circle, *Time* reported, welcomed these developments. "We believe children should begin sex at birth. It causes a lot of problems not to practice incest." David Thorstad, a homosexual spokesman for the pedophiliac movement, related his group's position in a classic phrase of radical feminism: the issue, he said, is the "rights of children to control their own bodies".[90]

---

[89] Gordon and Libby, *Sexuality Today and Tomorrow,* 427–28.
[90] "Cradle-to-Grave Intimacy", *Time,* September 3, 1981, 69.

Chapter Five

Planned Parenthood Competing with Religion

Margaret Sanger, the sixth child in a family of eleven, as we have already noted, was baptized a Catholic. Her father was an apostate Catholic, a man she described as "free-thinking". Biographer Madeline Gray has written that Sanger sought "poise and surcease for her recurrent depression through astrology, numerology, sex, religious cults . . . ";[1] attended seances;[2] and was a member of the Rosicrucian Society.[3] And she lent her name to the letterhead of a tribute to the free-thinking Robert Ingersoll.[4]

Sanger believed she had undergone numerous reincarnations, usually as a member of the social elite. One such nether-world inquiry placed Sanger in Phoenecia in 16 B.C.; Sumeria in 2000 B.C.; as wife of an Egyptian pharaoh in 4015 B.C.; as an American Indian in 6035 B.C.; in diverse incarnations in Ireland and Atlantis — as the daughter of an emperor of Atlantis around 15,000 B.C.; and another incarnation in a now non-existent continent with the elect of 50,000 B.C.[5]

With a background like this, it becomes easier to understand how her entire life's work became a calculated reaction to the teachings of the Catholic church on matters of sexual behavior and the family. Sanger biographer David Kennedy adds that "toward the Protestant churches Mrs. Sanger always displayed a lesser degree of antagonism, though until about 1930 they offered her little more encouragement than did the Catholic church".[6]

Before 1930 the parallel Catholic and Protestant views found social expression in the various federal and state "Comstock" laws that placed legal sanctions on the distribution, advertising, sale, manufacture, or interstate shipment

[1] Madeline Gray, *Margaret Sanger: A Biography of the Champion of Birth Control* (New York: Marek, 1979), 249.

[2] Gray, *Margaret Sanger,* 112–13.

[3] Letter of George Plummer, Societas Rosicruciana in America, asking Sanger for a piece of the Sphinx, December 1, 1934, SSCSC.

[4] Letterhead for a "Tribute to Colonel Robert G. Ingersoll", sponsored by the Freethinkers of America, sponsors: Thomas A. Edison, Roger Baldwin, Clarence Darrow, Prof. John Dewey, Margaret Sanger, August 1, 1931, MSCLC. She also paid a $10 membership fee to Freethinkers of America for 1932–33.

[5] Horoscope, dated birth September 14, 1883, Cabalscope of MLHSanger, "Visioned and indited by Hermes Trismegistus, Chief Scribe, Cosmic Council, Cave of Buddha, A.M. 400, 519, ideograph of MS from Ruby F. Remont, Los Angeles, CA, May 17, 1938", SSCSC.

[6] Kennedy, *Birth Control in America,* 153.

of birth control paraphernalia. A 1920 article by the Rev. John A. Ryan, a Catholic priest who later would become known as the "Right Reverend New Dealer", summarized the reasoning behind these laws. The occasion was one of Sanger's public lobbying campaigns, which produced a resolution by the New York State Federation of Women's Clubs. Approved by a large majority at the Federation's annual convention, the resolution favored "the removal of all obstacles to the spread of information regarding methods of birth control".[7] Catholic delegates opposed this resolution.[8]

Fr. Ryan cited several objections to birth control, and he made a number of remarkably prescient predictions. The married couple, he wrote,

> cannot help coming to regard each other to a great extent as mutual instruments of sensual gratification, rather than as cooperators with the Creator in bringing children into this world. This consideration may be subtle, but it undoubtedly represents the facts.
>
> ... the deliberate restriction of the family through these immoral practices weakens self-control and capacity for self-denial, and increases the love of ease and luxury. The best indication of this is the fact that the small family is much more prevalent in the classes that are comfortable and well-to-do than among those whose material advantages are moderate or small.[9]
>
> ... birth control leads sooner or later to a decline in population.[10]
>
> The further effect of such proposed legislation will inevitably be a lowering of both public and private morals. What the fathers of this country termed indecent and forbade the mails to carry, will, if such legislation is carried through, be legally decent. The purveyors of sexual license and immorality will have the opportunity to send almost anything they care to write through the mails on the plea that it is sex information; not only the married, but also the unmarried, will be thus affected; the ideals of the young, contaminated and lowered. The morals of the entire nation will suffer.
>
> The proper attitude of Catholics toward the demand made in the resolution of the New York State Federation of Women's Clubs is clear. They should watch and oppose all attempts in State legislatures and in Congress to repeal the laws which now prohibit the dissemination of information concerning birth control. Such information will be spread only too rapidly despite the existing laws. To repeal these would greatly accelerate this deplorable movement.[11]

For Sanger the proper attitude toward her critics was difficult to distinguish from personal vilification, character assassination, and old-fashioned

---

[7] Rev. John A. Ryan, D.D., "The Attitude of the Church towards Birth Control", *Catholic Charities Review*, vol. 4, no. 10 (December 1920): 299.

[8] Ibid., 299.

[9] Ibid., 300.

[10] Ibid.

[11] Ibid., 301.

bigotry. Sanger, a constant fellow-traveller with anti-Catholics, provided ideological cannon fodder for like-minded thinkers. The July 1924 issue of H. L. Mencken's *The American Mercury* carried an article reprinted from the *Birth Control Review* that noted: "Today the chief warfare against birth control is waged by the Roman Catholic clergy and their allies. . . . Public opinion in America, I fear, is too willing to condone in the officials of the Roman Catholic Church what it condemns in the Ku Klux Klan."[12]

The intolerance Sanger was willing to accept among her anti-Catholic allies was much more intense than the indulgence she claimed the American public was willing to grant the Catholic bishops. A favorite Catholic-baiter of hers was Norman E. Himes, who had contributed four articles and six book reviews to Sanger's magazine from 1926 to 1929, and who collaborated with her on projects during the 1930s. Himes claimed there were genetic differences between Catholics and others. Himes asked:

> Are Catholic stocks in the United States, taken as a whole, genetically inferior to such non-Catholic libertarian stocks as Unitarians and Universal . . . Freethinkers? Inferior to non-Catholic stocks in general? . . . my guess is that the answer will someday be made in the affirmative . . . and if the supposed differentials in net productivity are also genuine, the situation is anti-social, perhaps gravely so.[13]

In 1925, under Ryan's direction, the National Catholic Welfare Conference, predecessor of the current United States Catholic Conference, produced a steady stream of material countering the general birth control push. The NCWC's primary opponents were feminists and procontraception supporters, largely native-born scions of native-born families, white, Republican, educated, upper-income, liberal Protestants with small families.[14] Obviously, such a coalition could not be successfully opposed solely on grounds of Catholic moral teaching. Ryan and the NCWC, therefore, met the opposition largely on their own grounds with the publication of various one-page "fact sheets", each of which took on a different facet of the birth control debate. They dealt with such subjects as the pitfalls of birth control from an acknowledged birth control proponent; condemnations of birth control by general medical authorities; opposition to birth control on moral/ religious grounds by an Anglican bishop; and the sources of Catholic teaching on birth control traced back to a formal condemnation in the sixteenth century.

---

[12] *Birth Control Review* (September 1924): 246, 248, from *The American Mercury*, "The War Against Birth Control" (July 1924).

[13] Norman E. Himes, *Medical History of Contraception* (Schocker paperback ed., c. 1970), 413.

[14] Kennedy, *Birth Control in America*, 100.

One of Ryan's fact sheets was directed at the U.S. labor movement that, in socioeconomic terms, represented the social antithesis of the birth control protagonists. The NCWC pamphlet took issue with a pro-contraception publication entitled *Unemployment and Birth Control,* which said: "Society is not organized so as to assure even every willing worker enough wages, during the course of his working life, so that he can take care of the everyday needs of himself and his family from the time he begins to work until his death." The fact sheet rejoined:

> If this is true, and it is true, then the conclusion is: Society should be reorganized . . . the labor unions should be supported in their efforts to organize society on this basis.
>
> Birth Controllers do not say this. . . . Their conclusion is a strange one, and an entirely different one.
>
> "Every baby born," they say, "is going to compete for a job some day. If you do not suffer from that competition, it is simply because you have died before that baby has grown to the working age, but your children and those who succeed you in your trade union are going to suffer for it even if you do not. . . . The next time the boss tells you there are ten men at the gate looking for your job, remember that those ten men are sons of fellow-workers who had more children than the labor market could absorb."
>
> . . . [T]he [Birth Controllers'] leaflet closes with telling the working people . . . that the fathers of the workers are really responsible, that birth control would be the cure now had it been practiced a generation ago, and that it would be a cure a generation hence if it were practiced now.
>
> . . . but they have made the admission that the fundamental wrong is the way society is organized.
>
> Why not, then, spend the generation reconstructing our society . . . to fall back on birth control is to despair . . . it is to despair of unions, legislation, education, and cooperation. For this very reason, the birth control movement is a knife in the back of the labor movement.[15]

But the flashpoint for the clash of Sanger's views and her religiously inclined opponents was not reached until she launched her efforts to amend federal and state anti–birth control laws.

One series of clashes occurred during 1929 at a hearing attended by over one thousand persons on a bill introduced in the New York legislature by Assemblyman Remer to allow married women to receive birth control on request.[16] George H. Kennedy, representing the Catholic bishop of Buffalo, pointed out that the New York law " . . . was written at a time when Protes-

---

[15] Fact sheet, published 1925, issued by the NCWC, 1312 Massachusetts Ave., N.W., Washington, D.C., no. 4, *Birth Control and the Labor Movement,* MSCLC.

[16] Special to the *New York Times,* February 20, 1929, *New York Times,* "Birth Control Bill Stirs Bitter Clash", MSCLC.

tant churches were crowded to the door, and when that time comes again, legislation of this kind will not be introduced".[17] Also appearing in opposition was the Rev. William R. Charles, of St. Vincent de Paul Church, who said that: "Advocates of birth control pander to modern feminism. I have nothing to say about the modern woman in business but I know married women who hold positions which men should be filling. I know women who have limited their families in order to pursue careers."[18]

The Rev. John R. Straton, pastor of the Calvary Baptist Church of New York City, said: "This bill is subversive of the human family. . . . It is revolting, monstrous, against God's word and contradicts American traditions."[19] He added that he was proud to stand with Roman Catholic priests in opposition to the Remer bill "against the revolutionists, spoliators and radicals who would enact this into a law . . . great civilizations of the past have gone down fast when they attempted to tamper with natural laws; they have decayed when they put the flesh above the spirit".[20] That the Catholic position was not isolated was illustrated by the fact that the New York State Medical Society also opposed the bill.[21]

But the ecclesiastical and medical walls against the ideology of birth control were soon to be breached. In 1930 Anglican bishops, meeting in Lambeth, England, voted 193 to 67 to issue a nonbinding directive to Church of England members allowing for artificial birth control by married persons under very limited circumstances. Three prior conferences at Lambeth—in 1908, 1914, and 1920—had rejected birth control. The tradition against artificial contraception, held by all denominations but most vocally enunciated by the Roman Catholic Church,

> influenced Protestant Churches to such a degree that no religious body claiming to believe in the Divinity of Christ and the binding force of Holy Writ was known to declare that there are conditions when "the use of scientific methods for preventing conception" is permissible before the recent century of the Protestant era.[22]

Perhaps in partial response to this Anglican departure from a previously unbroken Christian tradition, Pope Pius XI, on December 31, 1930, issued his famous encyclical, *Casti Connubii,* in which artificial birth control was condemned and abortion along with it, in apparent anticipation of Sanger's

---

[17] Ibid.

[18] "Birth Control Hit in Talk", Albany newspapers, February 19, 1929, MSCLC.

[19] "Straton Assails Birth Control at Albany Hearing", February 29, 1929, MSCLC.

[20] "Fiery Debate on Birth Control", *Albany Sun,* February 20, 1929, MSCLC.

[21] "Straton Assails Birth Control at Albany Hearing", February 29, 1929, MSCLC.

[22] David Goldstein, *Suicide Bent: Sangerizing Mankind* (St. Paul, Minn.: Radio Replies Press, 1945), 84.

long-range efforts. Within eight days Sanger was urged by the editor of the *Portland [Maine] Evening News,* and later senator from Alaska, Ernest Gruening, to issue her own reply to the Pope's statement.[23] Sanger responded to Gruening on January 10, 1931, "I am now working on a statement for the press".[24]

By June 1931 she had finished a long reply. After describing the Pope as a bachelor relying upon the theories of another bachelor, St. Augustine, she wrote:

> The Pope made it perfectly plain that Catholics are expected to give up health, happiness, and life itself while making every other conceivable sacrifice rather than to have dominion over nature's processes of procreation. His letter denies any claims of poverty, sickness, or other hindrances to proper rearing of children that are valid reasons for the scientific limitation of offspring. As for the breeding of criminal, diseased, feeble-minded, and insane classes, the Pope opposes every method of control except that of suggesting to these unfortunate people to please not do it any more.[25]
>
> One must deplore the fact that Pope Pius should have chosen this time of the world's distress from unemployment, poverty and economic maladjustment to advertise doctrines and advise conduct which can only tend to aggravate that distress.[26]
>
> Assume for the sake of argument that God does want an increasing number of worshipers of the Catholic faith, does he want the throng to include an increasing number of feeble-minded, insane, criminal and diseased worshipers?[27]

She also noted that birth control is not timed abstinence, and that the Pope should not have confused it with abortion.[28]

Sanger received another boost from religious circles in March 1931, this time much closer to home, in the form of an endorsement of birth control for married couples from the majority report of the Committee on Marriage and the Home of the Federal Council of Churches of Christ (later called the National Council of Churches). The majority report commanded the assent of twenty-two of the twenty-eight-member committee, largely composed of social elite Protestants, including Mrs. John D. Rockefeller, Jr., who supported the move. Three members voted against the report, which never did meet with the formal approval of the Federal Council, largely because of the

[23] Special delivery letter of Ernest Gruening, editor, *Portland [Maine] Evening News,* to Margaret Sanger, January 8, 1930 [1931], MSCLC.

[24] Sanger letter to Ernest Gruening, January 10, 1931, MSCLC.

[25] Margaret Sanger, "Birth Control Advances: A Reply to the Pope", June 1931, 1, MSCLC.

[26] Ibid., 2.

[27] Ibid., 10.

[28] Ibid., 13.

commotion caused by the majority report in certain member churches of the Council.

The Rev. Worth Tippy, Council executive secretary and author of the report, told Sanger in April 1931 that

> the statement on Moral Aspects of Birth Control has aroused more opposition within the Protestant churches than we had expected. . . . Under the circumstances, and since we plan to carry on a steady work for liberalizing laws and to stimulate the establishment of clinics, it is necessary that we make good these losses and also increase our resources.
>
> Could you help me quietly by giving me the names of people of means who are interested in the birth control movement and might help us if I wrote them?[29]

Sanger immediately wrote Tippy that she would be "glad to select names of persons from our lists whom I think might be able to subscribe".[30] Tippy replied to Sanger a week later, offering to give her some names for fundraising and thanking her for the offer of "names of people who are able to contribute to generous causes and who are favorable to birth control".[31] He also related that they had expected some reaction from the "fundamentalist groups", but nothing like what had happened.

Sanger hand-wrote a note on Tippy's letter to her secretary, Florence Rose, "Send good list of 1,000 well-to-do Protestant names, N. Jersey Penna Mass & N Y about 200 each state." Tippy agreed with Sanger in June 1931 to have money from wealthy individuals "be assured to us as from individual givers not as a subsidy from the Birth Control League? You will see the advisability of doing this I am sure."[32] He also wanted two $1,000 gifts backdated to April 1, 1931, to coincide with dates of importance to his superiors.

Tippy had reason to worry. The majority report was repudiated by the Methodist Church South; the United Lutheran Church of America; the Northern Baptist Convention at Kansas City; the Presbyterian Synod at Pittsburgh; the Southern General Assembly of the Presbyterian Church at Montreat, North Carolina; the General Synod of the Reformed Church; and other Protestant bodies.

William Gerry Morgan, a Protestant and president of the American Medical Association, was quoted as saying: "I read in the morning press with surprise and regret the action taken by the Council of Churches on birth

---

[29] Letter of Worth M. Tippy to Margaret Sanger, Committee on Federal Legislation, April 14, 1931, MSCLC.

[30] Sanger letter to Worth M. Tippy, April 18, 1931, Federal Council of Churches, MSCLC.

[31] Tippy letter to Margaret Sanger, April 22, 1931, MSCLC.

[32] Letter from Tippy to Sanger, June 4, 1931, MSCLC.

control. I cannot believe any considerable number of the 23,000,000 individuals making up the 27 American Protestant churches will endorse the findings of that Council."[33]

Sanger and her associates, skilled as they were in exploiting and exacerbating sectarian rivalries, made the most of this public crack in the traditional Christian position on birth control. During the spring of 1932, a Sanger associate, one "Miss Moore", met with members of Congress to seek support for Sanger's amendments to the federal Comstock law. She reported on her contacts with Congressmen Allen Treadway of Massachusetts and Charles Timberlake of Colorado, making express appeals to them as Masons.[34]

Sanger and her friends wanted sympathetic Catholic speakers, but they could not find persuasive ones. One friend suggested that she secure the assistance of a Catholic and "former Jesuit", E. Boyd Barrett, to speak at the upcoming congressional hearings. Scrawled across the bottom of the letter is a handwritten note "very poor speaker—spoke for the ABCL luncheon, 1930".[35]

Instead, Sanger tried to get notable Protestant leaders to testify in support of amending the federal Comstock law, including the Reverend Tippy. In May 1932, Tippy had told Sanger that two factors kept both him and Council chairman Reinhold Niebuhr from testifying:

> First . . . the Baptist, Presbyterian, and Southern Presbyterian Assemblies are meeting in May. Six Presbyterians have memorialized the General Assembly to come back into the Federal Council. They went out, as you remember, on account of the Birth Control Statement. We were censured by both the Northern Baptist Assembly and the General Assembly of the Southern Presbyterian Church . . . if I go to the hearings then we shall seem to defy them. . . .
> . . . if I go on the stand . . . the chairman . . . will draw out the fact that the Federal Council spoke for itself, and not authoritatively for the denominations. . . . At present, the effect of our statement has been to carry the influence of the Federal Council, and largely the influence of Protestantism. . . . [36]

Sanger eventually did convince two other liberal Protestants to testify for the Federal Council of Churches, thus helping to reinforce the appearance of a "Catholic only" opposition. The Senate Judiciary Subcommittee, chaired by Sen. Daniel O. Hastings of Delaware, held three days of hearings in May to discuss the bill. Specifically, it would have revised federal law to allow interstate shipment of contraceptives and information to doctors, druggists,

---

[33] Goldstein, *Suicide Bent,* 90.

[34] Memo from "Moore" re congressional meetings, April 20, 1932, MSCLC.

[35] Letter from Hasirle[?] to Sanger, April 22, 1932, MSCLC.

[36] Tippy letter to Margaret Sanger, Commodore Hotel, Washington, D.C., May 5, 1932, MSCLC.

hospitals, and clinics. The American Federation of Labor remained opposed to this modified version of the previous year's bill and said it would be so as long as church leaders denounced it as immoral and medical leaders did not support it.[37]

Sanger testified in favor of the bill, claiming that responsible citizens practiced birth control, while "in the other family group we have overcrowding, illiteracy, ignorance, slums, infant and maternal mortality and child labor. Almost all our social problems are entrenched in this group and these problems are perpetuated from generation to generation."[38] Dr. William Morgan, past president of the AMA, opposed Sanger, as did Dr. Howard Kelly, professor emeritus and chair of gynecology at Johns Hopkins University. Kelly predicted quite accurately that if contraception were accepted that

> failing in this immediate end of prevention of conception, abortion becomes the next step.... The passage of such a law ... would give Government sanctions to immorality. Our young people would point out ... the fact that 'well, this is generally acknowledged to be uncontrollable, and it must be provided for ...'. Abortionists will undoubtedly thrive under such a scheme.... [39]

Sanger was also opposed by Fr. Ryan, who met her on her own terms and underscored the class politics of Planned Parenthood. He said:

> The proponents of this bill have frankly stated that their main object is to increase the practice of birth-prevention by the poor.... It is said that the present birth-prevention movement is to some extent financed by wealthy, albeit philanthropic persons. As far as I am aware, none of these is conspicuous in the movement for economic justice. None of them is crying out for a scale of wages which would enable workers to take care of a normal number of children.[40]

This bill did not pass, but another version was taken up in Congress during 1934. Advocates of the bill again pressed the "no opposition but Catholics" line of attack. On January 19–20, 1934, the House Judiciary Committee held hearings on H.R. 5978, another of Sanger's anti-Comstock amendments to let

[37] Edward M. McGrady, American Federation of Labor representative, *Senate Judiciary Committee Hearing on S. 4436,* May 2, 1932, 6.

[38] Margaret Sanger, national chairman, Committee on Federal Legislation for Birth Control, *Senate Hearings on S. 4436,* May 1932, 11–12.

[39] Testimony of Dr. Howard Kelly, *Senate Judiciary Committee Hearing on S. 4436,* May 19, 1932.

[40] Dr./Rev. John A. Ryan, D.D., Washington, D.C., professor of moral theology and industrial ethics, Catholic University of America, director, Social Action department, National Catholic Welfare Conference, May 14, 1932, *Senate Judiciary Committee Hearings on S. 4436,* May 1932, 72.

doctors prescribe birth control for health reasons. Reporting on the first day of the hearings, the *New York Times* noted:

> Representative Mary T. Norton of New Jersey, Mrs. Arthur Mullen, wife of the Democratic Committeeman from Nebraska, and Father John A. Ryan ... of the Catholic University of America, led the almost solidly Catholic opposition to the measure.
>
> This is now, according to Margaret Sanger ... the only organized opposition to the proposal.
>
> With two exceptions all of the speakers presented by the opposition today were representatives of Catholic Church groups.[41]

The "Catholic only" opposition to Sanger was disputed by H. Ralph Barton, a non-Catholic from the National Patriotic League who wrote the *Times,* pointing to opposition from the International Reform Federation, the Lord's Day Alliance, the United Lutheran Church, the United Danish Evangelical Lutheran Church in America, the Evangelical Lutheran Synod, and the chairman of the Southern Baptist Convention's Social Service Committee. Barton also noted that:

> Two Protestant Bishops made known their opposition. ... The Rev. Warren A. Chandler of Atlanta, Bishop of the Methodist Episcopal Church South, also expressed his disapproval. ...
>
> The American Medical Association made known ... that it had taken no part in either preparing or promoting the enactment of the bill ... of the eight eminent physicians who appeared or made known their disapproval of the bill but two were Catholics.[42]

In March 1934, a Senate subcommittee held a hearing on S. 1842, another of Sanger's proposals for medical birth control. Sanger cited the experience of Weld County, Colorado, in using birth control to reduce welfare costs, alleging that for $300 spent on birth control for two hundred women, some $10,000 in public expenditures were saved.[43] Fr. Ryan, speaking once again, noted:

> The bill under discussion has been advocated as a means of recovery from the industrial depression. ... To advocate contraception as a method of bettering the condition of the poor and the unemployed is to divert the attention of the influential classes from the pursuit of social justice and to relieve them of all responsibility for our bad distribution and other social maladjustments.[44]

[41] "Birth Control War Hit as Commercial", *New York Times,* January 20, 1934, 17.

[42] Letter to the Editor, January 29, 1934, from H. Ralph Barton, *New York Times,* 14.

[43] Margaret Sanger, *Senate Judiciary Subcommittee Hearings on S. 1842,* March 20, 1934, 19.

[44] Fr. John A. Ryan, D.D., Washington, D.C., *Senate Judiciary Subcommittee Hearings on S. 1842,* March 20, 1934, 103–4.

Sam Saloman, a self-read, incisive Sanger critic who worked at the U.S. Government Printing Office, pointed out some of the moral consequences:

> ... birth control, Janus-like, presents two decidedly different faces to the world.
>
> Appearing before congressional committees ... its propagandists appear as the benign, motherly type of women. ...
>
> Before sex radicals, they appear as sophisticated women, demanding sex equality for women and men ... demanding also that society safeguard sex from the inevitable consequences of indulgence. ...
>
> Mrs. Sanger not long ago was asked to join a group of 30 sex radicals in a symposium on sex. ... This is her conception of the new morality and the part played by birth control: "... what they consider 'morality' we consider 'moral imbecility' ... our morality is an 'ethics of the dust' ... a morality of reality. ... It is not a morality concerned with melodramatic rewards and punishments, with absolute rights and wrongs, with unhealthy lingering interests in virginity and chastity ... but a morality insisting that men and women shall face honestly and realistically the intimate problems of their own lives, and that they themselves, on the basis of their own experience and their own desires, solve these problems with the instruments of intelligence, insight, and honesty."
>
> Now comes birth control [Saloman added], indispensable cog in the mechanism of the alluring morality that is to be.[45]

The Rev. Thomas E. Boode, a member of the Home Mission Board of the Southern Baptist Convention, spoke against the bill, specifically denouncing Sanger's obvious efforts to foment a Catholic-Protestant confrontation. He read to the committee a letter from Sanger to her "Friends, Co-workers, and Endorsers" reporting on the progress of birth control legislation. The letter lauded her supporters as presenting their case "with logic, reason, and courtesy, bring[ing] forth the facts of science. ... There was no doubt that the common sense and justice and humanity of the question was on our side." Sanger's letter then proceeded to portray (and lambaste) the opposing testimony as the work of Catholics determined

> not to present facts to the committee but to intimidate them by showing a Catholic block of voters who (though in the minority in the United States) want to dictate to the majority of non-Catholics as directed from the Vatican in social and moral legislation. ... American men and women, are we going to allow this insulting arrogance to bluff the American people?

Boode then related how he had been asked by a fellow non-Catholic Christian not to testify in opposition to the amendments. Boode had replied

[45] Excerpts, testimony of Sam Saloman, *Senate Hearings on S. 1842*, March 20, 1934, 112–16.

that as it was a matter of conscience with him, he would appear before the committee. He added:

> I could not prevent the conviction, in light of other information, that this was but part of the program further to bolster their effort to lead public opinion to the conclusion that the lines were drawn pro-Protestant versus anti-Catholic. From my point of view this is an unfair manner of procedure.[46]

The letter Boode quoted was not an unusual sample of Sanger's writings; in fact, it was, for her, a fairly typical anti-Catholic screed. It was not an accurate portrayal of previous congressional hearings or the legislative status quo, but it carried the tone and thrust of anti-Catholic bigotry that has reappeared in Planned Parenthood literature and advertising throughout this century.

Sanger was given an opportunity by the Senate committee to have the last word. She once again made her "Catholics only" charge, and added:

> We could respect and understand, though profoundly disagree with our opponents, if they came here and said, "This is our conception of morality. It is our religious belief that birth control is wrong. We cannot concede to any interference with the laws of nature and we prefer slums, child labor, prostitution, illiteracy, unemployment, crime, imbecility, national decadence, and wars to any change in these laws."

She repeated her charge that only "Catholic morality" argued against birth control.[47]

Though Sanger's congressional efforts had stalled, her flamboyant charges continued to bring greater notoriety to the birth control movement—as well as endorsements. Faced with this growing influence, Catholic leaders employed a variety of tactics, most of which would seem strident by today's standards.

For example, in August 1935 priests in the Roman Catholic Archdiocese of St. Paul, Minnesota [283,000 members in Minnesota, North and South Dakota, and part of Montana] read at Sunday Masses a letter from Archbishop John G. Murray warning his flock: "Persons employed in any position that involves co-operation of any kind effecting either birth control or sterilization must withdraw from such employment. Relief workers . . . must refuse to become agents of such anti-social and demoralizing activity."[48]

Sanger, claiming that seven hundred groups nationwide endorsed birth control and that 24% of her clinic attendees were Catholic women, told the

---

[46] Rev. Thomas E. Boode, *Senate Hearings on S. 1842*, March 20, 1934, 136–38.

[47] Margaret Sanger, further statement, *Senate Hearings on S. 1842*, March 27, 1934, 160–61.

[48] Clippings, "Catholics: Archbishop Denies Rites to 'Prenatal Murders'", *Newsweek*, August 24, 1935, MSCLC; "Catholics Told to Avoid Aid of Birth Control", *New York Herald Tribune*, August 10, 1935, AP wire, MSCLC.

press: "If Catholics follow the orders of Archbishop John Gregory Murray, they will have to withdraw completely and irrevocably from public life. . . . Catholics will soon have to emigrate from America to some less enlightened country."[49]

Archbishop Murray, sensing that Sanger's real goal included abortion, shot back, likening birth control organizations to the Dillinger mob. Both groups, he said, were "organized to commit murder".[50]

In the Catholic Diocese of Rochester, New York, the January 6, 1936, issue of the *Catholic Courier* devoted 90% of its front page to a broadside against birth control. The headline read: "Launch Race Suicide Drive Here—Club Women Begin Their Evil Campaign". Another article, "The Brazen Birth Controllers", noted that "The corruption and perversion of human nature implied in this doctrine which Carlyle would call 'pig philosophy' make it necessary to give special attention to this question". It went on to say that: "Birth Control is the spawn of atheism and thrives only where practical belief in God has been smothered in the soul. . . . Birth Control historically has been identified with atheism. Two notable atheists, Charles Bradlaw and Annie Besant, gave birth control its first notable impulse in 1876." Another article noted that Sanger wanted to issue child licenses before married couples could have any children; it also warned that birth control would lead to mercy killing.

Similar press coverage about the birth control controversy could be seen in the secular papers, and it made no difference that a federal court drove a stake into the federal Comstock law, allowing birth control for ostensibly "health" reasons in December 1936. The establishment of a birth control clinic just five months later in Stamford, Connecticut, produced sensational headlines, and this story in the Sunday, May 9, 1937, *Bridgeport Herald:*

> Stamford birth control advocates, including some of the most prominent citizens, are under fire for openly advocating and aiding wholesale violations of the state law forbidding use of contraceptives.
>
> Stamford is split into two warring camps over the moot topic.
>
> Many prominent people are shocked at the flouting of the law by the Maternal Health center. . . .
>
> Quite openly the clinic has been described as a "birth control" clinic.
>
> His attention called to the publicity, Bishop Maurice F. McAuliffe of the Hartford diocese of the Roman Catholic Church last week sent a letter about it to Stamford churches.

The Maternal Health Center in Stamford included a typical piece of pro-birth-control, Depression-era propaganda: a photograph of a squalid

---

[49] Sanger birth control release, National Committee for Federal Legislation for Birth Control, August 13, 1935, MSCLC.

[50] Clippings, *Newsweek,* August 24, 1935, MSCLC.

tenement room with a family of eight children, a work-worn mother, and a helpless despairing father; the other side of the display showed a happy family with four children, courtesy of birth control.[51]

That Catholic efforts eventually were successful in shutting the Connecticut maternal health (birth control) clinics was later pointed out by the Rev. Cornelius P. Trowbridge, a member of the PPFA National Clergy Committee:

> In June, 1939, the Catholic Clergy Association of Waterbury, Connecticut, passed a resolution condemning birth control and demanding that the Waterbury Maternal Health Center be investigated and prosecuted "to the full extent of the law." The resolution was read at Mass in every Roman Catholic Church in Waterbury on June 11. On June 12, the Health Center was raided and the staff arrested and brought to trial. Although the action was later dropped, the Connecticut Supreme Court held the law to be constitutional, and every birth-control clinic in the state was closed ever since.[52]

Though the initial battlefield was birth control clinics, many nonclerical Protestants and Catholics could see through to the real goal of Planned Parenthood, namely abortion on demand and all that that entailed. When the Louisville, Kentucky, *Courier-Journal* in April 1941 ran the pro-birth-control ad that had appeared in the New York papers (see chapter 1), it was criticized by the Catholic bishop of Louisville, the Rev. John A. Floersh, in a letter he asked to be read at all Sunday Masses. What most surprised officials of the Birth Control Federation of America (BCFA) was the hostile reaction of the Jefferson County Grand Jury, which reviewed the ad and forwarded a complaint to criminal court judge Laraine Mix.

The grand jury, whose members came from all faiths, unanimously viewed the ad as an invitation to further the very things that would lead to abortion or other criminal acts, whether by laymen or physicians. The BCFA memo suggested that for such a strongly Protestant state to endorse the "bigoted views" of a Catholic bishop was proof the grand jury was no different from its counterpart at the Scopes monkey trial.

The BCFA collected clippings about this incident from Arkansas, Illinois, Iowa, Kentucky, New Jersey, North Carolina, Tennessee, Texas, Virginia, West Virginia, and other states. Interestingly, when secular papers ran the Associated Press story, the section mentioning that the BCFA ad had been an invitation to abortion was omitted, but it appeared in Catholic

---

[51] "Birth Control Rocks Stamford: Clinic Hit by Bishop: Catholics Warned Not to Aid Maternal Health Center", *Bridgeport Herald*, May 9, 1937, MSCLC.

[52] Cornelius P. Trowbridge, "Catholicism Fights Birth Control", *The New Republic*, January 22, 1945, 107.

papers.[53] This was but one volley in the birth control debate between Planned Parenthood and its diverse religious opposition, including a most vocal Catholic contingent.

The conflict moved into greater prominence in the national print media during the 1940s. For example, the Rev. Edgar Schmiedler O.S.B., Ph.D., director of the Family Life Bureau, National Catholic Welfare Conference, sent a strongly denunciatory letter to *Parents* magazine for a pro–birth control article by Helena Huntington Smith in its September 1942 issue. The fireworks had only begun with the resignation from the magazine's advisory board of the Rev. John H. Cooper, head of the Anthropology Department at the Catholic University of America.

Fr. Schmiedler told *Parents* magazine that birth control:

> ... is but one of many forms of uncontrol, all closely linked together. Break down the moral code in regard to sex in one field and the way is paved for infractions in other fields. ...
>
> You have aligned yourself with forces that are rapidly making of us a decadent nation, a selfish and undisciplined people ... that cannot but prove ultimately suicidal to the moral qualities of the individual and the nation.[54]

For his temerity in attacking Planned Parenthood, Schmiedler was described by both Sanger and PPFA president Dr. J. H. J. Upham as part of the reactionary Roman Catholic Church hierarchy "which", they said, "has fought practically every important social advance since the turn of the century — including prohibition of child labor, preventive measures in regard to venereal disease, sex education in the schools, and countless others".[55] That Upham and Sanger had a "facts be dammed attitude" in this case — as in others — is apparent, as both Sanger's nemeses, Msgr. John Ryan and U.S. Senator Tom Walsh of Montana — a Catholic — vigorously supported ratification of the Child Labor Amendment to the U.S. Constitution.[56] And of course the reader is to understand that the achievement of all these "social advances" was integrally related to the legalization of birth control.

But if Planned Parenthood were to get anywhere in many states, a policy would have to be formulated to deal successfully with the "Catholic opposition", real or imagined. Sanger had said,

[53] "Anti B. C., R. C. Opposition, Report on Louisville Incident", May 16, 1941, three pages, SSCSC.

[54] "Condemns Article in 'Parents Magazine'", *The Pilot,* October 3, 1942, official paper of the Archdiocese of Boston, SSCSC.

[55] PPFA press release, "Religious Leaders Give Reply to Birth Control Attack", September 29, 1942, SSCSC.

[56] James M. O'Neill, *Catholicism and American Freedom* (New York: Harper and Brothers, 1952), 65.

In Washington, and in almost all Government activities, as well as health and welfare organizations, the intimidation is tremendous. One Roman Catholic Committee of twenty-five can silence any criticism . . . I have watched it at work . . . it is growing to such an extent that unless the American public becomes awakened to its dangers it will have freedom of the press and of speech throttled within our lifetime.[57]

Furthermore, many persons did not like to be publicly known as opposing the Catholic Church because "organization and discipline are so alien to Protestants, the efficiency and power of the Catholic Church terrifies them"; and some feared that their efforts would "resemble the Ku Klux Klan or the nativist movement".[58]

In part to preempt such criticism, Planned Parenthood sought the endorsement or "quiet support" of clergy for two main reasons: (1) Clergy had a position of prestige in community affairs and, as members of community planning groups, could be influential in securing or blocking support for birth control because opposition comes from religious or moral grounds; (2) clergy endorsement would necessarily reduce moral opposition to birth control, by conferring at least the veneer of moral legitimacy.[59] Also, local clergy would lend support more readily when told of the PPFA's National Clergymen's Advisory Council.[60]

In private at least, PPFA officials recognized that Catholics were the main, though not their only, opposition because myopic and utopian views of parenting and sex "among members of other religious faiths and the unwarranted fear of increasing immorality are also operative".[61]

But the question still remained how religious, including Catholic, opposition to birth control should be handled. With Sanger more and more in the background, the PPFA board suggested in April 1943 that the PPFA avoid controversy with the Catholic Church and emphasize the health and social benefits of birth control instead.[62] This strategy did not set well with Sanger. In July 1943 she wrote the PPFA in New York to complain:

I do not see how I could possibly work under such policy. To me it represents a leadership lacking in vision, experience and courage. . . . The

[57] Margaret Sanger letter to Franz[k] Emerich[k] January 24, 1939, MSCLC.

[58] Letter of Frank Emerick [Franz Emerich, above] to Sanger, Tuscon, Arizona, April 25, 1940, MSCLC.

[59] "Plan for Organization of Clergymen for Support of Idea of Responsible Parenthood and for Cooperation with Planned Parenthood Federation and Its State Leagues and Local Communities", March 5, 1943, Exhibit A, SSCSC.

[60] Ibid.

[61] Ibid., 3.

[62] "Suggested Policy on The Catholic Church, As Approved at the Executive Committee meeting on April 6, For Referral to the Board, 1943" (the words, "Not to initiate", are handwritten in for "To avoid" on Sanger's copy), SSCSC.

World Population Conference held in Geneva in 1927, which I organized, nearly exploded thru Roman Catholic intrigue and interference, and only a daring boldness of counterattack and freedom on our part kept the conference intact. Some subtle influence within the Federation recently more and more tends to a deadly appeasing policy toward the Catholic Church. The history of the Birth Control Movement shows that we have never attacked any religion, but we have never feared to defend our truths and policies. . . . To palliate the intolerance and bigotry of the Roman Catholic Hierarchy is an expression of craven timidity, and I for one could not cooperate with such an attitude.[63]

In its final policy on handling religious opposition, approved in November 1943, the PPFA Board dropped, apparently at Sanger's suggestion, the words, "To avoid controversy", and instead accepted a policy of not initiating, or at least not appearing to initiate, controversy. The PPFA also posed for itself a goal to be alert and to counterattack any Catholic plots to enforce their minority opinion.[64] By this time the PPFA had a National Clergymen's Advisory Council with over nine hundred members to help carry out its policies.[65]

With the birth control controversy gaining in public attention, as a practical matter the PPFA could claim it was merely answering an attack on birth control; in fact, however, it was precipitating one with its Catholic opponents in violation of its own pretended claim of merely answering charges. One such venture into the public arena came from the PPFA president, Dr. J. H. J. Upham, writing about "The Catholics and Planned Parenthood" in *The American Mercury* for February 1944.

Once again seeking to isolate the Catholic opposition, he said that birth control was not inherently against religion because it had been endorsed by "practically all religious bodies except the Roman Catholics".[66] Therefore, opposition represented merely a taboo and not a moral principle, because no one is compelled to use birth control.[67] Such an attempt to force religious tenets on nonbelievers would be "repugnant to a democratic nation".[68]

---

[63] Margaret Sanger letter to Mrs. Morris Hadley, 50 Madison Ave., N.Y., N.Y., July 5, 1943, MSCLC.

[64] "Program for Increasing Support and Interest of Religious Leaders", PPFA, November 1943; "Suggested Policy on The Catholic Church, As Approved at the Executive Committee meeting on April 6, For Referral to the Board", 1943 (see Sanger's handwritten observations on this draft), SSCSC.

[65] Ibid., PPFA policy, November 1943.

[66] J. H. J. Upham, M.D., president, PPFA, "The Catholics and Planned Parenthood", *The American Mercury*, February 1944, 1.

[67] Ibid.

[68] Ibid., 2.

Yet that is precisely the attempt being made . . . by the Catholic Church, directly and through Catholic organizations and individuals under its domination. Its aggressive, relentless campaign to deny birth control information and guidance to those who may want it is not restricted to Catholics but is directed to the entire American people.[69]

Its full force as a powerful minority group is being used to influence legislation, to bar medical advice on birth control from public hospitals. . . . [70]

I submit that this sort of activity by the Roman Catholic hierarchy is a direct and dangerous invasion of civil rights, as well as a startling infringement of the American principle of separation of church and state. . . . [71]

One Catholic critic, Msgr. Matthew Smith, pointed out several of Dr. Upham's errors in a southern Catholic diocesan newspaper:

His statement that Catholic efforts to "outlaw" advice on birth control invade civil rights is hardly in line with the facts. Catholic efforts have been opposed to legalizing what has been considered an outlaw practice. Nevertheless, there would be nothing wrong if we did try to get a repeal of civil statutes that are opposed to the law of nature.

. . . If we have no right to fight birth control, we have no right to fight murder or theft. . . . We would urge Dr. Upham to remember that all Americans, even Catholics, even Witnesses of Jehovah, even Methodist bishops, enjoy the right to sway legislation and public opinion. The American Medical Association takes the right for granted; it never stops legislating activity.

. . . Upham strives to make out that Catholics have the right to fight contraception among themselves, but "there is nothing in the planned parenthood program which compels any one to acquire or use birth control knowledge." If that be true, we would advise him to get the information to certain social workers, clinic nurses, doctors, etc., who do their level best to make people contraceptionists and do try to compel them by threats of no more aid unless they submit. The propaganda has sheer fanaticism behind it.[72]

Not only Catholic clerics, but Catholic hospitals and physicians were

---

[69] Ibid.

[70] Ibid.

[71] Ibid. 3.

[72] Letter to the Editor, *The Register,* Tennessee ed., vol. 20, no. 8, sect. two, February 20, 1944, SSCSC.

The Monsignor's letter also noted that Upham had mischaracterized the Catholic position on the "Rythm System: by saying that the Church had "endorsed" it since 1932. For a detailed discussion of this subject, see Herbert Ratner, M.D., "Nature, Mother and Teacher: Her Norms", *Listening: A Journel of Religion and Culture,* vol. 18, no. 3 (Fall 1983).

active as well in the fight to defend the integrity of the family and the natural law in conjugal matters. In April 1943 at St. Elizabeth's Hospital in Elizabeth, New Jersey, physicians who wanted hospital privileges in assigning patients were required to sign a statement agreeing not to disseminate birth control or belong to any group that favored "birth control or other eugenic activities at variance with Catholic morality . . . both in this hospital and in all my professional activities".[73]

At a 1944 meeting of the Catholic Physicians Guild, almost two hundred physicians issued a protest against the appearance of articles in AMA publications—*Hygeia* and the *Journal of the American Medical Association*—endorsing birth control. The Guild doctors said that these "have become immoral and anti-religious publications which can no longer receive the support of that portion of our population which belongs to the Catholic Church".[74]

But the cleavage between Catholics holding to the traditional position on birth control and the number of Protestants and Jews abandoning it had grown. The fall from a nineteen-hundred-year tradition based on an anti-contraceptionist understanding of the thirty-eighth chapter of Genesis had been rapid since 1931. This consistent understanding of Scripture had been subscribed to by Catholics like Augustine (354–430), Pope Gregory IX (1170–1241), and Thomas Aquinas (1225–1274), as well as Reformed theologians Martin Bucer (1491–1551), John Calvin (1509–1564), Robert Dabney (1820–1898), Franz Delitszch (1813–1890), Matthew Henry (1662–1714), Johann Keil (1807–1888), Martin Luther (1483–1546), Cotton Mather (1663–1728), Charles Spurgeon (1834–1892), John Wesley (1703–1791), and others.[75] This "new" understanding of Holy Writ proposed by the liberal, higher criticism of the Bible made possible the clerical departure from the traditional Catholic/Protestant understanding of Onan's sin (Gen 38:9). Sanger's sexual revolt was just one of the fruits of modern biblical scholarship.

Fully accepting the implications of this newer "understanding" of Scripture, Bishop G. Bromley Oxnam, president of the Federal Council of Churches, told a PPFA anniversary dinner that birth control affirmed the sacredness of human personality and would make a large contribution to the world's future peace.[76] By 1946 the 900-member PPFA Clergyman's Advisory Council had grown to 3,200.

---

[73] Cornelius P. Trowbridge, "Catholicism Fights Birth Control", *The New Republic,* January 22, 1945, 106.

[74] "Catholic Doctors Protest Harmful Medical Articles", *The Register,* Tennessee ed., vol. 20, no. 23, June 4, 1944, SSCSC.

[75] Charles D. Provan, *The Bible and Birth Control* (Monongahela, Penn.: Zimmer Printing, 1989), appendix 1.

[76] "Oxnam Sees Important Role for Planned Parenthood in New World Order", Press Room, 25th Anniversary Meeting, January 24, 1946, MSCLC.

Local clergymen on the PPFA Advisory Council would regularly receive assistance with their community relations efforts on behalf of birth control. For example, the PPFA prepared a model press release for local clergy committees to issue, leaving blank spaces to be filled in with the names and numbers of local clergy. A 1946 clergymen's model press release stated:

> The clergymen's manifesto recognizes that minority religious opposition to planned parenthood . . . frequently prevents hospital boards, nursing and welfare agencies from making use of essential services. . . . The failure of the community services to offer expert guidance and counsel in planning parenthood is a peril to community health and welfare. There are 568 planned parenthood centers and 7 states offer child-spacing information as part of their public program.[77]

At the national level, the PPFA warned that clergy who are solicited to support Planned Parenthood should be apprised of the un-American tactics of the Roman Catholic Church.[78] Planned Parenthood's drive to change the remaining state anti–birth control laws during this period grafted Protestant support for birth control onto medical arguments and pushed this alliance against Catholic opposition. This tactic was used in 1947 in an unsuccessful attempt to change Connecticut's 1879 birth control law to allow physicians to give birth control to a woman whose life would allegedly be jeopardized by a pregnancy.

On the surface of things, the Planned Parenthood League of Connecticut (PPLC), while giving heavy administrative support and advice, formally stayed out of the Connecticut legislative battle to minimize criticism that birth control was being sought for economic or emotional reasons. The bill was introduced in February 1947 by state representative Alsop, at the behest of the "Physicians Committee of 100". This, however, was a front, as "the nucleus of the Committee was the Medical Advisory Committee of Planned Parenthood".[79]

It so happened that six doctors on the "Physicians Committee of 100" were on the staffs of three Catholic Hospitals in Connecticut. On March 6, 1947, the diocesan director for hospitals, Fr. Skelly, told the six Protestant doctors that either they would have to resign from the Physicians Committee or be removed from the "courtesy staffs" of the three Catholic hospitals in question. They declined and were dismissed on April 2, 1947. Fr. Skelly told the doctors that:

[77] "Local Clergy Join Nationwide Demand for Planned Parenthood Services", for release to AM's of November 13, 1946, MSCLC.

[78] PPFA digest of minutes of operating committees, January 22–April 30, 1947, SSCSC.

[79] *Doctors Vs. Politicians—A Connecticut Episode,* issued by the Planned Parenthood League of Connecticut, June 1947, 1, MSCLC.

The action taken by the hospital has nothing to do with your opinion or belief on any matter. . . . Were the hospital to have ignored your action, the public would have been gravely misled as to the actual importance we attach to our fight against this evil in the community. . . . While a member of the courtesy staff and therefore to that extent acting under the aegis of the hospital, you gave your name publicly to the support of a movement which is directly opposed to the Code under which the hospital operates and which the hospital believes to be gravely against the public interest as well.[80]

The PPLC memo noted that the dismissal was immediately censured by Protestant clergymen, ministers' Federations and associations, and local Connecticut Councils of Churches. These same groups also supported "both the stand of the six physicians and the Alsop Bill itself. Suggestions were made in the General Assembly that hospitals which thus abridged free speech of their staff should be barred from receiving state funds."[81]

The funds involved were for charity cases accepted by the hospitals. The bill passed the Connecticut house but was defeated in the senate. Planned Parenthood blamed "the Catholic Majority in the Senate" for the loss.[82]

Another attempt to pass a similar bill in 1949 also failed, as did the efforts of members of the Planned Parenthood League of Connecticut to defeat state senator Alice V. Roland who voted against the bill. Sen. Roland, who ignored her doctor's advice not to have children, said that her victory disproved "the contention that a minority—meaning the Catholic Church—is forcing its views on the majority".[83] The 1949 bill was endorsed by the Connecticut Council of Church Women, the Connecticut Council of Churches, the Northern Middlesex Council of Churches, the Congregational Churches Social Action Committee, and the New Haven Section of the National Council of Jewish Women.[84]

The PPFA sought to better its working relationship with liberal Protestantism in 1949 through a financial agreement with the Beacon Press, which had published Paul Blanchard's *American Freedom and Catholic Power*. Under the agreement, the PPFA would receive a percentage of all sales made through its offices.[85] Blanchard's book was a thinly disguised attempt to revive latent

[80] *Record,* Meridian, Connecticut, "Catholic Hospitals Dismiss Six Protestant Physicians Who Gave Support to Birth Control Measure", April 8, 1947; *Gazette,* Worcester, Massachusetts, "Claim Dismissal Because of Views on Birth Control", April 8, 1947, MSCLC.

[81] *Doctors Vs. Politicians,* 3.

[82] Ibid., 4.

[83] Don Ross, "Doctors Differ on Connecticut Birth Control", *New York Herald Tribune,* April 13, 1949.

[84] Ibid.

[85] PPFA memorandum to state leagues and local chapters, from David Loth, public information director, March 4, 1949, MSCLC.

American nativism. Part of Blanchard's program for American Catholics included the following demands: Catholic medical schools and teaching hospitals were to be shut down unless they performed "therapeutic abortions"; teachers in Catholic schools were to be certified by secular public colleges; censorship of Catholic school books would insure that "textbooks do not distort history, science and sociology in an un-American manner" . . . ; the registration of all Catholic bishops with the U.S. government as agents of a foreign power; opposition to the "appointment or election of Catholic judges in all states where sterilization laws, applied to the unfit, are still on the books. . . . "[86]

Part of the indictment against Catholic interests in America included the following: "the parochial school . . . is the most divisive instrument in the life of American children";[87] the hierarchy was trying to get the pope to rule America "in moral, educational and religious matters"; Catholics venerated "statues by Canonical order";[88] "the hierarchy is bigoted in regard to both Protestantism and Jewry";[89] the Catholic birth rate is a menace to real Americans.[90]

New York's Cardinal Spellman had the temerity in 1947 to state that birth control leaders divorced sex from morals and ethics and that they were training people "to be sexually promiscuous with least risk of pregnancy or venereal disease";[91] the Catholic Church is trying to engineer "the capture of *our* public school system"[92] [emphasis added]; Pius XI and Pius XII were closet fascists and the majority of the American hierarchy may have been during the 1930s;[93] " . . . there were more Catholics who fought against the United States in the last war than for it . . . ";[94] the Catholic hierarchy exploits "the superstitions of the ignorant";[95] Catholic leaders oppose euthanasia, "a humane practice that many high-minded physicians and clergymen accept as entirely moral";[96] and " . . . Jesus never said anything specific about birth control, large families, sexual perversion, masturbation or sterilization."[97]

Showing that it also was capable of perverse Scripture interpretations, the National Clergymen's Advisory Council of the PPFA opened the decade

[86] Paul Blanchard, *American Freedom and Catholic Power* (Boston: Beacon Press, c. 1950), 304–5.
[87] Ibid., 302.
[88] Ibid., 299.
[89] Ibid., 301.
[90] Ibid., 285–86.
[91] Ibid., 142.
[92] Ibid., 285.
[93] Ibid., 240–53.
[94] Ibid., 241.
[95] Ibid., 212.
[96] Ibid., 125.
[97] Ibid., 134.

of the 1950s with a twisted Bible commentary and reading for Mother's Day:

> "Thou hast multiplied the nation . . . and not increased the joy". . . . There is little joy in hungry, overcrowded homes during Family Week—or any other week during the year. . . .
>
> We can be thankful . . . that . . . the principle of Planned Parenthood has become an integral part of democratic living. . . . Protestant and Jew alike have affirmed the moral rightness of Planned Parenthood, because this great ideal, based upon modern science and upon the dignity of the human personality, strengthens family life. . . . [98]

Just as determinedly, Catholic opposition to birth control was visible and equally combative during the 1950s. A "puff" piece entitled, "Margaret Sanger: Mother of Planned Parenthood", in the July 1951 *Reader's Digest* is a case in point. The article recounted the story of Sadie Sachs and sympathetically portrayed the dedicated, compassionate young Sanger vowing to help the poor women of the world; the fearlessness of her beliefs that led her to face prison rather than recant; the long fight she waged against the forces of reaction to bring enlightenment and health to the women of America; and the campaign to raise birth control to its present position of social dignity. The last sentence in the article read: "The world will always be in debt to her for her inspired crusade."[99]

Displeased responses to the article appeared in numerous Catholic publications. A summary of these was printed in the December 1951 *Reader's Digest,* as collected by Douglas J. Murphey, president of the Coordinating Committee of Catholic Lay Organizations for the Archdiocese of New York. Murphey noted that:

> The article makes repeated references to abortions—and fails to mention that the incidence of such criminality has increased proportionately and numerically since the advent of the Sanger movement.
>
> Inferences that "fewer mothers and babies are lost," or that "children grow up healthier and stronger" because of birth prevention practices, are examples of dishonest journalism.
>
> And the claim of children starving to death "can scarcely be reconciled with the fact that New York City's vital statistics contain no record of children dying from starvation during the years in question. . . . "[100]

[98] "Thoughts on Family Week, 1950", Executive Committee, National Clergymen's Advisory Council of the PPFA, MSCLC.

[99] Lois M. Miller, "Margaret Sanger: Mother of Planned Parenthood", *Reader's Digest,* vol. 59, no. 351, July 1951, 27–31.

[100] "The Case Against Margaret Sanger", condensed from a letter from Douglas J. Murphey, president, the Coordinating Committee of Catholic Lay Organizations for the Archdiocese of New York, *Reader's Digest,* vol. 59, no. 356, December 1951, 139–42.

In a letter to DeWitt Wallace of *Reader's Digest,* Sanger swiftly reacted to the publication of Catholic views that dissented from her orthodoxy:

> Now comes the onslaught by the most arrogant, benighted, religious group in America. Over the years I have had to endure this arrogance as well as the suppression of speech, and of assembly wherever even one of their members occupied a position of authority, but I think on the whole this assembled expression through their various magazines is about as abusive in its implications as they have ever dared express. I regret that *Reader's Digest* felt compelled to spread this dogma which is on a par with communistic dogma and arrogance.[101]

This testing of each other's will and resources was not limited to magazines. Two more fronts were soon established in New York. Early in 1952, seven doctors with staff privileges at St. Francis Hospital in Poughkeepsie were told to sever their association with either the hospital or the Planned Parenthood chapter of Dutchess County.[102] Three of the seven did resign, but four refused.[103] At this point PPFA national director William Vogt asked the AMA to back the doctors.[104] The AMA initially refused comment and viewed the matter as a special case, but the Dutchess County Medical Society charged that St. Francis Hospital violated the rights of the seven doctors as citizens.[105] The Planned Parenthood Federation/chapter filed a discrimination suit against St. Francis with the New York State Commission against Discrimination, but Commissioner Edwards doubted the validity of the protest as state law specified that an aggrieved party must file the action.[106]

The dispute was resolved in January 1953, with St. Francis Hospital renewing staff privileges for the seven doctors. The announcement came from the Planned Parenthood League of Dutchess County. Dr. John Rogers, a former president of the County Medical Society and one of the three who resigned from St. Francis, said that the hospital faced threats from many county physicians to withdraw their affiliation. Dr. Albert Rosenburg, chairman of the Dutchess County Planned Parenthood medical committee, and Dr. Florence Gottdiener, assistant director of the Planned Parenthood clinic, had refused to resign.[107]

A second defeat for Catholic resistance also began in March 1952, after an

---

[101] Letter to Mr. DeWitt Wallace from Margaret Sanger, *Reader's Digest,* Pleasantville, New York, December 3, 1951, MSCLC.

[102] *New York Times,* February 1, 1952, 1.

[103] *New York Times,* February 2, 1952, 15:8.

[104] Ibid., February 3, 1952, 40.

[105] Ibid., February 4, 1952, 15:1; Ibid., February 5, 1952, 27:2.

[106] Ibid., February 9, 1952, 15:6.

[107] "Seven Doctors Win Poughkeepsie Hospital Fight over Their Support of Planned Parenthood", *New York Times,* January 22, 1953, 25.

amalgamation of the previously separate State Welfare and Health Councils. Since 1949 the Planned Parenthood Manhattan–Bronx affiliate had been a member of the Health Council of Greater New York, as had the Catholic Charities Offices of New York and Brooklyn.[108] In March both councils merged with the stipulation that members of the two separate groups that did not receive money previously from the Greater New York fund would have to reapply for membership in the newly formed Welfare and Health Council of New York City.[109] The Planned Parenthood membership application was eventually rejected by the Welfare and Health Council on December 2, 1952. The Council acknowledged that the Catholic Charities of New York and Brooklyn had threatened to withdraw from membership because they "would not be justified in cooperating with Planned Parenthood as a member of the Welfare and Health Council".[110]

A spokesman for the Welfare and Health Board said that the decision was taken

> in the interests of maintaining and further developing the council's broad cooperative approach to many important problems for which there is ground for unity. . . . It was the considered judgement of a majority of our board members who endorsed Planned Parenthood organizations, that their cause can best be served by promoting it outside the membership of the Welfare and Health Council of the City of New York. To disrupt the planning and coordination of over 370 other agencies by bringing the issue within the council's program would be a disservice to the millions of New York City citizens whose health and welfare depend upon the smooth and effective performance of our program.[111]

Reacting to this, the Rev. Albert Panner, a member of both Planned Parenthood and the Protestant Council of New York, said that a resolution condemning this move would be circulated by Protestant and Jewish members of a "Citizens Committee for Planned Parenthood".[112] The Charities Office of the Brooklyn Diocese told the Queensborough Council for Social Welfare on March 2, 1953, that if Planned Parenthood remained in the Council, the Charities Office would withdraw.[113] The Queensborough Council was a subunit of the New York Council. The Planned Parenthood affiliate then refused to withdraw.

Attempts to resolve the dispute to the satisfaction of all concerned proved

---

[108] *Planned Parenthood News,* no. 2, Winter 1952.

[109] Lillian Bellison, "Catholics in Welfare Body Bar Birth Control Agency", *New York Times,* January 15, 1953.

[110] Ibid.

[111] Ibid.

[112] Ibid.; *Planned Parenthood News,* no. 2, Winter 1952.

[113] "Catholic Agencies in Welfare Fight", *New York Times,* March 13, 1953.

futile. On May 6, 1953, the PPFA warned its affiliates that Roman Catholic dioceses were preparing to challenge Planned Parenthood nationwide if the New York Catholic Charities succeeded in keeping the Planned Parenthood affiliate out of the Welfare and Health Council.[114] The next day, on a scheduled vote electing a new board of directors, a slate of directors who supported the inclusion of Planned Parenthood on the Welfare and Health Board was voted in by 317 to 289.[115]

Prior to the vote, Thomas F. Keogh, a Council member representing the New York and Brooklyn Dioceses, addressed some of the issues raised in the controversy:

> The first allegation is that the Catholic agencies are using pressure. . . . It has been suggested that for the Catholic agencies to consider withdrawal of membership is undemocratic. . . . Under our democratic processes of government both the right to associate and the right not to associate in voluntary organizations are equally recognized and protected. . . .
>
> There is a long history of Catholic objection to membership of Planned Parenthood organizations in the Council. That fact was well known in the welfare field. . . .
>
> It is a matter of record that a spokesman for the Catholic agencies announced the position of the Catholic groups only when asked what attitude they would take. . . .
>
> Is it pressure to conclude that if an objectionable organization is admitted to a voluntary group, you will withdraw? Is it pressure . . . to decide and follow one's own religion and moral principles . . . ?
>
> . . . The second unfounded allegation is that Catholic groups are inconsistent in . . . not cooperating here when in other localities . . . they have done otherwise. . . .
>
> The principles followed by the Catholic groups have continued the same. Circumstances and the situations confronting them have been varied and have changed. In each situation responsible authority . . . has determined how far the Catholic agencies could go in material or seeming cooperation . . . with an organization established and operated to attain and foster practices . . . which Catholics and others judge to be gravely immoral.
>
> . . . In Catholic opinion, the attainment of the principal program of the Planned Parenthood group . . . would also do a disservice to family life and the nation.
>
> . . . Throughout the country . . . Catholic organizations have considered themselves bound to reach the same conclusion made by the Catholic agencies in New York.[116]

[114] "Roman Catholic Church Accused of Obstructing Parenthood Group", *New York Times,* May 7, 1953.

[115] Edith Asbury, "Planned Parenthood Backers Win in Welfare Council Vote", *New York Times,* May 8, 1953, 1, 22.

[116] *New York Times,* May 8, 1953.

From this distance, these objections can be seen as prophetic.

The Planned Parenthood victories at the St. Francis Hospital and in the New York Welfare and Health Council fight were significant turning points in public opinion. It was not that all Catholic resistance to the pro-birth-control agenda was thereafter doomed to fail. Even in 1959, Dr. Crawford Campbell, a Planned Parenthood board member, was successfully barred from the Roman Catholic St. Peter's Hospital because of his Planned Parenthood affiliation. The New York State Commission against Discrimination said it was powerless to reverse the decision.[117]

But with this event, the string of Catholic successes in isolating Planned Parenthood from community support was stopped, largely due to Planned Parenthood's persistent efforts at coalition building. Second, in the welfare fight, the proposition that birth control was harmful in itself and detrimental to marriage and family life was rejected by social agencies entrusted with the public welfare. The clear implication was that birth control was becoming acceptable to wider circles of supporters and that it was something that was either good in itself or preserved other goods like the family, etc.

This was not lost on pro-birth-control leaders, especially liberal clergy. Methodist Bishop G. Bromley Oxnam told the 1955 National Family Life Conference that the opponents of birth control "do themselves commit sin. Christian parents are morally obligated to plan for the coming of their children."[118] The conversion of birth control from a sin to a moral duty had taken only twenty-four years for these liberal Protestant clergy.

It would take only three more years for doctors to claim it was their professional duty to prescribe birth control—enter the New York City Hospital fight outlined in Chapter Two.

Like many other cities, New York had a policy of not providing birth control in publicly supported hospitals.[119] In response to a charge by a pro-birth-control physician, New York Hospital Commissioner Morris A. Jacobs said in November 1957 that, "I do not consider it the function or responsibility of the municipal hospitals of this city to disseminate birth-control information."[120] In January 1958 a doctor from the New York Academy of Medicine asked Dr. Jacobs to place on the Commission's agenda the subject of contraceptive counseling in public hospitals.[121] Jacobs

[117] Ibid., December 30, 1959.

[118] "Family Planning Is Moral Duty, Religious Leaders Say", *Planned Parenthood News*, no. 10, Winter 1955, 3.

[119] Rev. Richard Regan, S.J., *American Pluralism and the Catholic Conscience* (New York: MacMillan Company, 1963), 232.

[120] "City 'Unchanged' on Birth Control", *New York Times*, May 3, 1958, 27.

[121] Ibid.

replied to the request in April, but did not directly address the birth control issue.[122]

Despite Planned Parenthood's liberalizing efforts, but also because of its efforts, birth control was still considered a medical issue only. Thus, the *New York Times* reported that the New York Catholic Archdiocese was at one "extreme" in opposing birth control in public hospitals. It added that,

> At the other extreme in the controversy are doctors who agree with the view of the Planned Parenthood Federation that birth-control counseling should be prescribed not only to women who are medically unable to have children but to those who have less urgent health, economic or family reasons for postponing or avoiding a pregnancy.[123]

Dr. Jacobs refused to budge or elaborate on his recent statement. Two Planned Parenthood physicians, Dr. Louis Hellman and Dr. Alan F. Guttmacher, each indicated they would press for a definitive resolution of the question. One unnamed doctor said he had ordered a contraceptive for a non-Catholic patient.[124]

The Rev. Dan Potter, executive director of the Protestant Council of the City of New York, said that Protestants and those of others faiths should not be denied "medically therapeutic information", including birth control, in the city's hospitals.[125] No resolution had been forthcoming from Commissioner Jacobs, so on July 18 he was asked by Mayor Wagner's office to explain why he had issued an order denying a doctor's request for a contraceptive for a diabetic Protestant patient. Jacobs declined a public answer. The Protestant Council of the City of New York then began its own investigation into the city's policy on birth control. The 162 Protestant chaplains in the public hospitals were asked to examine the situation and report to the Council.[126] On July 23 the Archdiocese of New York issued a statement reaffirming the traditional Catholic position, citing Pope Pius XI and also stating that: "Catholics cannot accept such a procedure, nor can any Catholic, in or out of our hospitals, condone or cooperate in assisting others to this unnatural and immoral practice."[127]

The Catholic Physicians Guild supported the birth control ban, stressing that "The policy of every hospital . . . should be one of hopeful progress in the treatment of diseases complicating pregnancy rather than suppression or

[122] Ibid.

[123] Edith Asbury, "City Edict Sought on Birth Control", *New York Times,* May 22, 1958, 33.

[124] Ibid.

[125] "Hospitals Scored on Birth Control", *New York Times,* May 26, 1958.

[126] "Mayor Asks Jacobs Report on Dispute on Birth Control Therapy in Hospital", *New York Times,* July 19, 1958.

[127] "Church Cites Pope on Birth Control", *New York Times,* July 24, 1958, 27, 51.

prevention of conception. It is certain that the best interests of humanity lie in the eradication of disease and not in the elimination of function."[128]

The Association of Medical Boards of the Department of Hospitals of the City of New York also endorsed the ban because contraceptives were not "emergent matters of therapy and are available in private and voluntary agencies throughout the city—free of cost to those who cannot afford to pay".[129] The Planned Parenthood Association of Manhattan and the Bronx (PPMB), however, balked at the idea of helping the poor it professed to serve. In declining to fulfill its mission, PPMB representative, Mrs. Walter Andrews, suggested that the affiliate was not equipped to provide birth control to all of the 35,000 women giving birth in New York City's twenty-two municipal hospitals.[130] This reference to all 35,000 women giving birth in public hospitals, rather than to just the diabetic ones at issue in the dispute, gives some idea of the real thrust behind the PPMB drive for placing birth control in the city's hospital system.

Adding to the pressure to lift the birth control ban was the unanimous vote by the Baptist Ministers' Conference of Greater New York. Failure to provide birth control, they noted, was a violation of the "American doctrine of separation of church and state".[131]

Finally on September 18, the New York City Hospital Board reversed its long-standing ban on birth control by a vote of eight to two.[132] The Department of Hospitals stipulated that: birth control was not to be made available for non-medical reasons; before a woman could be given contraceptives in municipal hospitals two doctors would have to certify her need; the woman would have to request birth control in writing, and her husband's consent would also be solicited; she would be advised to see her spiritual counselor; physicians, nurses, and others who objected to this policy did not have to participate.[133]

Writing five years later in 1963, Fr. Richard Regan, S.J., questioned the policy:

> The compromise does not truly assure neutrality of the public hospitals: institutions supported by public funds are committed to provide both contraceptive advice and devices. . . . Catholics may wonder at the logic by

[128] Ibid.

[129] "Policy Advocated on Birth Control", *New York Times,* July 27, 1958, 48.

[130] Edith E. Asbury, "Parenthood Unit Bars Jacobs Idea", *New York Times,* August 27, 1958.

[131] Philip Benjamine, "Therapy Is Upheld to Control Birth", *New York Times,* September 4, 1958.

[132] "Groups Laud Vote on Birth Control", *New York Times,* September 19, 1958.

[133] Peter Kihss, "Birth Control Rule Says 2 Physicians Must Certify Need", *New York Times,* September 23, 1958, 1, 30.

which non-Catholics object to the prohibition of contraception by the public authority on grounds of religious pluralism but demand the prescription and supply of contraception by public institutions without regard for the moral susceptibilities of Catholics.[134]

In what must now be classified as "famous last words", Regan suggested that:

On the practical side of the problem, however, we should note that the New York City compromise does not affect too large a number of patients and certainly will not make birth-control clinics of the public hospitals. The compromise is, in fact, closely restricted to those cases where the willing patient would be in danger of life or health from a future pregnancy.[135]

Within four years of Fr. Regan's prediction, Boston City Hospital hosted a Planned Parenthood nurse to distribute birth control every week. The hospital was under the direction of the all-Catholic Boston City Council and was supervised by a four-man board of trustees, which included Richard Cardinal Cushing.[136] Things were going just as Sanger had hoped.

The Rev. Billy Graham said in 1959 that birth control was an acceptable answer to the "terrifying and tragic" overpopulation problem. And, he noted, there was nothing in the Scriptures that forbade the responsible use of birth control. "But", he added, "when a segment of the citizenry is opposed to birth control the problem should be handled privately and not as a 'political issue'."[137] This was the identical view taken by then-President Eisenhower who rejected, as none of the government's business, a suggestion by former general William Draper that federal money be used for birth control in U.S. foreign aid programs. Of course Sanger was provoked by Eisenhower's remarks and gave the *New York Times* her standard fare:

Birth control, family planning and population limitation are most important in any effort to bring real peace to the world. Less population will bring less war. Fewer people means more peace. Population planning through Government health and welfare departments . . . provide[s] the essential foundations for world peace.
    . . . The Draper Report recommended to President Eisenhower that the United States as a matter of Government foreign policy should help other nations [that] request such aid.
    Then a few dozen Roman Catholic Cardinals, Archbishops and Bishops

---

[134] Regan, *American Pluralism*, 232.
[135] Ibid., 232–33.
[136] Alan Guttmacher, *Presidential Letter*, no. 24, July 31, 1967, 4.
[137] *New York Times*, December 13, 1959.

gathered and proclaimed an edict to the effect that the United States Government cannot give such recommended aid.

... Only a minority oppose this plan for world peace. The short-sightedness of the Roman Catholic hierarchy in this country shows their bold assault upon the Draper Committee's report about a medical and welfare project for the well-being of the entire world.[138]

Six months later Sanger had a few choice words for the Democratic Party, too. Commenting on Senator John F. Kennedy's presidential campaign, she said that "a Roman Catholic is neither Democrat nor Republican. Nor American, nor Chinese; he is a Roman Catholic". Sanger added that a Roman Catholic President would "make impossible America's most important contribution to world peace — the dissemination of birth control information".[139]

Sanger's long-time lawyer, Morris Ernst, was, however, overjoyed to have a Catholic of Kennedy's persuasion as president.[140] And with good reason.

Cass Canfield, chairman of the PPFA and chairman of the editorial board at Harper and Row, was also optimistic. He told John Rockefeller III that he believed President Kennedy would more likely support a presidential conference on population if there were more public discussion on the matter between Catholics and non-Catholics.[141]

In July 1962 Canfield set about to bring such a dialogue to fruition. He wrote the Rev. John Considine of the National Catholic Welfare Conference, who had previously told a meeting of the Council on Foreign Relations that the federal government should seek to establish a policy on population problems and find areas of firm agreement.

Canfield told Fr. Considine that PPFA president Dr. Alan Guttmacher had made a similar call on "CBS Reports" for Catholics and others to talk about the population problem and related concerns. This, Canfield pointed out, was similar to a proposal made by another NCWC priest. The ostensible immediate purpose of such a meeting would be for a small group of Catholics and non-Catholics to meet in New York to discuss the population problem with others, including Planned Parenthood officials.[142]

Canfield solicited a number of Catholic officials in the United States and Europe for the same purpose, even relating that in June 1962 Planned Parent-

---

[138] Margaret Sanger, Letter to the Editor, *New York Times,* January 3, 1960.

[139] *Baltimore Evening Sun,* July 16, 1960, Honolulu, AP.

[140] Morris Ernst letter to Dr. Alan Guttmacher, 1185 Park Avenue, New York, N.Y., November 16, 1961, CLHMS.

[141] Cass Canfield letter to John Rockefeller III, June 6, 1962, CLHMS.

[142] Cass Canfield letter to Rev. John Considine, M.M., NCWC, July 9, 1962, CLHMS.

hood representatives scored a first with their participation in the yearly National Catholic Family Life Convention. Canfield also expressed his interest in extending such a dialogue.[143]

Though his goal of getting President Kennedy to call a population conference was not met until President Nixon did so at the behest of Congress in 1970, Canfield's efforts eventually met with some success among Catholic journalists in the East and Catholic family-life leaders in the Midwest.[144]

Compared to past battles, the warm reception accorded by some Catholics to these new Planned Parenthood initiatives was indeed revolutionary. This was perhaps aided by careful Planned Parenthood affiliate intelligence work in identifying sympathetic or friendly Catholics, pursuant to a request from the PPFA to send in the names of Catholics on affiliate boards or committees.[145]

To further these efforts, a series of public relations approaches were undertaken to either co-opt or soften Catholic opposition to birth control. A few of them had remarkable impact with major figures in the American Catholic hierarchy. The first of these was the book written by Dr. John Rock who, as one of three co-developers of the Pill, was Margaret Sanger's kind of Catholic. The book contained a great amount of medical and theological credentialing. The foreword to Rock's book was written by Christian A. Herter, who said Rock was "a Roman Catholic immensely devoted to his church, a physician more than nominally devoted to the Hippocratic Oath. . . . "[146] Rock related in the foreword that his entire life had been guided by the words of a kindly, saintly, Irish priest, Father Finnick, who had told him as a mere youth: "John, always stick to your conscience. Never let anyone else keep it for you . . . and I mean anyone else."[147] But, Rock adds, "With increasing frequency I was disturbed by the realization that the voice of my conscience was not always telling me what the priests of my Church kept telling me".[148] Hence, he proceeded to work on the Pill, in response to his "conscience" and, by inference, to the pastoral and priestly advice of Fr. Finnick.

Throughout the book Rock trots out a host of tolerant, scholarly "Catholics" whose arguments and articles point toward acceptance of the Pill for personal

[143] Cass Canfield letter of July 9, 1962 to Fr. Stanislas de Lestapis, S.J., Harvard; Cass Canfield letter to Rev. George A. Kelly, Archdiocese of New York, July 9, 1962; Cass Canfield letter to Rev. John A. O'Brien, Notre Dame, July 9, 1962 (O'Brien was on CBS telecast with Guttmacher), CLHMS.

[144] Msgr. George Kelly, *The Battle for the American Church* (Garden City, New York: Image Books, Doubleday & Co., c. 1981), 139.

[145] PPWP Field Dept. to all affiliates, memo (M-8126), request that names of all Catholics on affiliate board or on Planned Parenthood committee, or state committee, or volunteers be sent to the PPFA, May 11, 1964, SSCSC.

[146] John Rock, M.D., *The Time Has Come* (Avon Books, 1964), by agreement with Alfred A. Knopf, Inc., N.Y. N.Y., v.

[147] Ibid., x.

[148] Ibid.

use by Catholics or acceptance and legal use of the Pill by others. A Catholic philosophy teacher, Dr. Thomas Flynn, is quoted saying that for a solution to the "human, moral problem of overpopulation we must humbly beseech you medical scientists and practitioners".[149] Fr. John Courtney Murray's words are cited to condemn the nineteenth century Connecticut anti–birth control use law: "Since it makes a public crime out of a private sin, and confuses morality with legality, and is unenforceable without a police invasion of the bedroom, the statute is indefensible as a law."[150] Lastly, Rock inverted the traditional Catholic argument from nature to claim:

> The steroid compounds are the first physiologic means of contraception . . . they merely serve as adjuncts to nature . . . the pills, when properly taken, are not likely to disturb menstruation, nor do they mutilate any organ of the body, nor damage any natural process. They merely offer to the human intellect the means to regulate ovulation harmlessly, means which heretofore have come only from the ovary and, during pregnancy, from the placenta.[151]

In addition to the Rock book, which was directed at a Catholic audience, Alan Guttmacher told readers of his inaugural presidential newsletter that Catholics were changing their views. He related that the Catholic Association for International Peace had graciously received Planned Parenthood associate medical director Gordon Perkin, along with co-delegate Gen. Draper, at a population conference. Another conference attendee was Boston College law dean Robert J. Drinan, S.J., who favorably impressed his Planned Parenthood observers as someone to watch in the future.[152] The assessment was accurate, as Fr. Drinan proved later as a Democratic Congressman from Massachusetts with an unswerving record of support for federally funded abortion.

Lastly, writer Dorothy Dunbar Bromley's 1965 book, *Catholics and Birth Control,* contained a foreword by Richard Cardinal Cushing, Archbishop of Boston. Cardinal Cushing wrote:

> If there is to be any "change" (I would prefer the word "refinement") in the traditional presentation of the Church's position on birth control, it is imperative that our people be prepared for it. To that end, it is necessary that they be acquainted with all the discussions that have been going on concerning the matter for the past few years. . . . Those who will honestly and sincerely reflect upon the points of view which [this book] presents cannot fail to appreciate the reality of the problem posed by the various authors cited and the logic of the solutions they present.[153]

[149] Ibid., 65.
[150] Ibid., 107.
[151] Ibid., 149.
[152] Alan F. Guttmacher, *Presidential Letter,* no. 1, December 31, 1964, PPWP no. 1, 4.
[153] Dorothy Dunbar Bromley, *Catholics and Birth Control* (1965).

Moreover, Planned Parenthood had proposed the subject of the book and also suggested Devin Adair as its publisher. Guttmacher crowed in his private newsletter to Planned Parenthood's major donors that Planned Parenthood was sponsoring a book that would produce a "powerful impact on the Catholic world."[154] Bromley's book also had a preface by Fr. John Thomas, S.J., of St. Louis University. Just the year before, Fr. Thomas had appeared with a Protestant leader and a prominent sociologist at the 1964 annual Planned Parenthood meeting in Dallas.[155] The outburst of Catholic–Planned Parenthood cordiality even resulted in Guttmacher's addressing a Chicago Cana Conference in January of 1965, apparently at the invitation of Fr. Imborski, a classroom sex education proponent.[156]

At this time, of course, as Catholic author and jurist John Noonan has pointed out, many Catholics (himself included) who favored liberalization of Catholic views on contraception expected that the Second Vatican Council might result in a different application of Catholic dogma on birth control. Noonan wrote that in April 1964 a Vatican II Conciliar draft document "not only avoided any direct condemnation of contraception; it also said that the number of children to have was the decision of each couple, to be made . . . 'with full and conscious responsibility'."[157] Moreover, four cardinals indicated they supported a reexamination of the traditional birth control doctrine.[158] In June 1964 Pope Paul VI himself said that:

> The problem—everyone talks about it—is that of so-called birth control; that is to say, of population increase on one hand and of family morality on the other. . . . It will be necessary to look attentively and squarely at this theoretical as well as practical development of the question. And this is what the Church is in fact doing. . . . It is under study, we say, and we hope to finish soon with the help of many and eminent scholars.[159]

Seizing the opportunity, Gen. William Draper wrote to PPFA chairman Donald Strauss in February 1965 at the suggestion of an unnamed Catholic priest who had formulated a plan of action designed, in conventional terms, to push or pressure the Pope into a favorable statement on birth control and, in particular, the Pill. A group of 182 prominent Catholic laymen from twelve

---

[154] Guttmacher, *Presidential Letter*, no. 1, December 31, 1964, 5.

[155] Ibid., no. 5, May 19, 1965, supplement.

[156] Ibid., February 26, 1965, no. 3., 1.

[157] John T. Noonan, Jr., *Contraception* (Cambridge, Mass.: Belknap Press of Harvard University Press, 1966), 508.

[158] Ibid., 511.

[159] National Catholic Conference News Service, June 23, 1964, cited by John R. Cavanagh, M.D., *The Popes, the Pill, and the People* (Milwaukee, Wis.: Bruce Publishing Company, 1965), 1.

countries had already petitioned the Pope for a reconsideration of the traditional teaching, especially as it applied to the Pill.

The plan consisted of securing the endorsement of a series of letters from renowned gynecologists, Nobel Prize winners, demographers, and prominent persons from science or public life supporting positive steps to address the population problem. The gynecology letter would depict the rhythm method as inadequate to the task, and point to the Pill's ability to regulate ovulation. The letters were to emphasize the gravity of the population problem and the need for remedial action.

Draper told Strauss this was an important project for Planned Parenthood that should be delicately handled, preferably by a committee and on a confidential basis.[160] He added that Strauss, Guttmacher, Canfield, and Dixie Cup magnate Hugh Moore could serve as an effective and confidential steering committee for the project. After suggesting how to prepare the actual letters, Draper added that by having demographers, doctors, and Nobel Prize winners do the public work, Planned Parenthood could avoid much criticism that could otherwise be expected.[161]

When word finally leaked out that the letters had been sent to the Pope, it was reported that no publicity was given the petitions "out of deference to the wishes of the Holy See".[162] The deference, of course, was to Planned Parenthood, whose efficient network had been able to implement the "inside" suggestion in short order.

As time went on, more and more aspects of the Planned Parenthood program became amenable to progressive-minded Catholics. When the Connecticut birth control case was awaiting final decision from the U.S. Supreme Court, Fr. Drinan was urging Catholics not to oppose public funding of birth control.[163]

The complete policy reversal came when leading Catholic intellectuals, lawyers, and priests opted for abolishing the Connecticut anti–birth control law that earlier generations of Catholics had ardently defended. Fr. John Courtney Murray, S.J., castigated the 1879 Connecticut "Comstock law" that criminalized the use of any drug or instrument to prevent conception by any person, subjecting them to a fine of not less than $50 and/or imprisonment of not less than sixty days. Murray criticized what he called the "characteristic Comstockian-Protestant ignorance of the rules of traditional jurisprudence".

In general, the "free churches" . . . have never given attention to this subtle

---

[160] William F. Draper, Jr., letter to Donald B. Strauss, PPWP, and attachment, "Letters to be sent to His Holiness, Pope Paul VI, Vatican City, Rome, Italy, February 13, 1965", CLHMS.

[161] Ibid.

[162] John Cogley, "Nobel Laureates Petition the Pope", *New York Times,* June 22, 1965.

[163] Guttmacher, *Presidential Letter,* no. 5, May 19, 1965, supplement, 2.

discipline . . . that mediates between the imperatives of the moral order and the commands or prohibitions of civil law. In fact, so far from understanding jurisprudence, these sects have never really understood law but only power. . . . In any case the Connecticut statute confuses the moral and the legal, in that it transposes without further ado a private sin into a public crime. The criminal act here is the private use of contraceptives. The real area where the coercions of law might, and ought to, be applied, at least to control an evil—namely the contraceptive industry—is quite overlooked. As it stands, the statute is, of course, unenforceable without police invasion of the bedroom, and therefore is indefensible as a piece of legal draughtmanship."[164]

Murray was wrong on several counts, and the great weight his name carried compounded the harm of his arguments. For all his complaints against the "Comstockian Protestants" and their supposed ignorance of the traditional rules of prudence and jurisprudence in public affairs, Murray was himself remarkably ignorant of the fact that the Connecticut law (1) had been enforced mainly against Planned Parenthood clinics, and (2) no police invasions of marital bedrooms ever happened, and (3) a spouse could not be compelled to testify against his mate. And Fr. Murray ignored or was ignorant of the long-standing and great practical importance Planned Parenthood placed on legal strategies to have the courts void it. Moreover, Murray did not acknowledge the need for some rule to determine when and where any so-called private sin—whether child abuse, prostitution, homosexual acts, suicide pacts, euthanasia, abortion, drug abuse, pornography, or wifebeating, all of which might just as readily fit Murray's description above—rises to the level of a criminal act.

But Planned Parenthood's lawyers were working from the textbook of a more farsighted theory. Their over two-decade-long effort to overturn the Connecticut statute would eventually become the legal occasion for the development of the constitutional right to privacy in the 1965 *Griswold v. Connecticut* case. Prior to that landmark case, Planned Parenthood's legislative and judicial efforts to overturn the law had met with continued defeat even in the U.S. Supreme Court. In a PPFA-inspired 1961 Supreme Court case *Poe v. Ullman* (367 U.S. 497), a husband and wife sought contraceptives from their doctor to avoid continued psychological distress because three previous, consecutive pregnancies ended in infants born with multiple defects who died shortly after birth.

The family doctor, who knew about contraceptives, believed them necessary for the Poes' (a pseudonym) health. However, the delivery or use of contraceptives was banned by Connecticut law. The Poes, who feared

---

[164] John Courtney Murray, S.J., *We Hold These Truths: Catholic Reflections on the American Proposition* (New York: Sheed and Ward, 1961), 157–58.

prosecution, sought a declaratory judgment that the law was unconstitutional.

Justice Felix Frankfurter, neither Catholic nor conservative, wrote for the Court and rejected their claim. He noted as fact the following: the Poes were not prosecuted; in the entire history of the Connecticut anticontraception-use law enacted in 1879 no married couples had ever been prosecuted for using birth control; prosecution of contraceptive use by a spouse would have been bizarre—as admitted by the Poes' counsel—and made more improbable by Connecticut's law prohibiting one spouse from being compelled to testify against the other.[165]

Frankfurter noted that the law did, however, operate against the efforts of Planned Parenthood to establish birth control clinics, which had been shut down as a result of Catholic efforts in 1939, surely not ancient history even for Fr. Murray. Justice William Brennan, himself Catholic, said as much in a concurring opinion: "The true controversy in this case is over the opening of birth-control clinics on a large scale; it is that which the State has prevented in the past, not the use of contraceptives by isolated and individual married couples."[166]

Justice Douglas dissented, claiming that the law represented an unconstitutional "invasion of privacy". However, he did not tie this assertion to a specific constitutional provision. Douglas had another chance four years later when another Planned Parenthood challenge to the Connecticut law again reached the Court, this time in *Griswold v. Connecticut* 381 U.S. 479 (1965). The appellants, Mrs. Griswold and Dr. Buxom, operators of the Planned Parenthood Center in New Haven, were convicted and fined $100 for abetting the use of contraceptives for the purpose of preventing conception. As Robert Bork has pointed out, this case arose not spontaneously from the operation of the Connecticut statute, but as a result of an initiative by the Yale Law School faculty in cooperation with the PPFA, the ACLU, and an organization called the Catholic Council on Civil Liberties.

This time Douglas wrote for the Court and held the same law unconstitutional. Employing techniques borrowed from fiction writing and police-state imagery from Fr. Murray, Douglas noted quite correctly, but needlessly, that most Americans would find abhorrent the circumstance of police searching a married couple's bedroom for evidence of contraceptive lawbreaking. That this had never happened in the almost one-hundred-year history of this law or was even alleged to have happened outside of conjectural social criticism of the law was apparently irrelevant. In now-famous words, Douglas reached for the novel insight the Court would use repeatedly over the next

---

[165] *Poe v. Ullman,* 367 U.S. 497, nos. 60, 61, October term (1960).
[166] Ibid, concurring opinion.

few decades to strike down state statutes affecting family life: "Specific guarantees in the Bill of Rights have penumbras, formed by emanations from those
guarantees, that help give them life and substance . . . various guarantees create
zones of privacy."[167]

Justice Potter Stewart dissented, noting in part that: "With all deference,
I can find no such general right of privacy in the Bill of Rights, in any other
part of the Constitution or in any case ever before decided by this Court."[168]

Interestingly, Douglas subsequently received a warm personal letter from
Margaret Sanger's niece, Olive Byrne Richard, congratulating him on the
pro–birth control result in *Griswold*. She told Douglas that her mother, Ethyl
Byrne, and Sanger had been arrested for opening a birth control clinic in
Brooklyn. Mrs. Sanger "would rejoice in this new pronouncement which
crowns her 50 years of dedication to the liberation of women from enslavement
born of bigotry".[169]

Msgr. John C. Knott, director of the Family Life Bureau, National Catholic Welfare Conference, had a similar view: "Aside from the fact that you can't
legislate morality, this law was a bad one . . . I am glad it was held unconstitutional".[170]

This entire debacle, which set the stage for *Roe v. Wade* and other like cases,
could not have happened without the willing collaboration of manipulated
and manipulating Catholics. First, Sanger's lawyer, Morris Ernst, told her
son, Dr. Grant Sanger, that the major brief in the *Griswold* case was the one he
suggested that the Catholic Lawyers Guild file before the U.S. Supreme
Court, adding that Planned Parenthood's brief received little attention from
the court while the "Catholic" brief was accepted in full.[171]

The amicus curiae brief to which Ernst referred was filed in the *Griswold* case
under the name of the Catholic Council for Civil Liberties, formed in 1958 by
Catholic laymen in Omaha, Nebraska. The brief was filed by an entourage of
Catholics, almost the exact mirror image of the Catholic coalition that Fr.
John Ryan's National Catholic Welfare Conference led in opposition to Sanger's
federal legislative efforts. Some of the signatories included: reporter John
Cogley, Center for the Study of Democratic Institutions; Rev. John F. Cronin,
S.S., assistant director, Social Action Department, National Catholic Welfare

---

[167] *Griswold v. Connecticut*, 318 U.S. 479, 1965.

[168] Ibid., 1965 dissenting opinion.

[169] Olive Byrne Richard letter to Justice William O. Douglas, June 9, 1965, Library of
Congress Collection (Manuscript Division), Papers of Justice William O. Douglas (hereafter
referred to as LCCJWOD).

[170] John Cogley, "The Catholic Church Reconsiders Birth Control", *New York Times
Magazine*, June 20, 1965, found in Population Crisis, Hearings, Subcommittee on Foreign
Aid Expenditures, Senate Committee on Government Operations, on S. 1676, part 1
(1965), 20.

[171] Letter from Morris Ernst to Dr. Grant Sanger, February 15, 1966, CLHMS.

Conference; Richard L. G. Deverall, Education Department, AFL–CIO; Rev. George H. Dunne, Georgetown University; Dean John C. Hays, Loyola University School of Law, Chicago; Sister Joan, S.N.D., Trinity College, Washington, D.C.; Rev. Benjamin L. Masse, S.J., associate editor, *America;* Edward J. McCormack, former attorney general of Massachusetts; and Dean Joseph O'Meara, School of Law, Notre Dame University.

The Catholic Council for Civil Liberties was an affiliate of the National Catholic Social Action Conference of the NCWC, and urged the

> ... Court to strike down the contraceptive statute in question as an impermissible invasion of married persons' privacy and thus an unreasonable deprivation of their liberty under the Fourteenth Amendment. This is a novel claim to some extent, with respect to the past decisions of this Court. ... [172]
>
> ... the Connecticut law ... can fairly be taken to represent the flat judgment of the state that the use of contraceptives is immoral and wrong per se.
>
> As a matter of public policy the Catholic Council on Civil Liberties would not advocate the retention of this statute, and indeed has sought to have similar laws repealed. ... [173]
>
> Commonly held convictions and understandings about sexual morality in marriage ... have changed so much. ... This has been particularly true of the Catholic community in the past ten years. As one commentator described it: "Up until about the middle of the fifties there was a remarkable harmony among the ideals of the magisterium, the theologians and the married laity. ...
>
> "Social realities ... soon unbalanced this equilibrium. Catholics finally realized how much the Protestant consensus had changed, so much so that now family limitation (by the most efficient means) is taken to be a Christian duty. Then the population explosion began to be noticed by demographers. ... Of more immediate concern to Catholic parents, it turned out that American society is simply not geared for very large families. ... A new perception of the importance of education, of the necessity that a wife be something more than a mother ... helped to round out the change of perspective."[174]
>
> The right of privacy as so invoked means that the state has no competence whatever, no power or jurisdiction in the bedrooms of agreeing spouses.[175]

Douglas' manipulation of the Constitution was made possible only with some "inside help" from Justice Brennan, the Court's only Catholic member.

---

[172] Amicus curiae brief of The Catholic Council for Civil Liberties, in *Griswold v. Connecticut,* October term (1964), no. 496, submitted by Robert B. Fleming, New York, 9.

[173] Ibid., 10.

[174] Ibid., 11, 12 of brief, citing Daniel Callahan, "Authority and the Theologian", vol. 80, *The Commonweal.*

[175] Ibid., 14.

For although Justice Douglas' name appears on the *Griswold* decision, Brennan supplied the intellectual rigor and constitutional underpinnings that Morris Ernst had originally suggested to his Catholic friends. Douglas' first *Griswold* draft proposed to strike down the Connecticut law by locating the "freedom to contracept" in a "right to association" that, Douglas thought, flowed from the First Amendment's guarantee of freedom of assembly.[176] Brennan wrote a flattering critique of Douglas' efforts, but suggested "a substantial shift in emphasis" to a "theory based on privacy" in order to successfully effect a reversal in this case:

> [W]hy not say [that] what has been done for the First Amendment can also be done for some of the guarantees of the Bill of Rights? In other words . . . the Bill of Rights guarantees are but examples of those rights, and do not preclude applications or extensions of those rights unanticipated by the Framers . . . we need not say how far it would extend . . . whatever the contours of a constitutional right to privacy, it would preclude application of the statute before us to married couples.[177]

Eventually Brennan found that he needed four amendments from the Bill of Rights in order to make this newly created right to privacy sufficiently appealing to Douglas and thus secure Planned Parenthood's goals.

But it was not only the Constitution that some Catholics were altering; many Catholics were also altering their birth control practices, according to the 1965 National Fertility Study funded by the National Institute of Child Health and Human Development. The results disclosed a liberalization of birth control practices from 1955 to 1965 among a national sample of white, married women aged eighteen to thirty-nine living with their husbands. "Catholicity" was measured by Mass attendance.

Following is a summary of the survey results:[178]

	All Catholic Couples				
	Number	% Conforming to Church Teaching	% Not Using Birth Control or Rhythm	% Using Rhythm	% Using Other Methods of Birth Control
1955	787	70	43	27	30
1960	668	62	30	31	38
1965	843	47	22	25	53

[176] Draft opinion, Justice William O. Douglas, no. 496, October term (April 1965), LCCJWOD.

[177] Memo of Justice William J. Brennan to Justice William O. Douglas, April 24, 1965, LCCJWOD.

[178] William T. Liu, ed., *Family and Fertility: Proceedings of the Fifth Notre Dame Conference on Population, December 1–3, 1966,* University of Notre Dame Press, 1967 167.

| | Catholic Wives, 18–39, Attending Mass Once a Week or More | | | |
	Number	% Conforming to Church Teaching	% Not Using Birth Control or Rhythm	% Using Rhythm	% Using Other Methods of Birth Control
1955	533	78	45	33	22
1960	525	69	32	37	31
1965	607	56	23	33	44

Defection from traditional Church birth control teaching by Catholic couples was matched by similar defections among the Catholic intelligentsia. The slide from past Church policy was a gradual process. The initial departure came in the area of publicly funded birth control programs, with suggestions similar to the non-opposition policy of Rev. Robert Drinan. But non-opposition eventually evolved into full-fledged support for tax-supported birth control programs. Thus, William V. D'Antonio, a Notre Dame University sociology professor, and the Rev. Dexter Hanley, S.J., of Georgetown University testified at a 1966 U.S. Senate hearing in support of S. 2993, introduced by Sen. Joseph Tydings (D–Md.), which made federal money available for birth control services.[179] Fr. Hanley even opined that though he opposed premarital sex, as a Catholic moral theology professor, he thought it was doubly sinful not to use effective birth control in such relations.[180] Guttmacher agreed.

Yet, Catholic efforts from the "old school" were still capable of inflicting defeats on Planned Parenthood, as when the Pennsylvania Catholic Conference took ads in nearly sixty Pennsylvania newspapers in 1966 and succeeded in rolling back welfare expenditures for birth control. A compromise was reached prohibiting unmarried women from receiving birth control and also prohibiting caseworkers from initiating birth control discussions. Alan Guttmacher said that this represented a "serious hardship" for the poor.[181]

The nation's Catholic bishops launched a nondoctrinal "civil liberties" attack on government birth control in mid-November 1966, claiming that under the Johnson administration welfare programs providing birth control would lead to coercion of the poor, infanticide, abortion, sterilization, euthanasia, and other social abuses. In a joint statement, George Lindsay and Donald Strauss of the PPFA denied the coercion charge, claiming instead that the bishop's policy of keeping the poor ignorant of birth control was itself cruel and coercive.[182] But Strauss and Lindsay took special exception to the specula-

[179] Guttmacher, *Presidential Letter,* no. 13, May 15, 1966, 1, 2.

[180] Ibid., no. 21, April 4, 1967, 3.

[181] Ibid., no. 15, September 23, 1966, 2.

[182] "Public Policy, Birth Control, and Freedom of Choice", *PP–WP NEWS,* George Lindsay, chairman and Donald B. Strauss, chairman, Executive Committee, PPWP, November 16, 1966, 3, SSCSC.

tive tone of the bishops' statement, taking them to task for predicting exactly what, it turned out, did happen. Strauss and Lindsay claimed there was no historical basis behind the bishops' assertion that government-supported birth control would lead to their litany of social horrors.[183]

But the Catholic bishops found themselves surrounded by defectors with noses alert for publicity. At the annual PPFA conference in 1966, Sister Mary A. Schaldenbrand, professor of Religion and Philosophy at Nazareth College, delivered an address in terms that may have made some PPFA delegates wonder if the recently departed Margaret Sanger had experienced yet another reincarnation. Sister Mary claimed that responsible conception control freed women from a narrow "species-preservative role" that unnecessarily restricted women's personal powers. Birth control, by diminishing fear and anxiety, resulted in "making more available person-creative sexual communion (its unique power to achieve the personal being of the partners involved) and . . . it liberates time and energy for the development of personal capacities and their exercise within the larger human community."[184]

Similar appearances and utterances proved almost too much even for Guttmacher, who was the only non-Catholic speaking at a two-day Planned Parenthood–Jesuit conference in Rochester, New York, in September 1967. Guttmacher related that Catholic nuns, priests, and college professors " . . . paralleled so closely the tried and true Planned Parenthood philosophy . . . that, had I closed my eyes, I would not have known where I was." He also noted that these Catholics publicly lamented that the pope had not changed his views.[185]

Regional Planned Parenthood chairman, Mrs. Harper Sibley, Jr., gladly told PPFA's Cass Canfield about the Jesuit–Planned Parenthood meeting, mentioning a "priceless" photograph they had of a nun standing before a Planned Parenthood banner.[186]

Such shifts were not isolated. The Jesuit magazine, *America,* in September 1967, opted for birth control. Thus, for a while, it did seem that the Catholic Church—certainly the American branch—was on an unalterable course to changing its position on birth control.

Then, on July 29, 1968, Pope Paul VI issued his encyclical, *Humanae Vitae (On Human Life),* condemning artificial birth control, stressing that economic and social development, not birth control, was the proper answer to those warning of the dangers of population growth, and pointing out the personal and social ills that birth control itself would produce in society. Dissent within Catholic circles was immediate, beginning with the man who was chosen to

[183] Ibid., 4.
[184] PPWP press release, New York, October 19, 1966, SSCSC.
[185] Guttmacher, *Presidential Letter,* no. 27, November 28, 1967, 2, CLHMS.
[186] Letter from Mrs. Harper Sibley, Jr., chairman, Northeast Region PPWP, to Cass Canfield, October 3, 1967, SSCSC or CLHMS.

release the encyclical in Rome, Msgr. Fernando Lambruschini. Twice on that very day, he claimed that *Humanae Vitae* was not an infallible document.[187] Just five days after the encyclical, Fordham University in New York sponsored a panel discussion for the secular media and leading contraceptionists.[188] The *Christian Science Monitor* reported on a Notre Dame study that claimed that 95% of assistant pastors under age thirty favored birth control.[189]

But with firm papal opposition to the Pill, the contraceptionists would have to be satisfied with more limited victories among the sergeants and sentries of the Church, seeing that its head remained intact. PPWP chairman George Lindsay said the Pope's encyclical marked a sad day in the Church's history.[190] Lindsay also cited figures to show that, if the Pope could not be converted to birth control, at least individual Catholics or Catholic institutions could. Here he was correct.

An exchange of letters in 1971 between Guttmacher and Dr. William Schwartz of St. Joseph Mercy Hospital in Pontiac, Michigan (Archdiocese of Detroit) is quite instructive. Dr. Schwartz was a member of an obstetrical/gynecological committee at St. Joseph's that was seeking to allow physicians to perform sterilizations there. Schwartz told Guttmacher that the St. Joseph's administration seemed to be quite liberal, as evidenced by their approval for resident physicians to assist at a local Planned Parenthood affiliate and an expressed willingness to have Planned Parenthood use the new hospital facilities when finished. Schwartz noted that if a plan could be developed that would both permit elective sterilizations and let the Sisters of Mercy to appear orthodox it would be seriously considered.[191]

No trouble, Guttmacher told Schwartz. Just write to his good friend, Dr. Andre Hellegers (a Kennedy family confidant who testified before Congress in favor of a human life amendment) at Jesuit-run, Catholic Georgetown University Hospital in Washington, D.C., where sterilizations were called by the name "uterine isolation operation", not a "hysterectomy".[192]

With the exception of sterilization, at present the birth control habits of most Catholics, as consistently measured by national surveys, are virtually identical to members of other denominations, and contraception is only slightly less prevalent than among those of no religious faith.

---

[187] Msgr. George Kelly, *The Battle for the American Church* (New York: Doubleday, 1981), 164.

[188] Ibid., 165.

[189] Ibid.

[190] "Planned Parenthood Leader Responds to Pope's Statement", George Lindsay, chairman, PPWP, Order no: 401/768, code: 6.11, July 29, 1968.

[191] Letter of Dr. William Schwartz, coordinator of education, St. Joseph Mercy Hospital, Pontiac, Michigan, to Dr. Alan Guttmacher, 51 Madison Ave., N.Y., N.Y., March 26, 1971, CLHMS.

[192] Guttmacher letter to William Schwartz, April 13, 1971, CLHMS.

From 1971 to the present, American Catholic social efforts in this area have been largely defensive, and directed primarily against abortion on demand. The situation of Catholics "coming to terms" with secular, American society has reached the point that the director of pro-life efforts for the Archdiocese of Hartford, Connecticut, recently supported a bill in the Connecticut legislature which codified *Roe v. Wade* in state law and removed criminal penalties from the old law that was still on the books. The diocese did so because the bill provided that girls under fifteen seeking abortions be counseled, and prohibited abortions "after the viability of the fetus except where necessary to preserve the life or health of the pregnant woman".[193] A consultant to the Hartford archdiocese who heads the Pro-Life Council of Connecticut also endorsed the bill, publicly calling it a pro-life victory.[194]

But the Catholic-endorsed bill did not require viability testing, nor did it even state when viability presumptively began. State representative George Jepsen said, "It was as though you had died and went [sic] to heaven: an abortion vote on which you could be supported by both sides."[195] Pro-abortion Rep. Nancy Wyman said, "I'm ecstatic ... I could never have guessed that would have happened."[196] Other legislators expressed similar surprise. Republican state chairman Richard Foley said that: "If I were pro-life, I would not be proclaiming victory on that vote.... Clearly they got snookered—the pro-life leadership, I mean—and they are not bright enough to know they were snookered."[197]

If Margaret Sanger were alive, like the perplexed Connecticut legislator, she undoubtedly would gaze with supreme pleasure at the spectacle of Catholic representatives hailing legislation providing for abortion on demand as a victory for life.

---

[193] Mark Pazniokas, "Abortion Bill Pleases Both Sides", *Hartford Courant,* April 22, 1990.
[194] Mark Pazniokas, "Abortion Foes Irate at Leader", *Hartford Courant,* April 27, 1990.
[195] Pazniokas, "Abortion Bill Pleases Both Sides", *Hartford Courant,* April 22, 1990.
[196] Ibid.
[197] Ibid.

Chapter Six

When "Choice" Infects Medicine

The guiding light in the realm of medicine for almost twenty-five centuries in the Western world was the Oath of Hippocrates, named after the Greek physician who is also called the Father of Medicine. This oath, though taken to a pagan god, embodied a "Natural Law" ethic compatible with orthodox Jewish and Christian thought and practice. Faced with this roadblock, it was inevitable then that Planned Parenthood could not effect its social revolt as long as the practice of medicine in the United States and elsewhere was guided by the Hippocratic ethic.

Alan Guttmacher himself said in 1971 that it was a decided advantage for Planned Parenthood not to be tied down by a venerated document like the U.S. Constitution or the constraints of the outdated Hippocratic Oath which forbade doctors from performing abortions or assisting suicide.[1]

But, of course, by 1971 American medicine had come a long way itself toward eventual complete abandonment of the Hippocratic Oath. And, as we shall presently discuss, the departure of American medicine from the "sanctity of life" ethic came by degrees, each step of the way paved with little concessions to Planned Parenthood's agenda for social betterment, until the means and goals were indistinguishable.

From its inception in 1847, the American Medical Association upheld the Hippocratic Oath as a norm of both professional practice and ethical conduct toward patients. As such, until well into the twentieth century, the AMA officially opposed both contraception and abortion.

In 1866 the American Medical Association decided to issue a brief but comprehensive statement on abortion for distribution among women. The task fell to Horatio R. Storer, an assistant in obstetrics and medical jurisprudence at Harvard and a leading antiabortionist of his day. Storer's resulting essay, "The Criminality and Physical Evils of Forced Abortions", which won an award, quoted Percivil's *Medical Ethics* to the effect that "to extinguish the first spark of life is a crime of the same nature both against our Maker and society, as to destroy an infant, a child, or a man". In addition, Storer cited a statement from 1653 that decried the putting to death of a being "in the shop

---

[1] Goals and Activities of Planned Parenthood-World Population, Dr. Alan Guttmacher, address to annual meeting of PPWP in San Francisco, October 28, 1971, reconstructed from notes, CLHMS.

of nature", i.e., the womb, as "a thing deserving all hate and detestation". With the full support of his colleagues, Storer declared that all "physicians have now arrived at the unanimous opinion that the foetus in utero is alive from the very moment of conception". The assumptions that "the child is not alive until quickening has occurred" or that it is "practically dead" until it has breathed were "both erroneous".

"Thus, whenever and wherever a practitioner of any standing in the profession has been known, or believed to be guilty of producing abortion, except absolutely to save a woman's life, he has immediately and universally been cast from fellowship, in all cases losing the respect of his associates."

Storer also contended that "the deliberate prevention of pregnancy" was "detrimental to the health and to the moral sense". He also lashed out at infanticide, which at the time was an "occasional occurence". The bulk of the essay, however, dealt with abortion and concluded with the suggestion that the AMA would again be "true to its mighty and responsible office of shutting the great gates of human death".[2]

In May 1870, the AMA denounced all physicians who performed abortions. In May of 1871, a similar denunciation referred to the preborn as "the child". In June of 1902, the AMA came out against advertisements of appliances to prevent or cut short pregnancy.

A slight but notable change came in 1928, some ten years after Margaret Sanger had begun her birth control crusade. In that year, the AMA board of trustees referred to its House of Delegates a resolution recommending a change in laws so that physicians could give contraceptive information to their patients. However, in 1932, 1933, and 1934 the House of Delegates disapproved resolutions recommending a study of birth control. In 1935, a resolution was approved that provided for the study of birth control without endorsing or opposing it. In 1936, the AMA disapproved of the propaganda from birth control agencies.

But after Sanger's success in federal court, the AMA began to reverse its policies, providing in 1937 for investigations into birth control and allowing information on fertility and sterility to be disseminated in medical schools. The following year, it recommended changes in the state laws to allow physicians to give birth control information to patients.

Ten years later in 1948, the AMA, pushing its own logic further, gave its approval to artificial insemination. Some two decades later, in 1967, it endorsed abortion for saving the health—including the mental health—or life of the mother, when the infant would be incapacitated, physically deformed,

---

[2] Horatio R. Storer, "The Criminality and Physical Evils of Forced Abortions", American Medical Association, 1866.

or mentally deficient. Abortion in cases of rape or incest was also recommended.[3]

In 1970 the AMA opposed the inclusion of health warnings in packages of the Pill and supported the distribution of birth control information to teenaged girls. It also stipulated that abortion should be performed by a licensed doctor or surgeon in an accredited hospital after consultation with two other physicians. This practically allowed for abortion on demand.[4] The medical rejection of the Hippocratic Oath would be recognized in American jurisprudence by the 1973 abortion decisions of the U.S. Supreme Court.

A 1977 statement by the American Academy of Pediatrics indicates the extent to which the Hippocratic Oath had been rejected. In response to the question, "Do you believe that the life of each and every newborn infant should be saved if it is within our ability to do so?" 80% of the Academy's surgical section answered in the negative.[5] Later, the Academy of Pediatrics also opposed the Reagan administration's efforts to mandate nondiscriminatory treatment of handicapped newborn infants.

In 1979 Congressman Ron Paul (R-Tex.), also a medical doctor, introduced an amendment to a bill extending the National Health Planning Act. Representative Paul stated: "...My amendment simply requires one thing: namely that the 205 health systems describe their plans in terms of the ancient and venerable Oath of Hippocrates, as restated by the World Medical Association at Geneva in 1948."[6] Representative Paul then read the Oath into the Congressional Record, and in view of the historical importance of this moral and legal watershed, we include a portion of that debate.

MR. PAUL: Mr. Chairman, medical scientist and educator A. C. Ivy said in 1949, "I realized for the first time at the Nuremberg Trials, the full meaning of the contribution of Hippocrates and his school to medicine and human welfare.... One cannot conceive of a sound society with medicine that does not have a sound moral philosophy."

In the years preceding World War II, German academic medicine was pre-eminent. Germany was the leading world center for postgraduate medical studies, just as the United States is today. The prostitution of German medicine occurred by degrees as collaboration with the Nazis proceeded. If we are not careful, the anti-moral elements that characterized Nazi medicine will become present in America to a degree not once

[3] American Medical Association, *Digest of Official Actions*, vol. 1, 1846–1958; AMA, Chicago, Ill.

[4] Ibid., vol. 2, 1959–1968; vol. 3, 1969–1978.

[5] Cited in a speech by Dr. C. Everett Koop, Right to Life Convention, Cincinnati, Ohio, June 23, 1979: See *Congressional Record*, 95th Cong., 1st sess., July 18, 1979, E3716–E3718.

[6] *Congressional Record*, daily ed., 95th Cong., 1st sess., July 19, 1979, H6243–H6247.

thought possible only a few years ago. The government talks inordinately of "cost control" in a vain attempt to neutralize government inflation and because the sanctity of life for one individual is subordinated to the quality of life for another.

Dr. Leo Alexander, an official medical expert at the Nuremberg Trials of German physician-executioners of Nazi atrocities, has stated: "Whatever proportions these crimes finally assumed, it became evident to all who investigated them that they had started from small beginnings. The beginnings at first were merely a subtle shift in emphasis in the basic attitudes of physicians. It started with the acceptance of the attitude, basic in the euthanasia movement, that there is such a thing as a life not worthy to be lived.

"The attitude in its early stages concerned itself merely with the severely and chronically sick. Gradually the sphere of those to be included in this category was enlarged to encompass the socially unproductive, the ideologically unwanted, the racially unwanted, and finally all non-Germans."

A physician is a human being and equally shares and suffers the human condition. He or she has no genetic immunity to vice, ignorance, or temptation. Dr. Herbert Ratner, Oak Park, Illinois, has stated: "Medicine has undergone an erosion since the post-Nazi holocaust on human experimentation. It is seen in the acceptance of killing as a new function of the medical profession, namely the killing of the unborn child and the promotion of active euthanasia among the born. To advance killing in medicine is just as monstrous as tolerating injustice in law."

Doctors need to be protected from becoming the tools of amoral health plutocrats. Patients need their sanctity of life respected by all physicians, not just a majority. . . .

When we emancipate ourselves from the Oath of Hippocrates, we liberate ourselves to commit atrocity. I urge adoption of the amendment.

Mr. [Henry] Waxman (D–Calif.): Mr. Chairman . . . I would like to engage the author of this amendment in some discussion so that I can understand what this amendment does.

Mr. Chairman, as I understand this amendment, the gentleman is asking that in the health plan there be a statement of how the goals affect this particular Oath; is that correct?

Mr. Paul: If the gentleman will yield, if what we spend the money on does not fulfill the goals stated in the Oath of Hippocrates at Geneva, a report to that effect is required. It would be like an ethical impact statement. You don't have to follow the Hippocratic Oath, but the purpose would be to say whether or not you are following it or not following it in all government health planning.

Mr. Waxman: The gentleman, I hope, understands that what health planning agencies do is not just what we spend money on, but the whole health care system in the area.

MR. PAUL: I think it would be wise for the whole health care system if they followed some type of ethical conduct.

MR. WAXMAN: But what the gentleman is suggesting is that the ethic as stated in this Oath be the official ethic of this country that we tell all health care officials to abide by.

MR. PAUL: Is there anything specific in the Oath that the Gentleman objects to?

MR. WAXMAN: I do not know. It seems to me that it is presumptuous of us to decide what the morality is for all health authorities in this country. There is a mention here about which I think there is some controversy, where it says, "I will maintain the utmost respect for human life from the time of its inception."

Certainly we want to respect human life, but with that I assume that the gentleman would be imposing the views that he may have on the question of abortions on all doctors in this country? Is the gentleman making a moral judgment and wanting us to put in the law his moral version of the law?

MR. PAUL: I am asking that we use this as the standard of ethical conduct in the practice of medicine when government money is involved, at least to the extent whether or not those standards are followed.

MR. WAXMAN: Government money is not involved in all of the practice of medicine under the health planning system. It is all the health care that is given in this country.

MR. PAUL: I think all of medicine should be under some ethical standards if the government is going to be regulating it, as they are.

MR. WAXMAN: I do not dispute they ought to be under ethical standards. I do question whether the gentleman should decide what ethical standards are appropriate.

It does provide a lot of paperwork for the agencies; it makes them go through a lot of busy work. I do not see that it does any good. On that basis, I would oppose it.[7]

Congressman Paul's amendment went down to defeat, receiving fewer than eighty votes. Thus, the question of paperwork and the notion of imposing an allegedly "private" set of values took precedence over the protection of human life. Mr. Paul was not "imposing" a set of values peculiar to himself. He after all would have needed a majority of the House and Senate to carry his amendment in the first place. But the standard for medicine he was suggesting had been normative in the Western world for ethical physicians at least since the time of Plato and Aristotle.

[7] Ibid.

Respect for medicine as practiced according to the Oath of Hippocrates is so complete that physicians regularly speak of "management options" when they are really talking about starving to death handicapped infants, euphemistically referred to as "nothing by mouth". The Indiana "Baby Doe" case back in 1982 drew national attention to this widespread practice. There, a tiny baby boy born with Down syndrome and a malfunctioning esophagus was denied food. He died six days later. All the formal, legal procedures had been followed: parental consent, judicial orders, and "prescribed medical procedures". A number of married couples in the area were willing to adopt the baby, but their efforts were rejected by society's agencies of social welfare, justice, and medicine.

It is not just for Down syndrome that babies are starved to death. Dr. C. Everett Koop, later surgeon general, has noted that 7.9% of doctors would acquiesce to similar parental wishes even in cases of intestinal atresia, the surgery for which is almost 100% successful, and life is completely normal following surgery.[8]

The American Medical Association also accepts the "quality of life ethic". The AMA officialy opposed a 1983 congressional bill requiring the nondiscriminatory treatment of handicapped children.[9] The AMA also opposed a similar proposal by the Reagan administration to use the U.S. civil rights laws to protect handicapped newborns. *Pediatrics,* the official journal of the American Academy of Pediatrics, ran an editorial by Australian bioethicist Peter Singer who concluded that

> if we compare a severely defective human infant with a nonhuman animal, a dog or a pig for example, we often find the nonhuman to have superior capacities.... If we can put aside the obsolete and erroneous notion of the sanctity of all human life, we may start to look at human life as it really is: the quality of life that each human being has or can achieve.[10]

Another measure of the distance American medicine has come from the Hippocratic Oath is perhaps best illustrated by a situation that took place the same month that Baby Doe was killed. The Maryland Board of Veterinary Examiners fined a veterinary doctor $3,000 and suspended his license for sixty days for starving a dog to death.[11] The American medical community seems

[8] See Rep. Robert K. Dornan, Extension of Remarks, *Congressional Record,* 95th Cong., 1st sess., July 18, 1979, E3716–E3718.

[9] James H. Sammons, M.D., executive vice president, AMA, letter to Rep. Henry Hyde, June 28, 1983, in opposition to H.R. 618, 98th Cong., 1st sess.

[10] Peter Singer, "Commentaries: Sanctity of Life or Quality of Life", *Pediatrics,* vol. 72, no. 1 (July 1983): 128–29.

[11] Sen. Jeremiah Denton, speech on Sen. Res. 101, *Congressional Record,* 97th Cong., 2d sess., vol. 128, no. 66, May 26, 1982, S6143–45.

to be at peace with a circumstance of a human life having less value than a dog's.

With the slide toward killing as a medical function, doctors have had to defend themselves from social recognition of this practice. Contemporaneous with these developments, state legislatures have passed laws providing that capital punishment may be inflicted by medical injection of lethal drugs. Dr. Donald Price, president of the Idaho Medical Association, testified against the passage of one such law, stating, without apparent irony, that "our jobs as physicians is to protect lives, not take them. We felt this had to be clarified."[12] That such a fundamental point had to be clarified at all indicates how confused the professional role of the physician has become.

Almost 2,500 years ago Aristotle pointed out the confusion that would ensue when medicine abandoned "health" as its formal goal. He wrote:

> Why do doctors continue their treatment only until health is restored? Is it because it is impossible for any other condition to be produced from health? The doctor . . . achieves a state which is such as to constitute a condition of health; and from this no condition can be produced except one which is intermediate between health and sickness. Neither the doctor's art nor any other art will create anything out of health; for either nothing would be produced, or else the opposite of health.[13]

Aristotle's words describe the situation that prevails in much of Western medicine today. Consider that women take a powerful drug, the Pill, not to cure a disease, but to prevent babies, a natural, physiological occurence. This in fact is the legitimization of drug-taking for other than medical purposes, i.e., curing a disease or alleviating pain. Doctors thereby draw the healthy to their services and not just the sick or potentially sick. Certainly the "Pill" is the most unique drug ever given to healthy women. Conventionally understood in normal medical therapeutics, drugs are chemical substances "used to counteract the effects of disease, or to reinforce the tissues in their struggle to maintain their functions".[14] What disease is prevented by the Pill? Indeed, if pleasure is the primary motivational factor accounting for the current social use of the Pill, how is this different from other forms of nonmedical, "recreational" drug use?

To retain the logical symmetry a physician is disposed to apply to his trade, it follows that the unwanted child must become the medical equivalent of a disease process. This is the subtle transference of meaning required to justify the Pill. Mary Calderone expressed this symmetry in the 1960s when she

---

[12] "Injection Death Has Become Ethical Issue", *American Medical News,* July 11, 1980, 19.

[13] Aristotle, *Aristotle Problemata,* book 30, vol. 7 (London: Oxford University Press), 965.

[14] D. L. Marsh, *Outline of Fundamental Pharmacology* (Springfield, Il.: Charles C Thomas, 1951), xi.

lamented that: "We have yet to beat our drums for birth control in the way we beat them for polio vaccine, we are still unable to put babies in the class of dangerous epidemics, even though this is the exact truth."[15]

Alan Guttmacher noted that physicians in general, prior to the advent of the Pill in 1960, resisted "becoming involved in the whole area of preventing conception". He gave six reasons for this, three of which had their direct origins with the Hippocratic Oath: the mandate to preserve life, the injunction to do no harm, and the refusal to "play God".[16] Guttmacher elaborated on each of these basic principles: Preventing the creation of a new life was perceived as antithetical to a doctor's primary purpose; the Hippocratic philosophy directed a physician to refrain from an action rather than "doing something when the action harms the patient";[17] and the following actions— "sterilization, therapeutic abortion, donor artificial insemination . . . withholding resuscitative techniques to seriously malformed infants in the delivery room" and, for some physicians, contraceptive practice, all constituted playing God.[18] Guttmacher was able to accept this expansive role, and elsewhere he endorsed euthanasia and served on the Medical Advisory Council of the Euthanasia Educational Council, as did other Planned Parenthood stalwarts.[19]

As the premier medical contraceptionist of the twentieth century, Guttmacher's linkage of artificial contraception to all of the other practices listed above is no accident. In each case, medicine is being used for a goal other than the preservation of life and the restoration of health.

Planned Parenthood's own journal has stated that pregnancy "may be defined as a disease . . . [and] . . . treated by evacuation of the uterine contents".[20]

But physicians who abandon the Hippocratic Oath will not, in the end, operate in a moral vacuum. They will simply choose another ethic while pretending to hold onto the old one. Other considerations, be they personal preference, social utility, population control, prevailing governmental cost control policies, inflation, or even the position of the stars—some basic standard—will become the new measuring rod.

[15] Cited in *Medical-Moral Newsletter,* February–March 1968, published by Dr. Frank Ayd (psychiatrist), Baltimore, Maryland.

[16] Alan Guttmacher, "Family Planning and Population Programs", in *Proceedings of the International Conference on Family Planning Programs,* Geneva, August 1965 (Chicago: University of Chicago Press, 1966), 455. The other three reasons were: popularity with colleagues, keeping in step with medical politics, and retaining ability to enjoy Catholic hospital staff privileges.

[17] Ibid, 457–59.

[18] Ibid, 457–58.

[19] Letter from Florence Clothier, M.D., to Dr. Alan Guttmacher, November 1, 1973, CLHMS; letter from Dr. Alan Guttmacher to O. Ruth Russell, Ph.D., February 8, 1971, CLHMS.

[20] Warren Hern, "Is Pregnancy Really Normal?" *Family Planning Perspectives,* vol. 3, no. 1 (January 1971): 9–12.

Thus, in the words of Planned Parenthood's Dr. Elizabeth B. Connell, who would later serve as a consultant to the Food and Drug Administration's Drug Advisory Committee:

> It would be unreasonable to expect those attempting to deal with the exigencies of the population crisis and the agonies caused by unwanted pregnancies to view the pill precisely the same way as medical traditionalists demanding a preparation proved 100 percent effective, safe and devoid of all side effects.[21]

In practice, this perspective, which can only be described as medical relativism, has the definite effect of making disease and bodily dysfunction a formal or acceptable goal of "health care". Dr. J. Robert Willson of Temple University gave a few examples of what it meant for the individual woman patient in terms of pathological consequences for physicians to shift their focus from the individual's health to the criteria of worldwide population control. At a 1962 IUD conference sponsored by the Population Council, he stated:

> . . . suppose one [patient] does develop an intrauterine infection and suppose she does end up with a hysterectomy and bilateral salpingo-oophorectomy [removal of an ovary and fallopian tube]. How serious is that for the particular patient and for the population of the world in general? Not very. Perhaps we have to stop thinking in terms of individual patients and change our direction a bit. . . . Again, if we look at this from an overall long-range view (these are things I have never said out loud before and I don't know how it is going to sound) perhaps the individual patient is expendable in the general scheme of things, particularly if the infection she acquires is sterilizing but not lethal.[22]

Medical director of the PPFA at the time, Mary Calderone, in partial response to the above statement, said, "It thrilled me to hear a clinician like Dr. Willson talk in terms of public health applications as I, a public health person, would not have dared talk, particularly in this assembly".[23]

Speaking further as to what degree of mayhem would prompt concern from the Planned Parenthood physician, Dr. Jack Lippes, inventor of the Lippes Loop IUD, told the conference:

> As you know, I have no reservations about ascending infection. This is not

[21] Elizabeth B. Connell, M.D., "The Pill: Facts and Fantasies, Books in Review", a review of five books on oral contraceptives, and the second FDA report on the "Oral Contraceptives", *Family Planning Perspectives*, vol. 2, no. 1 (January 1970): 45.

[22] "Intrauterine Contraceptive Devices", *Proceedings of the Conference*, April 30–May 1, 1962, New York City, ed. Christopher Tietze and Sarah Lewit, International Congress Series no. 54, Excerpta Medica Foundation, 124.

[23] Ibid., 125.

one of the things I worry about. However, should future studies show that a cervical projection does change the Pap smear, it may be necessary to go back to the Grafenburg principle of not bridging the gap between the uterus and the vagina. At any rate it would take a great deal of moral courage at such a time to stand up and still say that intrauterine contraception is good.[24]

After the devastating experience of millions of American women with the Dalkon Shield, such "moral courage" still stands in ready supply among the procontraceptive leaders. Except for certain Supreme Court briefs, that courage does not usually extend to telling women, as a kind of informed consent, that the Pill and IUD have the definite property of causing early abortions. As we point out elsewhere, the *device* used to save these contraceptive devices was the simple one of redefining the standard usage of such medical terms as "conception" and "contraception".

These word changes are the external sign of the internal transformation of medicine. If individuals can legitimately ask for, and doctors furnish, non-health-related medical interventions—e.g., birth control or letting a malformed infant die—because these represent "personal goods", why could not the government itself impose the same "goods" upon the general population? In other words, if the sanctity of human life is not a sufficiently powerful deterrent, then why would so relatively thin a principle as "personal choice" fare better, at least in the long run?

As Planned Parenthood leader Pramilla Senanayake stated, "where governments have taken steps to provide essential services for its [sic] population, society has a right to expect some kind of reciprocal responsibility from its citizens, in terms of how they space their children and determine final family size."[25]

Recall that Pope Paul VI said in 1968 that if individuals could choose birth control as a personal good, governments could also "choose" birth control for the common good, and we all know that implementing the common good sometimes requires the use of coercion. But this warning was lost in the criticism and complaints hurled at Pope Paul VI when he issued *Humanae Vitae*. Yet American medicine and our overseas population-control assistance programs have come a long way since 1968 and now appear prepared to go even further. It can be seen that medicine has less and less to do with "health", and instead has become a major tool for implementing a broad spectrum of amoral social policies.

[24] Ibid., 132–36.
[25] Pramilla Senanayake, "The Politics of Contraception", in *Future Aspects of Contraception,* proceedings of an international symposium, held in Heidelburg, September 5–8, 1984, pt. 2, Female Contraception, ed. B. Runnebaum et al. (Boston: MTP Press Ltd., 1985), 351–60.

This is no idle speculation. Former U.S. congressman and now World Bank president Barber Conable told a meeting of the International Monetary Fund that population issues "will be prominent in the World Bank's future decisions with governments" [i.e., loans to poor nations].[26]

But there is nothing new in finding medicine as the vehicle for implementing totalitarian visions. Approximately three hundred and fifty years before the birth of Christ, the Greek philosopher Plato described in *The Republic* the role that birth control would play in establishing a utopian, but totalitarian, state. It provides some remarkably useful insights for the present discussion.

In Book 5 (at 459), Plato records the following dialogue:

SOCRATES: I mean, I replied, that our rulers will find a considerable dose of falsehood and deceit necessary for the good of their subjects: we were saying that the use of all these things regarded as medicines might be of advantage.

GLAUCON: And we were very right.

SOCRATES: And this lawful use of them seems likely to be often needed in the regulations of marriages. . . . Now these goings on must be a secret which the rulers only know.

The discussion immediately following deals with the application of animal husbandry techniques to the human social order, starting with the need to expose handicapped babies, abort children from incestuous unions, abolish monogamous marriage and familial child rearing, separate mothers from their children, and even prohibit them from breast-feeding.

Elsewhere in Book 5, Plato specifies that if the sexes differ only in that men beget and women bear children, that "this does not amount to a proof that a woman differs from a man in respect of the sort of education she should receive". Plato also suggests that as men and women "differ only in their comparative strength . . . " that the wives of the guardians, the political elite, should "share in the toils of war and the defense of their country".

The irony is that medicine, pressed into the service of hedonism, becomes the singularly most important vehicle for creating and sustaining the demands of the totalitarian, hedonist state. Now, under the birth control ethos, a new, emasculated Hippocratic Oath is taken in many medical schools, where the doctor solemnly promises that "I will abstain from all that is illegal". Indeed, the plight of the medical schools is much akin to the moral relativistic plight of the seminaries: We teach medicine but not health, legality but not justice, philosophy but not wisdom, the current social gospel but not the real, timeless Gospel.

[26] Robert S. McCartney, "Conable Urges Curbs on Population", *Washington Post,* September 28, 1988, D-1, D-4.

Chapter Seven

Planned Parenthood and Medicine: Motherhood as a Disease

A critical mainstay of Planned Parenthood's public relations effort from its inception—with only minor lapses—has been a theme, repeated with several variations, that artificial birth control of any type is healthy for women. The propagation of this premise was in fact the wedge by which widespread social acceptance of birth control was achieved in the United States. Planned Parenthood sought to pit the ostensibly proven medical fact that birth control would save the lives of mothers and children against the conjectural moral opposition that birth control, and the resultant division of sexuality and reproduction, would wreak individual and social havoc.

At first it was claimed that birth control would reduce infant and maternal mortality.[1] This notion was later extended, as we shall see, to the proposition that any form of birth control, including legally induced abortion, would be "safer" than pregnancy and childbirth.

A standard strategy (which Planned Parenthood and its public policy spinoff affiliate, the Alan Guttmacher Institute, still use) is to point to the decades-long decline in infant and maternal mortality and attribute this decline to birth control. For many years now the nation's secular print and electronic media have uncritically accepted this claim, although an examination of sources and a little critical thinking could easily have shown otherwise.

For example, in December 1941 Planned Parenthood highlighted the almost 10,000 maternal deaths and 109,000 infant deaths during 1939 to make a case that birth control would reduce both maternal and infant mortality.[2] Their researchers gave particular weight to a 1925 study conducted by the Children's Bureau of the U.S. Labor Department, insisting it showed that birth control reduced both infant and maternal mortality.[3] Infant mortality figures cited from the study were held to be "conclusive evidence of the effectiveness of child-spacing to prevent child deaths". The following data are reproduced from the study:

[1] Lydia Allen DeVilbiss, M.D., "Medical Aspects of Birth Control", *Birth Control Review*, vol. 5, no. 12 (December 1921): 13.

[2] "A Memorandum on Planned Parenthood and the Nation's Population Situation", Birth Control Federation of America, N.Y., N.Y., December 1, 1941, 6–7, SSCSC.

[3] Ibid., 4–7.

Interval between Births	Infant Mortality Rate per 1000 births
1 year	146.7
2 years	98.6
3 years	86.5
4 years	84.9

While Planned Parenthood correctly cited the infant mortality figures, they offered explanations for them that were never mentioned by the Children's Bureau. First of all, the study neither discussed nor assessed birth control use, let alone suggested that it could lower infant mortality. Furthermore, where the study does offer causal explanations, they are at variance with the Planned Parenthood interpretation. For example:

Short Interval Births and Low Mortality: "In spite of the relatively high proportion of short-interval births among births second in order, this order had a lower infant mortality rate than any other.

"The proportion of short-interval births was higher—29.6 percent—in the group of second births than in that of any other order up to tenth and later, for which it was 30.6 per cent."[4]

Short Interval Births and Artificial Feeding: "The mortality among infants whose mothers became pregnant during the infants' first year of life was over two-and-one-half times the average rate during corresponding months for all infants. *This excess mortality was largely accounted for by the greater prevalence of artificial feeding* [emphasis added] but was due in part to the fact that the group included an undue proportion of infants of nationalities having high mortality rates as well as an undue proportion of those born in families with low incomes for which the infant mortality rates were markedly above average."[5]

Breast-Feeding: "The artificial feeding of infants, when commenced in the early months of life, was associated with a mortality between three and four times that found to prevail among the breast-fed infants. This excess was not explained by the slight over-weighting of the group of artificially fed with twins and triplets, prematurely born infants, and babies whose mothers died during the year, all of whom were characterized by high rates. The excess appeared in all nationality and earnings groups. . . . "[6]

Working Mothers: "The mortality for infants whose mothers have worked away from home during pregnancy was 176.1, as compared with 114.6 for

[4] Robert Morse Woodbury, *Causal Factors in Infant Mortality,* February 25, 1925, Children's Bureau, U.S. Dept. of Labor, 51. Data consisted of birth records for 23,000 infant births in eight U.S. cities. The infant mortality rate was 111.2/1,000 live births.

[5] Ibid., 70.

[6] Ibid., 103.

those whose mothers worked at home and with 98 for those whose mothers had not been gainfully employed."[7]

"The excess mortality among infants whose mothers were employed away from home was due in part to an unusual prevalence of artificial feeding. . . . When allowance was made for [income]. . . . There still remained an excess of mortality, due probably to lack of the care which only mothers who remained at home could give their babies."[8]

Income and Prenatal Care: "The infant mortality rates from all causes and from each principal cause of death were highest when the father's earnings were low and lowest when the father's earnings were relatively high."[9]

"After allowance was made for variations in order of birth, age of mother, and interval between births, the high correlation between infant mortality and father's earnings was still nearly as marked as before; *it could not therefore be attributed to association with unusual frequency of births* [emphasis added]. . . . Nor do other economic factors—housing congestion, employment of mother during pregnancy, and employment of mother during the infant's first year—account for all the relationship between low earnings of father and infant mortality, though they are responsible for it in part. . . . The intermediate factors . . . included . . . adequate care of the mother during pregnancy and confinement and the care of the infant's health during his first year. A close association was found to obtain between these factors and the father's earnings."[10]

Planned Parenthood also cited, or rather miscited, a U.S. Public Health Service survey of 258,500 births in New York state between 1936 and 1938 as further "proof" that a birth control program would reduce maternal deaths that show an increase after the fourth birth.[11] Yerushalmy, Palmer, and Kramer's study did show an uneven increase in maternal mortality after the fourth birth, but with a downturn in maternal mortality after the tenth child not mentioned by Planned Parenthood.[12] But that aside, again there is no mention of birth control in the study in any context, much less that it would reduce maternal mortality.

[7] Ibid., 7.

[8] Ibid., 8.

[9] Ibid.

[10] Ibid., 9.

[11] "A Memorandum on Planned Parenthood and the Nation's Population Situation", 6.

[12] Jacob Yerushalmy, Carroll E. Palmer, and Morton Kramer, "Studies in Childbirth Mortality: Age and Parity as Factors in Puerperal Fatality", Public Health Reports, vol. 55, no. 27, July 5, 1940. A total of 255,727 deliveries; 258,525 births; 251,348 live births; women who died from abortion, miscarriage, ectopic pregnancy, or who were undelivered were excluded. The complete mortality data are as follows:

Planned Parenthood further adduced a study by Nicholas Eastman, one of their own members, that suggested that birth control could reduce maternal and infant mortality. But Eastman only recommended it after a woman had had eight children, a qualification Planned Parenthood did not mention.[13]Eastman's real advice was far too conservative for Planned Parenthood. In 1940 only 4.5% of married women who were born from 1895 to 1899, and who were, therefore, at the end of their childbearing years, had nine or more children.[14] But Planned Parenthood could not be content with such a limited application of birth control, as that would never achieve the sexual and social revolution it sought.

Nor was Eastman content with Planned Parenthood's use of his study. In a later work, Eastman said that the 1925 Children's Bureau study was scholarly, highly influential, and had become the medical basis for birth control in America in spite of its failure to recommend any course of action, including birth control, to reduce infant mortality. But Eastman also observed that " . . . those interested in the furtherance of birth control were quick to see a remedy. . . . And forthwith the Woodbury [Children's Bureau] study became one of the cornerstones of the birth control movement and has remained so ever since."[15]

Eastman suggested that the twenty-eight-year-old [Children's Bureau] study might lack validity in light of intervening improvements in medical care. So he presented the results of his own study of 5,158 births at Johns Hopkins between September 1, 1936 and June 30, 1943. His conclusions, which contradicted Planned Parenthood's claim, were that:

Birth Order Puerperal Fatality (chart from p. 1198):

No. of children	Per 10,000 births
1	28.2
2	19.8
3	18.5
4	26.7
5	34.1
6 and 7	37.9
8 and 9	63.4
10 and over	44.2

[13] Nicholas J. Eastman, M.D., "The Hazards of Pregnancy and Labor in the 'Grande Multipara' ", New York State Journal of Medicine (December 1, 1940): 1712. Eastman's study of 45,514 conservative obstetric cases (no abortions included) had 191 maternal deaths, or 4.20 maternal deaths per 1000 births at Johns Hopkins Hospital from 1896 to 1939.

[14] Historical Statistics of the United States: Colonial Times to 1970, Series B 42–48, part 1, Washington D.C.: Government Printing Office, 53. 5.8% were listed as having seven to nine children; we assume that one third of this cohort had nine children and added this figure to the percentage having 10 or more.

[15] Child and Family, Oak Park, Ill., Fall 1969, 323–48, specific cite on 324. Reprint of Nicholas J. Eastman, M.D., "The Effect of the Interval between Births on Maternal and Fetal Outlook", American Journal of Obstetrics and Gynecology 47:445–66; read at a meeting of the Chicago Gynecology Society, November 19, 1943.

[1] Infants born from twelve to twenty-four months after a previous delivery . . . have at least as low a stillbirth and neonatal mortality as do infants born after longer intervals. [2] The longer the interval between births, the more likely the mother is to suffer from some form of hypertensive toxemia of pregnancy. The incidence of this complication is lowest when the interval is twelve to twenty-four months, significantly higher when it is twenty-four to forty-eight months, and much higher when it exceeds four years. . . . [3] In patients who have had a previous hypertensive toxemia of pregnancy, the likelihood of repetition become progressively greater as the interval becomes longer. [4] The incidence of the following conditions is no greater when the interval is twelve to twenty-four months than when it is longer: premature labor, anemia, postpartum hemorrhage, and puerperal infection; nor are mothers in this brief interval group less able to nurse their babies.[16]

Eastman stated that there were too few cases of subsequent pregnancies ended before twelve months of a previous birth to make any firm conclusions.[17] However, he did point out that only 35.8% of white patients giving birth within twelve months of a previous birth breast-fed their first child, as opposed to 66.3% of women giving birth after twelve months or more. Among black patients, only 27.0% breast-fed their first child before giving birth within twelve months, as opposed to 66.9% of women giving birth after twelve months or more.[18]

In summation, time between births was not the critical infant mortality factor; and rather than birth control, Eastman concluded that for infant and maternal health "youth is a better ally than child spacing".[19]

Planned Parenthood launched its counterattack within a year, but later authors have pointed out that Eastman's optimum interval of from twelve to twenty-four months has been reinforced, and not refuted.[20] Eastman's conclusion is all the more important because in 1943 he was the honorary president of Planned Parenthood.[21]

Proof or no proof, Planned Parenthood's message never changed, though its messengers would occasionally contradict it. Thus Dr. Alan Guttmacher wrote in 1956 that when a patient asks how many children one should have and what their spacing should be:

There is no pat answer, no precise formula. The physician can be certain [that] . . . youth is a respected ally of pregnancy and delivery. Second, no

[16] Ibid., 342.

[17] Ibid.

[18] Ibid., 336.

[19] Ibid., 343.

[20] Ibid., 347, citing J. Yerushalmy, "The Existence of an Optimum Interval between Births", *Human Fertility,* 10 (1945): 107–11.

[21] Ibid., 348.

physical harm has been proved to result from having children close together. Third, both great parity and a woman's relatively advanced reproductive age penalize the efficiency and safety of childbirth.[22]

In the same book he listed thirteen reasons why childbirth had become very safe in America in the late 1950s. Birth control was not one of them.[23]

Guttmacher would later tell attendees at a 1964 PPFA Board and Affiliate meeting that many of Planned Parenthood's fundamental arguments "are still based on logical hypotheses rather than proved facts".[24] Among them he included the "birth control improves maternal health" argument.[25]

Even today the more candid proponents of birth control acknowledge that "little is known about the effect of birth spacing on maternal mortality . . . ".[26] Take, for example, a public health program sponsored by Bangladesh that sought to measure the effect of birth control on maternal mortality. While the birth control program led to a 25% decline in births, it did "not appear to have substantially altered the mortality risks associated with pregnancy and childbearing . . . ".[27] This birth control program led to a shift in childbearing patterns, away from the older, high-parity woman, "but toward another subgroup with equivalent or even higher mortality risks (younger, nulliparous women)".[28]

Thus birth control of a type that is not inherently more dangerous than pregnancy and childbirth may reduce the maternal mortality ratio (maternal deaths/live births × 100,000) but "only to the extent that it reduces the proportion of pregnancies to high-risk women".[29] Finally, some of

[22] Alan F. Guttmacher, M.D., *Pregnancy and Birth,* 17th printing (Signet Books, 1956, 1962), 227.

[23] Ibid., 79–80. His list included more hospital births, elimination of the "granny" midwife, greater attendance of obstetric M.D. specialists, better prenatal care, more widespread use of antibiotics and chemotherapy to overcome or prevent infection, availability of blood transfusion to correct anemia and for hemorrhages, anesthesia, improved obstetrical teaching, professional societies and maternal mortality committees, and greater X ray use.

[24] PPWP, "Thoughts on Our Program for the Mid-Sixties", remarks at Affiliate and Board Meeting, January 24–25, 1964, 2–3, SSCSC.

[25] Ibid.

[26] James Trussell and Anne R. Pebley, "The Potential Impact of Changes in Fertility on Infant, Child, and Maternal Mortality", *Studies in Family Planning,* vol. 15, no. 6 (November–December 1984): 267–80.

[27] Michael A. Keonig, Ph.D. et al., "Maternal Mortality in Matlab, Bangladesh: 1976–85", *Studies in Family Planning,* vol. 19, no. 2 (March–April 1988): 69–80.

[28] Ibid.

[29] Judith A. Fortney, "The Importance of Family Planning in Reducing Maternal Mortality", *Studies in Family Planning,* vol. 18, no. 2 (March–April 1987): 109–14.

the underlying causes of maternal mortality may predate the onset of pregnancy.[30] Manifestly, this will not be corrected or even altered by birth control.

PREGNANCY AND CHILDBIRTH ARE POSITIVELY DANGEROUS TO THE MOTHER'S HEALTH

The inability to prove that maternal health would be improved by birth control did not stop Planned Parenthood from adding yet another claim to their list, that pregnancy and childbirth were themselves a menace to women's health. Sanger told the audience at a 1953 International Planned Parenthood gathering that "records" indicated that in 1912 and 1913 about 250,000 mothers died from causes related to pregnancy in the United States.[31] Her phrasing was a little imprecise, but under any analysis of the real data her figures were completely fantastic. The official public health records show 13,750 women dying from causes associated with maternity in 1912; and 15,000 women dying from causes associated with maternity in 1913.[32]

But such fantastic claims are not merely things of the past. Sanger's whopping error is kept alive in a recent Planned Parenthood fund-raising epistle. Dr. Hakim-Elahi, medical director for Planned Parenthood of New York City, opines that: "After a century of progress for family planning, America is at a crossroads. Some people want us to return to the way things were a hundred

---

[30] Halfdan Mahler, director general, United Nations Food and Agriculture Organization (UNFAO), World Health Organization (WHO), World Bank (WB), sponsored Safe Motherhood Initiative, "The Safe Motherhood Initiative: A Call to Action", *The Lancet* (Mar. 1987), 668–70.

[31] Fourth International Conference on Planned Parenthood, Stockholm, 1953, "The History of the Birth Control Movement in the English Speaking World", unedited translation from Sound-Mirror, by Margaret Sanger, 6, SSCSC.

[32] *Historical Statistics of the United States, Colonial Times to 1970*, part 1, U.S. Department of Commerce, Bureau of the Census, House document no. 93–78, pt 1, 93d Cong., 1st sess., series A 29–42 for population data; *Vital Statistics Rates in the United States, 1940–1960*, PHS pub. no. 1677, U.S. Department of Health, Education and Welfare, table 65, death rates for detailed causes, death-registration states, 1900–1932, p. 569 for puerperal figures; for 1912 the death rate associated with the puerperal state was 144.4 per 1,000,000 population per death-registration states with the resident U.S. population at mid year of 95,335,000; for 1913 the death rate associated with the puerperal state was 154.4 per 1,000,000 population per death-registration states with the resident U.S. population at mid year of 97,225,000.

years ago. The days when . . . the leading cause of death among women was pregnancy and childbirth . . . ".[33]

While the U.S. mortality data for 1890 are not available to the authors, the official records for 1890 from at least one state, Massachusetts, show that Hakim-Elahi is wrong.[34]

There were a total of 6,283 deaths to females aged fifteen to fifty in Massachusetts during 1890. Of these, 261 were related to childbirth or pregnancy: abortion, 5; childbirth, 147; miscarriage, 21; puerperal convulsions, 25; puerperal fever, 63. Thus, 4.15% of all deaths to childbearing-aged women in Massachusetts a century ago were related to pregnancy and childbirth. The following table provides more detail:

Cause	No. of Deaths to Females Age 15–50	% of Total Deaths to Females Age 15–50
Pregnancy, etc.	261	4.15%
Typhoid Fever	264	4.20%
Pneumonia	565	8.99%
Heart Disease	487	7.75%
Phthisis (Lung Consumption)	2300	42.87%
Nervous System Diseases (all)	432	6.88%
Urinary Organs	300	5.02%

Furthermore, cause-of-death data for 1900 for all of the states that registered deaths in the United States at that time also show that the leading cause of death for women at the turn of the century was not childbirth and pregnancy. There were a number of causes of death to women much higher than the maternal death rate, and several that were just below. In addition, the maternal mortality rate cited below for 1900 represents all maternal deaths from childbirth, pregnancy, and the puerperal state, including abortion.[35]

---

[33] Planned Parenthood of New York City fundraising letter, "A Century of Progress in Peril", referencing the October 21, 1989, veto of an abortion funding bill by President Bush. Received during the winter of 1989, with attachments.

[34] *Forty-Ninth Report to the Legislature of Massachusetts Relating to the Registry and Return of Births, Marriages, and Deaths in the Commonwealth,* for the year ending December 31, 1890, etc., Boston, Wright & Potter Printing Co., state printers, Public Doc. no. 1, 1891, table 11, 72–91.

[35] Forrest E. Linder and Robert D. Grove, *Vital Statistics Rates in the United States, 1900–1940, Sixteenth Census of the United States: 1940,* U.S. Department of Commerce, (Washington, D.C.: U.S. Government Printing Office, 1943), table 15, 258–64.

Cause of Death: United States, 1900 All Females:	
Cause	*No. of Deaths per 100,000*
Maternity	26.9
Typhoid and Paratyphoid Fever	26.6
Diphtheria	39.9
Tuberculosis (all forms)	168.8
Cancer, other malignant tumors	90.9
Intracranial Vascular Lesions	107.7
Heart Disease	133.7
Bronchitis	47.2
Pneumonia (all forms)	198.5
Nephritis (all forms)	81.0
Diarrhea, Enteritis, Ulceration of the Intestines	134.9
Senility	56.3

In conclusion, if the most elementary of Planned Parenthood's historical claims can be refuted by mere recourse to the public record, what possible credence can be given to their claims when they control access to the records and what will be reported, as they do today with much of the clinical data on abortion?

All Forms of Birth Control Are Safer for Women than Pregnancy and Childbirth

The final major fabrication that Planned Parenthood has foisted on the American public is that any form of birth control is safer and healthier than pregnancy and/or childbirth. The philosophical foundation of this perspective is often missed: that the creations of the created are more perfect, wonderful, and sure in their operation than those of the Creator. Never mind the incredible hubris here—the implication that a few human beings have, with all their assorted jams, coils, caps, pills, and surgical invasions, exceeded the contemplation, design, and operation of the human body as prescribed by the Architect of Nature.

Planned Parenthood won the U.S. government's seal of approval on this thesis by including in the pages of its own journal an article from Dr. Howard Ory, then deputy director of the Division of Reproductive Health at the Centers for Disease Control (CDC, part of USPHS). Ory claimed that the mortality rate for any birth control method, including sterilization and induced abortion, was lower than the risk of death from "childbirth and ectopic pregnancy when no fertility control method is used".[36] The only exceptions

[36] Howard W. Ory, M.D., "Mortality Associated with Fertility and Fertility Control: 1983", *Family Planning Perspectives,* vol. 15, no. 2 (March–April 1983), reprinted by the U.S. Public Health Service.

to this finding were nonsmoking Pill users over forty and Pill users thirty-five and over who smoked.[37]

Ory was not reporting on a case-by-case national survey of causes of death that have been verified by autopsy. His article was based on estimates of what should happen if his assumptions were correct.

What are those assumptions? Using British data on complications, Ory assumed that American women would not be given the Pill if they had diabetes, hypertension, or certain other cardiovascular impairments. He then proceeded to reduce by one-third the potential mortality attributable to such diseases in combination with Pill usage. Traffic officials using Ory's reasoning could, by a stroke of the pen, eliminate a like number of deaths attributable to speeding because drivers are not supposed to speed.

Dr. Fred E. Mecklenberg has noted that in the United States the Pill is used by varying groups of women, some of whom are diabetics, are prone to hypertension and coronary heart disease or, lastly, are smokers.[38] Additionally, recently developed data from the second National Health and Nutrition Examination survey showed that 44% of women on oral contraceptives smoked. Also, that one in seven users of oral contraceptives in the late 1970s had at least two of the three main cardiovascular risk factors.[39]

The second of Ory's "qualifications" was to limit abortion mortality to the published rate for first trimester abortions only. Figures published by CDC claim an abortion maternal mortality rate of 0.98/100,000 legally induced, first-trimester abortions performed from 1972 through 1980. Abortion mortality for 13- to 15-week abortions for the same time period is 4.80/100,000 abortions; 12.80/100,000 for 16- to 20-week abortions; and 15.30/100,000 for ≥21-week abortions. Approximately 8.5 to 10% of all abortions in the United States are performed past the first trimester.[40]

Third, Ory used a cumulative figure for mortality calculations because it enabled him to include some of the alleged health benefits of the Pill. For example, Ory claimed that the Pill "protects" women from ovarian and endometrial cancer and that the "protection" lasts until age fifty-four.[41]

Fourth, Ory did not include deaths from sterilization in his cumulative figures, apparently because he lacked data to make them age specific. Yet he did claim that sterilization, along with other fertility control methods, is safer than childbirth. The reported non–age specific mortality rate for female

[37] Ibid.

[38] *Family Practice News,* May 15–31, 1985.

[39] *Obstetric Gynecologic News,* June 1–14, 1985.

[40] *Statistical Abstract of the United States: 1988,* U.S. Department of Commerce, Bureau of the Census, table 105, "Legal Abortions by Selected Characteristics", 70.

[41] Ory, "Mortality Associated".

sterilization is 4/100,000, which we will include in our adjustments of Ory's claims.[42]

Fifth, he included death from ectopic pregnancy in the maternal death category. Yet CDC has identified ten deaths caused by ruptured ectopic pregnancies after attempted legal abortion.[43] In spite of this, or perhaps because of it, CDC altered its previous abortion-related death classification to exclude deaths to women having ectopic pregnancies and undergoing induced abortions.[44,45,46]

Sixth, Ory "adjusted" the deaths attributed to maternal mortality by increasing them one-third because, he claimed, nonabortion maternal deaths were underreported by that much nationwide. Support for his "increase-and-multiply thesis" came from Willard Cates and other abortion advocates at CDC.[47] Yet Cates and colleagues, in turn, base their one-third underreporting hypothesis on two articles. One deals with the accuracy of reported deaths in New Jersey. The other one concerns childbearing in Georgia.[48] Cates concluded that these two articles "probably reflect what is happening in other areas". An extrapolation from two to fifty states certainly is a leap of faith, if not of science.

But what Cates, and Ory as well, did not tell the reader is that an expanded definition of maternal death was used in the Georgia article. For example, the Georgia Vital Records Unit classified maternal deaths as "those deaths resulting from complications of pregnancy, childbirth, or the puerperium" [usually three to six weeks after birth]. However, Rubin et al. employed the more expansive maternal death definition used by the World Health Organization, i.e., "the death of a woman while pregnant or within 42 days of the termination of pregnancy, from any cause related to or aggravated by the pregnancy or its management, but not accidental or incidental causes".[49] Rubin also included deaths up to 189 days after delivery that were believed to be related to childbirth.[50] Increasing from 42 to 189 the number of days a death is

[42] Jordan M. Phillips, "Female Sterilization by Laparoscopy: The State of the Art", in *The Safety of Fertility Control,* ed. Louis G. Keith (New York: Springer, c. 1980), 234.

[43] George L. Rubin et al., "Fatal Ectopic Pregnancy after Attempted Legally Induced Abortion" *Journal of the American Medical Association,* vol. 244, no. 15(October 10, 1980), 1705.

[44] U.S. Centers for Disease Control, *Abortion Surveillance Report for 1978,* issued November 1980, 7–9.

[45] Ibid., issued May 1980, 9.

[46] *Administrative Guidelines for Investigating Abortion Deaths,* U.S. Centers for Disease Control, Abortion Surveillance Branch, September 1981, 1.

[47] Willard Cates, M.D., et al., "Mortality from Abortion and Childbirth: Are the Statistics Biased?", *Journal of the American Medical Association,* vol. 248, no. 2 (July 9, 1982): 194.

[48] George Rubin et al., "The Risk of Childbearing Reevaluated", *American Journal of Public Health,* vol. 71 (1981): 712–16.

[49] Ibid.

[50] Ibid.

attributed to childbirth would of course, "expand" that risk. (Would these authors have done the same for abortion or birth control deaths?)

Seventh, Ory lumped all childbearing women, of whatever underlying health status (i.e., diabetes, renal failure, multi gravida women, poor women, women who smoke, etc.), into a single category, unlike his statistical division of women on the Pill into smoking and nonsmoking groups, with correspondingly different mortality rates.[51]

Eighth, his statistical model assumed that all women began sexual intercourse at age fifteen.[52] Even with today's liberal sexual standards that is not the case. In fact, a 1986 study by Marsiglio and Mott reported that by their fifteenth birthday, 6.6% of American teenaged girls had experienced intercourse. Ory also picked pregnancy rates for older, married contraceptive users that are at the low end of the spectrum, and then applied these low rates to all women. Using this technique, for teens at least, he could postulate even higher maternal mortality rates and lower mortality rates from birth control use, especially the Pill and IUD. Yet Ory most certainly knew that the major risk factor from childbirth for teens is their social situation, not their biological maturity. This is not mentioned, however, in his analysis.[53]

Ninth, he very neatly contrasted all deaths resulting from or related to childbirth with a single method of fertility control.[54] But, as Ory's dichotomy was having sexual intercourse and children or having sexual intercourse and no children, he should instead have contrasted the mortality from all methods of child avoidance with the mortality from having children. That he did not do. Had he done so, it would not merely weaken his point, it would literally have destroyed it.

With that in mind, let us take Ory's mortality figures for all methods of birth control, add the sterilization deaths that he omits, and reduce maternal deaths by one-third to eliminate Ory's unjustified increase.

Contrasting pregnancy and childbirth with pregnancy avoidance or induced abortion and making no other adjustments as noted above, we arrive at figures which differ from Ory's conclusion (see table on page 199).

No other adjustments have been made in these computations as could have been done, with justice, in the following areas: restoring ectopic pregnancy deaths resulting from legal abortion but attributed to maternal mortality; figuring in second-trimester abortion death rates for all ages, in particular teens who have a higher percentage of such abortions than older women;

[51] Ory, "Mortality Associated".
[52] Ibid.
[53] Ibid.
[54] Ibid.

| | Maternal Ages | | | | | |
	15–19	*20–24*	*25–29*	*30–34*	*35–39*	*40–44*
Ory's "adjusted" pregnancy and childbirth deaths/100,000	12.9	12.0	15.3	26.5	53.9	89.1
Reduce by one-third pregnancy and childbirth mortality	8.6	8.0	10.25	17.75	36.1	59.7
Add sterilization deaths (4/100,000)	7.8	9.5	13.5	21.9	72.0	155.9
Mortality from all fertility control methods	3.8	5.5	9.5	17.9	68.0	151.9

increasing the death rate from Pill mortality to account for those deaths eliminated by Ory because of his erroneous assumptions about diabetes, etc.; and finding a more realistic age for onset of sexual intercourse.

Surgical Abortion Is "Safer" than Childbirth or, Killing Children Is Safer than Having Them

The American College of Obstetricians and Gynecologists (ACOG), as part of a new abortion "white paper" prepared for the enlightenment of the nation's state and federal legislators, cites a Planned Parenthood study to the effect that a "1989 study of 170,000 abortions performed by physicians at three New York City clinics showed it to be an extremely safe procedure. No deaths were reported. The most common complication, mild infection (in one out of every 216 cases), was treated with antibiotics at the clinics. There was no fertility loss."[55]

At the date of the ACOG publication, the referenced Planned Parenthood study had not been published. Nor was it available from the ACOG except in a one-page, three-paragraph clinical abstract.[56]

While the printed Planned Parenthood abstract does not make the claim, though it possibly was made during a Planned Parenthood presentation at the ACOG convention, ACOG nevertheless reports that "there was no loss of fertility" from 170,000 elective abortions. This is an interesting assertion, since

[55] Kathryn G. Moore, ed., *Public Health Policy Implications of Abortion: A Government Relations Handbook,* copyright American College of Obstetricians and Gynecologists, 1990, 9. (Published on behalf of the Health Professionals Coalition on Reproductive Health consisting of the following organizations which have provided information: American College of Obstetricians and Gynecologists; American Fertility Society; American Medical Association; American Medical Student Association; American Medical Women's Association; American Nurses' Association; American Psychiatric Association; The Organization of Obstetric, Gynecologic, and Neonatal Nurses; National Association of Nurse Practitioners in Reproductive Health; National Student Nurses' Association.)

[56] E. Hakim-Elahi, M.D., and Harold M. M. Tovell, M.D., "Complications of First-Trimester Abortion: A Report of 170,000 Cases", clinical abstract presented at the ACOG Annual Clinical Meeting, May 1989; one-page summary from ACOG.

there are several difficulties, such as the following, that impede collecting this and other types of data to accurately measure abortion morbidity/mortality sequelae.

Planned Parenthood's follow-up procedures are limited to immediate or short-term postabortion complications, and they do not include verifying postabortion childbearing capabilities. Moreover, a majority of Planned Parenthood's abortion clients accept contraception that is offered as part of the abortion service.[57] How was the return of their fertility verified? Additionally, an acknowledged 54% of the abortion patients at the Planned Parenthood centers comprising the "study" did not return to the Planned Parenthood of New York Center (PPNYC) for a postabortion examination. How fertility loss could be measured in these supposed 54% of 170,000, or 91,800, cases is not stated. Nor is there any explanation how long women who had undergone abortion were ostensibly "followed" to ensure that their fertility returned to normal. Did the "no loss of fertility" simply mean the return of menstruation, however irregular, or did it mean successful childbirth?

Also, the Planned Parenthood medical "follow-up" can be done by phone or mail, as requested by the patient.[58] Thus, it must be asked if the "data" thus collected are derived from the patients' own self-reporting or are they, in any clinical sense of the term, physician verified? And note the following: "Patients who come to the PPNYC centers with severe post-abortal bleeding are referred directly to the back-up hospital."[59] As will be seen below, when Planned Parenthood's patients go to a hospital, they are no longer Planned Parenthood's responsibility. It is unlikely that Planned Parenthood lists complications to patients no longer their own.

There are two potentially large classes of Planned Parenthood patients who may not even have been solicited by mail or phone for medical sequelae, and who were not considered "lost-to-follow-up". The initial group consists of women who refused to be contacted postabortion. At PPNYC, "If a patient has asked not to be contacted, her choice must be respected".[60] The other group consists of all those women who leave the Planned Parenthood clinic before the recommended three-hour, postabortion recovery period. This rate may be as high as 75% of all women undergoing abortion, as was reported during a PPNYC conference workshop on abortion in 1972.[61] Women are

[57] Ibid.

[58] *Workbook of the First National Affiliate Workshop of Planning and Providing Abortion Services,* prepared by PPWP and PPNYC, foreword by Susan Dickler, director, National Pregnancy and Abortion Services; Jerim Klaper, PPNYC, April 1973, conference held in September 1972, NYC-11, 13.

[59] Ibid., A/G 26.

[60] Ibid., A/G, 27.

[61] Ibid., WS-4.

required to sign a "hold harmless" agreement with PPNYC.[62] Complications Planned Parenthood denies any responsibility for might not be reported as part of Planned Parenthood's abortion complications. While "hold harmless" agreements are routine in some areas of medical practice, if abortion is as safe as PP claims, and safer than the pregnant condition in which the woman came in, why would PP insist on a "hold harmless" form at all?

There are further problems with follow-up. At a 1971 Planned Parenthood–sponsored abortion conference, several speakers either objected to follow-up as an invasion of privacy or said it was too difficult and costly. Their reasons were not limited to the issue of interstate travel for abortions *ante Roe.* For example:

> Adequate follow-up of abortion patients obviously presents special problems because of the exquisite sensitivity of many abortion patients with respect to their pregnancy and its termination [Dr. R. T. Ravenholt (Agency for International Development, Washington, D.C.)].[63]
>
> One of my objectives in life is to have this procedure regarded no differently than any other gynecological surgery.... I don't like to see these patients set aside and subjected to close questioning. Let's just treat them ... without invasion of their privacy [Dr. Allan C. Barnes].[64]
>
> Dr. Schwartz and I attempted to follow-up a number of patients post partum.... We were unable with the best techniques available to us, in association with Planned Parenthood, to find better than 50 percent of the Harlem group we attempted to locate. It cost between $200 and $300 a case to locate the ones that we did find.... In general, you cannot do this even if you wanted to, and I don't think we should anyway [Dr. Elizabeth B. Connell].[65]

In light of Planned Parenthood's conditions and finesses, what can we say is the real percentage lost to follow-up, and how many women really had complications?

As already mentioned, the Planned Parenthood abstract on behalf of "safe and legal" abortion claims that there "were no mortalities among the 170,000 charts reviewed".[66] While this claim might technically be

---

[62] Ibid., PC-12, e.g., see PPNYC Abortion Record: "This certifies that I, [*Name*], am leaving the [*Name*] Planned Parenthood Center, against the advice of the physician/surgeon in charge of my case, and hereby agree not to hold the physician/surgeon or Planned Parenthood of New York City, Inc., or any of its personnel responsible for any harm or injury that may result from my unauthorized departure."

[63] *Abortion Techniques and Services: Proceedings of the Conference,* N.Y., N.Y., June 3–5, 1971, sponsored by the American Medical Women's Association, APHA, ASA, Natl. Med. Assoc., PPWP, ed. Sarah Lewit, *Excerpta Medica,* 1972, 28.

[64] Ibid., 29.

[65] Ibid.

[66] Hakim-Elahi and Tovell, "Complications of First-Trimester Abortion".

true, women could nevertheless have died after undergoing an abortion at PPNYC.

First, a review of *charts* prepared monthly is not the same as a review of all *patients* undergoing abortion. Second, whatever the real extent of loss to follow-up is, PPNYC admits at least 8%, or 13,600, women not contacted.[67] Third, at the New York Planned Parenthood affiliate, women who undergo abortions and are referred to Planned Parenthood's backup hospital because of an emergency are no longer considered to be Planned Parenthood patients.[68] Fourth, PPNYC representatives have expressed an unwillingness to be completely forthcoming about "inside" information that might be the occasion of controversy. This was made apparent in a PPNYC abortion workshop where prospective abortion clinic operators were told that they would have "to deal with . . . people in the community . . . that you want to have know what you're doing . . . and the ones you really don't want to have know what you're doing at all."[69]

A fifth reason that might be operative here, and that may be gleaned from the meager ACOG abstract, is that "[t]he eligibility of patients undergoing abortion has been strictly enforced so that no person with major medical problems undergoes abortion in the clinic".[70] At the PPNYC clinics, a pregnant woman was considered medically *ineligible* for elective abortion who

> has severe *anemia* . . . symptomatic asthma . . . is taking anti-asthmatic drugs . . . has had more than one *Cesarean section* . . . heart disease or has had *cardiac* surgery . . . is being treated for diabetes . . . a history of epilepsy . . . wants or requires *general anesthesia* . . . has *hypertension* . . . been hospitalized for *mental illness* . . . is being treated for any serious medical illness.[71]

Lastly, Dr. E. Hakim-Elahi, who co-authored the cited ACOG report, has shown elsewhere that certain of his claims cannot be supported by objective, readily available data. For example, as PPNYC's medical director, Dr. Hakim-Elahi has stated:

> I lived through the days of illegal abortion in New York State. . . . In 1961, I began my Ob/Gyn residency at Queens General, a city hospital serving low-

---

[67] Ibid.

[68] *Workbook of the First National Affiliate Workshop,* HA-1; see January 11, 1973, Agreement between Planned Parenthood of New York City, Inc. and the New York Hospital: "1. The Hospital will accept all referrals from PPNYC for emergency treatment where such emergencies arise out of procedures administered by PPNYC to its patients. . . . Upon such admission of such a patient to the Hospital's emergency service, the patient shall thereupon become a patient of the Hospital. The Hospital will have responsibility for all subsequent treatment and medical management of the patient."

[69] *Workbook of the First National Affiliate Workshop,* NYC-6.

[70] Hakim-Elahi and Tovell, "Complications of First-Trimester Abortion".

[71] *Workbook of the First National Affiliate Workshop,* A/G 2–3.

income areas of Queens. . . . *When it was illegal for a woman to end a pregnancy, one out of every 40 women who had abortions died. Today the death rate is one in 400,000. At Planned Parenthood's three clinics in New York City, we've done 170,000 abortions in the past 18 years. Not one woman has died* [emphasis added].[72]

Hakim-Elahi's claim that 1 in 40 women died from illegal abortion is even more fantastic when contrasted to known deaths for females from all causes and the numbers of women said to have had illegal abortions. This latter figure is said to range from 600,000 to 1.2 million women per year in the 1960s, according to Planned Parenthood's president, Faye Wattleton, who repeated these figures before the 1990 American Bar Association annual meeting.[73] So the number of women allegedly dying per year from illegal abortion in the United States, at the ratio of one to forty, was at least 15,000 if there were 600,000 illegal abortions, and possibly 30,000 for 1.2 million illegal abortions. A minor problem with this claim is that it virtually crowds out deaths to females of childbearing age from all other causes. For example, in the United States during 1965, there was a total of 50,456 deaths to women aged fifteen to forty-four.[74] What Hakim-Elahi with his rates and Wattleton with her figures would have us believe is that 29.7 to 59.4% of all deaths to females aged fifteen to forty-four in the United States were caused by illegal abortion. This is simply not believable.

Using Hakim-Elahi's rates and Wattleton's figures for black abortions and black abortion deaths produces a complete absurdity. Wattleton said that during the 1960s the majority of women having abortions were "my poor, African-American sisters". The numbers of black women dying aged fifteen to forty-four in 1965 was 13,056. Using Wattleton's unspecific claim, black women must have had at least 51% of all abortions. Applying this figure to Hakim-Elahi's death rate would yield a minimum of 7,650 abortion deaths for black women, or 58.6% of all deaths among black females aged fifteen to forty-four. If Wattleton's higher abortion figure is the correct one, then 15,300 black women aged fifteen to forty-four died from illegal abortion, or, almost 2,000 more black women than died from all causes in that age bracket during 1965.

Lastly, it is questionable whether, on medical grounds, induced abortion has improved public health.

With the introduction of abortion on demand, no significant change has been detected in the maternal mortality rate which could be attributed to legal abortion.

[72] Planned Parenthood of New York City fundraising letter, "A Century of Progress in Peril", referencing the October 21, 1989, veto of an abortion funding bill by President Bush received during the winter of 1989 (with attachments).

[73] *Washington Post,* February 14, 1990.

[74] *Vital Statistics of the United States for 1965,* mortality table 7-3, 7–78.

Beginning in 1973, the year of the Supreme Court decision on abortion, there was a stabilization or plateau in the number of maternal deaths related to abortion (all causes). No such plateau was observed for nonabortion related maternal deaths.

In spite of a legal abortion policy . . . maternal deaths related to illegal abortion have not been eliminated.

In analyzing the trend in maternal deaths due to induced abortion, it has been shown that while maternal deaths stemming from criminal abortion appear to be decreasing, they have been replaced, almost one for one, by maternal deaths due to legal abortion. The results of this study indicate that there has been no significant impact on the relative frequency of abortion related maternal deaths due to induced abortion since the legalization of abortion.[75]

Chemical Abortion Will Help Third World Women

Old habits die hard. The "pregnancy is not as safe as man-made substitutes" apothegm has also been applied to newly developed killing technologies such as the experimental French abortion pill RU-486. The lethal RU-486 antichild pill, which geneticist Jerome LeJeune has labeled the first "human pesticide", is an antiprogesterone steroid developed in France by Etienne-Emile Baulieu of the pharmaceutical firm Roussel-Uclaf. It is used in combination with a prostaglandin to induce abortion up to forty-nine days from the last menstrual period. This combination of drugs has a "kill" ratio of 95%. Proponents of RU-486, Planned Parenthood among them, want to make this drug widely available in Third World countries.

Once more the Planned Parenthood public relations machinery of "safety" swung into high gear. A news report about RU-486 in the nation's paper of record, the New York Times, gives the flavor: "Family planning experts said evidence indicated that when used in the first trimester the drug was safer than surgical abortion, as well as less expensive".[76] Dr. Louise Tyrer of Planned Parenthood said that "it's really quite a benign medication".[77] Pramilla Senanayake of the IPPF claims that: "Abortion related morbidity and mortality are frequently the most significant factors for women in developing

---

[75] Thomas W. Hilgers M.D., and Dennis O'Hare, "Abortion Related Maternal Mortality: An In-Depth Analysis", New Perspectives on Human Abortion, ed. Thomas W. Hilgers, et al. (Hyattsville, Md.: University Publications of America, c. 1981), 90.

[76] Gina Kolata, "France and China Allow Sale of a Drug for Early Abortion", New York Times, September 24, 1988.

[77] Ibid.

countries."[78] Up to 50% of all estimated maternal deaths or 250,000 women are said to die yearly from illegal abortion in developing nations.[79] Supplying women with RU-486 will allegedly cut these deaths.

Unfortunately for the proponents of global distribution of RU-486, intensive surveys of actual maternal deaths in poorer nations do not support these claims. In a rural Egyptian province, a survey of physicians, surviving family members, and the vital registration system identified 437 maternal deaths. Of these just 17, or 3.8%, were caused by induced abortion, both legal and illegal.[80] Even in one of the world's poorest nations—Bangladesh—another intensive survey of maternal deaths, in the Matlab health service area for the period 1976 to 1986, showed that 15.2% of maternal deaths were attributable to all induced abortions, whether legal or illegal.[81] Both of these figures are a far cry from the soaring illegal abortion death ratio claimed by RU-486 supporters.

Furthermore, maternal mortality and abortion deaths are not known with any great reliability in developing nations. Newspaper headline estimates of maternal lives allegedly salvageable by RU-486 abortions cannot be substantiated. The World Health Organization (WHO) estimates that 500,000 women die annually in developing nations from complications of pregnancy, abortion, and childbirth. "However, national estimates of maternal mortality in most developing nations are based on limited and defective data. Data bases are incomplete or inaccurate in many developing countries and no improvement can be envisioned in the near future."[82]

"Only a few countries report annual maternal mortality rates. In general, African and Asian countries publish statistics about the age, sex, and cause of death for only 10% of their population. Only half of the Latin American countries have reliable statistics."[83] In the Middle East, with the exception of Israel, none of the maternal mortality rates for countries "are based on accurate registration and certification of cause of death. All proceed from surveys or other estimates."[84] Therefore, conjecture aside,

[78] Pramilla Senanayake, "Politics of Contraception" in *Future Aspects in Contraception: Proceedings of an International Symposium Held in Heidelberg, September 5–9, 1984*, ed. B. Runnebaun, Thomas Rabe and L. Klesel (Boston: M&P Press, 1985), 354.

[79] Mahler, "The Safe Motherhood Initiative", 668–70.

[80] S. Gadalla, Ph.D., et al., "Maternal Mortality in Egypt", *Journal of Tropical Pediatrics*, vol. 33, supp. 4 (1987): 11–13.

[81] Koenig et al., "Maternal Mortality in Matlab, Bangladesh", 69–80.

[82] J. Tiers Boerma, M.A., M.D., associate regional advisor, UNICEF/WHO, "Levels of Maternal Mortality in Developing Countries", *Studies in Family Planning*, vol. 18, no. 4 (July–August 1987): 213–21.

[83] Ulf Hogberg and Stig Wall, "Secular Trends in Maternal Mortality in Sweden from 1750 to 1980", *Bulletin of the World Health Organization*, vol. 64, no. 1 (1986): 79–84.

[84] Robert Cook, "Current Knowledge and Future Trends in Maternal and Child Health

No one knows exactly how many women die each year as a result of becoming pregnant. Most of those who die are poor, live in remote areas and their deaths are accorded little importance. In those parts of the world where maternal mortality is highest, deaths are rarely recorded and even if they are, the cause of death is usually not given.[85]

How can Planned Parenthood's "facts" be so far from reality, and yet receive so little criticism from the major media? Has government censorship produced this situation? Obviously not. Have medical or other research libraries been closed to the press and the public? Not really, though we have noticed that some material relevant to the history of Planned Parenthood in the United States has been removed from the U.S. Public Health Service's National Library of Medicine in the past few years.[86]

Where does Planned Parenthood get the teflon coating for its studies? Why do the nation's print and electronic media, which can find cost overruns in the Pentagon procurement process, count the number of shoes in Imelda Marcos' closet, and maintain an ocean of celebrity trivia, apparently have virtually infinite credulity when it comes to assessing objectively anything dealing with human sexuality?

One answer might be the personal biases of those in the journalism profession. A survey of the views of 238 journalists, the media elite so to speak, from the *Washington Post, New York Times, Time, Newsweek, U.S. News and World Report,* the *Wall Street Journal,* and the news organizations at ABC, NBC, CBS, and PBS during 1979 to 1980, disclosed the following

---

in the Middle East", Family Health Division, World Health Organization, *Journal of Tropical Pediatrics,* vol. 33, supp. 4 (1987): 3–10.

[85] Erica Royston and Alan D. Lopez, "On the Assessment of Maternal Mortality", *World Health Statistics Quarterly* 40 (1987): 214–24.

[86] The author [RGM] has been using the National Library of Medicine since at least 1970. After the introduction of the computer instead of 3" × 5" card catalogue hard file public access, the author noticed with increasing frequency a curiosity about Planned Parenthood file searches. Many of the items of historical interest previously catalogued, whereby earlier policies could be verified, were listed as "No longer in the NLM collection". Inquiries revealed that the items were not stolen. No other information was available.

The American Medical Association has implemented a similar policy regarding the published collections of its past actions and official policies, etc. I have tried, unsuccessfully, to purchase volume I of the published *AMA Digest of Official Actions,* which lists its prior position against abortion and birth control. A lawyer in the Chicago office of the AMA indicated it was no longer available, the reason being that it would "confuse" the public. Without this finding aid, researchers are faced with reading the many volumes of official transactions to find records of these past pro-life policies, which is no easy task.

about their attitudes concerning a cluster of issues relevant to Planned Parenthood and its mission:[87]

- 97% agreed that government should not regulate sex
- 90% agreed that a woman had a right to an abortion
- only 25% said homosexuality is wrong
- only 19% said that environmental problems are overstated

When the next generation of journalists was surveyed—the 1982 degree candidates at the Columbia School of Journalism—even more liberal attitudes were prevalent:[88]

- 93% agreed that government should not regulate sex
- 96% agreed that a woman had a right to an abortion
- only 18% said homosexuality is wrong
- only 14% said that environmental problems are overstated

American humorist Will Rogers once said that most people only know what they read in the newspapers. Today he would have added TV—or maybe substituted it for newspapers altogether. The current set of media biases gives a decided advantage to Planned Parenthood in the great cultural war now taking place between the normative tradition of right and wrong and what we would call the "wilderness of secular relativism".

Abortion Deaths and Morbidity Unknown and Unknowable

Abortion-related deaths are only the proverbial tip of the iceberg. *Nationwide information on the incidence of nonfatal complications of legal abortions, including major complications requiring inpatient care, is far less complete than information on abortion-related mortality. This is so because there is no agreement among investigators as to what constitutes a major complication, and no system of survelliance is in place* [emphasis added].[89]

This was the authoritative assessment of Dr. Christopher Tietze of Planned Parenthood, in a book assessing the U.S. abortion experience from 1973 to 1980. Even more recently, Surgeon General C. Everett Koop noted that

---

[87] S. Robert Lichter, Stanley Rothman, and Linda S. Lichter, *The Media Elite* (Bethesda, Md.: Adler and Adler Publishers, 1986), 29.

[88] Ibid., 47.

[89] Christopher Tietze, M.D., "Demographic Experience and Public Health Experience with Legal Abortion: 1973–80", in *Abortion, Medicine and the Law,* 3d ed., completely revised, ed. J. Douglas Butler and David F. Walbert (New York: Facts on File, Publications, 1986): 303.

"No comprehensive system exists for collecting data on abortion in the United States . . . for medical . . . complications resulting from . . . abortion".[90]

Currently in the United States only about thirty-five states (California not included) require abortion providers to submit to public health officials even minimal data regarding abortion procedures and complications.[91] Compliance is voluntary, and there is virtually no supervision. Moreover, for several reasons, the data requested are not sufficient to establish the true incidence of abortion mortality and morbidity even in those states were data collection is relatively thorough.

For example, the U.S. Public Health Service standard instruction manual for recording abortion complications by reporting states seeks information only about complications occurring "at the time the report is completed. . . . This item will provide data regarding the risk of induced termination."[92] Furthermore, only the abortion provider is asked to list complications. If a woman has a complication and is treated later the same day by her abortionist or by another health care provider, neither of these interventions is required to be reported to health authorities.[93]

The name of a woman undergoing abortion is not to be listed on any state abortion reporting form, though this information *is* requested for births, whether marital or nonmarital.[94] Thus, if a woman dies after an abortion, but the death does not occur at a reporting abortion clinic, there would be no way to match her name with a standard death certificate, though this could be routinely done after a birth.

Most abortion complications occur after a woman leaves the abortion provider. For example, even abortionists acknowledge that, "As a rule, little blood is lost during the vacuum aspiration procedure itself and the bleeding due to retained tissue usually does not occur for several days after the procedure."[95]

In addition, of the 1.6 million abortions during 1985, to examine just a single year, 83% were done in clinics and 4% in doctors' offices on an out-

[90] Report to President Reagan, "Final Report on Abortion", January 17, 1989, C. Everett Koop, surgeon general of the United States, final draft, abortion report, prepared by George Walter.

[91] Sen. Gordon Humphrey, *Congressional Record* insert accompanying the District of Columbia appropriations bill, 1987.

[92] *Handbook on the Reporting of Induced Termination of Pregnancy,* U.S. Public Health Service, PHS 79-01117, 11.

[93] Ibid.

[94] Robert Marshall's personal examination of state abortion reporting forms from 26 states.

[95] Jane E. Hodgson and Kathy C. Pormann, "Complications of 10,453 Consecutive First Trimester Abortions: A Prospective Study", *American Journal of Obstetrics and Gynecology,* vol. 120, no. 6 (November 15, 1979): 803–6.

patient basis.[96] Only 13% were done in hospitals, and many of these are also outpatient procedures. Thus, abortions in the United States are not performed in a setting likely to capture and report complications even where the provider is willing to do so.

A 1973 report by Margaret and Arthur Wynn to the Lane Committee (Great Britain) on the working of the Abortion Act stands in marked contrast to the abortion-reporting practices in the United States. An editorial comment on the report in a British medical journal said:

> In Britain notifications of abortion include only the complications occurring in the first week—much too short a period on which to base estimates of morbidity, especially when the private sector patients are frequently seen only for one day. Moreover, nobody knows the extent of the failure to notify. The Wynns argue that there is enough evidence now available on which to base estimates of morbidity. Most importantly, they stress that the longer the follow up, the worse the results. With a really prolonged follow-up—that is several years—a 30% morbidity rate may not be an over-estimate.
>
> One aim of the Abortion Act was to get rid of backstreet abortions with all their bad consequences. The backstreet element may have been greatly decreased, but many of the bad consequences remain.[97]

More recently in 1985, a joint study by the British Royal College of General Practitioners and the Royal College of Obstetricians and Gynecologists noted that official abortion-reporting statistics "carry the minimum of comment, and complications are recorded only to within one week of operation and usually only prior to discharge from hospital thereby underestimating the complication rates".[98] Of the 6,105 women in the British study, 85% of whom underwent supposedly safer first-trimester abortions, there was a 10% (10 per 100 women) morbidity overall directly related to the abortion procedure, although 16.9% experienced some postabortion morbidity. Major complications occurred in 2.1% (2.1 per 100 women). This is starkly different from the rate of adverse sequelae published by the state of Minnesota that recorded complications—ostensibly those identified in the first twenty-four hours postabortion—of 0.375% (.375 per 100 women).[99] In the British study, abortion complications were tracked for twenty-one days postabortion.

[96] Dennis Hevesi, "How Debate over Abortion Evolved with Changes in Science and Society", *New York Times,* July 4, 1989.

[97] Editorial, "Latent Morbidity after Abortion", *British Medical Journal* (March 3, 1973): 506.

[98] Joint Study of the Royal College of General Practitioners and the Royal College of Obstetricians and Gynecologists, "Induced Abortion Operations and Their Early Sequelae", *Journal of the Royal College of General Practitioners,* vol. 35 (April 1985): 175–80.

[99] *Reported Induced Abortions:* The Minnesota Abortion Surveillance, 1976, Minnesota Center for Health Statistics, Department of Health, report no. 2, April 1977, table 12, p. 21.

In this way the complications of induced abortion recorded in the study have included not only the early complications usually encountered by the operator [abortionist], but also morbidity seen by the general practitioner during the first 21 days following the operation.[100]

As noted above, where tracking is extended even further, more problems are detected. For example in Finland, women undergoing legal abortion were examined two years later. Of 143 patients examined, 10% had some early complications (endometritis, bleeding, cervical and uterine rupture); 10% experienced cervical insufficiency; 18% had fallopian tubes considered pathological; and 7.7% of women aborting in another group had attempted pregnancy but without success.[101] In the United States abortion-induced, involuntary infertility is not required to be documented and reported to public health officials at either the state or federal level.

The American approach to abortion-reporting complications seems to be one of "see no evil, hear no evil, and say no evil" about abortion. Continuing this policy, in the face of documented harm to women, cannot be in the public interest.

---

[100] Joint Study, "Induced Abortion Operations".
[101] Pentti Jouppila et al., "Observations of Patients Two Years after Legal Abortions", *Obstetrical and Gynecological Survey,* vol. 30, no. 9 (September 1975): 629.

Chapter Eight

Planned Parenthood and the Pill

Sanger's pet phrase, "birth control", is a euphemism. It is the birth of people, after all, that is in question, and human beings, not "births" per se, are the entity to be controlled. But "people control" or "life control" has a sinister Big Brother ring. G. K. Chesterton wrote that he despised birth control "first because it is a weak and wobbly and cowardly word ... they dare not call it by its name [birth prevention] because its name is very bad advertising".[1] In any case, the prevention of births has been the overriding purpose of Planned Parenthood.

The Birth Control Pill

> The oral contraceptives present society with problems unique in the history of human therapeutics. Never will so many people have taken such potent drugs voluntarily over such a protracted period for an objective other than for control of disease.[2]

By the late 1940s, Margaret Sanger was a battle-wise veteran with three decades of experience in the birth control crusade and some stunning victories to her credit. But she remained unsatisfied. In business terms, she did not have the ideal "product".

The existing methods of birth control, such as the diaphragm, were inconvenient. Sanger wanted a simple birth control pill.[3] In this area, as in others, prevailing opinion opposed the idea.

That fertility could be controlled with hormones was not a new idea but one that had been apparent since the mid-1800s. The contraceptive possibilities of such knowledge were well known during the early twentieth century.[4] At the International Birth Control Conference organized by Sanger in 1930, a Dr. Taylor of Edinburgh University stated that it was easy, though dangerous,

---

[1] G. K. Chesterton, "Babies and Distributism", *G. K.'s Weekly,* November 12, 1932.

[2] U.S. Food and Drug Administration, Advisory Committee on Obstetrics and Gynecology, "Report on Oral Contraceptives", August 1, 1966, 1.

[3] Gray, *Margaret Sanger,* 396.

[4] Joseph W. Goldzieher and Harry W. Rudel, "How the Oral Contraceptives Came to Be Developed: Special Communication", *Journal of the American Medical Association,* vol. 230, no. 3 (October 21, 1974).

to disturb the delicate mechanism controlling fertilization (union of sperm and ovum) and reproduction with hormones that altered pituitary gland behavior. He added, however, that "It is doubtful whether we shall ever wish to obtain a point where these dangerous weapons will be at the disposal of man."[5] These warnings did not bother Sanger.

Sanger convinced steroid biologist Gregory Pincus that the danger of the so-called population explosion required development of "the Pill". Pincus later cited Sanger's visits to him as perhaps the primary factor in the Pill's development. Planned Parenthood money was soon to follow.

Sanger threw PPFA's resources behind three men: Gregory Pincus and Dr. Min Cheuh Chang, both of the Worcester Foundation for Experimental Biology at Shrewsbury, Massachusetts, and Dr. John Rock, clinical professor of gynecology at Harvard Medical School. Rock was also the director of the Fertility and Endocrine Clinic at the Free Hospital for Women in Brookline, Massachusetts. Planned Parenthood gave Pincus grants totaling $21,000 between 1949 and 1952. John Rock received $17,064 during the same period.[6]

The big money for the Pill project came from Katherine Dexter McCormick, the wealthy widow of Cyrus McCormick, Jr., whose father founded the International Harvester Company. At a June 8, 1952, meeting with Sanger, Mrs. McCormick promised $10,000 a year, later increased to $150,000 and then to $180,000. In addition, she left $1 million to the cause in her will.[7]

Because Planned Parenthood was still a controversial organization in 1953, the Dickinson Research Memorial was set up as a way to attract money from rich individuals who wanted to avoid publicity. McCormick gave some money in this way, but when G. D. Searle and Company began supporting Pincus with drugs and research grants, the stigma diminished, and she contributed directly. Though money was no longer an impediment, a public relations problem remained.

Getting the Public to "Swallow the Pill"

While Gregory Pincus labored in the laboratory, the selling of the Pill fell primarily to Dr. John Rock. In 1938 Rock had united human ova and sperm outside of a woman's uterus. He also obtained specimens of human embryos from women undergoing hysterectomies.

[5] Margaret Sanger and Hannah Stone, eds., *The Practice of Contraception* (Baltimore: Williams and Wilkins, 1931), 104.

[6] "Planned Parenthood Federation of America, Research Facilities, Activities and Accomplishments", memo, January 20, 1953, MSCLC.

[7] James W. Reed, *From Private Vice to Public Virtue* (New York: Basic Books, 1978), 340.

Dr. Herbert Ratner calls such procedures "a form of lethal human experimentation".[8] In 1947 Rock co-authored *Voluntary Parenthood* with the PPFA's public information director. He was elected to Planned Parenthood's board in 1954. Though willing to tinker with preborn human life, Rock still claimed to be a Roman Catholic. It was doubtless for this very reason Sanger thought him the perfect public relations pitchman, perhaps able to land religious sanction for the Pill.[9]

Both Rock and Pincus proselytized tirelessly in the early 1950s, presenting the Pill not only as a social and sexual panacea, but also as a sure form of relief for apocalyptic anxieties. On May 6, 1954, Rock said of the Pill that "if it can be discovered soon, the H-bomb need never fall".[10] He further believed that the struggle against communism in Southeast Asia resulted in part from overpopulation and that birth control would diminish military crises. The public lobbying caught the media's attention.

An October 7, 1952, a *Look* magazine article trumpeted the prospects for a birth control pill, as developed by PPFA scientists. The article was prepared with help from Planned Parenthood staff.[11] Under the aegis of G. D. Searle and Company, the long-prophesied Pill, later called Enovid, made its appearance. But the new product had yet to be tested.

Testing began in April 1956 with poor Puerto Rican women as the primary subjects.[12] Later, Planned Parenthood affiliate clinicians would participate in field testing the Pill in various U.S. cities.[13] Writing in the April 1958 *Fortune* magazine, Robert Sheehan reviewed the progress to date and predicted that it would take five years before the inventors would apply to the Food and Drug Administration (FDA), and five more years before the FDA would approve of tests.[14]

Likewise, Dr. Alan Guttmacher wrote in 1959, "It is our opinion that the oral tablet has not yet been proved medically safe or highly effective ... steroid drugs are aimed at the wrong target organ. To attempt to inhibit the pituitary, which has so many functions besides stimulating the ovary,

---

[8] Herbert Ratner, "The Rock Book: A Catholic Viewpoint", *Commonweal*, July 5, 1963, 392–95; and, John Rock and Arthur Hertig, "Human Conceptuses during the First Two Weeks of Gestation", *American Journal of Obstetrics and Gynecology*, vol. 55, no. 1 (January 1948): 6–17.

[9] Reed, *Private Vice*, 352.

[10] *Planned Parenthood News*, no. 8, Summer 1954, 1, 8.

[11] PPFA memo about article in *Look*, October 7, 1952, MSCLC.

[12] Senate Select Committee on Small Business, Subcommittee on Monopoly, *Competitive Problems in the Drug Industry*, vol. 2, pt. 16, 91st Cong., 2d sess., January 22, 1970, 6237.

[13] Alan Guttmacher, *Planned Parenthood–World Population Handbook*, PPFA, pt 1, October 1963, 9.

[14] Robert Sheehan, "Birth Control Pill", *Fortune*, vol. 57 (April 1958): 54–55.

is fraught with dangers."[15] But such warnings did not impede approval.

On April 22, 1960, Dr. Pasquale DeFelica, assistant chief of the FDA's New Drug Branch, sent G. D. Searle and Company a letter approving the marketing of Enovid for contraceptive purposes.[16] In a May 11, 1960, memo to FDA commissioner George Larrick, William P. Kesserich (FDA) wrote, "We have concluded that the drug is safe."[17] The conclusion was based on tests of 897 women who had used the Pill for 10,427 cycles. However, only "sixty-six patients have taken Enovid for twenty-four cycles or more to thirty-eight and an additional sixty-six women have continued medication for twelve or more cycles to twenty-one."[18]

This small sample providing the margin of supposed safety was kept from the public until the Kesserich memo surfaced in the course of Senate subcommittee hearings in 1962 and 1963.[19] Even then the revelation was practically ignored by the media.[20]

Thus, on the basis of 132 of 897 women who used the Pill for a relatively short period of time, a powerful oral steroid unique in the history of medicine was pronounced safe and beneficial for all women of childbearing age.

The previously hesitant Guttmacher, then chairman of PPFA's medical committee, became an eager convert. He wrote that it was "safe and proper to include these compounds in the armamentarium of medically prescribed contraceptives".[21] Much press publicity followed, along with hard-sell tactics from the drug industry.

For example, Searle urged its sales people to avoid any mention of side effects like cancer and nausea and to "make the doctors want to use" Enovid by portraying it as "the most effective contraceptive known to man".[22]

The Pill helped ensure the power, prestige, and profits of both Planned Parenthood and the drug companies. Supporters of the Pill followed a simple but effective strategy.

First, they created a pill-taking habit without apparent concern about how

[15] Alan Guttmacher and Hilliard Dubrow, "The Present Status of Contraception", *Journal of the Mt. Sinai Hospital,* vol. 26, no. 2 (March–April 1959): 124.

[16] Letter of Pasquale DeFelica to William Grassen of G.D. Searle and Co., April 22, 1960, Food and Drug Administration, Public Affairs Office, files.

[17] Senate Select Committee on Small Business, Subcommittee on Monopoly, *Competitive Problems in the Drug Industry,* pt 17, app. 15, 91st Cong., 2d sess., 1970, 7323.

[18] Ibid.

[19] Morton Mintz, *The Therapeutic Nightmare* (Boston: Houghton Mifflin, 1965), 276–78.

[20] Morton Mintz, "The Pill—Press and Public at the Expert's Mercy", *Columbia Journalism Review,* Spring 1969, 4–16.

[21] Quoted in *Planned Parenthood News,* PPFA no. 28, Fall 1966, 1.

[22] Senate Select Committee on Small Business, Subcommittee on Monopoly, *Competitive Problems in the Drug Industry,* pt 15, app. 15, 91st Cong., 2d sess., 1970, attachment to J. Harold Williams testimony, 6268–71.

the Pill achieved its antifertility effects. Second, they denied any connection between the Pill and adverse health consequences. Or, when forced to admit these consequences, they trivialized their effects while simultaneously attacking critics by name-calling. Third, new formulations of the Pill would emerge, making past studies demonstrating adverse effects supposedly irrelevant. For the most part, the tactics worked, but there were more than a few problems.

The Pill under Suspicion

"The Pill has the same side effects as pregnancy".[23]

—Dr. John Rock

"I would not hesitate to give the Pill to a member of my immediate family".[24]

—Dr. Alan Guttmacher

The first reports of serious medical complications such as thromboembolism (TE) from use of the Pill came from England, where Enovid was marketed as Conovid. The English reports also mentioned that a number of women on Enovid had apparently developed fatal thromboembolic complications.[25]

It subsequently emerged that the FDA had investigated the deaths of two Los Angeles women in December 1961. The agency also had the Pill under intense investigation to see if it were related to the deaths of six other women. On August 4, 1962, the *Chicago Sun-Times* reported that Searle, Enovid's manufacturer, had held an unpublicized conference of their experts on Pill complications in April 1962. When this came to light, the effect was devastating and Searle stock plummeted. On August 7, 1962, the company sent a letter of caution to U.S. physicians who had been prescribing their product. Two days earlier, Searle claimed to be unaware of any "deaths caused by the Pill".[26] The company's line continued to be that "there is no evidence to suggest this causal relationship . . . between Enovid therapy and the development of thromboembolism".[27]

---

[23] Dr. John Rock, "The Hand That Rocked the Cradle", *Family Circle* (January 1968): 33, 79–81, 86.

[24] Alan Guttmacher, "Yes, I'll Still Prescribe the Pill", *Good Housekeeping,* vol. 162 (February 1966): 67–70.

[25] Herbert Ratner, "The Pill—I: Reluctant Admissions", *Child and Family,* vol. 12, no. 2 (1973): 98–99.

[26] Ibid.

[27] Ibid.; see also, *Proceedings of a Conference:* "Thromboembolic Phenomena in Women", sponsored by G. D. Searle and Co., Sept 10, 1962, 82–83.

Late in 1962, FDA officials began to monitor TE cases associated with Enovid. As a result, the FDA commissioner approved a recommendation that an advisory panel headed by Dr. Irving S. Wright be established to investigate the problem. By August 4, 1963, an ad hoc committee had submitted a preliminary report based on background material on more than 350 cases of TE and deaths from both FDA and Searle company files. The report stated that there was "no significant increase in the risks of (TE) death from the use of Enovid" in women under thirty-five, but that death from TE did appear to have increased for Enovid users over thirty-five.[28] This report also found that the incidence of TE death among Enovid users was 12.1 per million while the TE death rate for the general population was 8.4 per million. The difference was not considered significant.[29]

Critics pointed out that the Wright report considered all women to be equally at risk of TE whether they had taken Enovid for a month or a year. If a woman-year concept pioneered by Searle had been used by the Wright committee, the TE death rate would have been 22.32 per million, nearly three times as high as the general population.[30] Wright's response was to impugn the integrity, medical knowledge, and experience of the doctor(s) in question.[31] The Wright report appeared in the September 7, 1963, issue of the *Journal of the American Medical Association.* Ten months later the AMA endorsed the Pill in a Sunday newspaper supplement, "This Week".[32]

Though a number of articles in women's magazines proclaimed the Pill as entirely safe, linkage of the Pill to disease and death persisted. The FDA endorsed a collaborative study between Searle and PPFA at thirty-nine Planned Parenthood clinics. As might be expected, the two primary agents of Pill production and distribution gave their product a clean bill of health. But omitted from the study were any deaths and multiple pathologies that occurred in women *before* twenty-four months of use. As one medical observer commented: "This study was made despite the knowledge that the vast majority of the 132 cases of TE disease and death—which was the basis for the Chicago conference—occurred much earlier than the twenty-four

---

[28] Senate Select Committee on Small Business, Subcommittee on Monopoly, *Competitive Problems in the Drug Industry,* pt 15, app. 15, 91st Cong., 2d sess., 1970, 7235–46, reference to "Wright Committee Reports on Enovid".

[29] Ibid., 7240.

[30] E. Langer, "Enovid: Contraceptive Pill and Recent FDA Report Clearing It Stirs Continued Medical Dispute", *Science,* vol. 141, no. 3584 (September 6, 1963): 892–94.

[31] Senate Committee on Government Operations, Subcommittee on Reorganization and International Organization, 88th Cong., 1st sess., March 1, 1965, 3174, letter from Dr. Wright to Senator Hubert H. Humphrey, September 10, 1963.

[32] Ibid., 3187.

month period and predominantly within the first six months of Pill use."[33]

Since the FDA had endorsed the Pill, it was not surprising that it should participate in efforts to soothe public fears about possible adverse affects. The FDA's Advisory Committee on Obstetrics and Gynecology released a report on oral contraceptives on July 1, 1966. It found "no adequate scientific data, at this time, proving these compounds unsafe for human use".[34]

Significantly, of the ten committee members and three consultants, four had been publicly associated with Planned Parenthood. Most important, the committee's chairman, Dr. Louis W. Hellman, was a member of the PPFA's National Medical Committee from 1957 to 1966. Nicholas J. Eastman went back as far as the American Birth Control League and was also on the PPFA National Medical Council, as was Christopher Tietze. Schuyler C. Kohl was on the Budget and Finance Committee of the Association of Planned Parenthood Physicians.

Unencumbered by such partisan restraints, British journals kept producing articles on TE and other adverse effects resulting from the use of oral contraceptives. A second FDA report followed, with the same four Planned Parenthood allies as members of the Advisory Committee. Also included was Ralph M. Wynn, later president of Planned Parenthood Physicians. Their report, written by Dr. Hellman alone, concluded that "when these potential hazards and the value of the drugs are balanced, the Committee finds the ratio of benefit to risk sufficiently high to justify the designation 'safe' within the intent of the legislation".[35]

Yet "safe" was an elastic term, for as Dr. Herbert Ratner pointed out:

The incidence of death in white women of childbearing age from crimes of violence which include murder, forcible rape, robbery, and aggravated assault, is equivalent to the incidence of TE deaths from the Pill. . . . The Pill which the obstetrician prescribes contraceptively causes more deaths—approximately twice the number—than are prevented when the same obstetrician immunizes a pregnant woman against poliomyelitis. There are numerous additional lethal diseases in the U.S. to which public health devotes large sums of money and to which physicians devote great energy, in which the incidence of death is less than that caused by the Pill.[36]

From 1965 to 1980, approximately half of the members of the FDA's

[33] Herbert Ratner, "Recent Setbacks in Medicine", *Child and Family,* vol. 7, no. 2 (Spring 1968): 186.

[34] United States Dept. of H.E.W., Food and Drug Administration, Advisory Committee on Obstetrics and Gynecology, "Report on the Oral Contraceptives", 1966, 37.

[35] Ibid., "Second Report on the Oral Contraceptives", 1969, 8–9.

[36] Herbert Ratner, M.D., Editorial, *Child and Family,* vol. 7, no. 2 (Spring 1968): 182.

obstetric and gynecology advisory committees were affiliated in some way with Planned Parenthood.[37]

The Nelson Hearings

The furor surrounding the Pill culminated in a series of congressional hearings held in 1970 by the Senate Select Committee on Small Business, Subcommittee on Monopoly, chaired by Senator Gaylord Nelson, a Wisconsin Democrat. In testimony before the subcommittee, Planned Parenthood president Dr. Alan Guttmacher stated that "the Pill, in my opinion, and that of my colleagues, is an important prophylaxis, perhaps the most important, against one of the gravest socio-medical illnesses extant. That, of course, is unwanted pregnancy."[38]

The absurd and nihilistic notion that pregnancy and children are "illnesses" is a central theme of Planned Parenthood. Another is that, from the youngest age, people should be given full "knowledge about their bodies" as well as extensive information about birth control. Planned Parenthood has always charged its opponents with being obscurantist enemies of such information. These themes should be kept in mind during reading of the following excerpts of Guttmacher's testimony in the Nelson Pill hearings:

DR. GUTTMACHER: I do not think that you are going to be able to educate the American woman as to what she should or should not do with regard to the Pill. I think you can educate the American doctor. He is educable. . . . My feeling is that when you attempt to instruct American womanhood in this, which is a pure medical matter which I am afraid she has not the background to understand, you are creating in her simply a panic reaction without much intellectual background. And this is what I think has been unfortunate. . . .

Now you asked me whether special things should be done in, I suppose, packaging and labeling. I have the feeling that most patients do not read what is put into their Pill packages or medicines, and if they do, they have some difficulty understanding it.

SENATOR NELSON: What is the responsibility of the government which does the studies, licenses the Pills, approves the package insert which goes to the druggist and most of the time does not get to the physician because he does not get the package? The literature that is going out is inaccurate. It

---

[37] Copies of curricula vitae for members of the Advisory Committee on Obstetrics and Gynecology, U.S. Food and Drug Administration.

[38] Senate Select Committee on Small Business, Subcommittee on Monopoly, *Competitive Problems in the Drug Industry,* pt. 16, vol. 2, 91st Cong., 2d sess., 1970, Guttmacher testimony, 6561–31.

is misleading 8,500,000 women in this country, and it has been doing it for ten years.

DR. GUTTMACHER: I think that you probably have no right to impose what should be written in such a pamphlet. But if there were some way of clearing all medical throwaway data with the FDA before publication for their criticism, it might be a very salutary thing.

SENATOR JAVITS: Would you give us your recommendation as to whether the approval [for the Pill] should be withdrawn?

DR. GUTTMACHER: I am 100 percent certain that approval should not be withdrawn. That requires no thought on my part, sir. . . .

Guttmacher later detoured into warnings about the growing populations of places such as Latin America and Pakistan, the prospect that had so terrified Planned Parenthood's founders. The hearings, Guttmacher said, had created "panic" in such places [not, of course, among the general populace but in the select, small ranks of "population control" experts, who readily transformed medical science into a platform for social engineering]. Guttmacher reminded Nelson that the senator was himself "among the great protagonists of world population control". The attempt at flattery missed its mark.

SENATOR NELSON: There is no use going back to that. It is just a question of whether you believe the people of the United States should have all the facts or whether they should not. In my view, I think they should. . . . Would you agree with the letter sent out by Dr. Edwards, acting commissioner of the Food and Drug Administration, sent about the 18th of January, in which he states, "In most cases a full disclosure of the potential effects of these products would seem advisable, thus permitting the participation of the patient in the assessment of the risk associated with this method". This letter was sent to 324,000 doctors. . . . Do you agree or disagree?

SENATOR JAVITS: Do you not think the witness ought to see the letter?

DR. GUTTMACHER: I can evaluate that. I have not seen it, but we have discussed it before. I think it places a great burden on the patient. I think it is impractical, sir. I think the physician has to make the decision. . . .

SENATOR NELSON: What do your clinics tell the user of the Pill?

DR. GUTTMACHER: I think I have said in my testimony that I cannot say, because I do not visit the clinics and see them operate. . . .

SENATOR NELSON: I thought you referred, when the literature was handed out . . .

DR. GUTTMACHER: . . . this is covered by the literature. I am certain that if a doctor is terribly busy and the patient does not ask questions, he does not pause too long to tell her about the potential dangers. . . .

SENATOR NELSON: You are aware, I assume, that in the survey done for

Newsweek, two-thirds of the women in that survey stated that they were told nothing about side-effects by their doctors?

DR. GUTTMACHER: No. I do not remember that.[39]

Guttmacher's view of American women seemed to be that they were generally stupid beings unable to understand what are really quite simple facts about their own bodies. Such was their benighted state, according to Guttmacher, that vital information should be *withheld* from them, and doctors—primarily men—should continue to make important decisions for them, even though it might be the woman and her offspring who suffered.

While the publicity surrounding the Nelson hearings caused some to change their birth control habits, it did not end the love affair the FDA, Planned Parenthood, and the drug companies had with the Pill. By 1973 Guttmacher had dropped his support for "medically controlled" Pill usage and endorsed international schemes to "educate governments on the medical benefits to women and children of nonmedical methods of distributing oral contraceptives". The suitable distributors included "storekeepers",[40] presumably a group as "educable" as doctors. This was a far cry from his testimony in the Nelson Hearings, in which Guttmacher contended that:

> I would say that the physician should be made to understand and appreciate that unless he can see the patient who is on the Pill at least every six months, he should not prescribe it for her. I think there is a danger in allowing a patient to go for an indefinite period ... the doctor should be sufficiently well equipped to answer honestly and authoritatively the facts that have been presented about the Pill ... and if he feels that he cannot do this, then I think he should not dispense the Pill.[41]

From the original vision through research and funding, onward to government approval, around and over the medical objections, and finally arriving at unfettered mass distribution, often subsidized by tax dollars, the Pill has been a Planned Parenthood project. Without doubt, this has been one of Planned Parenthood's great victories.

Though many women are now cautious about the Pill, it remains something of an institution in the United States and a badge of modernity in much of the world, at least among governing elites. Perhaps two statements sum up Planned Parenthood's interest in keeping it that way.

The section "Achievements of the Federation", in PPFA's December 1971

---

[39] Ibid.

[40] "Population and Family Planning in Latin America", Population Crisis Committee, Washington, D.C., 1973.

[41] Senate Select Committee on Small Business, Subcommittee on Monopoly, *Competitive Problems in the Drug Industry,* pt. 16, vol. 2, 91st Cong., 2d sess., 1970, Guttmacher testimony, 6561–31.

Five Year Plan, states that "sales in oral contraceptives appear to have risen 10–20 percent in 1970 over 1969 sales". Or as Guttmacher triumphantly put it: " . . . our clinics have grown so magnificently since the Pill was introduced. . . . we now have a product which is extraordinarily acceptable to our type of patient."[42]

Medical Complications of the Pill

> King Lear: Hear, Nature, hear . . . Suspend thy purpose . . . To make this creature fruitful! Into her womb convey sterility! Dry up her organs of increase.

> (Shakespeare, *King Lear*, act 1, scene 4)

The initial ten years were only the beginning of troubles for the Pill. First, the Pill is an antiphysiologic chemical steroid that "differs markedly from that of natural oestrogen" and does not mimic the natural process of pregnancy.[43] The antiphysiologic action also holds for the new multiphasic Pills.[44]

The Pill's chemical steroids alter a woman's entire physiology as is evidenced by the Pill's ability to change the parameters of "normal" on over one hundred medical tests.[45] By 1969 more than fifty metabolic changes had been reported in women on the Pill.[46]

There are powerful economic reasons why women are told the Pill is natural. The Pill represents

> a very considerable financial investment, and the commercial interests backing these drugs have at their disposal a formidable machine of medical persuasion. . . . Women on oral contraceptives are, endrocrinologically speaking, in a state of medical castration. The advertizing campaigns . . . have been designed to direct thought along certain lines. . . . It is important for the sale of these drugs that the impression that they create an unphysiological state should not gain ground, so that the fanciful resem-

[42] Ibid., 6616; also see PPFA "A Five Year Plan", December 1971.

[43] Egon Diczfalusy, "Contraceptive Steroids and Their Mechanism of Action", from *Control of Human Fertility*, ed. E. Diczfalusy and Ulf Borell, Proceedings of the Fifteenth Nobel Symposium, May 27–29, 1970, at Sodergarn, Lidingo, Sweden (New York: John Wiley and Sons, 1971), 17–38.

[44] Daniel Mishell, Jr., "Symposium: Prescribing OCs for Safety", *Contemporary OB/GYN*, March 1986, 128–48. (Multiphasics are not physiologic.)

[45] John B. Maile and Jessie Kent, "The Effects of Oral Contraceptives on Results of Laboratory Tests", *American Journal of Obstetrics and Gynecology*, vol. 229, no. 13 (September 15, 1974): 1762–68; Leon D. Ostrander, Jr., et al., "Oral Contraceptives and Physiological Variables", *Journal of the American Medical Association*, vol. 244, no. 7 (August 15, 1980): 677–79.

[46] Editorial, "Metabolic Effects of Oral Contraceptives", *The Lancet*, vol. 2 (October 11, 1969): 783–84.

blance to the physiological state of pregnancy is constantly stressed. . . . This is largely nonsense.[47]

And though the Pill is likened to pregnancy, Planned Parenthood claims that teen pregnancy poses a greater health risk than the Pill.[48] Yet, Planned Parenthood obstetrician Dr. Louis Hellman, has said: " . . . the risk in having a baby is not the same for all individuals. A healthy young girl runs a very negligible risk, but someone who has serious heart disease . . . or who has hypertension, runs a real risk in having a baby. So to say the risk in taking the Pill is less than having a baby doesn't make much sense."[49]

And even Planned Parenthood's Dr. Christopher Tietze suggested that such comparisons are meaningless because contrasting the Pill to childbirth "may easily degenerate into a sort of 'numbers game' based on highly arbitrary assumptions".[50] The Pill-is-safer-than-pregnancy thesis is, in part, derived from fantastic fertility rates proposed by birth control luminaries such as the former president of the American College of Obstetricians and Gynecologists, Dr. Luella Klein, and, yes, also Dr. Tietze. They have suggested that a fertile sexually active woman using no contraception would average either thirteen to fourteen births or twenty-nine to thirty-one abortions over her lifetime.[51]

Sociologist Judith Blake observes: "As far as we know, such average rates of pregnancy and abortion are unprecedented in large-scale noncontracepting populations and, hence, the associated mortality risks are inflated."[52]

But in any case giving a young girl the Pill "seems safer than it really is, because young girls are less likely to be seriously ill".[53] Yet realistic health comparisons of Pill and non-Pill-taking women are difficult for two reasons. British and U.S. women who receive a Pill prescription are generally healthier than other women of similar age and background.[54] Therefore, comparisons will be biased in favor of the Pill unless women selected

[47] Arnold Klopper, "Advertisement and Classification of Oral Contraceptives", *British Medical Journal,* vol. 2 (October 16, 1965): 932–33.

[48] *Planned Parenthood Review,* Winter 1986.

[49] Louis M. Hellman, M.D., "A Doctor's View of Birth Control Pills", *Redbook,* vol. 132, April 1969, 60.

[50] Christopher Tietze, "Statistical Assessment of Adverse Experiences Associated with the Use of Oral Contraceptives", *Handbook of Oral Contraception,* ed. Eleanor Mears, (Boston: Little, Brown and Co., 1965), 698–715.

[51] Luella Klein, "To Have or Not to Have a Pregnancy", *Obstetrics and Gynecology,* vol. 65, no. 1 (January 1985): 1–4; Judith Blake, "The Pill and Rising Costs of Fertility Control", *Social Biology,* vol. 24 (Winter 1977): 267–80.

[52] Ibid.

[53] Ellen Grant, "Cancer and the Pill", *The Ecologist,* vol. 14, no. 2 (1984): 68–76.

[54] Howard W. Ory, "Letters to Editor", *Family Planning Perspectives,* vol. 15, no. 4 (July–August 1983): 155.

for the control group also do not have any medical contraindications to Pill use.[55]

But this is precisely what is not done. In the British Royal College of General Practitioners' study, women on the Pill were compared to controls who had venous thromboses 2.6 times as often as Pill takers at the start, and 2.06 times the rate of cerebrovascular accidents before entering the study. Both of these conditions were matters under study. But the College takes no account of this. Yet they did claim a bias against the Pill because of more frequent medical visits for Pill prescription renewals.[56]

Therefore studies that show the incidence of a particular disease is similar for Pill and non-Pill users do not exonerate the Pill. Rather, the fact that Pill users were healthier to start, but ended up with an equal incidence of a particular disease, suggests that the Pill has caused previously healthy women to become less healthy. With this in mind, we can now look at some of the medical misadventures associated with or attributable to Pill use.

AIDS

The risk of acquired immune deficiency syndrome (AIDS) may be increased for women on the Pill and their sexual associates. AIDS is thought to be caused by the human immunodeficiency virus-1. The HIV-1 attacks a key protective cell of the body's immune system, the T-4 helper cell. Though intravenous drug abuse and blood transfusions are vectors for spreading the HIV-1, AIDS appears to be primarily a blood-borne, sexually transmitted disease.

In a prospective study of prostitutes in Nairobi, Kenya: " . . . an increased risk of HIV-1 seroconversion was observed among oral contraceptive users independent of sexual activity, intercurrent sexually transmitted diseases, and condom use".[57] The Pill-using prostitutes seroconverted AIDS positive one-third more frequently than those not on the Pill.[58]

The U.S. Public Health Service funded Walnut Creek Pill study and The British Royal College of General Practitioners' 1974 *Interim Report* recognized the possible adverse effects of the Pill on the body's immune system.[59]

---

[55] Tietze, "Statistical Assessment of Adverse Experiences", 698–715.

[56] Valerie Beral, "Oral Contraception and Health", *The Lancet,* vol. 1 (June 22, 1974): 1280–81.

[57] Peter Piot et al., "AIDS: An International Perspective", *Science* (February 5, 1988): 573–79, citing among other things a paper presented at the 3d International AIDS Conference, June 1–5, 1987.

[58] Michael Specter, "AIDS Infection and Birth Control Pills", *Washington Post,* June 9, 1987.

[59] Irwin R. Fisch and Shanna Freedman, "Oral Contraceptives and the Leukocyte Count", *The Walnut Creek Contraceptive Drug Study: A Prospective Study on the Side Effects of Oral Contraceptives,* vol. 2, HEW pub. no. (NIH) 76-563, 47–60; Royal College of General Practitioners, *Interim Report,* 1974, chaps. 5 and 7.

The AIDS virus is known to be transmitted via parenteral exposure to infected blood or blood products.[60] The possible relationship of this to the Pill is that an increased incidence of bleeding of the gums (gingivitis) is found in Pill users.[61]

Pelvic Inflammatory Disease (PID)

...An episode of PID can have devastating consequences on a young woman's life, especially her reproductive health. In the post-PID state, the adolescent female is at risk for recurrent PID, chronic pelvic pain, infertility, and ectopic pregnancy.... Over one million women experience ... PID every year in the U.S.... 16–20% of these cases occur in teenagers.... the risk of PID in the sexually active fifteen-year-old female is estimated to have a one in eight chance.... This increased risk ... is reflected by ... more permissive sexual behavior by the cohort of adolescent women [and] ... oral contraceptives increase the risk of lower genital tract chlamydial infection ...they may predispose young women to increased risk for chlamydial PID.... if current trends in PID among teenage women continue, as many as 10 percent of [American] women will be sterile, and 3 percent will have had an ectopic pregnancy as a result of PID by the year 2000.[62]

The economic costs of PID for women fifteen to nineteen during 1984 was estimated by the U. S. Centers for Disease Control at $192,402,000.[63] PID is only one of more than fifty venereal diseases prevalent in the U.S. today. In 1955 there were only five known venereal diseases.[64]

Cancer

A recent Scandinavian study

which accounted for several possible confounding factors revealed a signifi-cant association between total duration of oral contraceptive use and breast

[60] James W. Curran et al., "Epidemiology of HIV Infection and AIDS Infection in the United States", *Science*, vol. 239 (February 5, 1988): 610–16.

[61] Bernard D. Lynn, " 'The Pill' as an Etiologic Agent in Hypertropic Gingivitis", *Oral Surgery, Oral Medicine, and Oral Pathology*, vol. 24 (September 1967): 333–34; G. M. El-Ashiry et al., "Comparative Study of the Influence of Pregnancy and Oral Contraceptives on the Gingivae", *Oral Surgery, Oral Medicine, and Oral Pathology*, vol. 30 (1970): 472; G. M. El-Ashiry et al., "Effects of Oral Contraceptives on the Gingiva", *Journal of Periodontology*, vol. 42 (1971): 273–75.

[62] A. E. Washington et al., "Pelvic Inflammatory Disease and Its Sequelae in Adolescents", *Journal of Adolescent Health Care*, vol. 6 (1985): 298–310.

[63] A.E. Washington, "The Economic Costs of Pelvic Inflammatory Disease", *Journal of the American Medical Association*, vol. 255, no. 13 (April 4, 1986): 1735–38.

[64] Elizabeth Connell and Howard Tatum, *Sexually Transmitted Diseases: Diagnosis and Treatment* (Stillwell, Okla.: Creative Informatics, 1985); see Introduction.

cancer risk. The relative risk of breast cancer after twelve or more years of use was 2.2 [1.4–4.0]. Oral contraceptive use for more than seven years before first full-term pregnancy entailed an increased breast cancer risk of 2.0 [1.2–4.2] which was of borderline significance. . . . The results suggest that long-term use of oral contraceptives may increase the risk of breast cancer in young women.[65]

And both the Pill and/or the sexual behavior made possible by the Pill have been implicated in the development of both invasive cervical cancer and its precancerous states (mild dysplasia, severe dysplasia, and carcinoma in situ). A 1980 British study noted that:

The relative risk among women who first had intercourse before seventeen years of age, compared to those starting at 21 or older was about 2–3 for risk of mild dysplasia, severe dysplasia and carcinoma in situ. . . . The risk of cervical abnormality was also found to increase with the number of sexual partners. . . . Women who reported pregnancy outside marriage, whether premaritally or at some other time outside legal marriage, were at increased risk. . . . Statistically significant linear relationships were seen for length of use of oral contraceptives and risk of severe dysplasia and carcinoma in situ.[66]

This view is not isolated: " . . . in young women the factors of sexual promiscuity and the prolonged use of oral contraceptives may interact over a period of time in a manner of increasing risk."[67] It is known that cervical tissues are responsive to the chemical steroids in the Pill, leading British researchers to write: " . . . we have observed a substantial relation between Pill use and invasive cancer. . . . We conclude that our data offer considerable support to the view that long-term oral contraceptive use may increase the risk of cervical neoplasia [new tumors]."[68]

Smoking and the number of past sexual liaisons of male consorts have also been identified as additional risk factors for cervical cancer.[69] In the United

[65] O. Meirik et al. "Oral Contraceptive Use and Breast Cancer in Young Women", *The Lancet,* 2 (September 20, 1986): 650–54.

[66] R. Harris, "Characteristics of Women with Dysplasia or Carcinoma in Situ of the Cervix Uteri", *British Journal of Cancer,* vol. 42, no. 3 (September 1980): 359–69.

[67] S. H. Swan et al., "Oral Contraceptive Use, Sexual Activity, and Cervical Carcinoma", *American Journal of Obstetrics and Gynecology,* vol. 139, no. 1 (January 1, 1981): 52–57.

[68] Martin P. Vessy, "Neoplasia of the Cervix Uteri and Contraception: A Possible Adverse Effect of the Pill", *The Lancet,* 2 (October 22, 1983): 930–34.

[69] C. Vecchia, "Cigarette Smoking and the Risk of Cervical Neoplasia", *American Journal of Epidemiology,* vol. 123, no. 1 (January 1986): 22–29; M. Zunzunegui, "Male Influences on Cervical Cancer Risk", *American Journal of Epidemiology,* vol. 123, no. 2 (February 1986): 302–7.

States nearly 6,800 women die yearly from cervical cancer.[70] The Pill may be a factor in some of these deaths.

Heart and Cardiovascular Problems

One of the alleged benefits of the Pill is that menstrual periods are lighter. Yet, as the monthly period is intended by nature, what happens in its absence? One answer might be that: "A reported 3.5 times greater risk of myocardial infarction could be attributable to higher iron stores." A study of forty-six never-pregnant Pill users aged eighteen to twenty-six and seventy-one matched non-Pill users showed that women on the Pill have significantly higher iron stores.[71]

Pill users also show higher cholesterol levels, which are associated with increased rate of myocardial infarction.[72] The increase in the low density lipids in Pill-using women is the same as is seen in women "that spontaneously develop myocardial infarction and have high levels" of these lipids.[73]

Quantifying these risks, Pill users aged thirty to thirty-nine have a three-fold greater chance of myocardial infarction than similar nonusers. And the risk of stroke for Pill users aged fifteen to forty-four is 47/100,000; the risk of stroke for a similar group of nonusers is 10/100,000.[74]

Even women who use the "low-dose" Pill have a higher incidence of stroke, which is unpredictable for specific women.[75] And the "newer oral contraceptive formulations increase the risk of deep vein thrombosis and pulmonary embolism".[76]

Dr. Ellen Grant, an early Pill supporter turned Pill critic, has said:

> We have experienced more than twenty years of unnecessary ill health in women. . . . But what is more alarming is the fact that . . . today younger

[70] David A. Grimes, "Deaths Due to Sexually Transmitted Diseases", *Journal of the American Medical Association,* vol. 255 (April 4, 1986): 1727–29.

[71] *Obstetric and Gynecologic News* (August 15–31, 1985), 19, citation of article in *American Journal of Clinical Nutrition,* vol. 41 (1985): 703–12.

[72] Robert B. Wallace et al., "Altered Plasma Lipid and Lipoprotein Levels Associated with Oral Contraceptive and Oestrogen Use", *The Lancet,* 2 (July 21, 1979): 111–15.

[73] FDA Fertility and Maternal Health Drugs Advisory Committee, *Transcript,* vol. 2 (February 9, 1984), 234.

[74] Bruce Stadel, "Oral Contraceptives and the Occurrence of Disease", *Contraceptive Steroids: Pharmacology and Safety,* ed. A. T. Gregorie and Richard Blye (New York and London: Plenum Press, 1986), 14–15.

[75] Eberhardt F. Mammen, "Oral Contraceptives and Blood Coagulation: A Critical Review", *American Journal of Obstetrics and Gynecology* (March 15, 1982): 781–90.

[76] S. Heimlich et al., "Deep Vein Thrombosis and Pulmonary Embolism in Relation to Oral Contraceptive Use", abstracts, *American Journal of Epidemiology,* vol. 120, no. 3 (March 1984): 465–66.

and younger women are now going on the pill even though six studies have found an increased risk of breast cancer from long-term use of oral contraceptives in women under twenty-five who had not yet had a baby. . . .

Preferred ignorance has caused us to close our eyes to the enormous increase in ill health of young women since the pill was introduced. . . . [77]

An analysis of mortality trends in twenty-one countries shows that since the Pill became available, changes in mortality rates from nonrheumatic heart disease, cerebrovascular disease, and hypertension among women fifteen to forty-four were found to be significantly associated with increasing oral contraceptive use in each country.

The risk of death from heart disease for Pill users versus nonusers is five to one; hypertension, two to one; cerebrovascular disease, and all cardiovascular diseases, three to one. These risks exist for both the high and "lower dose" pills. Other explanations were considered for these lethal health consequences, such as changes in diagnostic classifications, smoking, female employment, education, and lifestyle. But,

No association was found between changes in all cancer [excluding reproductive sites] mortality and pill use. On the other hand, there was a positive association between Pill use and changes in all-cause mortality.

The actual excess annual mortality from all nonrheumatic cardiovascular diseases may be 20 per 100,000 women aged fifteen to forty-four. This excess mortality is substantial when compared with the annual mortality rate of 70 per 100,000 from all causes, and of 1 per 100,000 from all causes associated with childbearing for women of comparable age in England and Wales in 1971–72.[78]

But this excess mortality would come to be tolerated as American medicine moved toward the maintenance of a "hedonistic" life style as its professional goal rather than the preservation of "health". This becomes apparent when the history of Pill use is traced. For example, after the Pill [Searle's Enovid] was on the market for approximately a year and a half, the only illness thought to be "possibly" associated with its use was thrombophlebitis. Readers of the *Journal of the American Medical Association* were cautioned: "But should the coagulation mechanism be proved to be disturbed, the oral contraceptives . . . would soon be only another memory".[79]

Obviously, that prediction went unfulfilled, and would continue to do so

---

[77] Ellen Grant, *The Bitter Pill* (London: Corgi Books, 1985), 15.

[78] Valerie Beral, "Cardiovascular-Disease Mortality Trends and Oral Contraceptive Use in Young Women", *The Lancet,* 2 (November 13, 1976): 1047–52.

[79] Edwin J. DeCosta, M.D., "Those Deceptive Contraceptives", *Journal of the American Medical Association,* vol. 181, no. 2 (July 14, 1962): 122–25.

even after many other diseases, ailments, and even death were found to be associated with the Pill. Thus,

> as a consequence of the broadening range of diseases for which the relative risk is higher among pill users, the cumulative absolute risk over all these diseases may be very much higher than was believed when only selected thromboembolic entities seemed to be involved. We cannot keep adding major diseases for which the relative risk is two to eight times greater among pill users and not begin to incur some absolute effects as well.[80]

However, proponents of the Pill were acutely aware that the implications of Dr. Beral's Pill critique threatened to unravel the claim of American medicine that the Pill was safer than pregnancy. Dr. Ory, of the U.S. Public Health Service, wrote:

> Applying the age specific death rates from Beral's report to U.S. women, I estimate that 6,000 of the approximately 8,000 cardiovascular disease deaths occurring annually in the United States to women of reproductive age would be attributable to OC [oral contraceptive] use. This does not seem possible. U.S. vital data . . . show that death rates from cardiovascular disease have been falling nearly equally since 1950. If oral contraceptives were as powerful a cause of cardiovascular disease as Beral's results suggest, death rates from these for men and women should diverge.[81]

To the untutored, Ory's defense appears plausible. But it is wrong. Planned Parenthood's Dr. Raymond Pearl long ago wrote: "There is ever present in vital statistics, and from the beginning always has been, an attempt to make the incidence of mortality a measure or index of morbidity. Mortality is not and can never be a good index of morbidity, generally speaking."[82] This is so because, in addition to one's general health status, the likelihood of dying [mortality] from a disease or illness [morbidity] is in part dependent upon the adequacy, availability, and quality of medical treatment.

Secondly, females usually live longer than males. In any particular year, the death rate from all causes for males is usually higher than that for females.

Using an analogy at some remove from sexuality may make this easier to see. For example, at first appearance most people would agree that a person making a million dollars a year was a financial success. But, if it were learned that in the absence of a drinking habit two million could be made, it could be

---

[80] Judith Blake, "The Pill and Rising Costs of Fertility Control", *Social Biology*, vol. 24, no. 4 (Winter 1977): 267–80.

[81] Howard W. Ory, "Health Effects of Fertility Control", in *Contraception: Science, Technology, and Application*, Proceedings of a symposium, 1979, pub. 1982, 110–21.

[82] Raymond Pearl, *Introduction to Medical Biometry and Statistics* (Md.: W. B. Saunders and Company, 1941), "The Raw Data of Biostatistics", chap. 3.

seen that the drinking was harmful financially no matter how much was made otherwise. The same with the Pill and health.

The nonaccidental death of a woman in her reproductive years is very alarming from a public health standpoint because this age period is usually the healthiest. In a large prospective study of 23,000 Pill users and 23,000 non-Pill takers [controls]

> the total mortality-rate in women who had ever used the Pill was increased by 40%, and this was due to an increase in deaths from circulatory diseases of 1 per 5,000 ever-users per year . . . or 20 per 100,000 . . . the increased mortality associated with oral-contraceptive use is much greater than the excess mortality (1.8 per 100,000 women per year) associated with the larger number of pregnancies in the controls.
>
> The deaths, all in oral contraceptive users, from subarachnoid haemorrhage, malignant hypertension, cardiomyopathy, and mesentericartery thrombosis in this study . . . have occurred despite a lower prevalence of vascular and other circulatory diseases in users than in non-users before recruitment into the stud[y]. These findings closely fit Beral's predictions in young women from twenty-one countries.[83]

Look at the following death rates for 1960, the year the Pill was first made available, and 1979, the year Ory was writing about:[84]

Age-adjusted Death Rates for Select Causes of Death—White Male/Female			
Year	1960	1979	*% reduction*
Males—white			
All causes	917.7/100,000	751.1/100,000	18.2%
Heart disease	375.4/100,000	281.2/100,000	25.1%
Cerebrovascular	80.3/100,000	46.5/100,000	46.5%
Females—white			
All causes	555.0/100,000	412.2/100,000	25.7%
Heart disease	197.1/100,000	134.8/100,000	31.6%
Cerebrovascular	68.7/100,000	36.8/100,000	46.4%

In the general health improvement and increase in longevity experienced by Americans after World War II, white females lead white males in decreasing death rates, *except for cerebrovascular diseases in which the rate is virtually identical.* Why did white female health improvement in this area change at the same rate of more-at-risk males when it improved at a greater rate in other areas? Is it just an accident that this is the very area of disease known to be a trouble spot for the Pill?

---

[83] Valerie Beral, "Mortality among Oral Contraceptive Users", Final report of Royal College of General Practitioners' Study, *The Lancet* (October 8, 1977), 727–31.

[84] "Health: United States", 1982, U.S. Dept. Health and Human Services, DHHS pub. no. PHS 83–1232, table 15.

Lastly, recent efforts to make the allegedly "safe" Pill "safer" have resulted in the new low-dose Pills. But even these may not be "safer" than previous formulations in spite of the estrogen decrease from 150 mcgc to 35 mcgc or less. Lowering the hormone component of the supposedly "safe" Pill was made necessary by health concerns that could not be explained away, successfully denied, or conveniently hidden by doctors or Pill companies. But part of the dose reduction occurred because chemicals in the present Pill are now micronised and are more efficiently absorbed by the intestine. Thus, dosage levels could come down (saving pharmaceutical companies money), but they still had to be potent enough to produce the same antifertility effects as high dosage Pills. "Obviously, women must be given large enough amounts of hormones reliably to block ovulation and to prevent endometrial bleeding. A truly low dose Pill is a myth."[85]

Adolescents and the Pill: Some Social Problems

> But if, in any of the laws which have been ordained, health has been preferred to temperance, or wealth to health and temperate habits, that law must clearly be wrong.
>
> Plato, *The Laws*, Book 5

The Pill has had four important social consequences. First, it enables individuals to be accountable only to themselves. Planned Parenthood supports giving the means of birth control to minors without parental knowledge or consent. This psychology of adolescent decision making assumes either that there is no objective moral order governing adolescent sexual conduct or that "right and wrong" must be subordinated to "health".

This is exemplified in a Planned Parenthood pamphlet ostensibly designed as an alternative to sexual indulgence, which reads: "The only question is: *What's right for you?* You decide. . . . Don't borrow your decisions. Make up your own mind. . . . Be honest."[86]

Note that the adolescent is not advised to consult the Ten Commandments, because that would imply a valid external behavioral norm. The implicit assumption here is that there are no objective moral standards or "duties" governing sexual behavior. Rather, there are only subjective "choices". So, the individual does not simply decide between right and wrong. Whatever sexual behavior the individual chooses, usually with the consent of another, is right or good for that person or persons. Thus,

---

[85] Ellen Grant, "Cancer and the Pill", *The Ecologist*, vol. 14, no. 2 (1984): 68–76.

[86] *Teen Sex? It's OK to Say No Way*, no. 99, 5–84/150, Planned Parenthood Federation of America, 1979.

the adolescent is isolated in his or her decision making from parents, society, and God.

And research has shown that adolescents who believe themselves less responsible to parents, society, or God are more likely to indulge in premarital intercourse.[87]

And when the individual acts out self-authenticating sexual norms, guilt is minimized or even eliminated depending upon how successful the indoctrination of radical moral autonomy has been. In a survey of 355 sexually indulgent single women aged thirteen to twenty, it was found that "sexual guilt from first to current intercourse was reduced from 41 percent to 8 percent".[88]

Guilt also inhibits consistent Pill usage, as is apparent from another finding in the previous survey: "Premarital sexual guilt was significantly related to seven of twenty reasons" for not using contraception.[89]

It becomes easy to see why Planned Parenthood's president Faye Wattleton believes "it is a mistake to enter into debates on questions of morality".[90] Minimizing the guilt that accompanies the departure from the moral order is also a convenient way to dull one's conscience. This occurs because conscience

> . . . states whether the act the person has in view is good or bad . . . conscience may stimulate, counsel, exhort to do what is right; it may warn that what seems to be a pleasure or a profit is evil. . . . [a]fter the decision has been made and the act decided upon has been accomplished, conscience . . . appears in the form of a judgment, stating that whatever was done was right or wrong, and this judgment is accompanied by feelings of approval or disapproval.
>
> A person who holds that he himself is the final norm by which to govern his conduct in moral matters can be expected to establish somewhat elastic rules, which will easily reflect his own inclinations.[91]

Secondly, availability of the Pill has facilitated a shift in the social acceptability of premarital intercourse. Carl Djerassi, the chemist who first synthesized the chemical steroids for the Pill in 1951, states that the Pill "clearly has had a tremendous impact on sexual mores . . . a desirable impact . . . in helping to

---

[87] "Teenage Pregnancy: A Comparison of Certain Characteristics Among Utah Youth", pt. 3, Utah State Office of Education, August 1981.

[88] Edward S. Herold, Marilyn S. Goodwin, "Premarital Sexual Guilt and Contraceptive Attitudes and Behavior", *Family Relations,* April 1981, 247–53.

[89] Ibid.

[90] "The Human Right to Family Planning", International Planned Parenthood Federation, November 1983.

[91] James H. VanderVeldt and Robert P. Odenwald, *Psychiatry and Catholicism* (New York: McGraw-Hill, 1952), 20, 23.

[92] Interview with Carl Djerassi, *Prism,* American Medical Association (February 1974): 20–23, 35.

liberate the younger generation."[92] Pro-birth control writer Susan Scrimshaw states that the Pill has been a catalyst for the

> most rapid and profound changes in sexual attitudes and behavior, in the altered dynamic of the male-female relationship, in the role of women in society. . . . Some of these changes might have taken place without the pill, "but they didn't". . . . The increased openness of sexual activity outside of marriage, which has accelerated since 1960, has clearly been linked by many adult participants to more effective contraception.[93]

Third, providing adolescents with the Pill increases the incidence of pre-marital intercourse. In 1963 Dr. Alan Guttmacher of Planned Parenthood, who had urged that teenagers be provided with birth control information, conceded that such information would bring about an increase in sexual relations among teenagers.[94] Dr. Michael Halberstam in 1970 told *Redbook* readers that " . . . when the use of contraceptives spreads through a society, one thing that happens is that the age of sexual intercourse and first exposure to unwanted pregnancy drops lower and lower."[95]

A Swedish researcher also notes the same effect of increasing sexual con-tacts for unmarried women relying upon oral contraceptives. "The second factor which might be responsible for the increase of venereal disease among university students is that they now are less afraid of pregnancy when P-pills are used (by 33–50 per cent of the females). They therefore have fewer inhibitions concerning sexual intercourse."[96]

And premarital sex has a tendency to spill over into extramarital sex. Alfred Kinsey noted in his famous study that 29% of the females with premarital sexual experience had had extramarital affairs as well. This was more than double the 13% of those who had had extramarital, but not premarital, sexual encounters.[97] This is supported by a study at a British venereal disease clinic of married women of all social classes who had taken the Pill for at least a year. They were asked: "(1) Have you had extramarital intercourse since taking the Pill? (2) Would you have thought twice about having extramarital sexual relations had you not been taking the Pill?" Of the ninty-two women questioned, sixty-three acknowledged having an extramarital affair, and forty-four of these said they would have thought twice if they had not been on the

[93] Susan C. M. Scrimshaw, "Women and the Pill: From Panacea to Catalyst", *Family Planning Perspectives*, vol. 13, no. 6 (November–December 1981): 254–62.

[94] David Gardner, "Speakers Discuss Modern Day Sex", *Knickerbocker News*, Albany, New York, December 6, 1963, 3B.

[95] Michael J. Halberstam, "Abortion: A Startling Proposal", *Redbook*, April 1970, 138.

[96] Lennart Juhlin, "Factors Influencing the Spread of Gonorrhea", *Acta Dermatologica Venereologica*, vol. 48 (1968): 82–89.

[97] Alfred C. Kinsey et al., *Sexual Behavior in the Human Female* (Philadelphia: W. B. Saunders, 1953), 427–28.

Pill. The majority had started taking the Pill simply to avoid pregnancy. The author of the survey notes:

> The majority of women taking the "pill" took it to prevent pregnancy. . . . With married women, promiscuity developed gradually with the increasing realization that they could no longer conceive. From the case histories it would appear that once a woman has started taking oral contraceptives, the likelihood of promiscuity is as great in the so-called stable university under-graduate as it is . . . [in lower social/economic, classes]. . . . In this manner sexual continence with one partner becomes jeopardized when oral contra-ceptives are taken.[98]

Finally, adolescents on the Pill become more active sexually. In the age of AIDS, that may be lethal. Teens aged thirteen to seventeen at a midwestern Planned Parenthood facility (87.5% using the Pill), for example, reported that their mean frequency of sexual intercourse increased from 4.3 to 6.8 times a month after clinic attendance and contraceptive prescription. Also, the mean number of sexual associates increased from 2.7 to 3.3.[99]

Another survey of girls aged eighteen showed an "undeniable increase" in the monthly frequency of sexual intercourse (7.1/month) compared to the nonclinic group (3.8/month) after receiving birth control. "[S]uch increases may reasonably be attributed to the peace of mind which effective contracep-tion can provide."[100]

The Intrauterine Device

The commercial availability of the IUD was hastened by the desire of popula-tion controllers to develop even simpler antifertility methods that could be set in motion so to speak, and "forgotten", and by medical problems associated with the Pill. Since the sexual revolt, there seems to be an unwritten law that as soon as problems with one method of artificial birth control are acknowledged or cannot be suppressed any longer, other methods are touted as trouble-free replacements. Thus, the IUD was thought to initially fit the bill for women who could no longer use the Pill.

But this did not last either. And the problems that were minimized or said to be statistically irrelevant become the selling point for the next antifertility intervention, as can be seen from a 1971 Planned Parenthood request for

[98] L. Cohen, "The Pill, Promiscuity, and Venereal Disease", *British Journal of Venereal Diseases*, vol. 46 (1970): 108–10.

[99] Paul A. Reichelt, "Changes in Sexual Behavior among Unmarried Teenage Women Utilizing Birth Control", *Journal of Population*, vol. 1 (Spring 1978): 57–68.

[100] C. Amechi Akpom et al., "Teenage Sexual Behavior: Perceptive and Behavioral Outcomes Associated with Receipt of Family Planning Services", *Journal of Biosocial Science*, vol. 1, no. 1 (January 1979): 85–92.

federal grant money to offer poor women the alleged benefits of sterilization! There, the IUD was cited as more problematic than the Pill, with contraindications including:

> Cancer of the cervix or uterus, endocarditis, rheumatic fever, pelvic inflammatory disease, cervicitis, purulent discharge, suspicious pap, history of uterine infection, pregnancy, polyps, prolapsed uterus, nulligravida woman, unexplained uterine or vaginal bleeding, uterine tumors, etc. Complications after insertion include pregnancy, intermenstrual bleeding and pain, spontaneous expulsion, embedding and perforation of the uterus, ectopic pregnancy, and disappearance of "tails" into the uterus.[101]

The intrauterine device is a metal or plastic mechanism inserted into the uterus to prevent pregnancy. The designation covers various designs such as the Dalkon Shield, the Lippes Loop, the Saf-t-Coil, the Majzlin spring, and many others.

In 1959 Alan Guttmacher wrote that "intrauterine devices are mentioned only to be thoroughly condemned because of their ineffectiveness as well as their carcinogenic potentialities. . . . It is believed that both intrauterine rings and cervical stem pessaries function by causing very early abortion after the egg implants."[102] But Guttmacher's critical assessments of the IUD soon changed, as had his negative evaluation of the Pill.

During January and February of 1963, International Planned Parenthood and the Population Council dispatched Guttmacher and his wife on a world tour to study birth control. Before long, Guttmacher advised the Population Council to support research into the IUD, which, of course, it was delighted to do.[103]

From the beginning, there was institutionalized deception about the ill-effects of the IUD and its mode of action in preventing pregnancy.

Dangers of the IUD

Alan Guttmacher's reversal on the IUD, which he had previously "thoroughly condemned" as a potential cancer-causing device, was soon complete.[104] He wrote in 1966 that

---

[101] PPFA to Warren Hern, Executive Office of the President, memo, Office of Economic Opportunity, Anderson County, Tennessee, Family Planning Project, 1970 grant request, no. 40482.

[102] Alan Guttmacher and Hilliard Dubrow, "The Present Status of Contraceptives", *Mt. Sinai Journal of Medicine,* vol. 26 (1959): 119.

[103] Alan Guttmacher, "Intrauterine Contraceptive Devices", eighth Olive Bird lecture delivered at the London School of Hygiene and Tropical Medicine, November 26, 1964, in *Journal of the Society for the Study of Fertility Research,* Committee of the IPPF Indian Society for the Study of Reproduction, 115–28.

[104] Guttmacher and Dubrow, "Present Status of Contraceptives", 118–24.

after six years of observation, there is no evidence that an IUD causes cancer or any other grave difficulty. Less serious medical problems have been encountered such as an occasional infection or, even in rare cases, perforation of the uterus by the device, but these and other complications can be safely cared for.[105]

In 1971 Aquiles J. Sobrero, a Planned Parenthood official and director of the Margaret Sanger Research Bureau in New York at the time, suggested that the IUD be inserted during the menstrual period because any resulting bleeding would then be "masked by the menses".[106]

One model, the Lippes Loop, was developed by Planned Parenthood official Dr. Jack Lippes. An article by another PPFA official, Miriam Y. Manisoff, promoted "improved designs" such as the Dalkon Shield and the Majzlin Spring".[107]

Unfortunately for Manisoff, on May 25, 1973, the FDA pronounced the Majzlin Spring a danger to women's health and ordered it removed from the market and the unsold products seized.[108] In June 1974, the FDA "requested" that the A. H. Robins Company, manufacturers of the Dalkon Shield, suspend sales of that device.[109] The following January, the Robins Company told its sales people that the problems with the Dalkon Shield were such that it should be returned to the manufacturer. The FDA also recommended against further use of the device.[110] Much adverse publicity followed, including an extraordinary class-action suit against Robins that resulted in $395 million in legal judgments against the company and its filing for bankruptcy protection in 1985.

The U.S. House of Representatives Government Operations Subcommittee on Intergovernmental Relations held hearings on the IUD in May and June of 1973. Dr. John G. Madry, Jr., a member of the Florida Obstetrics and Gynecologic Society, testified on the dangers of the IUD, a variety of which were in use in Planned Parenthood clinics.

Madry stated that "it became unmistakably and abundantly clear by early 1969 that IUDs were causing problems". Based on these problems, he

---

[105] Alan Guttmacher, "Birth Control Methods", *Report of the Victor Fund for the International Planned Parenthood Federation,* no. 4, December 1966, 22.

[106] Aquiles J. Sobrero, "Intrauterine Devices in Clinical Practice", *Family Planning Perspectives,* vol. 31, no. 1 (January 1971): 16.

[107] Miriam T. Manisoff, "Intrauterine Devices", *American Journal of Nursing,* vol. 73, no. 7 (July 1973): 1192.

[108] *Federal Register,* July 1, 1975, 27796.

[109] Statement of Alexander Schmidt, commissioner of the FDA, December 20, 1974, issued at a press conference; supporting documents.

[110] FDA *Drug Bulletin,* January–March 1975, 2.

set out to find the mortality rates for IUD users; his primary method was to make requests of "some twelve organizations dealing with health and contraception". In all the replies, Madry said, "there were no satisfactory answers to any of my questions" about the "number of deaths" related to IUD use.[111]

It was pointed out that George Langmyhr, medical director of Planned Parenthood–World Population, had said that "if the adverse reporting on oral contraceptives is somewhat inadequate, I can assure you that that for the IUD is even more so."[112]

Moreover, all the patients who were unavailable for the follow-up studies cited by Madry were "eliminated from consideration in presentation of final results on the basis that 'lost' patients are identical to those not lost". Madry added: "I am aware of no other studies related to patient care in any of its aspects where such a presumptuous, fallacious, mathematical formula has been applied to evaluation of experimental results obtained in human beings subjected to medical treatment of any kind."[113]

He went on to point out that a 1968 FDA report on the IUD "appears to have been authored by a committee predominantly composed of individuals having population control, rather than individual, or family planning, interests".[114] He was right.

In fact, the membership of the Advisory Committee on Obstetrics and Gynecology that issued the 1968 report was almost identical to the committee on the Pill mentioned earlier and was heavily weighted with Planned Parenthood officials and sympathizers. This time, however, another Planned Parenthood supporter was included, one Sheldon Segal.

Madry also commented on IUD injuries that were not only serious but also unusual. Examples included a Richter's hernia resulting from a displaced IUD and a uterine perforation by a Birnberg Bow IUD. "These reports", testified Madry, "are very frequent in the literature, and this is a serious complication requiring hospitalization posing danger to the life of the patient, and considerable expense." Madry told his own patients that "the only difference between the stone placed in the womb of the camel and the intrauterine device of today is the material, and there is no evidence that one is safer than the other". It also emerged in the hearings that physicians who discover IUD complications are under no obligation to report them to the FDA or to any other federal or state authority.[115]

Testifying at the hearings was Dr. Russell J. Thomson, who had worked in

---

[111] House Intergovernmental Relations Subcommittee, *Regulation of Medical Devices, Intrauterine Contraceptive Devices,* 93d Cong., 1st sess., June 1973, 4–48, 167–78, John Madry testimony.
[112] Ibid.
[113] Ibid.
[114] Ibid.
[115] Ibid.

Planned Parenthood clinics and was at one time an enthusiastic promoter of IUDs. He spoke of the "disastrous nature of IUD-induced pregnancies" and their "dire consequences" that were "absolutely omitted from any mention in either advertising for the medical profession or patient information pamphlets put out, I might add, by the drug companies or by such organizations as Planned Parenthood".[116]

About 40 to 60% of pregnancies occurring with IUDs in place, Thomson said, "terminate in spontaneous miscarriages" that are "serious medical emergencies requiring surgical completion with or without anesthesia, frequently the transfusion of whole blood, and often the use of massive doses of antibiotics because of infection".[117] Thomson had seen "a number of women faint following IUD insertion and particularly from the Dalkon Shield". In addition, X-rays were frequently necessary to locate displaced IUDs.

> I am sure that no one can calculate the genetic harm or carcinogenic harm done to American women and future generations by the yearly exposure of 40,000 ovaries to X-ray. But only a fool would claim that those X-rays are good for ovaries and the eggs they produce.[118]

For every woman who claimed that her IUD had increased her enjoyment of the marital bed by relieving fears of an unintended pregnancy, Thomson cited "two or more whose prolonged menses, unpredictable bleeding, and pelvic pain had either lowered the satisfaction of the sexual experience or basically compelled her to refrain from sexual expression until her IUD complications were resolved."[119]

Just as Planned Parenthood had conceded that IUDs cause early abortion in order to argue for legalization of postimplantation abortion, the organization also admitted the many serious medical problems with the IUD when it had other goals in mind. The statement used as an epigraph to this section acknowledged that the IUD had "more complications than the Pill"; these complications were mentioned as a reason for sterilization in a 1971 Planned Parenthood affiliate request for a federal grant to be used for the permanent sterilization of poor people in Tennessee.

The Planned Parenthood input to the federal government's major administrative and advisory bodies on the safety of the IUD continued in the 1970s. Members of a 1975 FDA task force on IUDs included four Planned Parenthood officials: Louise Tyrer, Theodore King, Robert Steptoe, and Richard Dickey.

The FDA's Obstetrics and Gynecology Drug Advisory Committee, which produced the second IUD report, included three Planned Parenthood staffers:

[116] Ibid., Russell Thomson testimony, 48–66.
[117] Ibid.
[118] Ibid.
[119] Ibid.

Gordon Griggs, Sheldon Segal, and Roman Garcia Celso. A fourth member, Howard Ory, had written for PPFA publications.

The FDA's Ob-Gyn Devices Classification Panel included five people either members of or connected with Planned Parenthood: William E. Brenner, Luella Klein, John B. Josimovich, John T. Queenan, and Richard M. Soderstram. Panel consultants included three Planned Parenthood representatives: Elizabeth B. Connell, William Cooke Andrews, and William J. Ledger.

The high number of PPFA people (approximately half the members from 1965 to 1980) involved in FDA advisory committees concerning products that in many cases PPFA had helped develop and in all cases vigorously promoted represented a rather unique circumstance in government regulation. In no other field of government regulation, whether air safety or interstate commerce or securities, could such a cozy arrangement have prevailed without public outcry.

One of Planned Parenthood's standard horror stories is the back-alley abortionist with his coathanger at the ready. It seems clear from expert testimony that the IUD is a kind of internal abortionist and coathanger all in one, able to do its work automatically and largely undetected, but with many if not all of the same dangers to the mother and her developing child.

Were any new food product or children's toy to cause even a fraction of the injuries, let alone deaths, due to the Pill and the IUD, it would surely be stripped from the shelves and banned from the marketplace.

The testimony of Russell Thomson revealed the stake that IUD manufacturers and promoters had in its continued sale, why they had fought so fiercely for it, and why they airily blame the "product-liability crisis" for the non-marketability of these devices now. Thomson pointed out that, with sufficient unit volume, it costs a company a paltry thirty-five to forty cents to manufacture, sterilize, and package an IUD. Most IUDs in the late 1960s and early 1970s sold for $3.00 or $3.50. "That is, let it be understood, a markup for Julius Schmid Pharmaceuticals of about ten times—or 1,000 percent—over production costs". And that markup, Thomson testified, "has come with little or no expenditure by the manufacturer for medical testing of the safety of its product. It might appear callous—but it is true—the name of the game in the IUD industry is profit."[120] It would appear that serious medical complications and human suffering are acceptable overhead.

[120] Ibid.

Chapter Nine

Evolution of the "Right to an Abortion"

In 1971, Dr. George Langmyhr, Planned Parenthood medical director at the time, acknowledged that

> Planned Parenthood Affiliates have long been involved in programs of abortion information, counseling, and referral. Before the recent change in abortion laws, these activities were, necessarily, unpublicized . . . [and] most professionals and volunteers associated with Planned Parenthood have accepted for a long time the necessity of abortion as an integral part of any complete . . . family planning program.[1]

Dr. Langmyhr wasn't talking about a sudden switch in policy after Margaret Sanger's death in 1966. Abortion involvement began under her leadership at least as early as 1913.

When the topic of abortion came up, Sanger's flair for the dramatic helped her to draw a line just where her particular audience wanted it. This line was different for each new audience, a testimony to her ability to adapt her birth control crusade to the needs of the moment.

Her method was deceptively simple. First, she would personalize her message with a horror story from 1913 about Sadie Sachs, a mother of three whose husband, Jake, apparently ignored the doctor's prior advice to "sleep on the roof". Though poor, Sanger related in her speeches, he phoned her after Sadie attempted a second, and this time unsuccessful, self-abortion. Sanger arrived ten minutes after Sadie died. The Sadie Sachs case, with its real or exaggerated pathos, provided all the arguments a selfless crusader for the downtrodden needed to go about unchallenged in her motives and methods—a bereaved husband, three motherless children, grinding poverty, a determined woman who felt another child would jeopardize her ability to care for those she already had, etc., Sanger wrote:

> I walked home in a daze, weary and heartsick. I walked and walked, all the while the resolve got stronger. . . . The dawn was rising as I reached my room and I stood at my window and looked over the sleeping city. . . . I could feel myself the awful fear pressing on these families . . . women always

[1] George Langmyhr, "The Role of Planned Parenthood–World Population in Abortion", in *Implementation of Legal Abortion: A National Problem*, ed. Gerald Holzman, vol. 14, no. 4 of *Clinical Obstetrics and Gynecology* (New York: Harper and Row, Medical Department, December 1971), 1190–91.

pregnant ... men, unable to take care of their ever-increasing families ... I threw my nursing bag across the room ... and made up my mind.... Women had a right to know about their own bodies; they should know about birth control. I would tell the world what was happening. I would be heard.[2]

Agile use of numbers was her second tactic. Sanger was enthralled by numbers, whether dealing with astrology, or the span of her previous reincarnations, or as "proof" of her birth control thesis. In this case, she claimed there were a whopping 2,000,000 abortions per year in the United States in 1912 and 1913.[3] There were no records to support this claim, but Sanger deftly countered sceptics, using another set of numbers to charge them with insensitivity. She claimed a toll of 250,000 maternal deaths per year from pregnancy, illegal abortion, and childbearing.[4] Surely, something had to be done to stop this appalling devastation.

It was a year-in, year-out variation of this standard script that led many commentators to believe that Sanger was actually opposed to abortion. But, in fact, her apparent opposition to abortion was a tactic for public relations purposes. She had a long record of support for hygienic abortion performed by "competent" personnel. In March 1914 in a publication called *The Woman Rebel*, Sanger hinted at approval of abortion. She suggested that feminists would "claim the right to be lazy ... an unmarried mother ... to create ... to destroy ... ".[5] The very next issue of her newsletter claimed that woman had to be "absolute mistress of her own body ... to procreate or to suppress the germ of life".[6]

In 1916, making slight of the difference between contraception and abortion, Sanger said:

> No woman can call herself free who cannot choose to be a mother or not as she sees fit ... knowledge of birth control was obtained and prac-
> ticed among the women of wealth while the working women were deliberately kept in ignorance of this knowledge ... I found that the women of wealth were able to have abortions performed on them if it became necessary, while such care and attention was given them that seldom did a death occur among them ... I found that the women of the work-

[2] Margaret Sanger and John Connolly, Jr., "Does the Public Want Birth Control?", *True Confessions*, April 1936, 78.

[3] Fourth International Conference on Planned Parenthood, Stockholm, 1953, "The History of the Birth Control Movement in the English Speaking World", unedited translation from Sound-Mirror, by Margaret Sanger, 6, SSCSC.

[4] Ibid.

[5] *Woman Rebel*, vol. 1, no. 1, March 1914, Margaret Sanger, pub. and ed., found in Margaret Sanger, *The Woman Rebel and the Rise of the Birth Control Movement in the United States*, (New York: State University of New York, 1976), 1.

[6] Victor Meric, "The First Right", *Woman Rebel*, vol. 1, no. 2 (April 1914): 10, Ibid.

ing class were as anxious to obtain this knowledge as their sisters of wealth.[7]

This speech begged all of the questions Sanger was presuming to answer with birth control. Why, it may be asked, did the rich "need" abortions if they had access to birth control to prevent pregnancies? And was it really the poor who "needed" birth control (and abortion as a back-up) or was it the rich who wanted the poor to divest themselves of children?

A few years later, Sanger's magazine, the *Birth Control Review*, noted that when it came to rich women, a skilled abortionist "brings almost no danger to the life of the patient".[8]

This on-off attitude toward abortion did not escape the notice of famed marriage counselor Dr. Paul Popenoe, who pointed out:

American Birth Control propagandists, for tactical reasons, usually lay great emphasis on the appalling evil of abortion, representing that their panacea would cure this as well as all other maladies of society. But as the same propagandists are often believers in the desirability of free abortion, the weight of their testimony is somewhat diminished. Occasionally one of them speaks right out in open meeting.[9]

Such "speaking out" occurred at a 1921 birth control conference in New York City sponsored by Sanger's nascent Planned Parenthood group, then named the American Birth Control League. At this event, the "official" versus "private" Planned Parenthood abortion position surfaced. Dr. Andre Tridon said:

I also believe one thing, that the meaning of the perfectly insignificant operation called abortion should be made clear to all women . . . the operation is extremely insignificant, much less dangerous than having your nails manicured or having your face shaved in a more or less antiseptic barber shop. You may tell me . . . that we will be breaking the law. . . . Well . . . the law was an ass . . . breaking the law is not a crime, but a public duty.[10]

Sanger, who presided at this session, said: "I think the question of legality is quite settled in the principles and aims of the League . . . we know we have to change the law. There is no question about that."[11] State and federal statutes

[7] Margaret Sanger speech, Washington D.C., MSCLC. (This speech was first given in 1916 and delivered some 119 times.)

[8] Margaret Sanger, "Why Not Birth Control Clinics for America?", *Birth Control Review* (May 1919): 10.

[9] Paul Popenoe, *The Conservation of the Family* (Baltimore: Williams and Wilkins, 1926), 119.

[10] "Birth Control, What It Is, How It Works, What It Will Do", *Proceedings of the First American Birth Control Conference*, pub. by the *Birth Control Review*, 104 5th Avenue (New York: Gothic Press, 1921), 145.

[11] Ibid., 146.

at that time uniformly forbade abortion except to save the mother's life. Another speaker, Dr. Vaughan, added:

> The bringing about of an abortion should never be necessary; can never be moral; and must rarely be legal . . . [but] as long as children brought into the world are throttled by poverty, rocked by inherited insanity, snuffed out by inherited diseases, wasted by wars and by our social system, thoughtful mothers choose abortion when they feel it necessary, unless they are given some better alternative.[12]

At another Sanger-sponsored conference, this time in Zurich, Switzerland, the abortion question came up again. On this occasion Dr. Norman Haire of London asked his colleagues whether a woman should continue her pregnancy despite having an IUD in place or, likewise, when an IUD had been unknowingly inserted into an already pregnant woman. Dr. Manes of Hamburg, Germany answered: "The pregnancy should be interrupted in the interests of the child."[13]

Dr. Norbert Neufeld of Breslau reported that a colleague had been prosecuted for inserting an IUD, and he wondered if the German penal code made any distinction between prevention of implantation and prevention of fertilization.[14] Other physicians present also assumed the IUD was a method for early abortion. IUD inventor, Dr. Ernst Grafenberg, said that it prevented implantation and not fertilization. Yet he denied this was an abortion.[15] Grafenberg also suggested that "we never know whether complications of the woman will arise from a pregnancy. In such cases we are justified in the interests of the woman to prevent the progress of the pregnancy."[16]

Ironically when the subject of prevention of abortion was discussed, two papers were read that dealt with new abortion techniques. Dr. Stone, of Sanger's Birth Control Bureau in New York, talked about the American experience in inducing abortion by X ray.[17] Dr. Van de Velde responded, "The reproach will at once be hurled at us that we, who say we are working for the control of conception, are in reality for abortions."[18]

Meanwhile, back in New York at the Sanger Bureau, some very pragmatic steps were being taken during 1932 to assist women with untimely pregnancies. Marjorie Provost, assistant director of the clinic, wrote to Sanger about a

---

[12] Ibid., 19, 21.

[13] Margaret Sanger and Hannah Stone, eds., *The Practice of Contraception, an International Symposium and Survey, Proceedings of the Seventh International Birth Control Conference,* Zurich, Switzerland, September 1930 (Baltimore: Williams and Wilkins, 1930), 55–56, 61.

[14] Ibid., 60–61.

[15] Ibid., 40.

[16] Ibid., 70–71.

[17] Ibid., 190–91.

[18] Ibid., 196.

"high-class", pregnant, unmarried woman who had arrived at the clinic and who was urged to see her fiance after confirming her pregnancy. She did, but he fled. Returning to the clinic, she was sent to a friendly doctor. Provost told Sanger of the splendid outcome of the problem pregnancy.

But as these things had to be done sub rosa, Provost let Sanger know how careful she had been, relating that she had the young woman write down the doctor's name and address herself on blank paper.[19]

This gave Sanger an idea. Within a month, she told Dr. Stone that women with "medical indications" for dealing with problem pregnancies should have their medical records note any transmissible disease known [most likely claimed] in the husband's family. This would help the woman "protect herself against diseased progeny".[20]

Within a year, even more plans were afoot to help pregnant women "control" their fertility. In 1933 Sanger wrote to Dr. Stone about

> the overdues. Every clinic in the country is having an overwhelming number of these cases which . . . are receiving no attention from us but sent away . . . I want to make a special study of all overdue cases applying to us either in person or over the telephone . . . I should like to put one doctor in charge at the noon hour and that doctor to be chosen for her contact with hospitals or doctors who may, in therapeutic cases, give proper attention to those coming under that term. I should also like our cases classified according to indications of transmissible disease of either parent, disease of mother or father, condition of the children and the economic condition. This is not technically stated but you will no doubt be able to make out. You or the physician taking the patient will make out the technical terminology.
>
> I believe that if we can make a study of about 1,000 cases and get the data concerning their physical condition, why they want termination and the facilities in the community for same, we will be able to make a contribution that may justify further action.[21]

James Reed, author of a survey on birth control in America since 1830, said of this letter that "the law did not catch up with Margaret Sanger's vision until 1973", i.e., with the *Roe* and *Doe* Supreme Court abortion decisions.[22]

In spite of Sanger's claims on both sides of the Atlantic that birth control would prevent abortion, there were doubters in the medical profession. D. Beckworth Whitehouse, a British physician, noted in 1932:

[19] Letter from Marjorie Provost, assistant director, Margaret Sanger Clinical Research Bureau, to Margaret Sanger, February 15, 1932, SSCSC.

[20] Sanger letter to Dr. Hannah Stone, March 10, 1932, copy to Marjorie Provost (in MS's handwriting), SSCSC.

[21] Letter from Sanger to Stone, 41 Fifth Ave., N.Y., N.Y., January 31, 1933, MSCLC.

[22] James Reed, *From Private Vice to Public Virtue*, comp. James Reed (New York: Basic Books, Inc., 1978), 119.

within recent years I have been rather impressed with the attitude of mind of the woman who has practiced contraception and who has failed to attain her object. Such a woman instinctively seems to feel that she has the right to demand the termination of an unwanted pregnancy. The criminal aspect of the matter does not appear to enter her mind in the least.[23]

Dr. Cecil Vogue in 1934 at a Washington, D.C., birth control conference observed that the high abortion rate was in large part due to birth control failure.[24]

This abortion-birth control link was measured in 1936 by Planned Parenthood board member Dr. Raymond Pearl, who noted that "the number of induced abortions per 100 pregnancies experienced, and the percentage of reproductive wastage due to induced abortions, are from three to four times greater, generally speaking, among contraceptors than among non-contraceptors. . . . Negroes, generally speaking, resorted to induced abortion only about half as frequently. . . . "[25]

A second study published in 1940, focusing on Planned Parenthood's flagship birth control clinic, the Margaret Sanger Clinical Research Bureau, was even more damaging to the "birth control prevents abortion" thesis. It was conducted, by two researchers sympathetic to birth control, on 991 women who experienced 3,255 pregnancies. Of the contracepting women, 41% of the pregnancies terminated in illegal abortion. Of the noncontracepting women, 3.5% of the pregnancies terminated in illegal abortion.[26]

In spite of these studies, Morris Ernst, Sanger's lawyer, and Harriet Pilpel (who would later become Planned Parenthood's premiere attorney for over forty years) co-authored an article in December 1939 explaining how contraception came to be legal. Perhaps with feigned surprise, they wrote: "Oddly enough, the first ray of light filtered through in a case involving abortion, which is of course the antithesis of contraception, but which was lumped together with it in the Comstock laws."[27] Yet Pilpel would later "reverse" herself, acknowledging that legalized abortion was the logical culmination of

---

[23] Beckworth Whitehouse, "A Paper on the Indications for the Induction of Abortion", *British Medical Journal* (August 20, 1932): 337–40.

[24] Cecil I. B. Vogue, Ph.D., F.R.S.E., London School of Hygiene and Tropical Medicine, "Factors in the Measurement and Evaluation of Commercial Contraceptives", Conference on Birth Control and National Recovery, Washington, D.C., January 15–17, 1934, National Committee on Maternal Health, 1, SSCSC.

[25] Raymond Pearl, *The Natural History of Population* (London: Oxford University Press, 1939), 222, 240–41.

[26] Regina K. Stix and Frank Notestein, *Controlled Fertility* (Baltimore: William and Wilkins, 1940), 79–87.

[27] Morris Ernst and Harriet Pilpel, "Release from the Comstock Era", *Birth Control Review* (December 1939): 24.

such earlier court decisions, and in fact was the long-range goal of legal contraception on demand.[28]

The complete disproof, then or now, of Sanger's thesis by her own disciples and associates did not stop Planned Parenthood from claiming in pamphlet after pamphlet that birth control would prevent abortion, and that, in fact, abortion was not birth control. A 1939 brochure noted:

> Birth Control prevents conception, that is, the fertilization of the female egg or ovum through the union of the ovum and sperm, while abortion destroys life after the ovum has been fertilized. . . . Abortions are responsible for one-fourth of the high maternal death rate in America. The spread of reliable contraceptive knowledge will reduce this unnecessary waste of life.[29]

Yet spokesmen did occasionally stray from the text, usually at semipublic gatherings. "At the 1942 meeting of the Birth Control Federation of America in New York, Alan F. Guttmacher of Johns Hopkins suggested that the medical profession relax its barriers against therapeutic abortion, in order, as he put it, 'to cheat the criminal abortionist.' "[30] But in case statements like Guttmacher's confused anybody, Planned Parenthood was reassuring in a 1943 booklet aimed at social workers, *Confusing Abortion with Contraception.* It said:

> Therapeutic abortion, or abortion to save the life of the mother, is a medical procedure which can be resorted to with complete legality. All other abortions are illegal. Their toll in death, sterility and illness is appalling. The public is confused about the two types of abortion, and about either with birth control . . . proper accessibility of birth control information to married women through physicians would reduce the large proportion of abortions that occur among married women.[31]

The mention of reducing abortions "among married women" was a tactical necessity to reinforce in the public mind that illegal abortion primarily affected the "responsible, married woman" whose love led her to this drastic means to "protect" the children she already had from being subjected to a family-wrecking crisis. Sanger, in yet another and earlier "birth control prevents abortion" tract, had denied that birth control was abortion and would

---

[28] Harriet Pilpel, "Abortion: U.S. Style", *Journal of Sex Research,* vol. 2, no. 2 (May 1975): 118.

[29] *Questions and Answers about Birth Control,* Birth Control Federation of America, April 1939, SSCSC.

[30] Rev. Edgar Schmiedler, O.S.B., Ph.D., *25 Years of Uncontrol* (Huntington, Indiana: Our Sunday Visitor Press, 1943), 36. Schmiedler was director, Family Life Bureau, National Catholic Welfare Conference.

[31] *The Case Worker and Family Planning,* PPFA, April 22, 1943, 26, Library of Congress holdings.

lead to immorality among the unmarried. Instead, she claimed, it would lead to earlier marriage and decreased immorality.[32]

Nevertheless, Guttmacher's "therapeutic" approach eventually prevailed under the guise of the hospital abortion committee system. "At the end of World War II, there were no abortions, not even therapeutic ones, being done in hospitals under surgically clean conditions. The committee system that he [Guttmacher] and others had designed was a tiny but significant fracture in the monolithic wall built against abortion by the late 40's and early 50's."[33]

What the committee system gradually produced was a situation under which private patients with money and connections could get a therapeutic abortion for some "medical indication". Poor women, or ward patients, would be aborted far less often. Eventually the committee system, at least among private patients, would embrace not only physical health maladies, but mental ones as well. There is more than a little irony here. Guttmacher would come to deplore the hypocrisy of the very system he helped to establish because the more socially advantaged patients got more abortions than the poor. Legal abortion would change that, however, and make of the committee system merely one stage along Planned Parenthood's methodical progression toward legal abortion on demand.

Credentialing the "need" for a reassessment of the nation's abortion laws, a Planned Parenthood–sponsored conference of medical experts in 1955 decried the "contradictory" abortion situation in the United States. An abortion would be therapeutic at one hospital but denied elsewhere.[34] However, the public would have to wait until 1958 before the conference proceedings were published. When they were, it was quite apparent that recommendations had been adopted that could result in more liberal access to abortion. Pursuing the hypocrisy theme, the pro-birth-control experts "deplored" the wider access to contraceptives and abortion the rich and better-educated enjoyed relative to the underprivileged. The conference recommended that a model law be drawn up to "correct" the situation. This was the genesis of what eventually became the abortion "reform" movement, scoring its first legislative victory with the passage of a liberalized abortion law in Colorado in 1967.[35,36]

It may be unique in social history that the very creators of a situation

[32] *The Case for Birth Control, Questions and Answers,* Birth Control International Information Centre, London, Margaret Sanger, president, undated, SSCSC.

[33] Bernard Nathanson, M.D. and Richard N. Ostling, *Aborting America,* comp. Nathanson and Ostling (Garden City, N.Y.: Doubleday and Co., 1979), 147.

[34] *Planned Parenthood News,* no. 13, Fall 1955, 8.

[35] *Planned Parenthood News,* no. 21, Spring 1958, 8.

[36] Mary Calderone, ed., *Abortion in the United States* (New York: Harper and Row, 1958), 183.

assigned themselves the leading role in proposing an answer to the dilemma they had helped to frame. Somehow this maneuver escaped public notice.

A model abortion law was proposed at a May 1959 meeting of the American Law Institute (ALI). The model law allowed abortion until the twenty-sixth week of pregnancy if the doctor believed that the mother's physical or mental health would be gravely impaired; if the child would be born with grave physical handicap, or the pregnancy resulted from felonious intercourse, i.e., rape or incest. Abortions were to be performed in a hospital. The proposed code revision specifically exempted from the abortion restrictions drugs or devices that prevented implantation of the fertilized ovum. The wording used posited two beginnings for the same pregnancy, i.e., fertilization and implantation.[37] This double beginning of pregnancy apparently posed no problem for these solons.

Alan Guttmacher's brother, Manfred, a psychiatrist, was a member of the ALI law revision panel. So was Judge Learned Hand, who, along with two other U.S. Appeals Court judges, had overturned the congressional ban on importing contraceptives in 1936, if done for health reasons (*U.S. v. One Pessary*). Hand's wife was a member of Sanger's Birth Control League, and his daughter, Mrs. Robert Ferguson, later became president of the PPFA from 1953 to 1956.[38] Judge Hand complained to Guttmacher that the ALI proposal was "too damned conservative".[39]

This Planned Parenthood–spawned ALI proposal added some interesting nuances to the meaning of "health". First was the provision that if the child was not healthy, he could be put to death. Second, the child — and this is not explained — was held capable of causing the mother's mental health to deteriorate, and therefore he could be killed.

It would take several years of behind-the-scenes lobbying before the phalanx of state life-of-the-mother-only abortion laws gave way to reform. And it was during this same period that the internal contradictions of Planned Parenthood's leaders became more acute.

Alan Guttmacher's own views are quite instructive. By 1961 he clearly wanted "therapeutic" indications for abortion broadened. By this time he was tired of subterfuge in the abortion approval process and even expressed a preference for a head-on attack on tough abortion laws dating from 1803 because they were not in harmony with contemporary medicine and morals.[40]

---

[37] Model Penal Code, Proposed Official Draft, The American Law Institute, May 4, 1962, c. ALI, 1962, 189, 191.

[38] Obituary notice for Mrs. Learned Hand (mentioning Mrs. Robert Ferguson), *New York Times*, December 13, 1963, and early Birth Control League Stationery.

[39] Quoted in Alan Guttmacher, "Abortion: Odyssey of an Adventure", *Family Planning Perspectives*, vol. 4, no. 4 (1972): 6.

[40] Alan Guttmacher letter to Dr. Clay H. Johnson, Dallas, Texas, October 5, 1961, CLHMS.

One major impediment to legal change that Guttmacher identified in 1963 was the Catholic Church, which he believed was so well organized and populous in the Northeast, that several decades would pass before abortion laws could be changed.[41] Guttmacher opined that even Planned Parenthood was some distance from supporting a major shift in abortion laws.[42] But he did not let this hesitation or his role as national Planned Parenthood president deter him from advocating the establishment of, and being willing to join, a nationwide abortion reform organization.[43]

In 1965 he told his newsletter readers that "CBS Reports" would examine the world-wide abortion situation, placing Guttmacher in a leading role covering post-conception birth control. Included was a segment with Dr. G. Lotrell Timanus, a retired abortionist from Baltimore.[44]

Hyping the problem of illegal abortion—worsened by increased access to birth control, courtesy of Planned Parenthood—would become the policy instrument to hasten legalized abortion. During the 1960s the abortion argument was usually posed as follows:

1. There are millions of women faced with an unwanted pregnancy who cannot be deterred from abortion.
2. But illegal abortion is unsafe and thousands of women will die.
3. While medically induced abortion is socially and morally repellent, illegal abortion is more so. Therefore, the lesser evil of legal abortion [called "moral" by some] is to be preferred to the greater evil of illegal abortion.

This Planned Parenthood thesis, both pre- and post-*Roe v. Wade*, has required its advocates to perform a careful balancing act involving the creative manufacture and fabrication of "facts" to convince the public of its validity. First of all the social problems had to be of such magnitude that the public could be manipulated into clamoring that, indeed, "something had to be done".

This was accomplished by touting the number of illegal abortions, and ensuing maternal deaths. There were plenty of figures for any occasion or audience. Dr. Robert Hall, associated with Planned Parenthood and president and co-founder of the Association for the Study of Abortion, said in 1967 that

---

[41] Alan Guttmacher letter to Mrs. A. Falini, New York, New York, April 17, 1963, CLHMS.

[42] Alan Guttmacher letter to Arthur M. Jackson, Lebanon, Oregon, December 8, 1964, CLHMS.

[43] Ibid.

[44] Alan Guttmacher, *Presidential Letter,* February 26, 1965, no. 3, 4.

there were 1,000,000 illegal abortions annually.[45] Also in 1967, Harriet Pilpel had suggested there were from 1,000,000 to 1,500,000 illegal abortions.[46] Alan Guttmacher placed the number of illegal abortions in 1967 between 500,000 and 2,000,000.[47]

A Realistic Abortion Maternal Death Toll Assessment

The second set of figures used to intimidate the public into accepting legal abortion was the alleged numbers of maternal deaths from illegal abortion. Whatever the death toll was from illegal abortion in the 1930s, it had dropped considerably in the 1950s and 1960s. In 1950 the AMA published figures clearly demonstrating the decreasing death rates from illegal abortion: Data for abortion with mention of infection in 1933 showed 2,037 deaths, or 0.98 deaths per 1,000 live births, comprising 15.8% of total maternal mortality. Data for abortion with mention of infection in 1948 showed 289 deaths, or 0.08 deaths per 1,000 live births, comprising 7% of total maternal mortality. This represented a 92% decrease in death rates attributed to illegal abortion from 1933 to 1948.[48]

At New Orleans' Charity Hospital, maternal deaths from illegal abortion in that period decreased because of "the liberal use of chemotherapy and antibiotics, the availability of blood for transfusion, and recognition and prompt treatment of complications".[49] During the four and one-half years prior to 1941, the death rate from illegal abortion was 1.06% of women aborting. By 1951 that figure had dropped to 0.46%.[50]

Louisiana is of particular interest as the antiabortion law there did not allow for the life-of-the-mother exception. Did this have an adverse effect on maternal health? In 1949 the maternal mortality for whites was 0.7/1000 live births and 2.1/1000 for nonwhites.[51] The maternal death rates for the entire United States were almost identical: 0.68/1000 live births for whites, 2.3/1000

[45] Robert E. Hall, M.D., "Abortion in American Hospitals", *American Journal of Public Health* (November 1967): 1933–36.

[46] Harriet F. Pilpel, "The Abortion Crisis", *The Case for Legalized Abortion Now,* ed. Alan Guttmacher (Berkeley, Calif.: Diablo Press, 1967), 97–113.

[47] Alan F. Guttmacher, M.D., *Pregnancy, Birth, and Family Planning, A Guide for Expectant Parents in the 1970s* (New York: Viking Press, 1967), 165.

[48] Frank G. Dickinson and Everett L. Welker, "Maternal Mortality in the United States in 1949", *Journal of the American Medical Association,* vol. 144, no. 16 (December 16, 1950): 1395–1400.

[49] Jason H. Collins, "Abortions—A Study Based on 1,304 Cases", *American Journal of Obstetrics and Gynecology* (September 1951): 548–58.

[50] Ibid., 558.

[51] John S. LeMasson and J. D. Martin, "Maternal, Fetal and Infant Mortality in Louisiana", *New Orleans Medical and Surgical Journal* (December 1950): 234–43.

live births for nonwhites.[52] This is all the more remarkable because at that time Louisiana ranked fortieth out of the forty-eight states in per capita personal income.[53] Income is a usually reliable indicator of quality medical care.

It was precisely data such as these, which were available to knowledgeable medical and public health leaders, that led the more honest of them to question the allegedly high incidence of illegal abortions. For example, Peter Diggory relates:

> The medical profession has tended to say that criminal abortion is exceedingly dangerous, and indeed that belief was responsible, in England at any rate, for the medical establishment doubting the high numbers of criminal abortions estimated by the police, demographers and others, simply on grounds that there were not as many deaths as they would have expected. . . . [54]

Diggory also suggests that illegal abortionists had access to antibiotics by 1965.[55]

But none of the above is the stuff of which a sexual or legal revolution can be made. Dr. Bernard Nathanson, former abortion practitioner and now an ardent pro-lifer, has laid bare the rather utilitarian nature of illegal abortion death claims. He has written:

> How many deaths were we talking about when abortion was illegal? In N.A.R.A.L. [the National Association for the Repeal of Abortion Laws, now known as the National Abortion Rights Action League] we generally emphasized the drama of the individual case, not the mass statistics, but when we spoke of the latter it was always "5,000 to 10,000 deaths a year." I confess that I knew the figures were totally false, and I suppose the others did too if they stopped to think of it. But in the "morality" of our revolution, it was a useful figure, widely accepted, so why go out of the way to correct it with honest statistics? The overriding concern was to get the laws eliminated, and anything within reason that had to be done was permissible.[56]

Lawrence Lader, who wrote a hagiographical biography of Margaret Sanger, worked with Nathanson on this "number-puffing" project, orchestrating the statistical hysteria leading to the pre-*Roe v. Wade* abortion "reform" laws. Lader wrote:

---

[52] Vital Statistics, series B 136–47, Bicentennial Edition, *Historical Statistics of the United States, Colonial Times to 1970*, pt. 1, 57.

[53] National Product and Income, series F 297-348, ibid., 243–45.

[54] Peter Diggory, "A Review of Abortion Practices and Their Safety" in *Second Trimester Pregnancy Termination*, ed. Marc J. N. C. Keirse et al. (The Hague: Leiden University Press, Martinus Nijhoff, 1982), 36.

[55] Ibid., 37.

[56] Nathanson and Ostling, *Aborting America*, 193.

Unable to obtain a safe hospital abortion, a woman may resort to the horrors of self-abortion — rubber tubes, knitting needles, soap solutions and other chemicals which invariably lead to mutilation and often death. Or she may turn to the filthy back rooms of untrained, nonmedical abortionists where infection [remember Dr. Diggory's antibiotics], lack of anesthesia, and lethal techniques create similar butchery. At least 350,000 patients are admitted to hospitals annually with complications from such abortions. From 500 to 1,000 die.[57]

Fifty-two pages later, Lader cited a much-inflated illegal abortion maternal death toll from an April 1967 *New York Times* article about then Colorado legislator — and later governor — Richard Lamm's abortion liberalization bill. The article stated, "It [the bill] offers dignity and decency in place of present pitiless restrictions thoughout the nation which have resulted in . . . the needless death of four thousand mothers each year."[58] Lader did not bother to correct the nation's paper of record in its transparent news advocacy. Why should he? Fact-checking had long been rare activity in the abortion advocacy field.

In 1966 Lader wrote that "One recent study at the University of California's School of Public Health estimated 5,000 to 10,000 abortion deaths annually. Dr. Tietze places the figure nearer 1,000. Yet almost half of all childbearing deaths in New York City are attributed to abortion alone."[59] Such efforts were commonplace. During the campaign to legalize abortion during 1967 and 1968, the California Committee to Legalize Abortion produced a brochure which read in bold letters, "8,000 Women Die".[60]

Still, during the early 1960s, Planned Parenthood's public tack was officially not supportive of liberalized abortion, though long-working undercurrents would gradually place the organization in the forefront of the abortion fight. Thus, Alan Guttmacher felt no apparent conflict when he referred to an early obstetrical practice as "intrauterine murder" (he was describing the ancient procedure of dissecting the baby in utero, prior to the development of the cesarean section, whenever labor came to a halt).[61] Guttmacher noted that moralists reasoned that such babies had forfeited their claim on life because they didn't cooperate in the birth process, which was looked at as evidence of their morally deficient character.[62]

---

[57] Lawrence Lader, *Abortion II: Making the Revolution* (Boston: Beacon Press, c. 1973), 13.

[58] Ibid., 65.

[59] Lawrence Lader, *Abortion* (Boston: Beacon Press, c. 1966), 3.

[60] From California Committee to Legalize Abortion, single page brochure in the author's possession, courtesy Dr. Herbert Ratner.

[61] Speech of Alan Guttmacher, president, Planned Parenthood–World Population, "The Challenge for Family Planning", San Francisco, Calif., May 15, 1962, 4, CLHMS.

[62] Ibid.

In 1963 Planned Parenthood produced one final version of its standard "What Is Birth Control" brochure, which stated that abortion took the life of a child before it was born.[63] After this, it seems, the truth was too painful or embarrassing for the organization.

As indicated above, spurred by intensive planning and lobbying by pro-abortion activists, Colorado became the first state to adopt the American Law Institute's abortion reform bill. The ALI model said that

> A physician is justified in terminating a pregnancy if he believes there is substantial risk that continuance of the pregnancy would gravely impair the physical or mental health of the mother or that the child would be born with grave physical or mental defect, or that the pregnancy resulted from rape, incest, or other felonious intercourse. All illicit intercourse with a girl below the age of 16 shall be deemed felonious. . . . [64]

As noted above, the ALI proposal did not apply to drugs or devices "for avoiding pregnancy, whether by preventing implantation of a fertilized ovum or by any other method that operates before, at or immediately after fertilization".[65] All other abortions were third degree felonies, except that abortion past twenty-six weeks was a second degree felony.[66]

Besides the abortionists hammering away and conjuring up the specter of illegal abortion, an undoubted assist to the cause of abortion liberalization was what became known as the "thalidomide tragedy". Thalidomide was a drug approved in West Germany for use as a tranquilizer. The FDA never approved it for use in the United States. The problem was that pregnant women who took it ran a significantly increased risk of bearing a child with limb reductions. Because thalidomide had been initially distributed without prescription as a sedative mixed with aspirin, contemporary estimates of the number of West German children affected ranged from 4,000 to 6,000.[67] The 1962 case of an Arizona woman, Mrs. Sheri Finkbine, who took thalidomide while pregnant and who had initially secured approval and was then later denied a therapeutic abortion, produced an avalanche of publicity. She later went to Sweden and was granted an abortion after a week's delay.[68]

The second crack in the abortion laws came from the long-range liberalizing effects of Guttmacher's "therapeutic abortion" committee system. Germain

---

[63] *Plan Your Children for Health and Happiness,* (New York: Planned Parenthood, 1963, 1965).

[64] American Law Institute, *Model Penal Code, Prepared Official Draft,* May 4, 1962, 1962, 189.

[65] Ibid., 191.

[66] Ibid.

[67] Helen B. Taussig, M.D., "The Thalidomide Syndrome", *Scientific American,* no. 2 (August 1962): 34.

[68] Lader, *Abortion,* 10–16; interestingly, Lader, in his second abortion book (Lader, *Abortion II,* 43), changes both the year in which and state where Mrs. Finkbine was denied her abortion (a Colorado hospital in 1964).

Grisez has pointed to Guttmacher's statement that over 85% of the abortion operations performed at New York's Mt. Sinai Hospital from 1952 to 1956 "at least bent the law, if they did not fracture it". Guttmacher "also said that abortion laws make hypocrites of us all".[69]

Another indication for therapeutic abortion was rubella, or German measles. New York City seems to have been a mecca for therapeutic abortions of this variety. One of every 19 abortions performed from 1951 to 1953 was for this reason, rising to one in every 10 to 12 abortions during 1954 to 1959. And 1964 was an epidemic year for rubella in New York City with 329, or 57% of 579, therapeutic abortions that year performed for this indication.[70]

Of course none of the physicians performing these abortions, who were acting with the blessing of their colleagues, were prosecuted for such "therapeutic" activity. Thus, abortion reform proponents argued that they simply wanted the law to reflect what was already happening "quietly" in hospitals. But "reform" would do several other things as well. First, it would acclimate the American public to accept abortion for what purported to be "medical" reasons other than a threat to the mother's life. Social reasons masquerading as secondary health reasons were advanced to justify abortion of children thought to be physically or mentally handicapped. Thus, the eugenic wedge Planned Parenthood had long sought to apply as a precondition to participating in the American dream was legalized, and the "right" to a perfect baby was acknowledged in state laws. The difference between this and the ancient pagan practice of infant exposure to the elements was the timing and manner of the killing, papered over with deft rhetoric about allegedly saving desperate women from illegal abortion. American medicine was being used simply as a tool for killing the unhealthy.

Having already won acceptance of medicalized categories for social abortion, abortion advocates found it easier to propound the thesis that one's origin alone could justify withdrawal of legal protection before birth. Thus, abortion was made legal for pregnancies claimed to have been the result of rape or incest.

The Planned Parenthood–American Law Institute abortion reform proposal, or modified versions of it, were enacted in: Arkansas (1969); California (1967, by statute except for fetal handicap, but court decisions expanded it); Colorado (1967); Delaware (1969); Georgia (1968); Kansas (1969); Maryland (1968); New Mexico (1969); North Carolina (1967); Oregon (1969); South Carolina (1970); and Virginia (1970).

---

[69] Germain Grisez, *Abortion: The Myths, the Realities, and the Arguments* (New York: Corpus Books, 1970), 75, citing "Therapeutic Abortion in a Large General Hospital", *Surgical Clinics of North America* 37 (April 1957): 468; "The Law That Doctors Often Break", *Redbook,* August 1959, 24–25, 95–96.

[70] Grisez, *Abortion,* 87, citing Edwin M. Gold et al., "Therapeutic Abortions in New York City: A 20-Year Review", *American Journal of Public Health,* vol. 55 (1965): 965.

But the catalogue of social problems that could be reduced in scope or eliminated by legalized abortion was steadily expanded after the reform laws passed. In 1968 Alan Guttmacher told a Chicago abortion conference that abortion on demand would cut in half the out-of-wedlock birth rate and the numbers of "unwanted" children born within marriage.[71] Except for extraordinary circumstances abortion on demand would be performed only in the first three months, in approved hospitals by licensed doctors.[72] Guttmacher stated that it would be important to mandate that physicians at the hospital where the abortion was performed carefully prepare a detailed report including any post-operative problems so that accurate state and national public health records could be amassed.[73] Thus, Guttmacher continued his process of cautiously expanding the abortion "right", and all of these "qualifications" are now rejected by the PPFA and public health professionals.

That same year Guttmacher had been selected to be a member of New York governor Nelson Rockefeller's Abortion Law Reform Panel. His views at this stage could best be characterized as a liberalized version of the ALI proposal providing for: only hospital abortions; maternal life and health including mental health; severe fetal handicap or deformity; rape with police notification within thirty days; a woman with three or more children if she had not had an induced abortion in the previous twelve months; a woman of 40 or more if she had not had an induced abortion in the previous twelve months; and any single female under 17.[74] His averred goal was to reduce illegal abortion and eliminate socioeconomic and ethnic discrimination that impeded access to legal abortion.

Only in 1969 did Planned Parenthood finally come out of the closet to endorse abortion openly.[75] When it did, it did so with zeal.

Guttmacher and three other physicians sued the New York City district attorney and the hospital abortion committees for a "declaratory judgment to test the constitutionality of New York's abortion law".[76] The City of New York then had a "life of the mother" statute, as did the state of New York.

Planned Parenthood and its abortion coalition eventually prevailed in the New York legislature, securing Governor Rockefeller's signature on a bill on April 11, 1970, allowing abortion on demand up to twenty-four weeks'

[71] Alan Guttmacher, transcript of a talk given at a University of Chicago abortion conference, April 1968, 3, CLHMS.

[72] Ibid., 4.

[73] Ibid.

[74] Memorandum, Alan Guttmacher's views on abortion as a member of the Rockefeller panel, February 2, 1968, CLHMS.

[75] Langmyhr, "Role of Planned Parenthood–World Population in Abortion", 1190.

[76] Alan Guttmacher, Presidential Letter, no. 44, December 15, 1969, 2.

gestation—the nation's most liberal abortion law at that time. It was scheduled to take effect July 1, 1970.[77]

In the months leading up to this zero hour, discussions took place among abortion leaders as to how the law should be implemented. The major question was whether abortions should be performed only in hospitals or in facilities attached to them.[78]

Dr. Robert Hall of Planned Parenthood, who was also head of the Association for the Study of Abortion, did not want Planned Parenthood of New York City to do abortions in its clinics because, in his view, abortions done in any clinic would produce higher mortality rates than hospital abortions because of complications that, he argued, could only be handled in a hospital. Complications would be very high because American doctors were not experienced with outpatient abortion, local anesthesia, and suction curettage techniques. He also noted that abortion was not a harmless procedure, pointing to the nearly universal opinion that it should be done in hospitals. Further, even the best-staffed clinic would set a bad precedent in the drive for abortion law repeal.[79]

Guttmacher's own views on the question of abortion safety were similar. He acknowledged in November 1970 that he and his colleagues knew nothing about abortion morbidity and little about mortality, and at this time he still held that abortions past the eleventh week without menstruation should only be done in a hospital.[80]

But such cautious, even sceptical, appraisals of the safety of legal abortion, though regularly discussed in closed meetings or letters to medical colleagues, were not replicated in public view. Guttmacher responded to an inquiry from the National Urban Coalition with a different emphasis. To the press he claimed that performing an early abortion required the same skill as inserting an IUD. He therefore thought that nurse-midwives could safely perform abortions.[81]

There were a few stressful public relations moments during that first year (July 1, 1970, to June 30, 1971) as, for example, when forty-seven infants were

---

[77] Lader, *Abortion II*, 144.

[78] Memorandum and notes of meeting with attachments, "The Special Committee to Study Abortion Laws and Sterilization"; meeting held at chairman Dr. Locke L. Mackenzie's house, May 13, 1970, Alan Guttmacher not present (excused absence), CLHMS.

[79] Ibid., Robert Hall, attached paper "Independent Abortion Clinics".

[80] Alan Guttmacher letter to William Welch, Boulder, Colorado, November 2, 1970, CLHMS.

[81] Alan Guttmacher letter to Melina P. Hamilton, National Urban Coalition, August 14, 1970; see also, letter of Melina P. Hamilton, National Urban Coalition, to Alan Guttmacher, July 27, 1970, CLHMS.

reported live born after either saline or hysterotomy abortions.[82] These live births prompted Bernard Hirsh of the American Medical Association to say, "It's just horrible, whether you call it murder or anything else. It's just horrible."[83] Hirsh added that the AMA opposed the twenty-four-week limit and that most doctors believed it was not right to abort a woman after twelve to fourteen weeks.[84]

In the face of these live births after abortion, what one East Coast newspaper would call "the dreaded complication", Planned Parenthood would have to defend its "gains" in New York against prolife efforts to retrench the new law. Alfred Moran of New York City's Planned Parenthood told a New York state senate committee in February 1971 that the twenty-four-week time limit should be eliminated, legal abortions should not be limited only to hospitals or approved clinics, and that Planned Parenthood would go to court to oppose any residency requirement. Restrictions would only make women return to illegal abortionists because women will lie about their addresses, he argued, making medical follow-up impossible.[85] Moran also opposed protective laws for doctors, nurses, or others who refused to do or assist at abortions; he stated that Planned Parenthood of New York City did not wish to compel medical professionals to act against their "personal, religious or moral convictions. . . . In our opinion, professionals are obligated to refer patients they will not serve."[86]

As mentioned earlier, the New York abortion leaders' assessment of abortion safety differed when they got together to "talk shop". At a June 1971 abortion conference sponsored by Planned Parenthood–World Population and the AMA, Dr. Jean Pakter of the New York City Health Department stressed that higher complication rates were being noted at resident-based facilities [hospitals]. This was so because "we are getting more accurate reporting. And this is why I reiterate that it would be fallacious to say that lower complication rates exist in freestanding clinics, which cater to the nonresident population who may develop their complications more frequently after they get home."[87] And of course, women could develop their complications in the

[82] Information bulletin, Gordon Chase, Health Services administrator, New York City, October 6, 1972.

[83] Ronald Kotulak, "A.M.A. 'Violently Opposes' Legal Late-Term Abortions", *Chicago Sun-Times*, December 19, 1970.

[84] Ibid.

[85] Testimony of Alfred F. Moran, executive vice president, PPNYC, before the New York State Senate Committee on Health, February 19, 1971, 2585/371 2.3.

[86] Ibid.

[87] *Abortion Techniques and Services:* Proceedings of the Conference, NY, NY, June 3–5, 1971, sponsored by American Medical Women's Association, American Public Health Association, Association for the Study of Abortion, National Medical Association, PPWP, ed. Sarah Lewit, *Excerpta Medica* (1972): 31.

cab on the way to the airport, etc., or even die after that. In fact, city officials estimated that only a fifth of the abortions done at freestanding clinics during New York's first year of legal abortion were ever reported.[88]

Dr. Joseph J. Rovinsky noted that New York City's "better" gynecologists reported a higher incidence of uterine perforation than poorer ones and doubted whether the official reports were accurate "where the question of perforation depends on the degree of suspicion of the operator and on his willingness to report the perforation".[89]

In spite of this known under-reporting of abortion complications, Guttmacher claimed in a draft article for American biology teachers that data from New York City were accurately noted and given to officials.[90]

The New York City experience also called into question long-standing claims of abortion enthusiasts. Dr. Christopher Tietze suggested there would be a "slackening of contraception" with the availability of legal abortion on demand, and that "this is not necessarily a bad idea ... the best way to minimize maternal mortality is to use a completely harmless but not necessarily 100% effective method of contraception, plus abortion when necessary".[91]

Of the approximately 85,000 abortions performed on New York City residents that first year, Tietze estimated that only one-third would have gone to illegal abortionists in the absence of legalization. This meant that legal abortion appreciably increased the overall incidence of induced abortion.[92]

One additional "benefit", according to Guttmacher, was that "24% of the abortions in New York City were done on black women, who form 18% of the total population. Formerly, without the benefit of liberalized abortion laws, the black women practically never got a legal abortion."[93]

But the first wave of abortion law reform came under heavy assault from pro-life forces. Even the New York legislature, in a relatively liberal state with considerable poverty of the kind abortion on demand was meant to solve, voted to overturn the 1970 statute. It took a veto from Governor Nelson

---

[88] Alan F. Guttmacher, M.D., Robert E. Hall, M.D., Christopher Tietze, M.D., and Harriet Pilpel, "Roundtable: Legal Abortion", *Medical Aspects of Human Sexuality*, August 1971, 65.

[89] *Abortion Techniques and Services*, 85.

[90] Alan F. Guttmacher, "Abortion on Request—Theories and Facts", draft article for *The American Biology Teacher*, July 14, 1972, 7, citing three sources: J. Pakter and F. Nelson, "The First Nine Months", *Family Planning Perspectives*, 3:4 (1971); trimonthly bulletins on abortion program issued by Dr. J. Pakter's office in the Bureau of Maternity Services and Family Planning, New York City Dept. of Health; and releases from the Office of Health Services for New York City, Gordon Chase, administrator, CLHMS.

[91] "Legal Abortion", *Medical Aspects of Human Sexuality*, August 1971, 60.

[92] Ibid.

[93] Ibid., 69.

Rockefeller on May 13, 1972, to save the measure from repeal.[94] Planned Parenthood spent a great deal of time analyzing this and other setbacks.

An official from Upjohn Pharmaceuticals told Guttmacher how pro-abortion forces lost the 1972 Michigan referendum calling for a liberalized law. Pro-lifers there had developed literature equating the born child with a preborn one. Thomas J. Vecchio, chief medical officer of Upjohn Pharmaceuticals, manufacturer of the abortion-inducing drugs called prostaglandins, told Guttmacher that although most women would not have an abortion, they should be sympathetic toward those who might need one. He also maintained that abortion should only be pushed as a back-up for birth control; it should not be promoted as a good in itself, but as "a lesser evil".[95] Guttmacher replied that at an upcoming meeting he would discuss with Governor Rockefeller the possibility of dropping the legal limit for abortion to eighteen weeks' gestation, except for "eugenic" reasons. Guttmacher believed this tactic would take the steam out of abortion opponents, as they wouldn't be able to imitate the successful pro-life efforts in Michigan.[96]

With the abortion victory thus secured, Guttmacher offered explanations as to how his personal views had evolved into support for abortion on demand. In a 1972 law review article he explained:

> The more I studied early results from the five states which had been the first to liberalize their laws, the more I began to espouse the opinion that abortion statutes should be entirely removed from the criminal code. . . . *I reluctantly concluded that abortion on request* — necessitating removal of "abortion" from the penal codes — *was the only way to truly democratize legal abortion* and to sufficiently increase the numbers performed so as to decrease the incidence of illegal abortions. *I reached this conclusion in 1969*... [emphasis added].[97]

But when writing to the Planned Parenthood faithful in 1974 he said he had championed the choice of legal abortion, and that he *"took this position long before it became Planned Parenthood policy in 1969"* [emphasis added].[98]

But as to why the Supreme Court legalized abortion on demand in the 1973 *Roe* and *Doe* decisions, he had only one explanation: "the excellent results achieved during more than two years of legal abortion in New York and California. Results from both show that modern abortion is safer than

[94] *Washington Post* wire story, May 14, 1972, A-28.

[95] Letter from Thomas J. Vecchio, chief of Medical Research, Upjohn International, Inc., to Alan Guttmacher, November 16, 1972, CLHMS.

[96] Alan Guttmacher letter to Vecchio, November 20, 1972, CLHMS.

[97] Alan Guttmacher, "The Genesis of Liberalized Abortion in New York: A Personal Insight", *Case Western Reserve Law Review*, vol. 23 (1972): 756–78.

[98] Alan Guttmacher, *Presidential Letter,* no. 69, February 28, 1974, Planned Parenthood–World Population, 2.

childbirth."[99] That the excellent results may have been a product of poor or unsought-for data was not mentioned.

Yet, the Supreme Court's 1973 decisions did not spell the end of Planned Parenthood's abortion activism. This was an irrevocable decision for the organization. Previously, in March 1972, PPFA had changed its charter, stating that its raison d'être was to "provide leadership in making effective means of voluntary fertility control, including contraception, abortion and sterilization, available and fully accessible to all".[100] After *Roe v. Wade*, Planned Parenthood would defend abortion year in and year out in every state legislature, the U.S. Congress and the federal courts. This, and their additional abortion involvement since *Roe v. Wade*, should lay to rest any notion that PPFA was merely pro-choice and not pro-abortion.

Margaret Sanger would have been proud of her followers. By 1988, (the latest reporting year available to the authors) the PPFA would perform 104,000 surgical abortions at thirty-eight of its clinics nationwide. But this only skims the surface of its abortion involvement. The PPFA's 1988 annual report also touted the following abortion involvement: $100,000 medical service grants for consumer loans for abortions; responsibility for putting the French abortion pill, RU-486, back on the market again in France; through its Justice Campaign, advocacy of the federal funding of abortions; "post-coital hormonal contraception" [attempted early abortion]; "second trimester abortion"; lobbies against a U.S. Senate amendment denying tax exempt status to abortion providers such as the PPFA; favorable court challenges of decisions against parental notice for minor's abortions; and challenged in court a federal law that funded "religious institutions to promote chastity and that forbids counseling about the option of abortion". Additionally, the PPFA represented the Planned Parenthood Association of Kansas City in *Webster v. Reproductive Health Services,* challenged a federal regulation prohibiting abortion counseling in the USPHS birth control programs, and established the Katherine Houghton Hepburn fund to keep abortion "safe and legal".[101] Quite an admirable record for a group that called itself pro-choice, but not pro-abortion.

Interestingly, the PPFA 1988 *Annual Report* shows that the PPFA broke new ground for that organization's transparent inconsistency on the question of maternal deaths from illegal abortion overseas. PPFA president Faye Wattleton claims that in the developing world "unsafe, illegal abortion claims 500,000 lives annually". Yet, a mere four pages later the reader is told that the French "Death Pill", "RU-486 holds great promise for women in the developing

[99] Ibid., no. 65, February 15, 1973, 1.
[100] "Restated Certificate of Incorporation of PPFA, Inc.", approved March 3, 1972, supreme court, state of New York.
[101] Planned Parenthood Federation of America, *1988 Annual Report*.

world, where unsafe, often self-induced abortions kill an estimated 200,000 each year. . . . "[102]

Illegal Abortions?

Because of adverse health consequences, the question of illegal abortion has long held a prominent place in discussions of making or keeping abortion legal. Presumably, persons with some medical training would be able to induce an abortion with fewer complications. Those abortionists who did not have such training would apparently produce the statistical cannon fodder, real or contrived, of which the pre-1973 abortion reform movement was made and which TV news anchors routinely resurrect every time a threat to abortion on demand is raised.

Of course, the less "medically qualified" illegal abortionists are thought to be, the easier it is to convince the general public that abortion should be made or kept "safe and legal". In publications destined for the lay public, abortion proponents' usual tactic was to create the impression that most illegal abortions were being performed by nonmedical personnel from "madams" with their knitting needles to coat-hanger-wielding garage mechanics.

However, at medical conferences the degree of candor appears to have been higher, especially as some of those present had firsthand information about illegal abortion, i.e., they either did them or referred patients to colleagues. Thus, at the 1942 abortion conference sponsored by the National Committee on Maternal Health (NCMH) at the New York Academy of Medicine, NCMH chairman Dr. Robert L. Dickenson stated that 75% of all illegal abortions were performed by physicians.[103] His remark went unchallenged.

At the 1955 abortion conference sponsored by the Planned Parenthood Federation of America and attended by a host of birth control proponents and others who would play major roles in the legalization of abortion, the question of physician-induced abortion came up. The discussion leader on this point was the famed sex researcher, Alfred Kinsey, who was introduced by conference chairman Guttmacher as someone who could "give us the naked facts".[104] Providing a breakdown of illegal abortions, Kinsey stated that 87% of induced abortions were performed by doctors and about 8% were self-induced, and these could be ignored and it would not change the overall illegal abortion picture.[105]

---

[102] Ibid., 3, 7.

[103] Howard C. Taylor, Jr., M.D., *The Abortion Problem:* Proceedings of the Conference Held under the Auspices of the National Committee on Maternal Health at the New York Academy of Medicine, June 19–20, 1942 (Baltimore: Williams and Wilkins, 1944), 51.

[104] Mary Steichen Calderone, ed., *Abortion in the United States* (New York: Harper Brothers, 1958), 50.

[105] Ibid., 53.

Dr. Mary S. Calderone, a conference participant and editor of the Planned Parenthood conference proceedings, accepted Kinsey's conclusions. She wrote in 1960 that

> the conference estimated that 90 per cent of all illegal abortions are done by physicians. Call them what you will, abortionists or anything else, they are still physicians, trained as such; and many of them are in good standing in their communities. . . . Whatever trouble arises usually comes after self-induced abortions, which comprise approximately 8 per cent, or with the very small percentage that go to some kind of non-medical abortionist. Another corollary fact: physicians of impeccable standing are referring their patients for these illegal abortions to the colleagues they know are willing to perform them. . . . [106]

Calderone herself knew at least one physician of impeccable standing who referred for illegal abortion. Planned Parenthood president Dr. Alan F. Guttmacher acknowledged that a Baltimore abortionist/physician, on trial for performing illegal abortions, had "offered to produce a list of 300 reputable physicians who had referred cases to him. I assume my name was among them."[107]

As late as 1970, after abortion reform laws had passed several states, Dr. Guttmacher received an inquiry from an Ohio physician who asked about qualified gynecologists for a patient who did not want to have a psychiatric consultation, adding that he hoped his requests were not out of line.[108] Guttmacher responded within a fortnight. He assumed the doctor wanted the names of doctors operating outside the law. He provided the names of two proficient abortionists in New York City.[109]

In light of Kinsey's figure that 90% of all abortions were done by bona fide doctors, Guttmacher's reference to only two physician abortionists in all of New York City leads to an interesting situation: either illegal abortion was not as big a problem as Planned Parenthood claimed it was, or even doctors could not do them safely. But as Guttmacher believed in the safety of physician-induced abortion, that leaves a smaller illegal abortion problem. Cross checking these various "stories" at the time could have put the illegal abortion thesis to rout.

But "finesses" still come from Planned Parenthood officials. Faye Wattleton, the current president of PPFA, claimed in a January 22, 1979 letter to members

[106] Mary Calderone, "Illegal Abortion as a Public Health Problem", *American Journal of Public Health*, vol. 50, no. 7 (July 1960): 948–54.

[107] Alan F. Guttmacher, "Abortion: Odyssey of an Attitude", *Family Planning Perspectives*, vol. 4, no. 4 (October 1972): 5–7.

[108] Letter of Dr. Kenneth Rowley of Hamilton, Ohio to Alan Guttmacher, March 12, 1970, CLHMS.

[109] Letter of Alan Guttmacher to Dr. Kenneth Rowley, March 20, 1970, CLHMS.

of Congress celebrating legal abortion that: "Illegal abortions have virtually disappeared. Estimates are that fewer than two percent of all abortions in 1975 were conducted illegally by unlicensed practitioners (compared with 95 percent or more in the late 1960s)."[110] Kinsey's authoritative 90% estimate for physician-performed illegal abortions was reduced to less than 5% by a stroke of Ms. Wattleton's pen.

And even Planned Parenthood's own Christopher Tietze has disputed the claim that legal abortion eliminates illegal abortion:

> One of the major goals of the liberalization of abortion laws in northern Europe was to reduce the frequency of illegal abortions. A further objective was to reduce the total number of induced abortions, legal and illegal combined, by establishing contact with the pregnant woman and making available to her a broad range of social services. There is no agreement among Scandinavian authors to what extent the first of these objectives has been achieved in any of the countries concerned, and it is even less likely that the second goal has been realized.
>
> In eastern Europe, the reported number of "other abortions", which include criminal as well as spontaneous abortions and are based on hospital admissions, have not changed drastically in any of the countries for which statistics are available. . . . The total number of induced abortions, legal and illegal, has probably increased in the countries with permissive legislation.[111]

None of this emerged intact from Planned Parenthood's abortion propaganda machine. In December 1973 a Planned Parenthood "fact sheet" claimed:

> Most legal abortions are replacements of illegal ones: Contrary to the belief of some people, the impact of liberalizing abortion is largely a shift from dangerous and costly procedures, rather than the generating of abortions which would not otherwise have occurred. An analysis of New York's experience with liberalized abortion . . . revealed that 7 out of 10 legal abortions replaced illegal procedures.[112]

The seven out of ten ratio comes from Tietze, who propounded it in 1973 and repeated it to a gathering at the University of Notre Dame in March 1975: "About 70 percent of the legal abortions (50,000 per year) obtained by New York City residents during the first two years under the new law replaced illegal procedures. . . ."[113] Previously, Tietze had said that one third of the

[110] Faye Wattleton, circular letter to members of Congress, January 22, 1979, author's personal copy.

[111] Christopher Tietze, "Statistics of Induced Abortion", mimeographed copy of a talk presented at an abortion symposium, September 18, 1967, 10–11.

[112] Planned Parenthood Federation of America, *Facts and Figures on Legal Abortion of Importance to All Americans,* no. 1445, December 1973.

[113] Christopher Tietze, "The Effect of Legalization of Abortion on Population Growth

85,000 New York City residents who had a legal abortion during the first year of legalization would have had an illegal one if the legal alternative had not been available.[114] If only up to a third of legally aborting women would have aborted their children illegally, then legal abortion was significantly increasing the actual overall incidence of abortion, a political "no-no". Therefore, the illegal abortion replacement figure had to be at least 70% replacement of illegal abortion by legal ones. But mathematically, Tietze's own words put him in a box. Even if 100% of all abortions in the second year of New York's abortion legalization were replacement ones, this would have meant that, for two years, no more than 65% of abortions were replacements for illegal ones.

Why would such ratios happen? We think the reader will understand the necessity for yet another abortion "finesse" and possibly even sympathize with Dr. Tietze's self-induced predicament.

Continuing, Dr. Tietze also told his Notre Dame audience that:

> The experience for New York City can be extrapolated to the United States.... In 1973, about 745,000 legal abortions were performed, according to a nationwide survey of hospitals, clinics and physicians sponsored by The Alan Guttmacher Institute.... Allowing for an undercount of five to 10 percent, a total of 800,000 is probably a reasonable estimate.... If 70 percent of the new legal abortions replaced about 500,000 illegal abortions, the remaining 30 percent, or 250,000, could have replaced about 200,000 live births.... [This is so] because a higher incidence of abortion enables more women to return to the fecundable state sooner than if they had chosen to carry their pregnancies to term [i.e.,] more than one abortion is required to replace one birth.[115]

If a total of 800,000 abortions occurred in 1973, Tietze's own calculations of illegal abortion replacement would be 240,000 illegal abortions at 30% replacement, or 560,000 illegal abortions at 70% replacement.

Illegal Abortions Computed from Maternal Deaths

When the estimates of the numbers of women dying per 100,000 illegal abortions are brought into the discussion, the misuse of illegal abortion data becomes surreal.

---

and Public Health", adapted from *Family Planning Perspectives,* vol. 7, no. 3 (May–June 1975): 85–88. The article is a modified version of a paper presented at a conference on "Abortion: Public Policy and Morality", University of Notre Dame, March 20–21, 1975, and can be found in *Provisional Estimates of Abortion Need and Services in the Year Following the 1973 Supreme Court Decisions, United States, Each State and Metropolitan Area,* a report by the Alan Guttmacher Institute, copyright 1975 by the Planned Parenthood Federation of America.

[114] Guttmacher, Hall, Tietze, and Pilpel, "Roundtable", 60.

[115] Ibid., Christopher Tietze, "Legalized Abortion . . . ".

The following have been proposed as maternal death rates per 100,000 illegal abortions in the United States:

Author	Date(s)	Rate
Willard Cates, Jr.[116]	1972–74	30/100,000
Christopher Tietze[117]	1973	40/100,000
Christopher Tietze[118]	1960	66/100,000
Steven Polgar[119]	1965–67	3,416/100,000

Using the above maternal death rates supposedly resulting from 100,000 illegal abortions, an estimate of the total number of abortions may be derived. But this produces an unacceptable situation for abortion promoters. The higher the rate of maternal deaths per 100,000 illegal abortions, the lower the number of actual illegal abortions required to produce them.

For example, the National Center for Health Statistics (NCHS) has classified 114 maternal deaths in 1960 as resulting from illegal abortion. Applying the above maternal death rates would produce the following estimates for illegal abortions in 1960:

Cates at (30/100,000)   = 373,333 illegal abortions
Tietze at (66/100,000)   = 169,696 illegal abortions
Polgar at (3,416/100,000) =   3,279 illegal abortions

Cates, Tietze, and Polgar all have been featured in the pages of Planned Parenthood's journal *Family Planning Perspectives* as reputable and reliable sources for abortion information. How is it that these experts could disagree so radically and all be considered authoritative? All the figures above are at wide variance with the supposedly reliable estimates for the numbers of illegal abortions in what Polgar terms "the bad old days". Did this disturb anybody?

Take, for example, the typical 1960s claim that 5,000 women died each year from illegal abortion. That many maternal deaths would have extrapolated to the following figures for illegal abortion:

Cates at (30/100,000)   = 16,666,666 illegal abortions
Tietze at (54/100,000)   = 9,259,259 illegal abortions
Polgar at (3,416/100,000) =   146,370 illegal abortions

[116] Willard Cates, Jr., and Roger Rochat, "Illegal Abortion Deaths in the United States: 1972–74", *Family Planning Perspectives*, vol. 8, no. 2 (March–April 1976): 86–88, 91–92.

[117] Tietze, "The Effect of Legalization of Abortion", 86.

[118] Ibid., 87, based on Tietze's statement that puerperal sepsis and hemorrhage deaths corresponded to 10.2 per 100,000 live births in 1960, and declined to 6.2 per 100,000 live births by 1973, and matched to the 40/100,000 rate.

[119] Steven Polgar and Ellen S. Freid, "The Bad Old Days: Clandestine Abortions among

With legal abortion on demand, nowhere near the number of abortions that would have had to occur to achieve the number of maternal deaths derived from the maternal death rates for illegal abortion under Tietze's and Cates' estimates are reported. The illegal abortion figures become unbelievable. Of course, if Polgar's death rate had been correct the public relations impact of the illegal-abortion controversy would have lost some of its effect because of the diminished number of abortions.

There are other problems as well. Cates has stated that there were about 130,000 illegal abortions for 1972, 63,000 for 1973, and 17,000 for 1974.[120] But Planned Parenthood's research concluded that while 745,440 legal abortions occurred in 1973, there was a national "need" to kill at least 1,257,970 to 1,745,440 children by legal abortions based on assessments of the number of "unwanted" and mistimed pregnancies.[121] The same estimates for low and high abortion utilization are applicable to 1974.[122]

Applying Cates' illegal-abortion figures to Planned Parenthood estimates of births allegedly unwanted but not readily aborted legally, we can conclude the following:

1. Between 512,570 and 1,023,000 women were "in need of legal abortion but could or did not obtain one".
2. During 1973 only an estimated 67,000 of these women obtained an illegal abortion. This means that between 6.55% and 13.07% of women experiencing an unwanted or mistimed pregnancy will seek and obtain an illegal abortion if a legal one is not available. Whether this is from a lack of immediate availability or illegality is irrelevant.
3. During 1974 an estimated 16,700 women with an unwanted pregnancy procured an illegal abortion because a legal one was not available, which results in 1.63% to 3.25% of unwanted pregnancies being terminated by illegal abortion.

So, taking the extreme low and high figures provided by the Planned Parenthood experts, between 1.63% and 13.07% of women who experience an unwanted pregnancy or a mistimed one will seek and procure an abortion whether it is legal or not. This is according to the best estimates of the former chief of the Centers for Disease Control, Abortion Surveillance Branch, and

---

the Poor in New York City before Liberalization of the Abortion Law", *Family Planning Perspectives*, vol. 8, no. 3 (May–June 1976): 125–27.

[120] Cates and Rochat, "Illegal Abortion Deaths", 91–92.

[121] Christopher Tietze et al., "How Much of the Need Was Met in 1973", in *Provisional Estimates of Abortion Need and Services in the Year Following the 1973 Supreme Court Decisions, United States, Each State and Metropolitan Area*, a report by the Alan Guttmacher Institute, copyright 1975 by the Planned Parenthood Federation of America, 31–36.

[122] Ibid.

Planned Parenthood's top statistician. Neither of these "experts" has bothered to explain the wide variance regarding their own estimates in the percentage of women from year to year experiencing "unwanted" pregnancies who seek illegal abortions.

Nor have they explained that these illegal abortion figures are dramatically lower than their other figures. Nevertheless, if these percentages (which have a range of 800%) were applied to the estimates of "unwanted" pregnancy prior to *Roe v. Wade,* the number of unwanted pregnancies allegedly being terminated by illegal abortion would have dropped to a point too low to sustain a political drive to make abortion legal. For example, convert Harriet Pilpel's 1,000,000 "estimate" of the number of illegal abortions in 1968, label them unwanted pregnancies, and multiply that by the low and high figures for the ratio of women who will abort an unwanted pregnancy regardless of legality (1.63% and 13.07%, respectively). The resulting number of illegal abortions ranges from 16,300 to 130,700 for the year 1968. These numbers of women aborting are not pleasant to consider, but would they have sustained a nationwide case for abortion on demand? It seems highly unlikely.

Cates doesn't try to explain why there should be 16,700 illegal abortions in 1974 and 66,700 in 1973 even though the alleged "need" for abortion was the same for both years. Cates was trying to establish that "safe and legal" abortion had virtually replaced "unsafe and illegal" abortion, in spite of the fact that his own "proof" would play havoc with other parts of the abortion propaganda machine.

Who would cross check these data then or now? Certainly not proabortion Supreme Court justices. Hadn't reputable scientists like Tietze proved that abortion was safer than childbirth? The claims of pro-abortion partisans concerning the number of illegal abortions and the resulting toll in maternal deaths have been regularly presented to the public more like articles of religious faith than the unsubstantiated and contradictory fabrications that they were then—and still are.

Chapter Ten

Birth Control Will Prevent Abortion

Repeated to the point of mind-numbing boredom is the Planned Parenthood dogma that birth control will prevent the so-called "need" for abortion. But with more than seventy years of clinical evidence and experience, much of it from Planned Parenthood, what is consistently shown is that those who most frequently use "preventive" measures also most frequently resort to induced abortion.

In addition to the research of Pearl and Stix and Kopp cited earlier, we have the acknowledgment of this linkage by attendees at a 1955 Planned Parenthood–sponsored conference on abortion. At one point in the proceedings, famed sex researcher Alfred C. Kinsey said, "At the risk of being repetitious, I would remind the group that we have found the highest frequency of induced abortion in the group which, in general, most frequently used contraceptives".[1]

Later, the concluding statement of the conference, signed by Dr. Alan Guttmacher, Dr. Christopher Tietze, Dr. Louis M. Hellman (later HEW deputy assistant secretary for population affairs in charge of Title X), Dr. John Rock (co-inventor of the birth control pill), and other Planned Parenthood notables, acknowledged: "It was recognized by Conference participants that no scientific evidence has been developed to support the claim that increased availability of contraceptive services will clearly result in a decreased illegal abortion rate."[2]

In practical terms, all of the indications for illegal abortion in 1955 were indications for legal abortion after 1973.

In 1981 Dr. Malcolm Potts, former medical director of the International Planned Parenthood Federation, recognized the still-current validity of the contraception/abortion link in commenting upon two South American studies (1965, 1969). Potts wrote: "Requena showed in Santiago, Chile, that the poorest members of the community do not have a very widespread use of contraceptives, and the incidence of abortion is low. The middle classes

---

[1] Mary S. Calderone, ed., *Abortion in the United States, A Conference Sponsored by the PPFA and the New York Academy of Medicine,* at Arden House (New York; Harper and Row, 1958), 157.
[2] Ibid., 182.

attempt to control their fertility, and both the use of contraception and the incidence of abortion rise."[3]

Kristin Luker noted that of fifty white, middle-class, single women interviewed who aborted a first-trimester pregnancy, nearly "three-quarters had been using effective means of contraception before embarking on 'contraceptive risk taking' that resulted in pregnancy".[4]

In 1968, before the nationwide legalization of elective abortion, Planned Parenthood's Dr. Guttmacher said:

> [W]e find that when an abortion is easily obtainable, contraception is neither actively nor diligently used.... Therefore, if we had abortion on demand, there would be no reward for the woman who practices effective contraception. Secondly, abortion on demand relieves the husband of all possible responsibility; he simply becomes a coital animal.[5]

Guttmacher's view is not isolated. Writing in 1971, Sandburg and Jacobs stated that "during the past three years [1969 to 1971], as legal abortion has become increasingly available, it has become evident that some women are now intentionally using abortion as a substitute for contraception". They concluded that this "single-episode" approach to fertility regulation appealed to women who desire pregnancy but not reproduction, those who receive welfare abortions, who have erratic coitus, feminists who believe abortion to be a "right", and young "nonconforming social dissenters who declare, Why sweat? So it happens. So we'll take care of it.

"It seems certain that for some time to come there will be an increasing number of women who will reject contraception purely on the basis of the availability of legal abortion."[6]

Abortion proponents regularly link abortion to other forms of birth control by calling it a backup for "failed" contraception. Why are the Pill, etc. given out in abortion clinics? Or, alternatively, consider that postfertilization, abortion-causing antifertility drugs and devices are euphemistically designated as "contraceptives", "birth control", or even "family planning". One abortion doctor wrote that "attaching suction to a comparable cannula . . .

---

[3] Malcolm Potts, M.D., "Abortion and Contraception in Relation to Family Planning Service", in Jane Hodgson, M.D., ed., *Abortion and Sterilization: Medical and Social Aspects* (New York: Grune and Stratton, 1981), 490–91.

[4] "Says Physicians Are Mistaken in Idea of Who Will Seek an Abortion", *Family Practice News*, March 15, 1977; and Kristin Luker, *Abortion and the Politics of Motherhood* (Berkeley: University of California Press, 1984), 112.

[5] Alan Guttmacher, discussion, "Law, Morality and Abortion Symposium", held at Rutgers University Law School, March 27, 1968, *Rutgers Law Review*, Willard Heckel, moderator, vol 22, (1968): 415–43.

[6] Eugene C. Sandburg, M.D. and Ralph I. Jacobs, M.D., "Psychology of the Misuse and Rejection of Contraception", *American Journal of Obstetrics and Gynecology* (May 15, 1971): 227–37.

promises to be one of the most exciting advances in birth control imaginable, a procedure done before woman or physician is sure that pregnancy is present".[7]

Then there is the practical aspect of using abortion as a primary method of birth control. The Pill must be taken every day. Other methods must be used consciously and effectively at every intercourse. Abortion, in contrast, takes only one antifertility intervention. Coupled with the claim that abortion is "safer than childbirth", this advantage in convenience leads one to reasonably ask: Why not use abortion as a primary means of birth control? And if abortion is a moral right, what objection, other than emotional or possibly aesthetic can anyone have to repeat abortion? None. If abortion is a woman's right, why should anyone deplore or regret its exercise or seek to minimize its enjoyment or self-expression? Defenders of legal abortion are in the curious position, at least when they are seeking tax handouts from legislators for birth control, of wanting to minimize the exercise of the abortion right.

Planned Parenthood's premier researcher, Dr. Christopher Tietze, has acknowledged that

> a high correlation between abortion experience and contraceptive experience can be expected in populations to which both contraception and abortion are available and where some couples have attempted to regulate the number and spacing of their children. In such populations, women who have practiced contraception are more likely to have had abortions than those who have not practiced contraception, and women who have had abortions are more likely to have been contraceptors than women without a history of abortion.[8]

Denmark is a case in point. "During the fifteen months following the 1973 Danish abortion [liberalization] legislation, the mean annual rate of induced abortion was 23 per 1,000 women aged 15–44 compared with a mean annual rate of 14.5 during the preceding months."[9] Also Pill sales to drug distribution intermediaries decreased in this period. "Thus, whereas 15.9 more women per 1,000 aged 15–44 were using pills during each of the three and three-quarters years before the introduction of the 1973 abortion law, these women seemed to be abandoning use of oral contraceptives at an annual rate of 77.2 women per 1,000 after the law went into effect."[10] IUD sales increased, but as these act to cause early abortion, this intervention cannot be said to have decreased abortion. Second, some of these could have been used by women replacing an expelled IUD. Even if all the new IUD purchasers were new

[7] Harold Schulman, M.D., "A Critical Analysis of Induced Abortion", *Bulletin of the New York Academy of Medicine,* vol. 49, no. 8 (August 1973): 694–701.

[8] Christopher Tietze, "Abortion and Contraception", in *Abortion: Readings and Research* (Toronto, Canada: Butterworth, 1981), 54–60.

[9] Ronald Somers and Michala Gammeltoft, "The Impact of Liberalized Abortion Legislation on Contraceptive Practice in Denmark", *Studies in Family Planning* (1976): 222.

[10] Ibid., 218–19.

users (most unlikely), there still were not enough to compensate for the decline in Pill users.

Other researchers also suggest that the Pill played a part in increasing the social acceptance of abortion:

> Mariano Requena has found that in Latin America the introduction of more effective contraception led to an increase in the abortion rate. He argues that after couples have made a commitment to lower fertility, they are less willing to tolerate mistakes when they occur. In the United States, therefore, one could assume that the availability of the Pill—a virtually 100 percent effective contraceptive—would have created a population of people who had made important life commitments that depend on a very high level of fertility control.[11]

Viewed in this fashion, Pill users who abort unexpected pregnancies are simply disgruntled consumers who naively believed manufacturing claims and cannot tolerate disappointment. They were told that they could have 100% birth control effectiveness, and they will have it, even at the price of child homicide. The high expectation of near 100% birth control efficiency claimed for the oral contraceptive may predispose some women on the Pill to choose abortion when they do become pregnant. A survey of 320 predominantly white, middle-class women (mean age 24.6 years) undergoing abortion found that of the Pill "failures", 6% occurred in women who used the method correctly, and 94% occurred from Pill discontinuance because of undesirable side effects.[12]

The survey's authors suggest that women who choose birth control be given not only the technical or ideal "failure rates", but "also the number of human error failures among users" because the true effectiveness of a birth control method "is a function of both its technical efficiency and the user's propensity to use it correctly and consistently".[13]

Second, the ready availability of legalized abortion may lower the level of motivation necessary to use the Pill successfully.[14] And former Pill users may have an especially high rate of induced abortion even when compared to women currently using other forms of birth control. In the British *Royal College of General Practitioners Pill Study*, 20.98% of ex-Pill users reported at least one subsequent induced abortion, whereas in the control group, 55.18% of whom used another form of birth control, 12.28% reported at least one

---

[11] Potts, "Abortion and Contraception".

[12] Aris M. Sophicles, Jr., M.D., and P. A. Brozovitch, "Birth Control Failure among Patients with Unwanted Pregnancies: 1982–84", *Journal of Family Practice*, vol. 22, no. 1 (1986): 45–48.

[13] Ibid.

[14] Martin P. Vessy, "Randomised Double-Blind Trial of Four Oral Progestagen-Only Contraceptives", *The Lancet* (April 29, 1972): 915–22; and Tyler, *International Journal of Fertility*, vol. 13 (1968): 460.

abortion during the course of the study.[15] That former contraceptive users had higher abortion rates than nonusers was also shown in a Taiwan survey (1967) of women aged twenty to forty-four. Of these, 2,921 women had never used birth control, and their induced abortion rate was 3.5%; among users of birth control, 24.8% had an induced abortion.[16] The increase for induced abortion among former contraception users was consistently higher than nonusers, regardless of the number of pregnancies experienced.[17]

Potts et al. report that a survey by the Korean Ministry of Health and Social Affairs in 1968 suggested "that the number of Korean women in the 20–44 age group reporting that they have ever experienced one or more induced abortions doubled between 1964 and 1968, exactly paralleling the use of contraception".[18]

Moreover, the Pill itself is used as a postcoital menses inducer, or early abortion method. Birth control pills and other estrogens are routinely given to adolescents after "unprotected intercourse" to prevent the continued development of the preborn child after mid–menstrual cycle ovulation and conception but before or around the time of implantation.[19] This is acknowledged to be an intended early abortion, and it has also been suggested that clinicians not include this information in the patient's medical records and also not tell the patient of the abortifacient nature of the process.[20]

The regimen, not approved by the FDA, consists of giving two Ovral birth control Pills (Wyeth Pharmaceuticals) within seventy-two hours of "unprotected intercourse", followed by two more Pills within twelve hours.[21]

A report of an experimental program designed to influence aborting women subsequently to "contracept", presented at an American Public Health Association meeting, noted that none of the women were still on the Pill at fifteen months postabortion. The project's author, abortionist Dr. Michael Burnhill, tried to console his antifertility co-workers by noting that this failure to contracept was not their fault and that "altering fertility behavior is little-

---

[15] *The Royal College of General Practitioners Pill Study,* chap. 11 (23.67% used no birth control, almost 1% were sterilized, and 26.42% were pregnant or recently pregnant, as were 18.39% at recruitment).

[16] Malcolm Potts, Peter Diggory, and John Peel, *Abortion* (Cambridge: Cambridge University Press, 1977), 479.

[17] Ibid.

[18] Ibid., 458.

[19] Ruth Coles, "The Use of Oestrogens for Postcoital Contraception", *Journal of Biosocial Science,* vol. 9 (1977): 83–90; Dr. Jan Petty, former Medical Director [1977–80], Chicago Planned Parenthood, birth control training film *What's New and Useful,* Dept. of HHS, Title X program, USPHS, 1986. Reviewed by the author as a consultant to the Office of Family Planning, U.S. Department of Health and Human Services.

[20] Petty, *What's New and Useful.*

[21] Ibid.; and Richard P. Dickey, M.D., Ph.D., *Managing Contraceptive Pill Patients,* 4th ed. (Durant, Okla.: Creative Informatics, 1985), 192–95.

understood and difficult to accomplish".[22] One of Burnhill's co-presenters at the APHA public health conference stated that though the women undergoing repeat abortions usually denied using abortion as birth control, "you just know that's what they were doing".[23]

In another study of 101 adolescent patients who started taking the Pill at age thirteen to nineteen, similar results were obtained in the course of trying to discover factors associated with contraceptive compliance and nonuse: "Becoming pregnant and having an abortion before beginning oral contraception did not improve compliance in comparison to the never pregnant group."[24]

Abortion as a "Medical Matter"

Adolf Hitler wrote in his infamous tract *Mein Kampf,* "The great masses of the people . . . will more easily fall victims to a great lie than to a small one." Another practitioner of falsehood, a character in American writer Ring Lardner's "Ex Parte", noted: "I never lied save to shield a woman or myself."

While neither of these social opportunists were consulted by abortionists as they prepared to assault America's antiabortion laws in the 1960s, they honor, in common with abortionists, the use of language as a tool of deception. Because the physician is called upon to use his techniques and instruments as tools to implement the abortion decision, abortion has been mistakenly thought by some to be simply a medical matter, with the issue of the woman's "safety" surfacing as the central point of inquiry.

Abortion proponents, such as Planned Parenthood and other groups, usually adhere to the claim that "the early termination of pregnancy is a medical matter between the patient and the physician. . . . Abortion is a medical procedure and should be performed only by a duly licensed physician in conformance with good medical practice and . . . ."[25]

But to conclude that abortion is purely a "medical matter" is like saying that war is purely a military matter and that therefore only the generals should decide such issues; or that capital punishment is simply a concern of electrical engineers. Medicine, in effect, seeks to become a metaphysics of morals and

[22] Michael S. Burnhill, M.D. et al., "Impact of Counseling on Repeat Pregnancy and Contraceptive Use in Low SES Abortion Population", abstract.

[23] Personal communication, RGM.

[24] P. W. Scher et al., "Factors Associated with Compliance to Oral Contraceptive Use in an Adolescent Population", *Journal of Adolescent Health Care,* vol. 3 (1982): 120–23; only adolescents who chose the Pill at least three months before the study began were eligible. Compliance meant using the Pill without interruption after it was prescribed, or discontinuing use because not sexually active, or using another form of birth control. Noncompliance meant having "unprotected intercourse". Side effects occurred in seventy-seven patients after one month; 66% quit the Pill, and 42% of the noncompliants had an "unplanned" pregnancy after quitting the Pill.

[25] "The American Medical Association Policy Position on Abortion", ACOG, app. E.

ethics by answering profound and broad human questions with answers derived from a real or supposed technical competence in procuring an induced abortion. This is specious reasoning. For example, it could undoubtedly be demonstrated that a mother who stayed on a sidewalk, rather than pull her toddler from the path of a runaway car, would be less likely to be injured by a runaway car. But who would applaud this?

As human beings, we are called to seek not merely the "healthy" life, passing for the moment whether abortion is really "healthier" than childbirth, but rather the good and the just life. Were this not so, all social and legal decisions should be referred for resolution to the medical profession. This, manifestly, is not what most successful societies have chosen to do.

Planned Parenthood's tack is to identify mistakenly those who implement a decision with those who are "authorities" on whether such a decision should be made at all. In large part, American medicine is content with this misunderstanding. The authors of this book are not.

First, a doctor who performs elective abortions is not acting as a healer. In short, he is not practicing medicine; he is merely a biological technician who seeks to bring about the death of the human fetus (a Latin term for "offspring"). American medicine used to understand this fact. The American Medical Association, while not founded solely as an antiabortion organization during the mid-nineteenth century, nevertheless strongly defended the "pro-life" position. An 1859 AMA committee on criminal abortion, which was also concerned with a woman's health, stated that abortion was "the wanton and murderous destruction of her child".[26] Second,

> It would be a gross distortion . . . to believe that all or even most nineteenth-century laws were mainly attempts to protect a woman's health. An examination of the statements of those who most loudly urged the passage of restrictive laws during the latter two-thirds of the nineteenth century indicates that, in the minds of many, safeguarding the mother's health was held to be secondary to the protection of the foetus as a rationale for antiabortion laws. . . . One can infer from an analysis of nineteenth-century laws that the status of the foetus was a major concern of many State legislatures. A law which has maternal health as its sole or main consideration is not likely to be worded in such a way that the human status of the foetus is recognized, since such recognition would also require that the foetus be given human rights protected by law. In a law where the concern is with the woman's health, a woman is likely to be labeled as "pregnant" rather than as "being with child" or some other phrase which gives a human status to the foetus.[27]

[26] *Transactions of the American Medical Association,* instituted 1847, vol. 12, Philadelphia, printed for the Association, Collins, printer, 705 Jayne Street, 1859, 75–78.

[27] R. Sauer, "Attitudes to Abortion in America, 1800–1973", *Population Studies,* vol. 28, no. 1 (March 1974): 58.

But by 1981 the AMA would slough off its past and call elective induced abortion a "recognized medical procedure" and a "necessary medical procedure"; moreover, the AMA held that a constitutional amendment prohibiting or even allowing for restrictions on abortion would constitute an unacceptable "invasion of privacy".[28] Using this rationale, bank robbers could take a similar invasion-of-privacy view of television cameras monitoring their "financial transactions".

But what has happened is that the mere techniques of the physician, exercised here not for medical but for dubious social goals, have taken hold of his mission. His goal becomes to graft the goals of public health onto his techniques for establishing a "new" culture with individual autonomy as its major premise and which can be efficiently hedonist with minimal adverse consequences. Under this system, techniques and those who wield them become the measure of the new "morality"—really the old immorality. A 1970 editorial from *California Medicine* presaged the now partially completed slide away from the traditional sanctity of life ethic:

> This is seen most clearly in changing attitudes toward human abortion. . . . Since the old ethic has not been fully displaced it has been necessary to separate the idea of abortion from the idea of killing, which continues to be socially abhorrent. The result has been a curious avoidance of the scientific fact, which everyone really knows, that human life begins at conception and is continuous whether intra- or extra-uterine until death. The very considerable semantic gymnastics which are required to rationalize abortion as anything but taking a human life would be ludicrous if they were not often put forth under socially impeccable auspices. It is suggested that this schizophrenic sort of subterfuge is necessary because while a new ethic is being accepted the old one has not yet been rejected.[29]

Abortionists seek to replace the paramount question of the intentional homicide of the child in utero with the lesser question being addressed, namely, the partial "good" of a woman surviving an abortion with her "health" still relatively intact. These destructive labors are all the more appalling, taking place, as they so often do, half a corridor away from the wondrous interventions of perinatal specialists who see in both mother and child the focus of their healing and saving arts.

---

[28] Statement of the American Medical Association to the Senate Judiciary Subcommittee, December 14, 1981, "Constitutional Amendments Relating to Abortion", *Hearings before the Senate Judiciary Committee,* 97th Cong., 1st sess., S.J. res. 17, etc., vol. 2, app., serial no. J–97–62, 56–57.

[29] Editorial, "A New Ethic for Medicine and Society", *California Medicine,* vol. 113, no. 3 (September 1970); Official Journal of the California Medical Association, in *Abortion* pt 2, *Hearings,* Senate Judiciary Subcommittee, 93d Cong., 2d sess., on S.J. res. 119 and S.J. res. 130, 792–94.

Chapter Eleven

Planning for the Perfect:
Planned Parenthood and Eugenics

Margaret Sanger's birth control movement had as one of its major goals the elimination of live births of those, and among those, deemed inferior. Advertisements for the First American Birth Control Conference in 1921 and the Middle Western State Birth Control Conference at Chicago in 1923 promised that birth control would be an effective means to eliminate "mental defect, feeble-mindedness, low mental calibre morons, defectives, [and] paupers".[1]

Implicit in her appeal was the notion that physical, mental, moral, and social evils are hereditary and that the cure for these evils is "proper breeding on a scientific basis". With such obvious eugenic goals, it was only natural that Sanger found her efforts coinciding with those of existing eugenic organizations.

Sanger's roots and interest in eugenics were of long standing. She followed the career of pioneering American eugenicist Moses Harmon (1830–1910), a "free-thinking" preacher, abolitionist, and advocate of women's suffrage and sexual emancipation. Like Sanger, he ran afoul of the federal Comstock law and was arrested four times from 1886 to 1905 for publishing *Lucifer*, an incredibly avant-garde paper endorsing open marriages, birth control, and what the eugenicists diplomatically called "race betterment". After his last imprisonment, he went to Los Angeles and resumed publishing *Lucifer* under the name of the *American Journal of Eugenics*, continuing it until his death in 1910. The eugenics movement spread from Harmon's pioneering efforts.[2]

Sanger carried on her interest in eugenics in the pages of the *Birth Control Review*, which, under Sanger's editorship, was a virtual repository of articles and book reviews supporting the eugenic program. One prominent eugenic elitist and birth-control supporter, Harry Laughlin—a fellow traveller with

[1] Advertisements for the First American Birth Control Conference, November 11–12, 1921, and for the Middle Western States Birth Control Conference, Hotel Drake, Chicago, Illinois, October 29–31, 1923, MSCLC.

[2] Margaret Sanger's typed biographical notes on Moses Harmon; Moses Harmon Memorial, *The American Journal of Eugenics*, published by Lillian Harmon, Chicago, 1910, given to Margaret Sanger by Flora W. Fox, 1922, SSCSC.

Sanger on race purification policies—particularly stands out. Laughlin was cited by Guy Irving Burch, in commenting on congressional immigration hearings, as stating that over 70% of the immigrants to the United States from 1900 to 1925 were Italians and Slavs, each of whom had a high birth rate. Laughlin claimed that "in regard to all forms of social inadequacy, the foreign born and their children, who make up about 34 percent of our population, are even inferior to our native Negro population not long ago released from slavery".[3]

No recent convert to the gospel of "perfecting man", Laughlin had outlined the eugenic agenda for the First National Conference on Race Betterment in 1914, using terms quite similar to Sanger's:

> To purify the breeding stock of the race at all costs is the slogan of eugenics. The compulsory sterilization of certain degenerates is therefore designed as a eugenical agency complementary to the segregation of the socially unfit classes and to the control of the immigration of those who carry defective germ plasm. . . .
>
> . . . it is assumed that the lowest ten percent of the human stock are so meagerly endowed by nature that their perpetuation would constitute a social menace. . . .
>
> In addition to this body of persons, there is another group of persons who, though themselves normal, constitute a breeding stock which continually produces defectives; they are so interwoven in kinship with the lower levels that they are totally unfitted for parenthood. . . .
>
> The sex of the persons sterilized is an important eugenical factor. . . .
>
> The unprotected females of the socially unfit classes bear, in human society, a place comparable to that of the females of mongrel strains of domestic animals. . . .
>
> . . . at first only the very lowest would be selected for sterilization. . . . As time passes, and the science of eugenics becomes more exact, and a corps of experts, competent to judge hereditary qualities, are developed, and public opinion rallies to the support of the measures, a large percentage could, with equal safety, be cut off each year. . . .
>
> Unless all the states cooperated in the purging of the blood of the American people of its bad strains, and their cooperation is supported by the Federal Government in respect to immigration . . . we should not expect the program to work out. . . .
>
> . . . long before the end of two generations, the eugenic commissions of the several states should . . . extend their investigations and their selections for sterilization to the population at large. . . .
>
> . . . it is hoped that it will not be necessary to extend the authority of the

---

[3] Guy Irving Burch, notes about U.S. House of Representatives Immigration Hearing, 68th Congress, *Birth Control Review* (November 1926): 345.

eugenics commissions to the whole population immediately, however desirable such an extension would be in the future.[4]

Under Sanger's editorship the March 1928 *Birth Control Review* featured an article by Laughlin, at the same time extolling the benefits of sterilization and displaying the phrase, "Fewer But Fitter Children", on the cover. Showing that his fervor had not abated from earlier days, Laughlin pointed to the May 2, 1927, U.S. Supreme Court decision, *Buck v. Bell,* as a model of social legislation. That decision upheld a Virginia statute that provided for the compulsory sterilization of those having "degenerate" offspring. Laughlin noted that the Virginia law was not punitive as it did provide for due process, and he stated that the decision marked "a stage of fundamental importance in the advance of applied eugenics".[5] He cited Justice Holmes' words:

> It is better for all the world, if instead of waiting to execute degenerate offspring for crime . . . society can prevent those who are manifestly unfit from continuing their kind. The principle that sustains compulsory vaccination is broad enough to cover cutting the Fallopian tubes. . . . Three generations of imbeciles are enough.[6]

Laughlin had a practical interest in the outcome of the case because he had evaluated its findings. About Carrie Buck's family, he wrote, "[T]hese people belong to the shiftless, ignorant, and worthless class of anti-social whites of the South . . . ."[7]

Harry Laughlin is also interesting because he apparently provided Nazi Germany with the practical inspiration for the compulsory sterilization law passed in 1933, which was taken almost in toto from Laughlin's Model Eugenical Sterilization Law.[8] Laughlin's influence on the Nazi Germany sterilization program coincided with the height of his participation in the Planned Parenthood program. He is listed in the April 1938 *Birth Control Review* as a member of the Citizens' Advisory Committee for Planned Parenthood. And at least six other names on the Citizen's Advisory Commit-

---

[4] Harry Laughlin (superintendent, Eugenics Record Office, Cold Springs Harbor, Long Island, New York), "Calculations on the Working out of a Proposed Program of Sterilization", in *Proceedings of the First National Conference on Race Betterment,* January 8–12, 1914, Battle Creek, Michigan, published by the Race Betterment Foundation, ed. Emily F. Robbins, no copyright, excerpts, 478–94.

[5] Harry H. Laughlin, "Legal Status of Eugenical Sterilization", *Birth Control Review* (March 1928): 78.

[6] Ibid., Laughlin citing *Buck v. Bell,* 274 U.S. 200 (1927), 79.

[7] Laughlin, "Legal Status of Eugenical Sterilization", supplement, Annual Report of the Municipal Court of Chicago, 1930, 16–19, found in Allan Chase, *The Legacy of Malthus: The Social Costs of Scientific Racism* (New York: Alfred A. Knopf, 1977), 313.

[8] Ibid., 135.

tee were also listed in a publication of the advisory council of the American Eugenics Society (AES) for 1931.[9]

Lothrop Stoddard, a member of Sanger's American Birth Control League is also interesting. In 1940 he wrote a book, *Into the Darkness,* about his trip to Nazi Germany where he was accorded the privilege of witnessing the Nazi Supreme Eugenics Court in action. Stoddard later wrote, "On the evidence of that one visit, at least, the Sterilization Law is weeding out the worst strains in the Germanic stock in a scientific and truly humanitarian way."[10]

The close association between Sanger's ABCL and the American eugenics movement involved more than a handful of published articles. The ABCL *Birth Control Review* for March 1928 and the American Eugenics Society journal, *Eugenics, a Journal of Race Betterment,* show the following board members in common: C. C. Little, president, AES; Rosell H. Johnson, secretary-treasurer, AES; Edward M. East, Franklin H. Giddings, Samuel J. Holmes, Mrs. Helen Hartley Jenkins, Mrs. Otto Kahn, Dr. Adolph Meyer, Dr. Aaron J. Rosonoff, and Mrs. C. C. Rumsey.

Other board members, writers, and public supporters of both Sanger and the eugenics movement over the years included Norman Himes, Dr. Robert L. Dickenson, Dr. Hannah Stone, Rev. Fosdick, Rabbi Louis L. Mann, and Henry Pratt Fairchild, to cite a few. Both Sanger and the eugenics movement received money from the Brush Foundation, founded in 1929 for the purpose of "breeding out the unfit and limiting the numbers of those born into the world".[11]

Dr. Hannah Stone, of Margaret Sanger's own Clinical Research Bureau, chose the May 1929 *Eugenics* to paint a remarkably accurate picture of the future linkage of eugenics with birth control:

> The eugenicist, again, comes to birth control with a racial viewpoint. He sees in it an important aid towards controlling and improving the type and quality of the human stock. He looks at birth control, in its wider sense, to prevent the propagation of the physically and mentally unfit . . . the eugenicist also favors a certain type of birth release. Certain classes of the population he would even encourage to increased fertility. . . .
>
> It is [on] this biological basis that I believe the birth control clinics of the future will be organized. In connection with the birth control center there will also be a eugenic department, and both of these will, perhaps, be only a

---

[9] *Birth Control Review* (October 1938): 284. See also list of American Eugenics Society, Inc., Advisory Council, *Eugenics* Masthead, 1931 editions: common names included Leon J. Cole, Ellsworth Huntington, Mrs. Otto H. Kahn, Paul Popenoe, Charles R. Stockard, and Albert E. Williams.

[10] Lothrop Stoddard, *Into the Darkness* (New York: Duell, Sloan, and Pierce, 1940), 196.

[11] Dorothy Hamilton Brush, "The Brush Foundation", in *Eugenics,* vol. 2, no. 2 (February 1929): 17.

part of a more general "marriage advice station"....In such a center the racial aspect of reproduction could be stressed.[12]

The eugenic views of Planned Parenthood leaders also appeared in the mainline press, and not just academic or speciality journals. The *Chicago Daily Tribune* for September 7, 1933, contained an article by the Rev. John Evans about Margaret Sanger's advocacy of a "Baby Code" in order to bring about national recovery from the Great Depression.

A rough draft of her Baby Code from 1934 shows how she fashioned her efforts after President Franklin Roosevelt's National Recovery Act. The Sanger Baby Code was designed: (1) to prevent the overproduction of babies by the unfit so as to reduce the burden of charity and public relief; (2) to function through tax-paid birth control clinics; (3) to mandate that marriage licenses permit only a common household, not children; (4) to require permits for parents legally to have children, and to guide the issuance of these permits only to the healthy.[13]

Though Sanger had been absent from the editorship of the *Birth Control Review* since 1929 in order to devote more time to the pursuit of her federal legislative goals, the magazine had not abandoned her eugenic commitment. Among the articles published during this period were: "Let Us Take Stock" (December 1933), "Positive Eugenics" and "From Birth Control to Eugenics" (March 1934), and an entire issue styled as the "Eugenics Number" (April 1935).

Perhaps seeking guidance for the United States, delegates to the 1939 annual meeting of the ABCL heard from Mrs. Alva Myrdal of Sweden, who told them of that country's eugenic laws and policies. Mrs. Myrdal said that Sweden only wanted those children who were wanted by their parents. With the passage in 1934 of a compulsory sterilization law for Swedes with selected hereditary defects, the converse of this statement also appeared to be true, i.e., that Sweden would welcome the birth of only certain types of people. Mrs. Myrdal, however, said that social planners were looking next at how to deal with borderline undesirables, and they apparently had concluded that efforts would be made to persuade this group to limit family size strictly through propaganda and information on the use of birth control.[14]

Eugenic goals such as those described by Mrs. Myrdal were formally incorporated into Planned Parenthood's organizational objectives on a number of occasions both *before and after* the Nazi "Master Race" theories and

---

[12] Hannah Stone, M.D., "The Birth Control Clinic", May, 1929, *Eugenics*, vol. 2, no. 5 (May 1929): 11.

[13] "Baby Code" rough draft, March 6, 1934, MSCLC.

[14] "Safeguarding the Quality of Population by New Measures in Sweden", Mrs. Alva Myrdal, American Birth Control League Meeting, Biltmore Hotel, New York City, Jan. 19, 1939, 2, 5, SSCSC.

sterilization horrors had become public knowledge. In December 1938, the "Ultimate Objectives" for the newly named Birth Control Federation of America included discouraging those with inherited or transmitted diseases from increasing their numbers and promoting the increase of those healthy and bright persons from a favorable background.[15]

The week before the Japanese attack at Pearl Harbor, a BCFA planning document cited eugenics and population "authority" Brigadier General Frederick Osborn's report to the 1941 American Eugenics Society. General Osborn, chief of the Army Morale Division, estimated that two to three million Americans who had hereditary defects were burdens to themselves and others and cost the nation one billion dollars per year. As a partial solution to this problem, Planned Parenthood urged the distribution of birth control to the poor and an increase in the family size of middle- and upper-income Americans in urban areas.[16]

Part of the PPFA statement of goals for the United States in 1943 read, "[We will] foster selective pregnancy . . . and . . . will seek to offer the eugenically unsound means to avoid bringing offspring into the world who would become social liabilities."[17]

In 1945 a similar document outlining the goals of the PPFA noted that: "The weak and defective compose an alarming proportion of our present population . . . ."[18] This could be prevented by "providing reliable contraceptive advice for those who, because of disease, defectiveness or deficiency, are unfitted to bear children."[19]

That such ideas became palatable to American medicine only after its tacit and then increasingly explicit acceptance of birth control in the late 1930s is no accident. The 1957 *Report* of The American Eugenics Society, with Dr. Alan Guttmacher as its vice president and other prominent Planned Parenthood members, shows how Dr. Hannah Stone's prediction was coming to pass. The *Report* opened with a statement acknowledging that when the AES was founded in 1906 the scientific community gave it little support and even less came from a public that believed men were created of equal abilities. But a change occurred in the medical world after World War II toward greater

---

[15] Minutes of the meeting of the Joint Committee of the American Birth Control League and The Birth Control Research Bureau, Thursday, December 22, 1938, 10:00 A.M., at the League Headquarters, 501 Madison Ave., Recommendation on Objectives, MSCLC.

[16] Report at meeting, American Eugenics Society, New York, March 1941, in "A Memorandum on Planned Parenthood and the Nation's Population Situation", Birth Control Federation of America, N.Y., N.Y., December 1, 1941, 9, SSCSC.

[17] "A Statement of the Planned Parenthood Federation of America, Inc., for 1943", 9–10, SSCSC.

[18] "A Statement on Behalf of the Planned Parenthood Program for 1945", presented by PPFA, Inc., 1–2, SSCSC.

[19] Ibid.

acceptance of the possibilities inherent in genetic research. A practical step in the direction of public acceptance of eugenics was taken by the Eugenics Society with the promotion of genetic evaluation centers. There, counselors would not tell parents if they should have children; that would still remain a parental "choice".

On the positive side of eugenics, the AES *Report* noted:

> At present the birth of individuals with a likelihood of high genetic potential is blocked by many of our social, psychological, and economic conditions. ... The time when practical applications [are achieved] ... which will readily be accepted by an informed public may be nearer than anyone suspects.[20]

The AES officers were right. Already by 1955, medical investigators had "started prenatal sex determination based on the presence of X chromatin in the nuclei of amniotic fluid cells".[21] By 1966, the diagnostic technique of drawing fetal amniotic fluid from a pregnant woman and culturing fetal cells to help determine various fetal characteristics, including genetic abnormalities, had been described.[22]

The following chronological list describes the considerable overlapping of board memberships and interests among the leading figures in the Planned Parenthood Federation of America, the American Eugenics Society, and related groups and projects during the 1940s, 1950s, and 1960s.

From the 1940s: Frederick Osborn, Guy Irving Burch, Robert C. Cook, Henry P. Fairchild, found in the June, 1945 list of officers in the *Eugenical News,* American Eugenics Society.

From the 1950s: Dr. Alan F. Guttmacher, vice president, AES; Frederick Osborn, secretary, AES; Dorothy Brush; C. Lee Buxton (a plaintiff in the *Griswold* case); Mrs. Robert Ferguson, H. Bently Glass, Christopher Tietze, Sarah Lewit, J. Myron Stycos; from a November 25, 1958, letter from AES secretary Osborn to Margaret Sanger Slee, Tucson, Arizona, an acknowledgment that she had been a long-time AES member and considered it "one of [her] keenest interests".[23]

From the 1960s: Charles F. Westoff, Norman B. Ryder, Joseph P. Beasley, Larry Bumpass, found in *Eugenics Quarterly,* June 1963. The AES became the Society for the Study of Social Biology in 1973.

[20] The American Eugenics Society, "Five Year Report of the Officers, 1953–1957", 230 Oak Ave., NY, NY; Frederick Osborn was AES Chairman and at least six other Planned Parenthood members were prominent in the AES, 5–6, 10–11, 13.

[21] Gloria Sarto, M.D., Ph.D., "Genetic Considerations", in *Obstetrics and Gynecology,* ed. David N. Danforth (Hagerstown, Md: Harper and Row, 1977), 45.

[22] Ibid.

[23] Letter from AES Secretary Osborn to Margaret Sanger Slee, Tucson, Arizona, November 25, 1958; the statement cited was in Sanger's handwriting on the letter, SSCSC.

The collaboration went beyond personnel to policy and practicum. For instance, the AES helped another PPFA ally, the Population Council, providing it recommendations for the award of fellowships in medical genetics.[24] The Human Betterment Association of America (HBAA), a group seeking to make sterilization more available and/or legal, worked in tandem with the PPFA and the AES for eugenic goals, mostly by trumpeting the virtues of sterilization for social improvement.

In the 1950s the HBAA board of directors included prominent Planned Parenthood leaders such as Dr. Alan F. Guttmacher, Dr. Abraham Stone, PPFA national director William Vogt, and P. K. Whelpton.[25] An HBAA pamphlet supported sterilization as a way to solve "many personal, family and population problems". But it lamented the fact that progress in accepting this principle was slow. One sign of progress that was noted was that twenty-eight states had compulsory sterilization laws and that since 1907, when these statutes had first been enacted, 57,218 sterilizations had been carried out under them.[26] In December 1956, the PPFA Medical Committee recommended that the HBAA be permitted to notify Planned Parenthood affiliates that the HBAA would provide monetary help for sterilizations.[27]

The greatest advance in implementation of eugenic goals came with the development of the first major prenatal diagnostic tool, amniocentesis, in the mid-1960s. The technique involves inserting a hypodermic needle into a pregnant woman's abdomen to remove some of the amniotic fluid that surrounds the developing baby. The procedure is ordinarily carried out in the fourteenth to sixteenth weeks of pregnancy. Fetal cells that "shed" into the amniotic fluid are then cultured and analyzed, using various tests that, with varying degrees of accuracy, identify the presence of chromosomal abnormalities. Over 110 disorders and some structural defects can be identified in this way. Amniocentesis at this stage of pregnancy is done mainly if not exclusively to detect diseases for which there is no known cure or corrective course of treatment.

Based on earlier studies that measured the average rates of spontaneous miscarriage, the risk of miscarriage after amniocentesis was thought to be 0.5% higher than for nontested women. Proponents of amniocentesis state that "though this risk is small, it may exceed the statistical chances of giving birth to a child with certain disorders".[28] The one extra child who died for every two hundred pregnancies tested may have had a different view

---

[24] "Five Year Report", American Eugenics Society, 9, SSCSC.

[25] Brochure, *Sterilization for Human Betterment,* published by the HBAA, SSCSC.

[26] Ibid.

[27] Minutes of the PPFA National Medical Committee, December 5, 1956, 2, SSCSC.

[28] Mitchell S. Golbus, "The Current Scope of Antenatal Diagnosis", *Hospital Practice,* April 1982, 182.

of the magnitude of the amniocentesis risk. Moreover, the actual risk may be higher. A British study published in 1979 showed a fetal loss rate of 2.6% in amniocentesis procedures, versus 1.5% fetal loss in similarly matched women not undergoing the test.[29] Pro-life medical geneticist Dr. Hymie Gordon has stated that:

> A conservative estimate is that there is a 2 percent risk of either damaging the baby, tearing the uterus, introducing an infection, or precipitating a miscarriage.
> Even if the procedure itself does no harm, it is not always successful. Quite often it is not possible to obtain an adequate specimen either because the volume of fluid is insufficient or it has been contaminated with blood from the mother. There is a risk of at least 5 percent that an adequate specimen will not be obtained and then the procedure, with its risks, must be repeated.
> ... there is a substantial risk that the cells will not grow ... 10 percent at a minimum.
> Finally, errors in laboratory analysis are made ... including mistakes even in determining the baby's sex.
> One must take into account the serious emotional problems. ...
> I am not overstating this problem because there have been at least two (perhaps more) follow-up studies done by abortionists who have confirmed that the emotional trauma to mothers who have had an abortion after an amniocentesis is very considerable.
> ... try to imagine the parents' agonizing dilemma when they are told that the baby is likely to be normal but will be a carrier of a chromosome abnormality which could be passed on to the next generation.[30]

A decidedly different view of amniocentesis is, of course, taken by promoters of the eugenic agenda. The late Dr. Christopher Tietze wrote in 1982:

> At present, the number of abortions performed on the basis of prenatal diagnosis is quite small. ... In the United States, about 125 prenatal diagnosis units were active in 1978 ... but only 10 to 15 laboratories were adequately staffed and equipped for the diagnosis of Tay-Sachs disease or NTDs [neural tube defects]. The number of diagnostic amniocenteses performed in that year was on the order of 15,000, compared with 150,000 to 200,000 pregnancies at risk under currently accepted criteria. By 1982, the number of programs had risen to at least 155 and the number of amniocentesis procedures to at least 30,000. The number of abortions then performed on the basis of prenatal diagnosis was on the order of 1,500, or one-tenth of

[29] *Medical World News,* February 19, 1979, 25.
[30] Letter of Dr. Hymie Gordon, Mayo Clinic, to Kathy Hulst, Hudsonville, Minnesota, March 8, 1978.

1 percent of all legal abortions in the United States. However, each of these abortions averted a major catastrophe for a family.[31]

Even this number of selective screenings would not have happened without the passage in 1976 of the National Genetic Disease Act, public law 94–278. This law greatly facilitated the ability of the people planners to diagnose presently incurable genetic or structural defects of the unborn and then to offer abortion as a method of treatment. After the passage of this law, the PPFA restructured its own planning documents to reflect and implement this new policy, which it had done much to develop. Whereas the five-year plan of the PPFA prepared in 1975 had included no mention of genetic counseling or screening (in part because PPFA policy supported abortion on request), by 1977 the organization envisioned a much more active federal role in genetic screening.

In the first days of the Carter administration, PPFA officials worked feverishly to develop a broad policy paper to take advantage of the new administration's support for its agenda and the easy access it now enjoyed to the corridors of power. Sympathetic officials included White House aides Sarah Weddington, who had successfully argued the landmark abortion case, *Roe v. Wade*, before the U.S. Supreme Court, and Dr. Peter G. Bourne, a plaintiff in the *Roe* companion case, *Doe v. Bolton*.

The policy paper was called "Planned Births, the Future of the Family and the Quality of American Life: Towards a Comprehensive National Policy and Program". In terms Sanger would have found tepid, but stressing goals and methods she would have admired, the document suggested seven major new federal policy initiatives. Reducing retardation and infant disability could be accomplished, it said, by a "primary emphasis upon pregnancy testing and preventive services, prenatal diagnosis of fetal defects, genetic counseling, venereal disease prevention and other services".[32] The PPFA paper makes it clear that these "other services" would chiefly consist of second-trimester abortion.

The paper proposed a plan to increase federal money to at least $30 million in fiscal year 1979 for use by Planned Parenthood and other birth control providers to establish genetic counseling programs and to train genetic counseling personnel (the training presumably to come from Planned Parenthood and its allies). The final recommendation came close to establishing a national program of prenatal genetic disease detection and elimination by abortion. It

---

[31] Christopher Tietze, M.D., "Demographic Experience and Public Health Experience with Legal Abortion: 1973–80", in *Abortion, Medicine and the Law*, 3d ed., completely revised, ed. J. Douglas Buitler and David F. Walbert (New York: Facts on File Publications, 1986), 300.

[32] PPFA, "Planned Births, the Future of the Family and the Quality of American Life: Towards a Comprehensive National Policy and Program", June 1977, 3.

urged a national program to screen "older women and women at high risk of transmitting hereditary and other congenital disorders". To implement this massive screening, the federal government was to develop "suitable 'catchment areas' and prenatal diagnosis of fetal defects". This was important because diagnostic amniocentesis could not (and still cannot) be performed before roughly the fourth month of pregnancy, and hospitals in many areas of the country refused to perform mid-term abortions.

The "Planned Births" proposal amounted to a short- and long-term "solution" to the "problem" of local reluctance to perform these abortions. "Catchment area" is a term for a definite geographical area in which a particularly expensive or specialized form of medical treatment can be provided at a designated medical center. The Carter administration eventually cooled its ardor for such proposals in the face of internal divisions in the administration (most notably HEW secretary Joseph Califano) and the increasingly intense political clash over the abortion issue as the 1980 election approached.

"Planned Births" was unveiled at a July 1977 press conference. The clarion call of Margaret Sanger to limit the breeding of the unfit finally had a national planning document worthy of her name. Rife with the terminology of cost/benefit analysis, "Planned Births" aimed at nothing less than the virtual nationalization of reproduction.

The horizon at which "Planned Births" regularly hints, and occasionally explicitly grasps, is a world in which the provision of abortion, sex education without traditional ethics, genetic screening of couples, pregnancy "detection" to facilitate early abortion, and legal isolation of adolescents from their families are mandated by both federal and state law. The literal targets of Margaret Sanger's social betterment program, the "poor" and the "feeble-minded", have become, in the language of the bureaucratic social planners who wrote "Planned Births", the "low and marginal income" woman and the "retarded and disabled infant".

The PPFA's own *Standards and Guidelines,* dated December 15, 1977, incorporated the following: "Genetic counseling . . . should be an integral part of all family planning efforts in the United States and elsewhere."[33]

The "right" to have only a "wanted", healthy baby—coupled with the widespread availability of prenatal diagnostic techniques (amniocentesis, alpha fetoprotein (AFP) testing, chorionic villus sampling, ultrasound, fetoscopy) and "wrongful birth" suits—has virtually ensured a national policy of genetic screening along the lines PPFA suggested, even in the absence of the affirmative congressional legislation the organization dreamed about in 1977.

As a logical outgrowth of this trend, California presently mandates that

[33] PPFA, *Standards and Guidelines,* pt 1, sec. 12, "Genetic Counseling", December 15, 1977.

physicians offer to all pregnant women neural tube defect detection via alpha fetoprotein screening. While women may refuse the test (a 1987 report in the *New York Times* suggested that about half of pregnant women do so), the burden is on women to reject a course of action recommended by their physicians.

Thus, there are ample incentives both to offer and to agree to the test. But accuracy remains, or should remain, a considerable disincentive. While AFP screening has been implemented as a cost-saving measure, the procedure has been shown to be subject to errors when laboratories do fewer than five hundred specimen tests per week. For example, "laboratory reports to clinicians may lead to misdirecting 43% more pregnant women (with positive drift) into further (possibly invasive) diagnostic procedures".[34] And what of the anguish of parents whose children in utero initially test "false positive"? Will this impede the policy demands of eugenic planners?

While the current eugenic policies in the United States still officially call for "voluntarism", signs of coercion are already present in some government programs not normally associated with birth control. For example, nutritionists working with the U.S. Department of Agriculture's Women, Infants, and Children (WIC) Supplemental Food Program are involved with genetic screening.

The South Carolina Department of Health and Environmental Control (DHEC) is a case in point. South Carolina, it will be recalled, was one of the first two states to integrate birth control programs into the state welfare system. In late spring of 1983 nurses and nutritionists in the DHEC Maternal and Child Health Program at nine clinic sites within the four counties comprising the Low County Health District received some special in-service training. The training focused on how to make referrals to the South Carolina Genetic Disease Program within the DHEC's Bureau of Maternal and Child Health Care (BMCC).[35] A brochure from the BMCC specifies the following as indications for genetic referral:

> Pregnancies where there is: . . . divorce . . . maternal age (35 years of age or more when the baby is due) . . . Previous pregnancy . . . with multiple birth defects . . . multiple miscarriages . . . family history of . . . chromosomal abnormality . . . neural tube defects . . . a known single gene defect, dominant or recessive.
>
> Infant, child or individual with: major or multiple . . . birth defects . . . Short or immensely tall stature . . . Developmental delay . . . Failure to thrive . . . Primary amenorrhea after age 16 or delay in development of secondary sex characteristics.

[34] James N. Macri, M.D., et al., "Maternal Serum Alpha Fetoprotein Screening", *American Journal of Obstetrics and Gynecology*, vol. 156, no. 3 (March 1987): 533–35.

[35] Personal communication from James Hoffman of Port Royal, South Carolina to Robert Marshall, September 12, 1983.

Individuals with a positive family history for: ... mental retardation ...
Major psychiatric illness ... High risk for ethnically related specific disorders,
such as: Sickle Cell Anemia in blacks, Tay Sachs in Jewish ... [36]

Nurse and nutritionist social workers were given instructions on how
to handle referrals of a child or affected individual. They were to explain
the need for a genetic evaluation to the patients and give them any educational materials that may be appropriate and "motivate" them to keep the
appointment.[37] Borrowing sales techniques of striking while the iron is hot,
social workers who identified women with possibly inferior offspring were
told that "if the patient is in her 14th week or more, while you have the
patient there, call in the referral immediately ... ".[38] Presumably delaying the
testing too much longer would make the abortion of a possibly less than
perfect child a bit messier than usual.

Once the pregnant, gene-deficient ward of the state had been identified in
the WIC program, she was given an assessment of risks. According to the
official South Carolina genetic services handbook, "amniocentesis carries a
.5% (1/200) chance for the following: miscarriage, maternal infection or
complication, harm to the fetus".[39]

As can be seen, the risk assessment is below that of Dr. Hymie Gordon
cited earlier, and at the low end of the range found in subsequent studies for
fetal loss alone. It is doubtful that the loss of one of every two hundred
children of the poor due to amniocentesis-induced miscarriage is a matter of
great regret to at least some eugenic enthusiasts.

What happens when a program administrator becomes a program objector
can be seen in the story of James Hoffman, a public health nutritionist
employed by the South Carolina DHEC, who objected to making genetic
referrals after undergoing the prescribed training. Hoffman refused to implement the program because of professional, religious, and moral objections to
the abortions that often resulted from postscreening counseling. Furthermore,
Hoffman would not refer his WIC clients to other nutritionists. On July 7,
1983, he was told that unless he made gene referrals, his employment with the
DHEC, which began in 1980, would be terminated.[40] Hoffman responded
July 13, 1983, observing that the more able the educator is at personifying the

---

[36] *Indications for Genetic Referral*, Department of Health and Environmental Control,
Columbia, South Carolina, 29201.

[37] "The Process for Referral for Patients Needing Genetic Services", handout sheet,
Genetic Associate Division of Clinical Genetics, Medical University of South Carolina.

[38] Ibid.

[39] "Counseling, A Handbook for Genetic Services, Evaluation and Referral System", the
South Carolina Genetic Disease Testing and Counseling Program, 19.

[40] Dr. Forster McCaleb to James Hoffman, letter, July 7, 1983, personal correspondence
of James Hoffman made available to Robert Marshall.

fetus, the better the mother will eat. "It seems very inconsistent to me to treat the fetus like a baby when one is interested in feeding him/her, but to depersonify the fetus when the baby is 'unwanted' or has a genetic defect."

Hoffman, as the following statement makes clear, refused for other reasons as well: "I based my decision to refrain from making these referrals on religious grounds." He cited Deuteronomy 5:11 about killing the innocent, and cited the Psalms to show that God knits children in their mother's womb, and that "Jesus came to teach us to love, yes even the least of our brothers—including genetically defective ones".[41]

Hoffman was fired on July 16, 1983. In spite of his contempt for South Carolina's efforts at ridding the gene pool of defectives, he had the temerity to apply for unemployment compensation. Ironically, Hoffman's application was approved by South Carolina officials because, as they told him on August 4, his change in job duties had "caused a conflict with his religious ethical beliefs".[42]

His former employer appealed the decision. A hearing was held during September 1983, and a decision was rendered by the South Carolina Employment Security Commission Tribunal, which found Hoffman "to have been discharged for misconduct connected with his work" and reduced his unemployment benefits.[43]

The lesson of Hoffman's experience is that, in the world of the "perfect, the privileged, and the planned", protecting children from the lethal decisions of the eugenists is cause for dismissal. Government has come full cycle, existing now, it seems, to protect the strong from the weak.

What does the future hold? Increased genetic screening so it seems, with a U.S. Public Health Service recommendation that by the year 2000 all pregnancies be genetically screened. And medicine may help accomplish this with newer techniques of genetic screening such as chorionic villus sampling (CVS) for first trimester diagnosis of ailments, including being of the "wrong sex". A study to assess the "safety" of the procedure was reported in the March 9, 1989, *New England Journal of Medicine,* which gave the procedure a clean bill of health, so to speak.

The authors noted that other studies had reported a fetal loss rate after CVS

---

[41] Letter to Dr. Forster C. McCaleb from James Hoffman, July 13, 1983, personal correspondence of James Hoffman made available to Robert Marshall.

[42] Determination of South Carolina Employment Security Commission, account no. 126950, August 4, 1983, Ms. Lonnie Trakas, claims adjudicator.

[43] South Carolina Employment Security Commission, decision no. 83–A–7333, hearing date September 4, 1983, Martin G. Newborn appeals referee.

of from 2.2 to 5.4%[44] Their rate of miscarriage ranged from 0.9% in women who underwent CVS only once to 10.8% for women who had to take the CVS test three or four times to get accurate readings.[45] The overall excess risk for fetal loss was 0.8% above that for amniocentesis.[46] We also noticed that at the CVS centers

> pregnancies may be terminated for nonmedical reasons that include sex selection.... Of the 24 terminations of pregnancies in which the fetal karyotype was known, 11 were known or strongly believed to have been sought for purposes of sex selection (two male and nine female fetuses).... Four other abortions may also have been linked to sex selection, but we concluded that because less than one percent of the total pregnancies tested were aborted for sex-selection reasons, this reflects a policy of CVS centers not to participate in such abortions.[47]

This does not alter the fact, however, that almost 1% of CVS-tested pregnancies were artificially interrupted in the interests of preventing the birth of a child of the "wrong" sex.

The more things change, the more they remain the same. The July 4, 1919, *New York Times* carried an article about a severely disabled woman who quit her job at Planned Parenthood because of her coworkers' attitudes toward genetic screening and abortion of disabled fetuses. "There was a strong eugenics mentality that exhibited disdain, discomfort, and ignorance toward disabled babies", she said. The feeling at Planned Parenthood, she noted was that these were "bad babies".[48]

---

[44] George R. Rhoads et al., "The Safety and Efficacy of Chorionic Villus Sampling for Early Pregnancy Diagnosis of Cytogenetic Abnormalities", *New England Journal of Medicine* (March 9, 1989): 609–10.

[45] Ibid., 609.

[46] Ibid., 615.

[47] Ibid., 613.

[48] "Abortion Issue Divides Advocates for Disabled", *The New York Times*, National, July 4, 1991, A 11.

Chapter Twelve

Old Lies and New Labels:
When Contraception Is Abortion

Nowhere has the manipulation of the truth by population-control and abortion proponents been more evident than in the area of medical terminology dealing with antifertility drugs, devices, and social policies.

This policy of semantic gymnastics, successfully carried out over a period of decades, included efforts to redefine nearly every term in the lexicon of human reproduction: pregnancy, conception, abortion, and human being or person. These subterfuges were necessary because the prevalent social attitudes were against abortion, but the developing antifertility technology depended heavily upon it. The Pill and IUD, it was discovered, achieved their antifertility effects by methods besides preventing fertilization.

The definitional changes effected by Planned Parenthood and other notables were radical departures from prior, established medical knowledge. The "traditional" and previously noncontroversial understanding of some of these terms was clearly stated in 1952 by Planned Parenthood's own Dr. Abraham Stone, who had noted in a discussion of contraceptive research that

> the mechanical and chemical methods currently employed, or any biologic method that would prevent ovulation or fertilization merely prevent life from beginning. . . . Measures designed to prevent implantation fall into a different category. Here there is a question of destroying a life already begun.[1]

In the face of lingering antiabortion attitudes, a terminological shift was critically needed to obfuscate the difference between antiovulatory, anti-fertilization, and anti-implantation fertility control methods. This question was also related in a number of ways to the physiological problem of safely inhibiting fertility. This was evident in an internal memo from Searle and Company, an early leader in birth control research. This memo from the 1950s suggested that chemicals that interrupted the menstrual cycle and that would produce a "false" pregnancy would be rejected for human use.

---

[1] Abraham Stone, M.D., "Research in Contraception: A Review and Preview", presented at the Third International Conference of Planned Parenthood, Bombay, India, *Report of the Proceedings,* November 24–29, 1952, no copyright, Family Planning Association of India, 101.

I believe the only acceptable compound would be one which does not interfere with the cycle or ovulation but which might prevent either fertilization or possibly implantation [attachment to the uterine wall].[2]

But those most interested in redefinitions of reproductive terminology during this period were proponents of global population control. At a 1959 Planned Parenthood–Population Council joint symposium, Bent Boving, a Swedish fertility researcher, eloquently identified the importance of using *le mot juste* to mollify public concern about abortifacients: "Whether", he said, "eventual control of implantation can be reserved the social advantage of being considered to prevent conception rather than to destroy an established pregnancy could depend on something so simple as a prudent habit of speech."[3] Boving himself was not consistently able to manage the "prudent habit of speech" he urged. Earlier in the same discourse, Boving had said that: "Thus, the greatest pregnancy wastage, in fact by far the highest death rate of the entire human life span, is during the week before and including the beginning of implantation, and the next greatest is in the week immediately following."[4]

A "prudent habit of speech" was nevertheless needed because it was estimated, accurately as it turned out, by these early researchers that the physiological opportunities for developing antifertility drugs were limited, and the likelihood of achieving new ones that were safer, more effective, and totally nonabortive was slim indeed. The initial restructuring of medical terms was engineered to comport with the physiological reality of early abortion and to take advantage of religious/social opposition to abortion, but accommodation of "contraception". In 1962 Dr. Mary Calderone, the medical director of PPFA at that time, said that "if it turns out that these intrauterine devices operate as abortifacients, not only the Catholic Church will be against them, but Protestant churches as well".[5]

There were also legal implications in this matter, as can be seen from a 1963 U.S. Department of Health, Education, and Welfare survey that noted:

All the measures which impair the viability of the zygote at any time between the instant of fertilization and the completion of labor constitute,

---

[2] Memo to Dr. Drill from Dr. Saunders, re: "Effects of Drugs on Mating in Rats", December 9, 1954, Gregory Pincus Papers, Manuscript Division, Library of Congress.

[3] Bent G. Boving, "Implantation Mechanisms", in *Mechanisms Concerned with Conception,* ed. C. G. Hartman (New York: Pargamon Press, 1963), 386.

[4] Ibid., 321.

[5] Dr. Mary Calderone, discussion, "Mechanisms of Contraceptive Action", in *Intrauterine Contraceptive Devices: Proceedings of the Conference,* held April 30–May 1, 1962, New York City, ed. Christopher Tietze and Sarah Lewit, published by Excerpta Medica Foundation, 110.

in the strict sense, procedures for inducing abortion. Administration of such compounds whose mechanism of action is of this character to man as either an investigative procedure or as a practical birth control technique poses technical legal questions that have not yet been resolved.[6]

Eventually an answer to the question of how to effect a "prudent habit of speech" was suggested in 1964 at an International Population Council–sponsored symposium during a discussion between two physicians. Dr. Samuel Wishik stated: "In a Moslem country such as Pakistan, if it's considered that the intra-uterine device is an abortifacient, this obviously would have a bearing on national acceptance or rejection."[7] Dr. Tietze, affiliated with both Planned Parenthood and the Population Council, suggested not to "disturb those people for whom this is a question of major importance".[8] Dr. Tietze also indicated that theologians and jurists have always taken into account the prevailing medical and biological consensus of their times, and that "if a medical consensus develops and is maintained that pregnancy, and therefore life, begins at implantation, eventually our brethren from the other faculties will listen."[9]

Planned Parenthood's efforts at hidden persuasion were accepted by the American College of Obstetrics and Gynecology with the publication of its first *Terminology Bulletin* in 1965, which stated "CONCEPTION is the implantation of a fertilized ovum".[10]

Was there some shattering and revolutionary development in molecular biology during this period that necessitated ACOG's sudden shift in labeling? Dr. J. Richard Sosnowski, head of the Southern Association of Obstetricians and Gynecologists, a member group of ACOG, gave a clear answer in his 1984 presidential address:

I do not deem it excellent to play semantic gymnastics in a profession. . . . It is equally troublesome to me that, with no scientific evidence to validate the change, the definition of conception as the successful spermatic penetration of an ovum was redefined as the implantation of a fertilized ovum. It appears to me that the only reason for this was the dilemma produced by the possibility that the intrauterine contraceptive device might function as an

---

[6] *A Survey of Research on Reproduction Related to Birth and Population Control* (as of January 1, 1963), U.S. Department of Health, Education and Welfare, Public Health Service, publ. no. 1066, Washington, D.C.: U.S. Government Printing Office, 1963, 27.

[7] Discussion, *Proceedings of the Second International Conference, Intra-Uterine Contraception*, held October 2–3, 1964, New York City, ed. Sheldon Segal et. al., International Congress Series, Excerpta Medica Foundation, no. 86, 212.

[8] Ibid., 212.

[9] Ibid., 213.

[10] ACOG Terminology Bulletin, Terms Used in Reference to the Fetus, Chicago: American College of Obstetricians and Gynecologists, no. 1, September 1965.

abortifacient. Now that the intrauterine contraceptive device has lost popularity will we change the definition again?[11]

As Sosnowski's speech suggests, the ACOG and Planned Parenthood finesses are rejected elsewhere within the medical profession. The *American Journal of Obstetrics and Gynecology*, which is the official publication of nearly forty obstetrical and gynecological societies throughout the United States, publishes articles that use the traditional definition of pregnancy as beginning at fertilization. In a study of the preimplantation human embryo published in 1989, the following is reported:

> Early pregnancy factor and other factor(s) produced by the preimplantation embryo may play a role in suppressing maternal cellular immune response, thereby preventing maternal rejection of the embryo.
> However, other than the early pregnancy factor (EPF), present in the sera of pregnant women shortly after fertilization (24 hours), there is no other factor produced in significant amounts at time of implantation. Therefore this factor plays a possible role in the prevention of maternal rejection of the oligocellular embryo.[12]

And when different species of mammals are studied, such as rats, and no political agenda is at stake, fertilization and not implantation is readily recognized as the beginning of pregnancy: "Normally, fertilized rat eggs take about 3 days to pass through the oviduct, and on the 4th day of pregnancy they enter the uterus. . . . Day 5, attachment of the blastocyst to the uterine epithelium starts, and this we consider the beginning of implantation."[13]

No One Knows When Human Life Begins

The second facet of Planned Parenthood's redefinition involved the claim that no one really knows when human life begins. Yet, writing in 1933 when he had not yet accepted the doctrine of abortion on demand, Dr. Alan Guttmacher was perplexed that anyone, much less an educated medical doctor, would not know this.

> We of today know that man is born of sexual union; that he starts life as an embryo within the body of the female; and that the embryo is formed from

---

[11] Dr. J. Richard Sosnowski, "The Pursuit of Excellence: Have We Apprehended and Comprehended It?", *American Journal of Obstetrics and Gynecology*, vol. 150, no. 2 (September 15, 1984): 117.

[12] Ratna Bose, Ph.D., et al., "Purified Human Early Pregnancy Factor from Preimplantation Embryo Possesses Immunosuppresive Properties", *American Journal of Obstetrics and Gynecology*, vol. 160, no. 4 (April 1989): 955.

[13] Z. Dickmann and V. J. De Feo, "The Rat Blastocyst during Normal Pregnancy and during Delayed Implantation, Including an Observation of the Shedding of the Zona Pellucida", *Journal of Reproduction and Fertility*, official journal of the Society for the Study of Fertility, the Biological Science Committee of the IPPF, vol. 13 (1967): 3–9.

the fusion of two single cells, the ovum and the sperm. This all seems so simple and evident to us that it is difficult to picture a time when it was not part of the common knowledge.[14]

Guttmacher added that at least since 1875 two medical researchers "showed that the essential act of fertilization is not the union of the two cells, ovum and sperm, but the fusion of the two nuclei into one, the offspring beginning its career as a combination of the nuclei of its two parents".[15]

However, after his conversion to the "pro-choice" view and assumption of the Planned Parenthood helm, Guttmacher's past knowledge seemed to vanish. At a 1968 symposium he said:

> Dr. Marchetti and I are rarely together. . . . He believes that an abortion is murder, and under these conditions he does not feel that it can ever be justified.
>
> My feeling is that the fetus, particularly during its early intra-uterine existence, is simply a group of specialized cells that do not differ materially from other cells. I do not think they are made in God's image. I think they are made in man's image. . . . If one can justify shooting a burglar who enters your home . . . one can certainly justify the elimination of some cells, which from my point of view, have simply not yet become a human being, but simply have the potentialities of life. Philosophically we are too far apart to try to compromise; it is impossible.[16]

And he would add in his 1973 book that: "Scientifically all we know is that a living human sperm unites with a living human egg; if they were not living there could be no union. . . . Does human life begin before or with the union of the gametes, or with birth, or at a time intermediate? I, for one, confess I do not know."[17]

This view had its origins more in attitudes than knowledge. Guttmacher had noted that "many women who are opposed to abortion on request say that they do not regard the taking of a drug that will 'bring on their period' as an abortion.

"I believe the opposition of many doctors to abortion would be greatly diminished if there were a safe drug available."[18]

The "ignorance is bliss" posture has received widespread endorsement

---

[14] Alan F. Guttmacher, *Life in the Making: The Story of Human Procreation* (New York: Viking Press, 1933), 3.

[15] Ibid., 48–49.

[16] Willard Heckel, moderator, "Law, Morality and Abortion Symposium", held at Rutgers University Law School, March 27, 1968, *Rutgers Law Review*, vol 22 (Spring 1968): 436.

[17] Alan F. Guttmacher, M.D., *Pregnancy, Birth, and Family Planning: A Guide for Expectant Parents in the 1970's* (New York: Viking Press, 1973), 23

[18] Jane Ross, "Abortion and the Unwanted Child: An Interview with Alan F. Guttmacher, M.D. and Harriet Pilpel", *Family Planning Perspectives*, vol. 2, no. 2 (March 1970): 16–24.

throughout the medical community. The American College of Obstetricians and Gynecologists in their 1990 abortion "white paper" reported that 167 scientists and physicians told the U.S. Supreme Court in 1989 that "[t]here is no scientific consensus that a human life begins at conception, at a given stage of fetal development, or at birth. . . . When life begins cannot be tested by scientific method, but instead depends on each individual's beliefs and values."[19]

In essence, this claim of medical agnosticism is really an attack on the integrity of the biological sciences to which medicine is incontestably subordinate for its basic information regarding human physiology, development, and the healing process. In contrast to this formidable assertion of basic ignorance stands the published research of Erich Bleschschmidt who has stated that

the evidence no longer allows a discussion as to if and when and in what month of ontogenesis a human being is formed. To be a human being is decided for an organism at the moment of fertilization of the ovum. For this reason we have to regard the intrinsic quality of the fertilized ovum as an essential prerequisite, decisive for all future ontogenesis.[20]

And Professor Landrum Shettles, who has engaged in human in vitro fertilization projects, wrote a letter to the *New York Times* shortly after *Roe v. Wade* about the Supreme Court's indecision concerning the beginning of human life: "To deny a truth should not be made the basis for legalizing abortion."[21]

Over a century ago the *Journal of the American Medical Association* suggested that "this fallacious idea that there is no life until quickening takes place has been the foundation of, and formed the basis of, and has been the excuse to ease or appease the guilty conscience which has led to the destruction of thousands of human lives".[22] Every addition to medical knowledge that has occurred since the definitive discovery of fertilization in the first half of the nineteenth century has added to the weight of information in behalf of the humanity of the child in utero. Recent advances in ultrasound imaging should have taken away any vestiges of doubt on this part even among the uneducated (albeit public opinion polls uniformly indicate that it is the educated who have the most difficulty incorporating this knowledge). Abortion providers instinctively know this. Dr. Sally Faith Dorfman of Einstein Medical College has noted that during an abortion

[19] *Public Health Policy Implications of Abortion: A Government Relations Handbook*, Kathryn G. Moore, ed., American College of Obstetricians and Gynecologists, 1990, 38.

[20] Erich Bleschschmidt, *The Beginning of Human Life* (New York, Heidelberg, and Berlin: Springer-Verlag, 1977), 17.

[21] Dr. Landrum Shettles, Letter to the Editor, *New York Times*, February 14, 1973.

[22] Isaac M. Quimby, "Introduction to Medical Jurisprudence", *Journal of the American Medical Association*, vol. 9 (August 6, 1887): 164; see also N. C. Markham, "Foeticide and Its Prevention", *Journal of the American Medical Association*, vol. 11 (December 8, 1888): 805.

a compassionate and sensitive sonographer should remember to turn the screen away from the plane of view. Staff too may find themselves increasingly disturbed by the repeated visual impact of an aspect of their work that they need to partially deny in order to continue to function optimally and to concentrate on the needs of the women who come to them for help.[23]

Enacting Antiabortion Laws Will Deny "Contraceptives" to Women

Claims that prolife laws will outlaw "contraceptives" are not new. Previously, such discussions could be found only in arcane law journals, but they are becoming more prominent as the "threat" to abortion on demand increases.

For example, consider the amicus brief filed by the Planned Parenthood Federation of America and the Association of Planned Parenthood Physicians (APPP) in the 1973 *Roe* and *Doe* abortion cases. In that brief, PPFA and APPP lawyers noted that the states with antiabortion laws had not "made any effort to outlaw the use of the intrauterine device (IUD) which in fact may function to prevent implantation after fertilization has occurred".[24] The brief cited a 1964 law review article that pointed to the then-extant anti-abortion laws that

> apply to acts done with an intent to terminate pregnancy at any time, from the moment of conception. . . . The broad language of statutes and cases would suggest that to use pre-implantation means on a pregnant woman would be unlawful . . . under statutes where [proving] pregnancy is an element of the offence . . . manufacturers, distributors or sellers of the pre-implantation means might be prosecuted under ¼statutes prohibiting the manufacture, distribution or sale of abortifacients.[25]

Another law review article makes the point that where state laws such as that of Wisconsin criminalize abortion and refer to the "unborn child" as a human being from the time of conception,

> there would certainly be no question that under this enactment the vitalized embryo is legally protected before implantation and thus the use of any pills or intra-uterine devices to keep the fertilized ovum from implanting on the wall of the uterus is a violation of the statute.

[23] Transcript excerpts from a talk entitled, "Abortion Update" (talk no. 1065), given by Dr. Sally Faith Dorfman, director of Family Planning, Development, and Research at Albert Einstein Medical College in New York, at the American Public Health Conference, November 18, 1985, in Washington, D.C. Recorded by Robert G. Marshall, director of research, Castello Institute.

[24] Planned Parenthood Federation of America and the Association of Planned Parenthood Physicians in the 1973 *Roe* and *Doe* abortion cases, 44.

[25] Ibid., citing Sybil Meloy, "Pre-Implantation Fertility Control and the Abortion Law", *Chicago-Kent Law Review*, vol. 41 (1964): 183, 205–6.

Since the function of the pre-implantation means of fertility control is to interrupt pregnancy, their use would no doubt violate abortion statutes which do not require proof of pregnancy as an element of the offence. . . .

But with the problems of overpopulation facing us, as it is today, allowing society to legally expand methods of birth control to the instant of implantation does not seem unreasonable.[26]

In contrast to the *Roe* and *Doe* cases where "contraceptive" abortions were buried deep in legal briefs, the 1989 *Webster v. Reproductive Health Services* Supreme Court case brought the issue of abortion masquerading as "contraception" further out of the closet.

Frank Sussman, the lawyer who argued the pro-abortion side in the *Webster* case, told the Supreme Court that the Missouri antiabortion law would outlaw physician prescription of "contraceptives" such as the IUD and "progesterone only" Pill—the so-called mini-Pill—in public clinics.

Missouri attorney general William Webster flatly told the Court that Missouri's law was not enacted to restrict women's contraceptive options.

And Jack Willke, M.D., president of the National Right to Life Committee said that lawyers for his group "believe the Missouri law would not restrict access to birth control unless the state legislature passed another law specifically defining methods like the IUD and the progesterone only pill as abortifacients."

Such methods "fall in-between in the sense that they have both effects", he said. "One effect would be legal—contraception—and one effect would be illegal. It's our opinion that you could very easily defend those as contraceptives."[27]

All three of the responses above—Sussman, Webster, and Willke—betray a casual use of terminology that ultimately confuses the listener. After all, if a drug or device operates as both a contraceptive and an abortifacient, it makes little sense to call it one or the other. It is both. The public policy question is clearly one of determining whether the law should permit, fund, or allow research, development, or the use of occasionally or frequently abortifacient drugs or devices. For the birth control activist, the question is simple: Everything is permitted. The question for the defender of the right to life is at once more subtle and significant. If occasional abortifacients are acceptable, what possible objection is there to the frequently or nearly always abortifacient drug or device? This is a moral and political question that must take into account the general inability of the public to appreciate subtle though real

[26] John L. King, "Notes and Comment: Criminal Law—Abortion—the 'Morning After Pill' and Other Pre-implantation Birth Control Methods and the Law", *Oregon State Law Review*, vol. 46, no. 2 (February 1967): 211–18.

[27] *Washington Post*, May 28, 1989, A-19.

distinctions, and the profound question of possibly taking a life in ignorance, culpably or otherwise. But in any case, no moral or satisfactory practical solution will be forthcoming that ignores inconvenient physiological or pharmacological properties of various antifertility items.

The simple truth is that some of these drugs and devices are called contraceptives, but really cause the death of the human being by abortion shortly after the child's origin. But it is important to note here that Planned Parenthood and its supporters are sheepishly acknowledging their deception to a small proportion of their birth control market. Mr. Sussman and others submitting pro-abortion briefs in *Webster* omit any mention of the most "popular" birth control Pill, the combined estrogen/progesterone regimen, as also being in the abortion classification, even though the FDA patient and physician package inserts describe their mode of action in terms that mean abortion. Perhaps these opponents of Missouri's antiabortion law were unwilling to test the reaction of millions of women to the fact that even the most commonly used Pill, or "oral contraceptive", is sometimes a killer of children.

Each of these approaches looks to what is presumed to be the probable consequences of antiabortion laws in the lives of the "middle ground" public, which has largely accepted the practice of birth control. Each of these approaches seeks to maximize ignorance and confusion in order to maximize political advantage. Neither side is being completely candid. But we harken back to Professor Landrum Shettles' observation that "to deny a truth should not be made the basis for legalizing abortion".[28]

This curious right to be ignorant that has resulted from the abortion political standoff regarding contraceptives that kill has produced the incredible situation in the United States of doctors having the medical right to abort women without their knowledge or consent. In the 1984 Illinois case of *Diamond v. Charles,* a question in controversy was whether the state of Illinois could require physicians who prescribe or administer abortifacients to women to inform their patients that they have done so. By dismissing the case for procedural reasons, the Supreme Court effectively sustained without comment the decision of the U.S. Circuit Court of Appeals for the Seventh Circuit, which struck down the Illinois informed-consent provision.[29] Thus, Illinois women have no right to know what mode of action is responsible for the antifertility effect of the birth control drugs or devices prescribed to them.

Oddly enough, the American Medical Association, the American College of Obstetricians and Gynecologists, and others claimed the Illinois provision interfered with the physician's ability to provide medically relevant information to the patient.

---

[28] Shettles, Letter to Editor.
[29] No. 84–1379, Supreme Court, October 1984 term.

This "finesse" regarding the beginning of pregnancy is regularly displayed in medical journals as a matter of course. For example, when pregnancy is discussed in a neutral context, medical journals read as follows: "Highly sensitive early pregnancy tests that are positive at about the time of implantation (seven days after conception) are being used to estimate the extent of pregnancy losses that occur between implantation and the time after the first missed menses when standard pregnancy tests can be employed."[30]

But when a nonpregnant state is desired and the red flag of abortion is waving, the finesses recur. The following appeared a mere week later in the medical journal just quoted: "These preliminary studies suggest that RU-486 holds promise as a safe and effective form of fertility control that can be administered once a month."[31] The title of the article? "A Potential New Contraceptive Agent". This, for a drug that is administered postimplantation, after a pregnancy is suspected or definitively established.

Information regarding the abortifacient properties of both the Pill and the IUD are available to the public, even if presented in somewhat disguised language most of the time. When the FDA proposed in 1976 that mandatory physician and patient package inserts accompany the distribution of the Pill, it was stated that

> oral contraceptives are of two types. The most common . . . is a combination of an estrogen and a progestin, the two kinds of female hormones . . . this kind of oral contraceptive works principally by preventing release of an egg from the ovary . . . the second type of oral contraceptive, often called the mini-pill, contains only a progestin. It works, in part, by preventing release of an egg from the ovary, but also by keeping sperm from reaching the egg and making the uterus (womb) less receptive to any fertilized egg that reaches it.[32]

Note the omission of the word "abortion", used in 1963 by the same federal department to describe modes of action for antifertility drugs or devices that interfere with development after fertilization, such as the types of birth control pills.

This is all the more significant in light of the directives given by HEW that stated "the patient brochure will contain the latest medical information about 'the pill,' written in language understandable by the general public".[33] Seven years earlier in 1969, an advisory committee to the FDA for the Pill stated in

[30] Dorothy Warburton, "Reproductive Loss: How Much Is Preventable", *New England Journal of Medicine* (January 15, 1987): 158–60.

[31] Lynnette K. Nieman et al., "The Progesterone Antagonist RU-486: A Potential New Contraceptive Agent", *New England Journal of Medicine* (January 22, 1987): 187–90.

[32] *Federal Register*, vol. 41, no. 236, December 7, 1976, 53640.

[33] Press release, Dept. of Health, Education, and Welfare, December 3, 1976, contact Ed Nida, FDA.

definite if technical terms that, for the Pill: "The second major effect is on the endometrium. The progestin acts as an antiestrogen causing alteration in endometrial glands and as a progestin, causing pseudodecidual reactions. Both of these alter the ability of the endometrium to participate in the process of implantation."[34]

The FDA's suggested patient brochure on IUDs states that, "IUD's seem to interfere in some manner with the implantation of the fertilized egg in the lining of the uterine cavity. The IUD does not prevent ovulation."[35] Note again the avoidance of the word "abortion".

And Planned Parenthood reading materials for the "health consumer" identifies implantation and not fertilization as the beginning of pregnancy, which is clearly false.[36]

Old Habits Die Hard: The Abortion Pill, Killing as "Contragestion"

Gaining public acceptance for the French abortion pill, RU-486, is in part a matter of contriving and using acceptable euphemisms. Hastings Center author Lisa Cahill has written, "The method of reevaluation by redescription has assumed a significant role in the presentation of RU-486 . . ." She notes how the difference between abortion and contraception has been finessed "by the rhetoric designed to make the drug more acceptable to those who already accept conception prevention [i.e., contraception]."[37]

Indeed, RU-486 inventor Etienne-Emile Baulieu has acknowledged christening RU-486 a contragestive, partly in the hope that the term "may defuse the abortion issue".[38] His collaborators are even trying to extend the definition of "pregnancy prevention" to twenty-eight days after fertilization, again under the rubric of "contragestion".[39]

---

[34] Advisory Committee on Obstetrics and Gynecology, Food and Drug Administration, 1969, *Second Report on the Oral Contraceptives,* app. 4, "Report of the Task Force on Biological Effects", Philip Corfman, chairman.

[35] *Second Report on Intrauterine Contraception,* The Medical Drug and Device Advisory Committee on Obstetrics and Gynecology to the U.S. Food and Drug Administration, Department of Health, Education, and Welfare, December 1978, app. 1, 97, 101.

[36] PPFA, *Basics of Birth Control* (9-76/150), 1976, no. 150.

[37] Lisa Sowle Cahill, " 'Abortion Pill' RU 486: Ethics, Rhetoric, and Social Practice", *Hastings Center Report,* October/November 1987, 5–8.

[38] Etienne-Emile Baulieu, "Contragestion by the Progesterone Antagonist RU 486: A Novel Approach to Human Fertility Control", *Contraception,* supp. to vol. 36 (1987): 1–5.

[39] M. R. Van Santen, M.D. and A. A. Haspels, "Interception III: Postleutal Contragestion by an Antiprogestin (Mifepristone, RU 486) in 62 Women", *Contraception,* vol. 35, no. 5 (May 1987): 423–31 (see, "Only after the completion of implantation, i.e., after the 28th day of the menstrual cycle, should RU 486 be considered as an abortion). Moreover, organogenesis begins about two weeks after implantation."

This is a case in which the willingness to be deceived also plays a part. "Psychologically, the patients concerned consider themselves in no way pregnant and therefore do not regard the antiprogestins as abortifacient medication."[40] Failure to define correctly this pill's mode of action is reinforced by the fact that women can take the pill without a pregnancy test. "The psychological consequences of this uncertainty can be significant. 'We call it contragestion, not abortion', says Couzinet. 'Many women think of it as an induction of a menstrual period.' "[41]

Planned Parenthood decided to call RU-486 the "Interceptor Pill", because "it not only intercepts implantation, but it can also intercept further fetal development".[42]

Even the prestigious *New England Journal of Medicine* succumbed to designating RU-486 as a contraceptive. The study, conducted by researchers at the National Institutes of Health, noted that:

> The present studies were designed to test the contraceptive potential of RU 486. The ability of a single midluteal-phase dose to induce menses in women was established. Human chorionic gonadotropin (HCG) was also given concurrently to test whether RU 486 could induce menses in the presence of the enhanced corpus luteal function characteristic of early pregnancy.[43]

If RU-486 is being tested as a contraceptive why administer HCG in order to mimic the biochemical characteristics of an established pregnancy?

To quote Cahill once again, "The research team explained their project in a manner that presumed the disputed premise that expulsion of the embryo before implantation counts as 'contraception' rather than abortion. . . . This language may represent another attempt to redescribe an activity to make it less morally problematic."[44]

There is one additional major reason to call RU-486 a contragestive, and that is to obviate the impact of any existing antiabortion statutes.[45] This is semantic gymnastics on a scale to make even Nadia Comaneci envious.

[40] Ibid.

[41] "The Month after Pill", Medicine, *Time*, December 29, 1986.

[42] Dr. Louise Tyrer (vice president for medical affairs for Planned Parenthood), "General Discussion", *Contraception*, suppl. to vol. 36 (1987): 37–42.

[43] Lynnette K. Nieman et al., "The Progesterone Anagonist RU-486: A Potential New Contraceptive", *New England Journal of Medicine*, vol. 316 (January 22, 1987): 187–91.

[44] Cahill, " 'Abortion Pill' RU 486", 7.

[45] Tina Agoestina, "Prospective Usefulness of RU-486 in Fertility Control", *Contraception*, supp. to vol. 36 (1987), 33–36.

Chapter Thirteen

Conclusion:
What Planned Parenthood Has Wrought

This work has reviewed the seventy-year catalogue of personal and social "goods" that acceptance of the Planned Parenthood program was supposed to bring to the individuals and societies that accepted its premises and implemented its practices. We will briefly examine, in light of Planned Parenthood's promises, what the result of Planned Parenthood's success has been.

Availability of Birth Control Has Altered Teen Sexual Behavior and Increased the Incidence of Venereal Diseases

In 1965, Planned Parenthood national board chairman, Donald Strauss, warned his membership that "they could not escape the moral implications of widespread, easy-to-use contraceptives".

Strauss said, "The availability of contraceptives for all, which is our objective, is having a profound effect on the sexual attitudes and behavior of our time." He added that while birth control access was not the only factor, to pretend it had "no effect was to ignore the obvious".[1]

How else does one explain that today's teens and young people view premarital sex as "less wrong" than their counterparts in 1929 through 1949? Indeed, the change in the perceived relative wrongness of premarital sex by college students in a 1983 survey led the shifts in changes of moral judgments from American college students earlier in the twentieth century. "The only behavior for which current acceptance is far above previous levels of approval is having sexual relations while unmarried. . . . Half of the sample of current undergraduates rated premarital sex as '0' on the wrongness scale." Zero tallied with items held least wrong or not wrong, and "10" was most wrong.[2]

And medical authorities point out that

it is fair to acknowledge the role of our pharmaceutical technology in the

---

[1] Wherwein Austin, "New Moral Issue in Sex Presented", *New York Times*, May 7, 1965.

[2] Angela A. Aidala and Cathy S. Greenblat, "Changes in Moral Judgements among Student Populations: 1929–1983", *Youth and Society*, vol. 17, no. 3 (March 1986): 221–35. In previous years having an extramarital affair was perceived to be the most wrong of all behaviors contrasted; by 1983 the relative ranking drops, although the mean wrongness is rather constant.

sexual revolution of the 1960s. Changing social values merged with contraceptive advances to yield a new pattern of behavior. Liberalized sexuality of the 1960s begat the epidemic of sexually transmitted diseases of the 1970s and 1980s.[3]

Dr. Robert C. Barnes and Dr. King K. Holmes note that the increase in premarital intercourse among U.S. teens aged fifteen to sixteen "occurred with a simultaneous (and perhaps contributory) change in the pattern of contraceptive practices in the United States. Oral contraceptives and contraceptive intrauterine devices became widely available, and this has been associated with the increased sexual experience of unmarried women."[4]

Legal Abortion Has Increased the Incidence of Nonmarital Births

Prior to 1973, Planned Parenthood abortion proponents argued that abortion would strengthen the American family by reducing nonmarital births and allowing only wanted births to occur. The data initially seemed to support their case, at least on the first claim. Between 1970 and 1971 the rate of out-of-wedlock teen births dropped 10% in states with liberalized abortion laws, while it rose 0.3% in states where abortion was prohibited.[5] Selective state data further showed that nonmarital teen births "declined most in those [states] having the highest rates of legal abortion use (a reliable indicator, in general, of the availability of legal abortion).... In Arkansas and South Carolina, where legal abortion rates were the lowest of the states where abortion laws were liberalized, teenage" out-of-wedlock births (OWB) rose by 2% and 3%, respectively, between 1970 and 1971.[6] (Whether this was an actual rise in the OWB rate per one thousand females aged fifteen to nineteen or simply an increase in the raw number is unclear.)

New York and California were cited as early abortion "success" stories in reducing nonmarital teen births. The continued rise in out-of-wedlock births in New York City during the 1960s was not reversed until 1971, the first full year of New York's nonrestrictive abortion law. In that year, out-of-wedlock births for all ages dropped by 12%, with two-thirds of

[3] Robert Taylor, M.D., Ph.D., "Ectopic Pregnancy and Reproductive Technology", *Journal of the American Medical Association,* vol. 259, no. 12 (March 25, 1988): 1862–64. The authors point to more than one million annual cases of salpingitis (inflammation of the fallopian tube) in the United States. And because 50% of tubal pregnancies show evidence of chronic salpingitis, they point to the STDs as causative of ectopic pregnancy.

[4] Robert C. Barnes, M.D., and King K. Holmes, M.D., "Epidemiology of Gonorrhea: Current Perspectives", *Epidemiologic Reviews,* vol. 6 (1984): 1–30.

[5] June Sklar and Beth Berkov, "Teenage Family Formation in Postwar America", *Family Planning Perspectives,* vol. 6, no. 2 (Spring 1974): 80–90.

[6] Ibid.

the abortions for New York City residents and 90% of aborting teens being unmarried.[7]

Similar results were reported from California, where out-of-wedlock births fell 16% from 27.0 to 22.6 births per one thousand unmarried women between 1970 and 1971, the first decline since 1966. Along with this decline was an increase in the teen abortion rate from 30.8 per one thousand women aged fifteen to nineteen during the period July 1970 to June 1971 to 41.2 per one thousand in the period 1971 to 1972, or a 22.8% increase.[8]

What the pro-abortion authors of these reports failed to mention is that if *legal* abortion reduced the adolescent out-of-wedlock live birth rate, then: (1) Teens were *not* resorting to illegal abortion in the days prior to legalization to eliminate live births as Planned Parenthood abortion reformers claimed, or at least not to any great extent; or (2) for teenagers, abortion becomes a preferred method of birth control—even in the presence of legal contraception; or (3) prior to legal abortion the majority of teens were not having sexual intercourse, or not as frequently; or if they were, pregnancy did not occur when abortion was illegal, but for some reason did so after legalization—an unlikely situation.

In any case this abortion "victory" was short-lived in California, New York, and elsewhere. In 1971 the California out-of-wedlock live birth rate accounted for 12.1% of all births (black and white); the percent of such births to teens aged fifteen to seventeen was 45.2% and 23.8% for those aged eighteen to nineteen. However, by 1987 the California out-of-wedlock live birth rate accounted for 27.1% of all births (black and white); the percent of such births to teens aged fifteen to seventeen was 73.7% and 56.2% for those aged eighteen to nineteen.[9] Data for New York and other states all show an increase in nonmarital births in the presence of legal abortion. Why?

In the United States and in much of the Western world, "family planning" does not mean a course or program of action or preparation by married couples for childbearing and rearing. It means sexual intercourse without pregnancy or live childbirth. In a draft of a teen pregnancy study by Planned Parenthood's Alan Guttmacher Institute, the authors state that for some time the Scandinavian countries have served the United States as models for social change. They point to the simultaneous decline in marriage and rise in

---

[7] Jean Pakter et al., "A Review of Two Years' Experience in New York City with Liberalized Abortion Law", *The Abortion Experience: Psychological and Medical Impact*, Howard Osofsky and Joy Osofsky, eds. (Hagerstown, Md.: Harper and Row, 1974), 65–66, cited by Christopher Tietze, *Legalized Abortion and Public Health*, National Academy of Sciences, May 1975, 39.

[8] Jean Pakter and Frieda Nelson, "Factors in the Unprecedented Decline in Infant Mortality in New York City", *Bulletin of the New York Academy of Medicine*, 2nd ser. (July–August 1974): 851–52, cited by Tietze, *Legalized Abortion and Public Health*, National Academy of Sciences, May 1975.

[9] *Vital Statistics of California*, 1982, 1987, California Department of Health Services, marital/nonmarital birth tables.

informal cohabitation in Sweden, Denmark, etc., which has been accepted by the "U.S. white population and is already well established among American blacks. These, as well as other changes, perhaps imply that the United States will be following suit eventually in adopting more relaxed attitudes toward adolescent sexuality."[10]

So, the demise of the American family is to be achieved under "family planning" programs financed with tax money and sold to state and federal legislators and a Pill-swallowing public as a means for insuring family stability! Artifical birth control, whether pre- or postconception, is thus the driving force for the demise of the family structure, an institution that predates recorded history.

The adverse effects of birth control on marriage were noted by Sanger associate V. F. Calverton, who wrote in 1928 that:

> An important factor in the growth of the new morality, and the decay of modern marriage, has been the advancing perfection of modern contraceptives. A considerable part of the feminine revolt against the old morals has been fortified by this advance.
>
> ... The new morality and the spreading knowledge of contraceptives are closely associated.
>
> ... With the increasing use of contraceptives, the sex relation has rapidly changed in its emphasis. Regardless of the intention or desire of the individuals, the sex act has been insistently and inevitably associated with procreation. It was the procreative aspect, after all, that lent so much seriousness to the experience.
>
> Without question, it has been the advancing perfection of contraceptives, in their capacity to avoid, as well as control the number of children, which has provided a serious menace to the marital institution.[11]

In 1910, when Sanger was beginning her social misadventures, America was a contraceptive desert where there were 948,000 marriages and 83,000 divorces and annulments (8.75%). By 1976, with America well on the path to "reproductive freedom", there were 2,178,000 marriages (figures include remarriages) and 1,092,000 divorces (50.1%). For 1987 there were 2,477,000 marriages and 1,169,000 divorces (47.2%). This slight drop from 1976 in the percent of divorces versus marriages was more than matched by an increase in the number of couples "living together". That increased by a factor of 4.25 times, from 523,000 in 1970 to 2,220,000 in 1986. But the population aged eighteen and over increased

---

[10] Charles Westoff and Elsie F. Jones, et al. *Teenage Pregnancy in Industrialized Countries* (New Haven, Conn.: Yale University Press, 1986), 20.

[11] V. F. Calverton, *The Bankruptcy of Marriage* (New York: Macauley Company, 1928), 119–120, 123.

by a factor of only 1.3, increasing from 135,290,000 in 1970 to 178,325,000.[12]

We do not contend that birth control can account for all of the continuous increase in the divorce and cohabitation rate since 1910. But recall that Margaret Sanger claimed birth control would usher in an era of marital stability and a higher morality. Instead, the phenomenon of divorce has regularly occurred in other countries in proportion to the extent that birth control has gained acceptance.

This should bother us. The family is not an accidental contrivance discovered by the twentieth century and made an option for human existence. And until recently it was meeting the problem of childrearing and controlling adolescent sexuality quite well, despite the Planned Parenthood claims.

Kingsley Davis, in discussing the lower nonmarital adolescent pregnancy rates in the United States prior to 1960, the year the Pill became available, has noted that:

> The key to the old system seems to have been that teenagers were held responsible for any children they engendered. They were held accountable by parents and relatives, by neighbors and acquaintances, and by official representatives of the community. . . .
> Informal controls of teenage children . . . included ignorance . . . , fear (not only of pregnancy but also of venereal disease), and local surveillance (reducing opportunities). These controls got many girls and boys through the younger years without intercourse. . . .
> [The old system was lost because] nonfamilial agencies or third parties have tended to intrude themselves between parents and children, taking over all or part of what traditionally were parental functions and hence assuming parental authority. . . . They are usually arms of the Government. . . .
> Public health agencies and the medical profession also take over authority with respect to the child. Teenagers are not only given birth control devices and abortions without parental consent, but are also given "sex education" . . . conveying an implied approval of sexual relations among teenagers as long as a "method" is used.
> . . . the problem of teenage pregnancy will not be solved by further promotion of contraception and abortion for children.[13]

Birth Control and the Abolition of Parenthood

Several years ago two advocates of modern birth control wrote that British writer and population control enthusiast, Aldous Huxley, in his book, *Brave New World*,

---

[12] *Statistical Abstract of the United States, 1981; Historical Statistics of the U.S. from Colonial Times to 1976*, U.S. Dept of Commerce, citing marriage and cohabitation tables.

[13] Kingsley Davis, "A Theory of Teenage Pregnancy in the United States", in Catherine Chilman, *Adolescent Pregnancy and Childbearing: Findings from Research*, U.S. Dept. of Health and Human Services, NIH pub no. 81–2077, December 1980, 328–30, 332.

envisioned the abolition of parenthood and the family, which would take place with the full cooperation of society as it attempted to improve on natural reproduction. We are on our way to Huxley's vision, and 1984 saw ... the first surrogate embryo transfer ... [and] the first birth from a frozen embryo.... The year saw major reports by government-appointed panels on noncoital reproduction in the United Kingdom (the Warnock Report) and Australia (the Waller Report) and Congressional hearings on the subject in the United States.

Techniques for noncoital reproduction close a circle opened with the introduction of effective contraception that made sex without reproduction dependable. Society seems as supportive of the new techniques for reproduction without sex as it was of contraception.... [14]

That sterilization and abortion are needed to "back-up" so-called effective contraception mitigates but does not eliminate the utopian nature of such claims.

Thus the goal of having sexual intercourse free of the bothersome problem of babies has been followed by the development of techniques for having babies without sexual intercourse. Hence, we see the present-day phenomena of "alternative reproductive technologies" competing with conventional sexual intercourse in the generation of new humans in which the marriage or even the face-to-face meeting of the "seed donors"—parents may be inapt here—is unnecessary.

The patterns of thought, behavior, and values that have been derived from the widespread introduction of birth control, while certainly part of the present set of social "norms", were not always so. It has been only within this century and frankly, originating with Planned Parenthood's success within the United States, that the consensus in the culturally Christian Western world concerning the licitness of birth control was broken. Martin Luther, John Calvin, John Knox, and other of the Reformers all agreed with the popes, that human reproduction could not be separated from human sexuality without grave, objective moral fault, and with terrible social consequences, some of which could only be dimly, if at all, envisioned.

This consensus had previously found social expression in 1873, by an overwhelmingly Protestant United States Congress, which passed the Comstock Act and outlawed contraception, abortion, and pornography because of the social connection between them and consequent sexual immorality and family breakdown. Congress later reenacted the "Comstock law" on at least ten different occasions, with the final vestiges of that statute—barring unsolicited

---

[14] Sherman Eliar and George Annas, "Social Policy Considerations in Noncoital Reproduction", *Journal of the American Medical Association*, vol. 255, no. 1 (January 1986), 62–67.

mailing of contraceptive advertisements to minors—struck down by the Supreme Court in *Youngs v. Bolger* (1985).

That social understanding has been lost with the passage of time and the advent of technological innovations affecting conception and abortion. Yet, even secular social commentators were able to pinpoint birth control as a revolutionary social innovation. In 1929 liberal journalist Walter Lippmann opined that the Christian churches were correct in "recognizing that whether or not birth control is eugenic, hygenic, and economic, it is the most revolutionary practice in the history of sexual morals".[15] Another contemporary social philosopher, Will Durant, who knew Margaret Sanger, agreed. (Durant, like Sanger, abandoned the Catholic Faith, but unlike Sanger, he later returned to the Church.) Durant said that

> the invention and spread of contraceptives is the proximate cause of our changing morals. . . . The dissociation of sex from reproduction has created a situation unforseen by our fathers. All the relations of men and women are being changed by this one factor; and the moral code of the future will have to take account of these new facilities.[16]

But unlike the song from the prior generation, which noted that "love and marriage go together like a horse and carriage", the current separation of sex from reproduction has become so widespread that *Washington Post* columnist Judy Mann could write that "half of today's sexually active teens still don't know that sexual intercourse is a leading cause of pregnancy".[17] Unfortunately for the curious, Ms. Mann failed to mention "other leading causes of pregnancy". Earlier in this century Sigmund Freud wrote:

> . . . it is a characteristic of all the perversions that in them reproduction as an aim is put aside. This is actually the criterion by which we judge whether a sexual activity is perverse—if it departs from reproduction in its aims and pursues the attainment of grat fication independently.[18]

Contrast Freud with Dr. Mary Calderone's view of what sex is really for: "Communication, ego formation, self-realization, play, pleasure, celebration of life, ultimate intimacy, cooperative energy release, sensing principles and values, and balancing love against hate".[19] Why are children or marriage or even heterosexuality omitted from Calderone's list?

[15] Walter Lippmann, *A Preface to Morals* (New York: Macmillan, 1929), 291.

[16] Will Durant, *The Mansions of Philosophy* (New York: Simon and Schuster, 1929), 119.

[17] Judy Mann, "Family Planning Is Alive in the Reagan Budget", *Washington Post,* March 20, 1981, pages B-1–2.

[18] Sigmund Freud, *General Introduction to Psycho-Analysis,* Great Books of the Western World, vol. 54 (Chicago: Encyclopedia Britannica, 1952), 776.

[19] Darrell J. Bogue, ed., *Adolescent Fertility: The Proceedings of an International Conference,* copyright 1977 by Community and Family Study Center, see discussion, 100.

If children have nothing to do with human sexuality, her list looks odd beside the massive world-wide efforts to have a "perfect contracepting society" in which all men, women, and adolescents inject, swallow, absorb, inhale, or affix antifertility drugs and devices, and then later resort to sterilization (mutilation) or abortion (child homicide) when these fail.

The chief catchphrase by which we were lured into this morass was the slogan "Every child a wanted child", or "Children by choice, not chance". In either case sexual intercourse is "freed", except in cases of "contraceptive failure", i.e., a baby, from the previously "blind" and inevitable biological consequences.

Only the children, if any, of couples practicing birth control can be "voluntary" and "planned". Married couples who "slip up" or who do not use birth control have accidental pregnancies and unplanned families. Such persons are subject to nature, fate, or forces beyond themselves and are dependent, not autonomous. Controlling pregnancy thus becomes an exercise of the will to power, not a surrender of love or an entrance into the mystery surrounding the creation of persons.

Notice that when Planned Parenthood uses the "wanted baby" phrase, that such babies have rights. Unwanted babies have no rights and are morally equivalent to disposable property. But under the wanted baby scheme, where do rights come from? From being wanted, of course. But who is it that does the "wanting" that results in the conferring of rights? Not the father, nor a couple seeking to adopt. No, it is the pregnant woman alone who gets to confer rights. Planned Parenthood could never use the phrase, "Every child a valuable child", because that would implicitly recognize the intrinsic worth of the child irrespective of whether father, mother, etc., "wanted" the baby. And the next logical question would be: "Who put the value there and why is the child valuable?" That question was answered in Genesis 1:26: "Let us make man in our image, after our likeness."

Needless to say this does not sit well with persons who view themselves after the manner of the Deity, claiming that they are their own ultimate arbiters of right and wrong. Man, in other words, is made in man's image. Man does not merely measure, man is the measure. By claiming an inherent inequality among the human species, the "problem" of too many inferior men, i.e., overpopulation, can be "cured" by contraception, sterilization, abortion, and euthanasia. But since the Author of Genesis is correct, how can there be too many creatures made after the likeness of absolute goodness, or God?

Quite obviously, Planned Parenthood ideologues are not satisfied with the current arrangement of things in the universe. In 1955, Planned Parenthood national director, Dr. William Vogt, stated that the major article of his faith was "belief in the potentialities of man himself . . . he is going to survive a long time . . . if he will only take advantage of the powers he has evolved . . . I believe that . . . human nature can be changed. . . . Indeed, I believe we must change human nature—and at a far more rapid rate than we have in the past."[20]

English writer C. S. Lewis, with remarkable foresight, pointed out in *The Abolition of Man* that "in reality, if one age really attains, by eugenics and scientific education, the power to make its descendants what it pleases, all men who live after it are the patients of that power". Lewis also noted in a comment that applies to the technology of birth control, that all of the control over nature "generally turns out to be a power exercised by some men over other men with nature as its instrument".

Artificial birth control is such an instrument. For on the physical level it attempts to remove the child as the natural result of sexual intercourse and at the same time creates a dependency on the provider of birth control. And on the moral level artificial birth control implies that right and wrong depend upon consequences of actions, rather than the inherent agreement with or divergence from the good established for man by God.

A logical, if possibly lascivious example of this type of thinking, was articulated by long-time Planned Parenthood supporter, Episcopal theologian Joseph Fletcher, at the PPFA 1981 annual meeting held in Washington, D.C. Fletcher noted:

> I want to say carefully and without elaboration, sex is morally acceptable in any form; hetero, homo, auto, bi or poly . . . . that what makes any sexual act right or wrong is its consequences, because in and of itself sex is neither good nor bad, neither praiseworthy nor blameworthy, and its ethical significance depends upon the values it serves and seeks to realize.[21]

Note also how Fletcher's assumptions differ from the creation account in Genesis, where the various aspects of the creation were called "good" by God and not simply in virtue of their "consequences". And in fact, the only thing called "not good" was the man's being alone or lack of a suitable partner (Gen 2:17). And perhaps, if God had not been intolerant but had listened to Fletcher, he could have broadened his appreciation of pluralism by asking Adam and Eve what values they served and sought to realize by following the serpent's advice.

We know what happened; God imposed his values on them and the entire

---

[20] *Planned Parenthood News,* no. 11, Spring 1955, 4.

[21] "Serving Families, Preserving Freedom", Annual Meeting, 1981 Special Issue, Theology Workshop, *Planned Parenthood Review,* vol. 1, no. 4 (Winter 1981): 10.

natural order. For, although it is correct that at present all Nature groans under sin, all of the created order is still under the dominion of God. Yet, the Book of Nature is not always viewed in a normative sense even by many Christians, and is looked on as in need of "editing" by secular humanists.

Writing in 1940, Protestant theologian Dietrich Bonhoeffer has offered an insightful analysis about the consequences of the virtual abandonment of the natural order by Protestant theology:

> The significance of the natural for the gospel was obscured, and the Protestant Church was no longer able to return a clear word of direction in answer to the burning questions of natural life. She thus left countless human beings unanswered and unassisted. . . . The consequences of this decision were grave and far reaching. If there were no longer any relative distinctions to be made within the fallen creation, then the way was opened to every kind of arbitrariness and disorder, and natural life, with its concrete decisions and orders was no longer subject to responsibility to God. The sole antithesis to the natural was the word of God; the natural was no longer contrasted with the unnatural. For in the presence of the word of God both the natural and the unnatural were equally damned. And this meant complete disruption in the domain of natural life.[22]

With natural law or common-sense ethics abandoned, statistics replaced old norms with new ones. Dr. Herbert Ratner, a prominent and accurate Pill critic has written:

> Biologist Alfred Kinsey of the 1948 *Kinsey Report,* and a pioneer of modern sex surveys, and avant garde [Catholic educated] theologian Anthony Kosnik of the 1977 report, *Human Sexuality,* erred when they sought ethical norms of sexual behavior from what the majority of people did. For all they knew, they may have been measuring the sexual activities of a sick society. Germany, under National Socialism, exterminated Jews and other alleged inferior people, as well as "useless eaters", but this did not make extermination an ethical norm that corresponded to the nature of man as an individual or as a social animal.[23]

But the abandonment of nature as a minimal behavioral norm and guide also affects Catholic theologians as well. The Rev. Charles Curran, a prominent dissenter from orthodox Catholic teaching on birth control, claims, "In a pre-technological civilization, man found happiness by conforming himself to the rhythms of nature. But through science and technology contemporary man must interfere with the laws of nature to make human

---

[22] Dietrich Bonhoeffer, *Ethics* (New York: Macmillan, 1955), 143–44.
[23] Herbert Ratner, M.D., "Nature, Mother and Teacher: Her Norms", *Listening, a Journal of Religion and Culture,* vol. 18, no. 3 (Fall 1983): 195–96.

life more human."[24] Two years later in 1968, Fr. Curran gained national prominence by openly leading the dissent from Pope Paul VI's encyclical, *Humane Vitae*.[25]

This conformity of nature to man, most often attempted by public health and so-called medical practitioners in the vast efforts to isolate hedonism from Nature's revenge, is purely chimerical.

A mere thirty years ago, there were five clinically apparent venereal diseases. At present there are more than fifty disease entities caused by at least twenty microorganisms or viruses that are transmitted to sexual associates during intercourse and to babies during pregnancy or childbirth. Ectopic pregnancy, which can be life-threatening, has increased in America and the Western world. Sterility has increased among young women over the past twenty years. Cervical cancer is increasing among younger and younger sexually liberated women. And Acquired Immune Deficiency Syndrome, a lethal disease for which there is no magic bullet, has spread rapidly among homosexuals in America, and has made itself present among sexually indulgent heterosexuals and drug users, as well as children, blood transfusion recipients, and other bystanders who are innocent victims of the sexual revolt.

These few considerations point to the conclusion that not only is it not nice to fool Mother Nature, it is not possible. Any "victories" are merely apparent ones.

There are three reasons for this. First, God the Father is the Author of Nature (Heb 3:4). Second, the purpose which he placed in things cannot be destroyed: "Consider the work of God: who can make straight that which he hath made crooked?" (Eccl 7:13). Third, God constituted Nature to respond to man's actions in a proportional manner: "I call heaven and earth to record this day against you, that I have set before you life and death, blessing and cursing: therefore choose life that thou and thy seed may live" (Dt 30:19).

It is the moral norms that inhere in nature that many critics of the 1987 Vatican paper condemning artificial technological reproduction miss completely. For example, take Pulitzer prize winner Charles Krauthammer's article "The Ethics of Human Manufacture". He suggested that "nuance" will avoid both the Frankenstein consequences of modern reproductive technology and the sexual straitjacket Vatican celibates are preparing for us.[26]

Now here Krauthammer not only misses the main points, he manufactures some of his own that he proceeds to manipulate for the unwary. He states

[24] Charles Curran, ed., *Contraception: Authority and Dissent* (New York: Herder and Herder, 1969), 163.

[25] George Kelly, ed., *Human Sexuality in Our Times* (Boston: Daughters of St. Paul, 1979), 62–63.

[26] Charles Krauthammer, "The Ethics of Human Manufacture", *The New Republic*, May 4, 1987.

that allowing experimentation on a pre-fourteen-day-old in vitro human (IVH) allows clinicians to implant only the "best" IVHs into women, and that without the fourteen-day line, discarding the "spares" would be murder (he is correct about murdering the spares.) Krauthammer further states that this balancing of the social good of achieving fertility for a couple offsets the rights of, say, a "16-cell organism". Yet at seven to eight days after fertilization, the embryonic human has several hundred cells; and at eighteen days the fetal heart begins to beat. The rate of fetal growth "is enormous at first . . . in the first month after fertilization, the human zygote increases a million times in weight".[27,28] But of course, this injection of size as a criteria of who has rights obscures the real point, namely, that the lines drawn by the Deity as recognized by Catholic moral teaching challenge Krauthammer's right to draw his own "bright lines" of moral demarcation.

He rightly decries involuntary sterility and the real pain childless couples experience, but then he fails to note that a great number of couples are now involuntarily sterile because they resorted to allegedly reversible birth control or induced abortion—both condemned by "compassionless" Catholic teaching. Lastly, he states that "artificial sex [birth control] is a challenge to a personal relationship". Here he is correct, with a record number of venereal diseases (including at least three lethal ones), a 50% divorce rate, one out of three pregnancies aborted, and out-of-wedlock pregnancy rates higher than at any time in U.S. history.

Indeed, the Church is saying "No!" to man, because man is saying "No!" to God. Or, let's take a Catholic critic of the Vatican instruction, the *Washington Post*'s own Colman McCarthy, who claims that Pope John Paul II and Cardinal Ratzinger lack compassion because they have the courage to say "no" to technological degradations of human procreation.[29]

Now, compassion means "suffering together with another", not acquiescing to or applauding efforts to "go beyond the limits of a reasonable dominion over nature". Compassion, moreover, is possible only when predicated on a desire, respect, appreciation, and insistence on truth. When Christ was told by the Samaritan woman at the well that she had no husband, he replied that as she had had five previous "husbands" and her current male companion was not her husband, she had spoken the truth and was to be congratulated. And although she could have stood on her personal anguish in trying to find happiness, children, and fulfillment, her response was, "I see you are a prophet", and not, "Where is your compassion for my exceptional situation?"

[27] Dr. and Mrs. John C. Willke, *Abortion: Questions and Answers* (Cincinnati, Ohio: Hayes Publishing, 1985), 35, 44.

[28] Ernest W. Page et. al., *Human Reproduction* (Philadelphia, Pa.: W. B. Saunders, 1976), 194.

[29] Colman McCarthy, *Washington Post*, March 14, 1987.

But apparently McCarthy thinks that, when the Lord said "What God has joined together, let not man break asunder", God was not addressing journalists or infertile couples. The Vatican was so heartless as to suggest "adoption, various forms of educational work, and assistance to other families and to poor or handicapped children"—events which happened far more often among infertile couples when abortion was illegal and which socially conscious journalists then regularly applauded.

Curiously in McCarthy's column, no mention is made of the numerous couples that we referred to earlier, who are now sterile because they resorted to allegedly reversible birth control or abortion. Even the U.S. Centers for Disease Control has admitted sterility can be a Pill or IUD "complication".

Current estimates of the number of involuntarily sterile are one in every five to seven couples, or 15 to 20%. While not all such infertility is a result of a venereal disease, and not all venereal diseases cause permanent infertility, "the trends over the last twenty years show a definite correlation between the two". Lethal effects of sexual liberation also are felt by children, as five thousand newborns die each year from venereally transmitted group B streptococcus infection.[30]

Yet, the secular response to these technological violations of the moral law are further technological deviations to achieve the "wanted" baby after so many millions of allegedly "unwanted" ones have been discarded or destroyed. This has led to social arrangements like the salaried biological nine-month host or "surrogate mother", who carries but does not conceive the petri-dish-derived child obtained from male gametes masturbated and female gametes aspirated from the bodies of remunerated "donors" who never met. The surrogate mother then has a duty to relinquish the child, all pursuant to a contract, perhaps initiated because the contracting absentee "mother" wanted to maintain her figure and social contacts uninterrupted by the inconvenience of a pregnancy. We also have in vitro "hatcheries" charging $3,500 and more for their petri-dish experiments and claiming they are more successful than nature, some of who "overlook" the fact that as the check-writing couples still maintain conjugal relations the baby may have resulted from natural conception. Yet the Vatican is irrational and cloaked in prejudice and error!

Lastly, McCarthy claims that only Catholic politicians are asked to act as the "pope's lobbyists shoving legislatures around" to enact "church laws" on a pluralistic society. But the law is at once both something less and something more than legislation. The endowments of inalienable rights which belong to all human beings are surely as essential in the tent of the womb as they are at the lunch counter or the voting booth. McCarthy did not use such rhetoric about "papal lobbyists" when the issue was civil rights.

---

[30] Carolyn Keating, R.N.C, "The Impact of Sexually Transmitted Diseases on Human Fertility", *Health Care for Women International*, vol. 8 (1987): 33–41.

In its reasoned conclusions the Vatican Congregation did not rely only on principles of Faith as found in Scripture, which do apply to Catholic politicians even if some of them such as New York's governor Mario Cuomo think otherwise. Also noted was a correct and authoritative reading of the Book of Nature, which is applicable to all human persons and which should be defended by the public authorities of any or no faith as necessary for the individual and the common good.

As a nation we were once respected and admired for our ideals; now, after the birth control–fueled sexual revolt, we are merely envied for our machines. Currently we are in the position of poet Francis Thompson's incontinent lover who sought to derive the infinite from the creaturely, bending nature as if it were a plastic object to be molded by anyone brave enough to try. However, in the "Hound of Heaven", the idolator discovers that:

> I tempted all his servitors, but to find
> My own betrayal in their constancy,
> In faith to Him their fickleness to me,
> Their traitorous trueness, and their loyal deceit.
> To all swift things for swiftness did I sue . . .
> Fear wist not to evade as Love wist to pursue.
> Still, with unhurrying chase,
> And unperturbed pace,
> Deliberate speed, majestic instancy,
> Came on the following Feet,
> And a voice above their beat—
> "Naught shelters thee, who wilt not shelter Me."

Lastly, we realize that we are in a culture that operates under no or very few Christian presuppositions. Indeed, finding religious or biblical motivation behind legislation makes it constitutionally suspect, but only for some denominations and then mainly on issues that touch sexuality. Nevertheless, as pagan practices make further inroads, and as technological changes increase the reach of certain social principles, there will be additional questions to answer as the conception, bearing, rearing, nurturing, and educating of children become even further divorced. For example: (1) Although the term "surrogate mother" is applied to the woman carrying the child resulting from a petri-dish conception for which she may have supplied her own ovum, she is not a surrogate because she is not the "substitute" mother. In fact she becomes a temporary concubine. How is this not exploitative of women? (2) What is there to stop a single woman, say a lesbian, from seeking the "services" of an in vitro "hatchery" to conceive a child according to the eugenic specifications she stipulates? How is this good for children? (3) Should certain women be prohibited from attempting this, e.g., short women, lesbians? And if so what criteria are to be used? (4) How are married couples protected from deception and paying for a child "production" service they never actually received as in the case where they undergo petri-dish fertilization but with subsequent implantation of a child they naturally conceived?

The above are only a few of the many questions that can be asked because of recent technological innovations affecting human generation. Christian self-denial will seem like a spring picnic compared to the social nightmare that further tampering with the natural order will inevitably produce.

Planned Parenthood: The New Creators

A comparison of policy tenets of Planned Parenthood, of what it holds to be "good", shows its radical differences with traditional Christianity: Scripture considers children as a blessing and a reward (Prov 17:6; Dt 7:14; Is 48:19), but Planned Parenthood sees certain children as a social disease or an epidemic. Barrenness is considered an affliction in Scripture (Gen 48:5–6; Jg 13:2), but Planned Parenthood seeks to induce it. Adoption is promoted by the New Testament (Jesus and Joseph) and the Old Testament (Moses and Pharaoh's daughter), but Planned Parenthood opposes even a twenty-four-hour abortion waiting period during which a woman could be counseled about adoption. St. Paul condemns disobedience to parents and fornication, and Jesus says "lead us not into temptation", but Planned Parenthood facilitates and promotes all three with its policy of giving birth control to teens without mandatory parental notice. Christ says that only the sick need a doctor (Mt 9:12), but Planned Parenthood justifies the continued use of powerful antifertility drugs by millions of healthy women. While Scripture condemns homosexual acts (Gen 19:5–7; Lev 20:13; Rom 1:27), Planned Parenthood's sex-education policies proclaim heterosexuality and homosexuality as matters of "personal choice". And though St. Paul says that women will be saved by childbearing (1 Tim 2:15), Planned Parenthood claims that "contraception is liberation". And when Scripture counsels that "to every thing there is a season . . . a time to embrace, and a time to refrain from embracing" (Eccl 3:1, 5), Planned Parenthood claims that even temporary abstinence is either psychologically harmful of virtually impossible for most humans.

Scripture also notes that there is nothing new under the sun. So while the technology of the antifertility cultists may be innovative, the philosophy behind it is not. In fact the primary moral roots of Planned Parenthood go back to the Old and New Testaments, which condemned the practices and policies of Gnosticism.

> The ethical system of Gnosticism, like its speculative construction was grounded in the dualistic hypothesis. By this hypothesis the idea of morality,

in the ordinary sense, was excluded. All material conditions were regarded as necessarily evil. . . . Spiritual natures are called on to assert their independence of the material world by indulging in its pleasures without restraint.[31]

When Genesis is read, it becomes immediately apparent that the first effect of sin was the difficulty Adam and Eve had in controlling the sexual aspect of their bodies. So quite logically, the Gnostics return to the starting point of the effects of sin, human sexuality in its male- and femaleness, to in fact lay the ground work for the rebellion against the created order. And "success" consists of directing the exercise of human sexuality at any goal other than children and what that necessitates in the social order. And this ability to produce effects against the order of nature becomes a kind of measure of success against the one who orders nature. The Gnostics have challenged the Creator and Maker of the created order in their attempt to "be like gods".

And in order for Gnostics to achieve their goal, their antifertility policies must necessarily be cast over a wide area and operate both in the bedroom and out, and these policies must also operate directly and indirectly to achieve their desired result. In pursuit of this goal Planned Parenthood's Frederick Jaffe, in 1969, suggested various strategies for implementing a population policy for the United States:

1. payments for contraception, sterilization, abortion; distribute certain contraceptives nonmedically; abortion and sterilization on demand with birth control as a core element of health care
2. chronic economic depression; child tax; tax married more than single; extra tax on parents with more than two children in school; reduce or eliminate paid maternity leave and benefits
3. stock-type certificates for having children; compulsory sterilization of all who have more than two children, except for a few allowed three; discouragement of private home ownership
4. restructure family; encourage increased homosexuality; fertility-control agents in the water supply[32]

Frederick Jaffe complained when his memo was cited to a Senate subcommittee that neither he nor the PPFA advocated "any of the specific proposals . . . which go beyond voluntary actions by individual couples to space and limit births".[33] But Jaffe's denial for himself and the PPFA cannot be taken seriously. Consent for an abortion does not come from the "individual couple",

---

[31] William Crooke, "Gnosticism", vol. 6, *Encyclopedia of Religion and Ethics,* ed. James Hastings (New York: Charles Scribner and Sons, 1913), 236.

[32] "Family Planning Services and Population Amendments of 1973", *Hearings before the Senate Labor and Public Welfare Subcommittee on Human Resources,* 93d Cong., 1st sess., on S. 1708, S. 1632, May–June 1973, 501.

[33] Ibid., 492.

it is exercised by the individual woman even against the wishes of her husband, boyfriend, or parents. The same holds for sterilization or contraceptives. Moreover, with the notable exception of antifertility agents in the water supply, which still has numerous technical problems, most of the policies Jaffe listed were suggested at one time or another by Margaret Sanger or other Planned Parenthood spokesmen.

The following point clearly shows that Dr. Guttmacher did not completely reject forced population control:

> Predicting 20 critical years ahead in the struggle to control the population explosion, Dr. Alan Guttmacher, president of Planned Parenthood–World Population, continues to urge the use of all voluntary means to hold down on the world birthrate. But he foresees the possibility that eventual coercion may become necessary, particularly in areas where the pressure is greatest, possibly India and China. "Each country," he says, "will have to decide its own form of coercion, and determine when and how it should be employed. At present, the means are compulsory sterilization and compulsory abortion. Perhaps some day a way of enforcing compulsory birth control will be feasible."[34]

With the growth of the antifertility mentality and its acceptance in the United States, it has now become a debatable question in the U.S. Congress, and not a taboo one, whether or not U.S. taxpayer funds should go to assist the Red Chinese/Planned Parenthood compulsory population control program. This tolerance for a manifest evil, even by libertarian standards, is precisely what Pope Paul VI, in *Humanae Vitae* (1968), predicted would happen in the governmental sphere if couples on a large scale chose antifertility measures for themselves in their private sphere. Forced birth control is quite compatible with Planned Parenthood's program.

Consider that the IPPF has declined to expel the Red Chinese Planned Parenthood affiliate that works "to assist the government programme by motivating people to accept family planning, particularly at the grassroots level".[35] And the same IPPF Report states that "while the one-child family policy has been widely publicized, it is not generally believed that the vast majority of couples will follow the guideline".[36] The "volunteers" of the China Family Planning Association "are familiar with the national programme and, being government functionaries, have access to the highest levels".[37]

Planned Parenthood, which sings the song of voluntarism to Americans,

[34] "Compulsory Population Control Foreseen", "Outlook", *Medical World News,* June 6, 1969, 11.
[35] International Planned Parenthood Federation, *Financial Statements and Reports on Programmes of Grant-Receiving Associations,* vol. 2, October 1984, 924.
[36] Ibid.
[37] Ibid., 925.

dances to the tune of compulsion in China. The final goal of this program both in Red China and the United States has not been seen yet. But earlier in this century, Professor Harold J. Laski hinted at some of the ultimate goals his ideological kindred had in mind. Laski wrote to Justice Holmes, after the Supreme Court decision upholding Virginia's law sterilizing Carrie Buck against her will, advocating "steriliz[ing] all the unfit, among whom I include all fundamentalists".[38]

Those so at war with the order of creation eventually come to propound contradictions without the slightest awareness of doing so. Luke Lee, in a publication funded by the International Planned Parenthood Federation (IPPF), the United Nations Fund for Population Activities (UNFPA), and the U.S. State Department would write:

> But if a state can justify restrictions on the number of spouses on human rights grounds, it can similarly justify restrictions of the number of children each couple can have ... [and] can it not be argued that "in allowing children that are born to live a higher quality of life," compulsory sterilization may be considered as "reaffirming an individual's right to procreate"?[39]

Mandatory sterilization means freedom to reproduce. Up is down, good is evil, hatred is love. Big Brother, in George Orwell's totalitarian novel, *1984,* longed for this state of social affairs. We now have it. What is to be done?

Epilogue

What then can be done by those whose faith or good will takes offense at this sensually fueled death machine that has taken on worldwide proportions? First, our own "house" must be in order. And this starts with our lives and those of our families. We must ensure the strength of our own families so that we will have a suitable foundation from which we can at the same time reconstruct a sound social policy and dismantle the institutional edifices erected by the latter-day Gnostics and secular messiahs from Planned Parenthood.

Second, there is no inevitable reason in any historical sense why Planned Parenthood's social program should continue to hold sway or even extend its tentacles further into the social fabric. The human condition involves sin and suffering, but it also includes the will to resist. There is hope, then, in the response that good men and women take when confronted with the full

---

[38] *Holmes-Laski Letters: The Correspondence of Mr. Justice Holmes and Harold J. Laski, 1916–35,* ed. Mark DeWolfe Howe, with a Foreword by Justice Felix Frankfurter (Cambridge, Mass.: Harvard University Press, 1953). See especially 938–41.

[39] Luke T. Lee, "Compulsory Sterilization and Human Rights", *Tufts Law and Population,* Monograph ser., no. 43 (1977): 5–6.

implications of Planned Parenthood's program. And this especially includes those who have been lured to its message for a time.

As long as men and women of faith or good will act in a principled and prudent manner against the "glamour of evil" proposed to us by its program, Planned Parenthood cannot succeed. Other tyrannies have fallen; there is nothing about this erotic kingdom that makes it immune to failure, and there is much that makes it certain to fall.

In fact its philosophy openly embraces failure. For though Planned Parenthood's message promises a virtually unbridled freedom for sensate indulgence, its meaning is profoundly pessimistic.

If the world needs more food, Planned Parenthood proposes to kill more children or sterilize more couples. To cope with sexual desires, eliminate the consequences (children), because curbing sexual desire is impossible. More venereal diseases, rely upon antibiotics because chastity does not work. Fidelity is bothersome, take the Pill, get sterilized. If killing a child is morally bothersome, simply redefine the baby out of existence. The family is breaking down in the wake of the contraceptive-clad sexual revolt, appropriate more money for government day care. Faced with growing poverty, abort (kill), contracept, or sterilize the poor. Johnny and Jane cannot read, never mind, give them condoms and the Pill before they propagate any more of their like.

Talk show hosts, newspaper editorialists and reporters, and public officials must be challenged in their slavish reliance on Planned Parenthood's "facts". A series in the *Los Angeles Times* (July 1990) by James Shea underscored the problem of media bias on abortion and noted how the press unquestioningly relies on such resources as the Alan Guttmacher Institute while never mentioning its history as a Planned Parenthood subsidiary. If the editorially pro-abortion *Times* can recognize this syndrome, so can every other media outlet in America. This book provides the basis for a historical critique of Planned Parenthood's failure. You can supply the rest if you are willing to challenge the status quo.

French philosopher Etienne Gilson once said that "philosophy always buries its undertakers". Applying this adage to the present situation, we might say that the Planned Parenthood movement in all its social manifestations is its own best funeral director. It believes in death, it inflicts death; let this movement have what it has given others.

A simple program for action must begin with personal prayer and sacrifice, asking the Lord for wisdom and the resources to conduct these efforts. Second, we must approach this problem from the standpoint of the long haul. In the absence of direct providential intervention, there will be no quick fix to the social evils precipitated over three quarters of a century by the acceptance of the philosophy of Margaret Sanger and her followers. Third, working within your parish, church, and congregation is the initial place to begin your pro-life apostolate. Fourth, there are many functions and ministries needed to restore the right to life and the spiritual consensus that underlie its prior acceptance, and this requires some concentration or specialization of effort. We must know and initially accept people where they are before we can get them to go in another direction.

The point here is never to try to direct a volunteer who feels called only to picket abortion clinics, form life chains, etc., into activities they are not ready for or believe themselves ill-equipped to do. Some people will only write letters, and they may believe that their efforts will succeed in changing a legislator's views or voting pattern. They will never believe that the legislator must be replaced until they themselves diligently try and eventually fail in their efforts to change the lawmaker's views. At that point you will have a self-motivated believer who will work a precinct for your pro-life candidate and not simply write letters to a lawmaker who was merely pretending to have an open mind on life issues. However, volunteers will have to reach that point by themselves. So do not initially get frustrated or angry; give your letter-writers a host of things to write about, information or legislative alerts with which they may try to convince a congressman to vote pro-life. Encourage their efforts. As long as they do not lose heart, you can bring them to an awareness that additional work needs to be done.

Next, join a church group for pro-life, pro-family action. The reason this must be done is that Jesus directed his apostles to be aware of the leaven of the pharisees. This is simply to recall that the direction any society takes is derived from its moral reference points, and organized religion is the most important reference point any society has. So seek to activate your entire congregation by giving information to representatives of all parish clubs, fraternities, associations, etc. You also need to be constantly informed about current developments. Thus you need to receive information from pro-life, pro-family groups outside of your parish that monitor legislation and other policy developments in the private sphere and that can alert you to the need for letter-writing or other activities. Furthermore, it is smart to reinforce a friendly legislator, school board member, etc., who has to bear the brunt of criticism by sending a supportive letter now and again.

With the information documented in this book and that available elsewhere, you can call talk shows, write letters to the editor, and publicly confront proponents of the Sanger agenda. Even if you do not get on the show, even if your letter is not printed in the paper, even if your recommendation to a county school board is rejected, you cannot maintain silence or acquiesce placidly in the hedonist juggernaut of nihilism we now face.

The primary wedges you must use will be the very claims of our opponents. If abortion and birth control are so healthy for women, then why should not doctors be sued if a woman develops any of the complications or sequelae her physician informs her will not happen? Opposition to such informed-consent legislation by pro-abortion and birth control groups will help you cast doubt on these very claims. State public health reporting laws that require physicians, clinics, and hospitals to report abortion complications not just at the time of the procedure, but a week, a month, or a year later would put into true perspective the real health risks to women from induced abortion. The same should happen with artificial birth control.

And your state legislators need to be reminded that the social landscape of high rates of adolescent, nonmarital pregnancy and venereal disease did not exist prior to the change in laws that first allowed minors to get birth control and then paid for it with tax money. You should pick starting points of five and ten years before the base year in which access to birth control was liberalized for teens, tax-paid birth control was made available to teens, and the year in which abortion became available to teens (1973 or before in some states).

Moreover, as you now know how the Sangerites achieved their successes, you also know how to dismantle their ideological and organizational empire that reaches into all segments of American and Western society. And there can be no timidity about resurrecting the birth control debate once again. Anybody who resists striking at the root of Sanger's success is assured of only one thing: defeat. But even here prudence is counseled as you most likely will be dealing with persons who have invested quite a bit of their emotional lives in the practice and ethos of birth control. And if they are "pillars" of your church, you can expect some social ostracism and pressure on your pastor as well. So do not be taken by surprise.

There remains the final question of how we should attempt to implement principled proposals in a pragmatic society. To take the most pressing life problem, in short, what legislative measures may prudently be used to stop or reduce the planned, legally sanctioned killing of 1.6 million children in America by abortion every year? How far do we craft pro-life laws to meet public opinion? How far do we challenge public opinion? This question is of paramount importance in the aftermath of the Supreme Court's July 1989 *Webster* decision upholding a Missouri antifunding law and basically inviting further state legislation.

Some are asking whether in legislative proposals it is not better to save some children from abortion—since we cannot save all—rather than none. This partial-measures approach is not new.

But in considering partial measures to cut the numbers of legal abortion on demand there are two points to consider. A legislative proposal can be partial because it addresses only part of the abortion problem, but still itself be totally pro-life. Thus, in June of 1973 the U.S. House of Representatives voted on an amendment prohibiting the federally funded Legal Services Corporation from engaging in abortion litigation. We won. Another partial measure would be to eliminate the tax-exempt status for abortion clinics or public subsidies for them.

But some have suggested that pro-lifers go beyond this type of "partial" measure and be willing openly to propose legislation that contains antilife elements so as to gain the support of more Americans in stopping some abortions. These arguments are usually couched in terms of numbers: "Wouldn't it be better if there were 100,000 abortions rather than the present 1.55 million?" First, for the sake of clarity in thought and expression, we must state that killing 100,000 children is not "better" than killing 1,450,000 children. There are simply fewer murders, all of which are intrinsically evil.

Legislation that seeks or purports to protect children from death by induced abortion must be evaluated by four criteria: (1) Pro-life principles that stipulate that each child in the womb has an inalienable right to life from the Creator that must be recognized and defended by government action, and, (2) recognition of the fact that we live in a society that is in part hostile to such legal protection for the preborn child; (3) the good motives of even honest people are of themselves insufficient to produce just, enforceable laws; and (4) legislative proposals cannot in any way accept the central assumptions of *Roe v. Wade,* but rather must challenge them.

Legislative proposals can violate the above criteria in a number of ways. Laws may deny the personhood and humanity of the preborn child. Laws that assert that certain classes of preborn children can, should, and will receive legal protection from assaults on their life but that others may be killed, in fact accept and embody proabortion premises. Such proposals would include suggested state or federal laws that specify that legal protection shall not extend to certain classes of preborn children, i.e., those children conceived by rape or incest, those allegedly endangering the life or health of the mother, and those with physical or mental disabilities.

Laws may avoid coming to grips with the evil and reality of killing children by abortion. Legislation that would seek to prohibit abortion only where a pregnancy has been verified is of this variety. This has been suggested as a way around the charge that "pro-life legislation" really seeks to outlaw "contraception". However, this basically accepts as valid the linguistic manipulations of pro-abortionists who have redefined the beginning of human life in order to accommodate killing agents misnamed "contraceptives".

Laws may let abortionists redefine abortion. Laws that impose no obligation on doctors toward children that may be in a mother's womb do not seek to prohibit procedures that in fact kill a child. These procedures are euphemisms for killing and are called menstrual extraction, endometrial extraction, or aspiration. They amount to an intent to abort, but without a pregnancy test done to verify a known pregnancy. And requiring that a pregnancy test be done on a woman who expressly seeks an abortion will not protect a baby if in fact the same abortion procedure can be done under the pretext of the doctor's simply helping a woman "bring on her period" up to eleven weeks after a missed menstrual period.

Laws may not clearly state when abortion is outlawed. Such laws would include proposals that allegedly forbid abortion for reasons of birth control, but then fail to define birth control precisely. Would "birth control" mean the reason for not having a child or the means used for not having a child? And would it cover the situation of "birth control failure"? What if a man had a vasectomy or a woman were sterilized and pregnancy still resulted? Since they already had been using birth control, would abortion be allowed for birth control failure?

Laws that fail to challenge *Roe v. Wade* in all essential points still leave room for Supreme Court justices to keep abortion legal. Pre-*Roe*, antiabortion laws nationwide uniformly made abortion a criminal offense. Making abortion only a civil offense thus fails to directly challenge *Roe* on this essential point. While it admittedly has the advantage that it permits a private citizen to initiate a suit, it falls short in that civil remedies can only be imposed against property that may be attached. Making abortion merely a civil wrong and not also a criminal wrong will result in abortionists simply renting or leasing all their "equipment". Judgments against abortion providers will be unenforceable if there is no property in the abortionist's name to confiscate.

Additionally, proposals can sidestep the central legal holding of *Roe* if they fail to challenge the claim that there is a constitutional right to privacy that is broad enough to include a woman's decision to have an elective abortion.

In conclusion, pro-life groups should support only real pro-life proposals to outlaw abortion. Others are not even practical. Abortion proponents will only take comfort that we are arguing on their terms, and the question of killing the innocent child becomes one of permission by degrees, instead of opposition to any kind of killing of the innocent.

Trying to say that an exception-laden bill is a "reasonable" approach to opposing child killing is to condemn automatically any future efforts you support that are different from these "unreasonable" ones. We can expect no help from those who think it is reasonable to kill children at any time. Both prudence and moral principles suggest that:

1. It is better both in the short and the long run to stick to your principles and seek to apply them in a narrow area, rather than to abandon them or even look like you are abandoning them for what you think is a bigger gain in the short run.

2. Do not propose something you do not want, or you will eventually end up either defending it or having to backpedal in public, with all the loss of credibility that entails.

3. If we lose a battle and end up with abortion "compromise" legislation, that is one thing. But it is quite another thing for pro-lifers to offer compromises. One's past words will always be brought forth and measured by current actions. This is what happens when a goal is dropped or even rejected temporarily.
4. Remember when it comes to abortion, backtracking on your principles is both dangerous and deadly, no matter what the reason.
5. Let the politicians propose compromises, not pro-lifers.
6. Remember that the nation's public and private schools have to be recaptured from those who overtly or subtly inculcate the nihilistic message of Planned Parenthood.

Appendix I

Planned Parenthood and the Courts
(How Planned Parenthood Got What It Wanted)

A complete record of Planned Parenthood court cases and legal briefs surrounding the various aspects of contraception and abortion is beyond the scope of this book. However, some of the major cases where Planned Parenthood was a principal or participated as an amicus are outlined below:

Griswold v. Connecticut, June 7, 1965

Estelle Griswold, director of the Planned Parenthood League of Connecticut, along with the league's doctor, were fined $100 each for giving married persons information and advice, and for prescribing contraceptive devices. Griswold claimed that the statute under which they were charged was unconstitutional. An appellate court and the Supreme Court agreed.

The Planned Parenthood brief in the case contended that under the Connecticut statute, residents could limit their families only by "foregoing their marital rights" and that "medical authorities" considered abstinence "an evil". PPFA wondered how "the considered judgment of the medical profession" could have been outweighed by the court in the past. PPFA quoted one of their own, the Pill pioneer John Rock, as a "Catholic layman" who approved of the Pill for Catholics. PPFA also spoke of a "clear national consensus" in favor of family planning and regarded it as "necessary for the protection and preservation of the nation and the world". The PPFA amicus brief claimed, in pure Sangerite fashion, that abstinence is harmful to married couples; prescriptive contraceptives can be restricted to the married; and juvenile delinquency, poverty, unemployment, and other social evils could be alleviated by birth control. Harriet Pilpel would tell *SIECUS Newsletter* readers that the *Griswold* decision was more important for its future impact than for the case at hand.

Eisenstadt v. Baird, March 22, 1972

William Baird was convicted of violating Massachusetts law for exhibiting contraceptives to students at Boston University and for giving an apparently unmarried woman a package of Emko vaginal foam contraceptive at the end of his talk. The Massachusetts Supreme Court set aside the conviction for exhibiting contraceptives but convicted Baird for giving away the foam. The U.S. Supreme Court reversed the decision asserting that unmarried individuals also had a privacy right to birth control.

Planned Parenthood's brief in the case contended that "the right of access to medical services for contraception is a fundamental right", as was, in their view, "the choice as to whether or not to conceive and bear a child". There was "scant basis for assuming that forbidding dissemination of contraceptives for the unmarried will have any impact on the sexual mores of the citizen". Begetting a child could ostensibly be prevented by contraception. Deciding whether to bear a child already conceived clearly meant abortion. *Roe v. Wade,* a decision which would be nine months away, was a mere formality after *Eisenstadt.*

The PPFA brief also claimed that the Massachusetts law struck at the very basis of Planned Parenthood's purpose and that contraceptive availability would have no impact on the sexual mores of citizens. The brief specifically cited *Stanley v. Georgia,* a Supreme Court case that held that a person could have obscene material in the privacy of his or her own home as a basis for a parallel privacy right of the unmarried to use contraceptives.

Pilpel stated that "there is no ground for holding that the interests of Massachusetts in deterring fornication is compelling or even rationally based." So much for her previous contention in *Griswold* that birth control could be limited to married couples.

Roe v. Wade, January 22, 1973

A pregnant single woman ("Roe") challenged the constitutionality of a Texas statute forbidding abortion in all cases except to save the mother's life. The woman in question, Norma McCorvey, an astrology devotee, was not pregnant at the time and had already given birth, but was nevertheless granted standing to sue. She claimed that she had been raped, but much later acknowledged she had not been raped.[1]

The Supreme Court decided seven to two that, for the first trimester, abortion was a matter between a woman and her abortionist. States could regulate second-trimester abortion only in ways that were reasonably related to maternal health.

Justice Blackmun's majority opinion alluded to the *Griswold* case and upheld the "right of privacy" found in the "penumbras of the Bill of Rights". Such a right was "broad enough to encompass a woman's decision whether or not to terminate her pregnancy". Maternity or "additional offspring" could cause "a distressful life and future" or "psychological harm". Mental and physical health may be "taxed by child care".

[1] "Woman behind the Symbols in the Abortion Debate", *New York Times,* May 9, 1989, A18.

The Court need not "resolve the difficult question of when life begins" because "those trained in medicine, philosophy, and theology" were "unable to arrive at any consensus". Hence the judiciary "is not in a position to speculate as to the answer". The decision was "consistent with the relative weights of the respective interests involved and with the demands of the profound problems of the present day".

In his dissent, William Rehnquist noted that the court had found a new "right" that was not apparent to the drafters of the Fourteenth Amendment. He pointed out that the first state law dealing with abortion was enacted in 1821, and that by the time the Fourteenth Amendment had been adopted in 1868, thirty-six states had limited abortion. Framers of the Fourteenth Amendment did not question the validity of these laws.

Harriet Pilpel and Nancy Wechsler prepared a brief for Planned Parenthood that contended that there were "a whole host of reasons" why women might wish to have abortions, including "contraceptive failure". The "right to abortion must be viewed as a corollary of the right to control fertility", which had been recognized in the *Griswold* case. They also argued that the court "should expressly recognize the right of abortion". The differences on the question were "religious and philosophical" and could not be determined "by legislative fiat". Nor was it "constitutionally permissible for the state to adopt the metaphysical belief of some about the nature of the fetus". "The threat posed by population increases" was also cited.

Planned Parenthood v. Fitzpatrick, September 4, 1975

Planned Parenthood of Southern Pennsylvania challenged the Pennsylvania Abortion Control Act, passed over the governor's veto on September 10, 1974. The act provided for written spousal consent prior to an abortion, parental consent for abortions by minors, and a full report of information to spouses and parents. It limited abortions to licensed facilities and defined viability as the capability of an aborted baby to live outside the womb, albeit with artificial aid. Abortion after viability was banned except to save the life of the mother. Fetal remains were to be disposed of in a humane manner. There could be no abortion advertising except in the yellow pages and no state money for abortion except to save the life of the mother.

A three-judge federal court held that the act violated the right to privacy and held the viability statute to be "vague" and "overbroad". Moreover, Pennsylvania could not restrict the abortion subsidy because such a policy would "penalize" women who chose abortion.

T. H. v. Jones, May 24, 1976

Utah health regulations forbade Planned Parenthood from providing minors with birth control services without parental consent. "T. H.", a minor, challenged the law with a class action suit, supposedly on her own.

A federal district court held that the regulation violated the right of privacy of the minor in question and that Utah could not require that parents be notified. Utah's attorney general argued that the purpose of the act was to preserve the family, that no Supreme Court decision ever held that minors had a right to contraception, and that it was irrational to impose legal responsibility for the care of children on parents and then deny those parents control over children's conduct.

The judges, however, found the right of minors to receive contraception in the Social Security Act and also in *Roe v. Wade.*

Planned Parenthood of Central Missouri v. Danforth, July 1, 1976

The Missouri legislature mandated certain restrictions on abortion, similar to those in Pennsylvania, requiring life-sustaining care if the fetus should remain alive after the abortion. In addition, the fetus was not to be used in scientific experiments. Saline abortions were prohibited after the first twelve weeks.

The U.S. Supreme Court upheld the Missouri definition of viability, the informed consent provision, and the record-keeping requirements. It struck down the requirement of spousal consent and parental consent, the prohibition of saline abortions, and the requirement that a physician attempt to sustain the life or prevent the death of a child born alive after abortion.

Carey, Governor of New York et al. v. Population Services International, June 9, 1977

Population Services, along with Planned Parenthood Associates, challenged a law holding that New York state could restrict and/or prohibit the sale of nonprescription contraceptives to certain minors. A district court declared the law unconstitutional in its entirety, citing the "right of decision" upheld in the *Griswold, Eisenstadt,* and *Roe* cases.

Planned Parenthood's brief, submitted by the indefatigable Harriet Pilpel, again cited access to contraceptives as a "fundamental human right". In addition, many teenagers "do not have money enough to see a doctor or may be embarrassed to discuss contraceptives with a doctor or believe the doctor will inform their parents". Moreover, teenagers would be "embarrassed" at being refused contraceptives. Again PPFA found "no evidence" that teenage sexual activity rose in proportion to the availability of contraceptives.

Beal v. Doe, June 20, 1977

This case disputed whether Pennsylvania could, under the Medicaid act, deny assistance for nontherapeutic abortion. The Supreme Court struck down the state law as unconstitutional. Justice Powell wrote in his majority opinion that the restriction "denied respondents equal protection of the laws". Exclusion of nontherapeutic abortions from Medicaid coverage was "unreasonable on both economic and health grounds. The economic argument is grounded on the view that abortion is generally a less expensive medical procedure than childbirth. . . . The corresponding health argument is based on the view that an early abortion poses less of a risk to the woman's health than childbirth." However Powell wrote, "We do not agree that the exclusion of nontherapeutic abortions from Medicaid coverage is unreasonable under Title XIX", but he held that the state was free to provide such coverage if it so desired.

Planned Parenthood's brief took issue with the law, contending that the state's objections to funding were moral, not legal. "There is no physiological or psychological basis", they wrote, "for labeling the medical services attendant to birth more important or necessary than those attendant to abortion." Hence, "any attempt to perpetuate standards for 'medically necessary' abortions which is premised upon this quagmire of subjective and tenuous distinctions between 'medical' and 'nonmedical' decisions is both unwise and impermissible." In a "political system founded on the belief in a marketplace of ideas, in which all views are tolerated, the State may not impose one philosophy to the exclusion of all others on its citizens."

Edward Maher v. Susan Roe, June 20, 1977

Connecticut also acted to restrict abortion funding, and two indigent women who were unable to obtain a doctor's certificate of medical necessity for their abortions filed suit. The Supreme Court ruled that "the Constitution imposes no obligation on the States to pay the pregnancy-related medical expenses of indigents", and that the case "involves no discrimination against a suspect class . . . nor does the fact that the impact of the regulation falls upon those who cannot pay lead to a different conclusion". The court had "never held that financial need alone identifies a suspect class for purposes of equal protection analysis". In conclusion, it was "open to Congress to require provision of Medicaid benefits for such abortions as a condition of state participation in the Medicaid program".

Poelker v. Jane Doe, June 20, 1977

Another indigent sought unsuccessfully to obtain a nontherapeutic abortion in a city-owned hospital in St. Louis, Missouri, and subsequently brought a class action suit against the city. An appeals court ruled for the plaintiff, but the Supreme Court found "no constitutional violation by the City of St. Louis in electing, as a policy of choice, to provide publicly financed hospital services for childbirth without providing corresponding services for nontherapeutic abortions". Accordingly, the high court reversed the lower appeals court ruling.

A Planned Parenthood brief argued that the refusal to fund unnecessary abortions created an "invidious classification" and "discriminated against those women who would choose to have an abortion". They added that "preservation of the human race is not a legitimate ground for denying poor women access to abortions in the first two trimesters of pregnancy". The regulations in question were also held to be "forcing religious judgment on poor women".

Planned Parenthood of Northwest Indiana v. Town of Merrillville, Indiana, April 2, 1978

PPFA filed suit against the allegedly arbitrary and capricious efforts of Merrillville to prevent the construction and operation of an abortion clinic in the town. PPFA had spent over $60,000, and the court ruled that "the economic interests of this plaintiff" were "sufficient to confer standing in this action". The court ruled in favor of Planned Parenthood, adding that the town or third parties would not suffer substantial harm.

Bellotti v. Baird, July 2, 1979

Massachusetts had placed a parental consent restriction on unmarried women under eighteen who sought abortion. The restriction had been passed over the governor's veto. Writing for the high Court, Justice Powell recognized that "there are many competing theories about the most effective way for parents to fulfill their central role in assisting their children on the way to responsible adulthood". Indeed, "constitutional interpretation has consistently recognized that the parents' claim to authority in their own household to direct the rearing of their children is basic in the structure of our society."

But the question before the court was "a constitutional right to seek an abortion", and this decision "differs in important ways from other decisions that may be made during minority". The court concluded that "if the state decides to require a pregnant minor to obtain one or both parents' consent to an abortion, it also must provide an alternative procedure whereby authorization for the abortion can be obtained". The high court upheld the invalidation of the statute by a lower court. However, on February 9, 1981, the U.S. Court of Appeals decided that a twenty-four-hour waiting period and a different parental consent provision were both constitutional.

Planned Parenthood's brief stated that "the adolescent with an unwanted pregnancy is in an extremely difficult and emotionally charged situation". Parents who "cannot accept abortion as a method of terminating an unwanted pregnancy react to their daughter's condition in despair, disappointment, and even bitterness". Hence "in such circumstances, to compel a young woman to attempt to obtain the consent of parents who are nonsupportive or hostile to her own interests or needs will only further traumatize a person already upset by her pregnancy".

In any case, "the law already assures that every pregnant girl will have the guidance of her physician. Obviously these physicians can and will encourage parental involvement in those cases where they believe it will be in the girl's best interest." Unnamed "studies" had "documented the severe burden placed on adolescents who choose to keep their babies". PPFA observed that Massachusetts "has no law requiring parental consent or even prenatal consultation for medical services for a minor who chooses to carry her pregnancy to term". Therefore, "surely, if parental involvement is not required before a minor can obtain medical services in the more hazardous situation of carrying a pregnancy to term, it cannot be required for the less hazardous procedure of abortion."

Harris v. McRae, June 30, 1980

In this case the Supreme Court set out to decide whether the United States Congress could prohibit appropriation of Medicaid money for certain specified abortions. Justice Stewart, writing for the Court, noted that since September 1976, Congress had prohibited the use of any federal funds to reimburse the cost of abortions under the Medicaid program. This funding restriction was known as the "Hyde Amendment" after its sponsor, Representative Henry Hyde.

A district court had invalidated all versions of the Hyde Amendment on constitutional grounds. Ronald Reagan, then a presidential candidate, stated on February 21, 1980, that the court had permitted a single judge (John Dooling of New York) to "temporarily take away from Congress its exclusive authority over the expenditure of our tax dollars". Hence, according to Stewart, the controversy was no longer entirely about abortion but "whether the American people can hope to have any control over their government's expenditures".

Judge Dooling's decision was "astounding for its sweep, gratuitous assumptions, lack of clarity and logic, and claims of judicial power under the U.S. Constitution". Dooling had asserted that, with respect to abortion, the courts, not Congress, had power over the treasury because "poverty is a medical condition". He had also stated that abortion "is an exercise of the most fundamental of rights . . . her right to be . . . allied to the Fifth Amendment" and "in conformity with religious belief and teaching protected by the First Amendment".

The Hyde Amendment was upheld. It was "not the mission of this court or any other", Stewart said, "to decide whether the balance of competing interests reflected in the Hyde Amendment is wise social policy".

Planned Parenthood banded together with such organizations as the Gay Political Caucus, the International Socialist Organization, the National Council of Churches, the National Gay Task Force, the National Lawyers' Guild, the Workers' World Party, Youth against War and Fascism, and many other groups in an unsuccessful attempt to overturn the decision.

Williams and Diamond v. Zbaraz, June 30, 1980

Justice Stewart also delivered the opinion on whether the state of Illinois must pay for abortions other than those necessary to preserve a woman's life. Stewart reminded the parties that a district court had exceeded its jurisdiction in declaring the Hyde Amendment unconstitutional and concluded that Illinois was not obligated to pay for the abortions in question.

A Planned Parenthood brief contended that the Illinois statute conflicted with Title XIX of the Social Security Act and that the decision as to whether the abortion was medically necessary should be left entirely to the patient's physician.

Planned Parenthood of Minnesota v. the State of Minnesota, 1980

In 1979 a section of the Minnesota Family Planning Grants Act appropriated $1,300,000 for use as grants to cities, counties, or nonprofit corporations to provide birth control services. However, all nonprofit corporations that perform abortions were excluded. Federal judge Donald Alsop held that this restriction violated the equal protection clause of the Fourteenth Amendment, and the U.S. Court of Appeals agreed. They rejected the argument that giving the grant money to Planned Parenthood would free other money for abortion.

H. L. v. Matheson, Governor of Utah, March 23, 1981

"H. L.", a pregnant unmarried girl, challenged a Utah statute requiring a physician to notify parents or guardian if such a person sought an abortion. The Utah Supreme Court upheld the statute, as did the U.S. Supreme Court, by a six to three decision. Chief Justice Burger, writing for the court, said the fact that "the requirement of notice to parents may inhibit some minors from seeking abortions is not a valid basis to void the statute".

Planned Parenthood's brief had contended that the notification statute would "interfere" with abortion decisions and violate the patient-doctor relationship, which they held more sacred than the parent-child relationship. If parents were notified, "they may react in keeping with their own beliefs or prejudices, and not in their daughter's best interest". Thus the minor would be faced with the horror of being "influenced by the attitudes she encounters among her family".

Planned Parenthood Association, Chicago v. William Kempiners, Illinois Department of Public Health, December 7, 1981

Planned Parenthood brought action against the Illinois Department of Public Health statutes denying grant money to organizations that offered abortion counseling after pregnancy tests. Planned Parenthood contended that the denial "interferes with the rights of women". District Court Judge Marshall agreed, and contended that the statute violated free speech and interfered with doctor-patient relationships. The state "may not manipulate the woman's decision to have an abortion or limit her ability to make that decision knowledgeably".

City of Akron v. Akron Center for Reproductive Health, June 15, 1983

In February 1978, the Akron City Council passed an abortion ordinance providing that all first-trimester abortions be performed in a hospital. In the case of a minor, parental notification was necessary, and the attending physician would personally convey information about fetal anatomy in order to insure "informed" consent. A twenty-four-hour waiting period was also required, and fetal remains were to be disposed of in a humane and sanitary manner. Three corporations that operated abortion clinics filed suit.

In August 1979, the district court invalidated the parental notice, disclosure, and disposal of remains provisions, but upheld the others. The Sixth Circuit Court of Appeals upheld some parts of the decision and reversed other parts. The Supreme Court reversed the appellate ruling that upheld Akron's hospitalization requirement, but affirmed the invalidation of parental consent, informed consent, waiting period, and disposal of remains. The high Court also ruled that the word *humane* was "impermissibly vague".

The Planned Parenthood brief opposed the idea that the doctor be required to provide a detailed description of fetal anatomy. They pleaded for this enforced ignorance because "many patients may simply not want to hear this information prior to receiving an abortion". The right to speak freely "necessarily encompasses a right to refrain from speaking at all". By requiring doctors to provide information that, in their opinion, trained counselors could just as easily furnish, the statute was "raising the cost of abortions". And legal abortion was "the only safe means of terminating a pregnancy. To force a woman to choose between a legal abortion and an offensive state lecture is to violate both First and Fourteenth Amendment rights."

Planned Parenthood of Kansas City, Missouri et al. v. John Ashcroft, Attorney General of Missouri et al., June 15, 1983

PPFA of Kansas City challenged several sections of a Missouri statute: the requirements that abortions be performed in hospitals, that pathology reports be required for each abortion, that a second physician be present during abortions performed after viability, and that parental approval be secured in the case of minors. The Court ruled that the required second-trimester hospitalization provision was unconstitutional, but upheld the pathology reports, second doctor, and parental consent provisions.

Bolger et al. v. Youngs Drug Products Corp., June 24, 1983

A lower court had ruled that a prohibition of the mailing of unsolicited ads for contraceptives was unconstitutional. The Supreme Court agreed. Writing for the Court, Justice Thurgood Marshall noted that the restriction "is more extensive than the Constitution permits", and that "the level of discourse reaching a mailbox simply cannot be limited to that which would be suitable for a sandbox".

In a contrary opinion, Justice Rehnquist noted that Youngs could obtain permission to send its ads by conducting a "premailing". Planned Parenthood's brief contended that the material in question relates to the "fundamental right of all persons to decide whether to beget and bear children". The statute reflected "out-dated moralistic presumptions of what is suitable to travel through the United States mail" and would keep Americans from overcoming their "public ignorance concerning contraception". The problem was "self-evident—many Americans are ignorant of the availability of safe and effective contraceptive methods." This was one of the last vestiges of domestic legislation from the original Comstock law still in the U.S. statute books.

Planned Parenthood Federation of America v. Margaret M. Heckler, U.S. Department of Health and Human Services, July 8, 1983

At issue in this case was the validity of Health and Human Services regulations requiring all providers of family planning services that receive funds under Title X to notify parents of contraceptive services to minors, comply with state laws requiring parental notice, and "to consider minors who wish to receive services on the basis of their parents' financial resources, rather than their own". An appeals court upheld the ruling of a lower court that the parental notification requirement was invalid, as was the provision that the services be based on parents' income. The regulation "operates as a deterrent to teenage access to contraceptive services, thereby undermining Title X's goal of reducing the teenage pregnancy rate."

Webster v. Reproductive Health Services, July 3, 1989

In 1986 Missouri enacted a law regulating abortion and for other purposes. The statute provided that every abortion done at sixteen weeks of gestation or later must be performed in a hospital; that a doctor must determine whether the preborn child is viable (according to age, weight, and lung maturity) before performing the abortion on any woman whom the doctor believes is twenty or more weeks pregnant; no public funds, employees, or facilities could be used for "encouraging or counseling" a woman to have an abortion not needed to save her life.

The Court, in a plurality decision held that states could withhold public funding and the use of public facilities for abortion; the counseling section was moot because Reproductive Health Services could not claim it had been injured by the law, and so the constitutionality was not decided, and because the law was directed not at physicians, but at those officials responsible for disbursing public funds; Missouri could require tests for determining viability; the law's preamble, which stated that human life began at conception and that the laws of the state should be decided with protection of that life in mind, was not struck down because it was merely declaratory with no specific effect.

For the Record

As noted, this is not an exhaustive treatment of the legal efforts of Planned Parenthood. However, it shows the pattern of PPFA advocacy, from contraception to abortion on demand, along with the casuistry the organization employs. Clearly, Planned Parenthood has been the inspiration for much of the judicial activism along these lines of the past two decades.

Remarkable throughout the record is the judiciary's uncritical acceptance of PPFA's thoroughly bogus scientific and sociological assumptions, along with a reluctance to entertain any contrary opinions. Remarkable as well is *PPFA v. Merrillville,* in which the court avoided the merits of the case and cited PPFA's financial investment as sufficient to decide the matter at hand. Indeed, it is difficult to think of any corporation or special interest group in America whose interests and agenda have been so lavishly indulged by the courts and financed by public funds. Whatever this may be called, it is certainly not justice.

Judicial Origins of
the Privacy Right to Abortion

The *Roe v. Wade* decision did not state that a woman had a right to an abortion per se. Rather, the decision noted:

> The Constitution does not explicitly mention any right of privacy. . . . however . . . the Court has recognized that a right of personal privacy . . . does exist under the Constitution. . . .
> This right of privacy, whether it be founded in the Fourteenth Amendment's concept of personal liberty and restrictions upon state action, as we feel it is, or . . . in the Ninth Amendment's reservation of rights to the people, is broad enough to encompass a woman's decision whether or not to terminate her pregnancy.

Justice Rehnquist noted in his dissent that the Court found in the Fourteenth Amendment "a right that apparently was completely unknown to the drafters of that Amendment" in 1868 when thirty-six states and/or territories had antiabortion statutes. Where, then, did this privacy right come from?

The "fundamental" right to privacy, which the Court ostensibly found in the Constitution, is surely one of the more curious constitutional rights. For example, it is the only constitutional right that must be secured by a licensed physician in good standing (*Connecticut v. Menillo*, 423 U.S. 9 [1975]). The justices declined to point to any congressional debates on amendments or notes from delegates to the Philadelphia Constitutional Convention supporting their contention. The Court in *Roe* and *Menillo* did not rule on the alleged privacy right of a woman to abort herself. So it can be said that, in fact, what the Court did create through its own self-conferred legislative powers was not a privacy right of abortion for the pregnant woman, but a right immunizing licensed physicians against state prosecution for aborting women.

Moreover, the cases the Court cites in support of the privacy right proclaimed earlier in *Griswold v. Connecticut* (1965) asserted no such privacy right, but rather reached their decisions on other grounds. For example, in *Skinner v. Oklahoma* (316 U.S. 535 [1942]) no privacy right to procreate was asserted as the reason for striking down the Oklahoma statute providing for the compulsory sterilization of habitual criminals. Rather, Justice Douglas simply noted that while the law did apply its punishment to all persons convicted of larceny, habitual embezzlers were not sterilized even though the nature of the crimes was intrinsically the same. Indeed, far from asserting a right to procreate in *Skinner*, Justice Douglas made a favorable reference to *Buck v. Bell* (274 U.S. 200), upholding the Virginia statute providing for the compulsory sterilization of "feeble-minded" persons in institutions.

This silence is all the more telling against the privacy right because *Skinner* was written by the same Justice Douglas who also authored the *Griswold* decision creating the right to privacy. In any case, not only was this privacy claim novel, it contradicted the Supreme Court's earlier denial of a "privacy right" in *Prudential Insurance Co. v. Cheek* (259 U.S. 530 [1922]). In a case involving the validity of service letter contract laws, the Court noted "But, as we have stated, neither the 14th Amendment nor any other provision of the Constitution of the United States imposes upon the states any restrictions about 'freedom of speech' or the 'liberty of silence'; nor, we may add, does it confer any right of privacy upon either persons or corporations."

This course of judicial activism has not been without its critics. For example, Corwin and Peltason wrote that:

> The justices have not been too clear on what makes a right fundamental, but they have explained that it is not whether it is considered important. The rights to education, to shelter, and to food are basic, but in a constitutional sense they are not fundamental rights because they are not rights that the Constitution "explicitly or implicitly" guarantees. . . . Apparently, for example, the right to an abortion is fundamental because it is part of the right of privacy protected by the Constitution; however, the right to education is not fundamental, a distinction that some find difficult to draw [pages 200–10].

> And, while the Supreme Court has recognized that the Ninth Amendment

> protects the right to engage in political activity against unreasonable national regulation, until 1965 no law had been declared unconstitutional because of disparagement of any of these unenumerated rights, nor had there been a suggestion that this amendment limited the powers of the states. Then, the Court ruled that a Connecticut law forbidding the use of contraceptives violated the right of marital privacy and stated that this right is "within the penumbra of specific guarantees of the Bill of Rights" and is one of the fundamental rights reserved by the Ninth Amendment to the people against disparagement by a state or national government.

Corwin and Peltason cite the *Roe v. Wade* case as the best (really, the worst) modern example of a substantive due process approach, noting that "For some time the Court has been applying substantive due process but has been reluctant to admit that it has been doing so" (page 174). (Edward S. Corwin and Jack W. Peltason, *Corwin and Peltason's Understanding the Constitution,* 8th ed. [New York: Holt, Rinehart, and Winston, 1949, 1979].)

And, although the Court, in its privacy decisions, has tried to peg the privacy right to earlier Supreme Court cases, the effort is not supported by either the history of the Constitution or the Court. For example, the standard college-level history of the Constitution just prior to *Griswold* was that of Alfred H. Kelly and Winefred A. Harbison, *The American Constitution,* 3d ed. (New York: W. W. Norton and Co., Inc., 1948, 1955, 1963). And even the most recent revision of this book, written at a time when one would suppose an awareness of fundamental rights, at least among jurists or scholars, finds no express or implied right of privacy anywhere in the Constitution, or any of the Amendments, prior to the *Griswold* decision.

The closest the U.S. Constitution comes to asserting the particulars of what some hold to be derived from a general right to privacy, but without asserting such, is the Fourth Amendment to the Constitution, which states that "the right of the people to be secure in their persons, houses, papers, and effects shall not be violated; and no Warrants shall issue but upon probable cause, supported by Oath or affirmation, and particularly describing the place to be searched, and the persons or things to be seized".

The consistent and traditional judicial interpretation of this amendment had never proclaimed the existence of a separate privacy right apart from specific guarantees against compulsory self-incrimination, or against unreasonable search and seizure by government officials (*Boyd v. United States,* 116 U.S. 616 [1885]; *Wolf v. Colorado,* 338 U.S. 25 [1949]). And Chief Justice Taft, in the prohibition era, even narrowed the application of the Fourth Amendment, in a case which held that incriminating evidence obtained through telephone tapping was admissible evidence (*Olmstead v. United States,* 277 U.S. 438 [1927]).

This amendment grew out of the experience of American colonists' opposition to the use of the British "writs of assistance" that English colonial authorities relied upon in the course of enforcing revenue laws. They were "general warrants authorizing the bearer to enter any house or other place to search for and seize 'prohibited and unaccustomed' goods and commanded all ubjects to assist in these endeavors. The writs once issued remained in force throughout the lifetime of the sovereign and six months thereafter."

With respect to heterosexual relationships, the evolving Court-created privacy right would later surface in a March 22, 1972, decision authored by Justice Brennan. There, in *Eisenstadt v. Baird,* the Court reversed a Massachusetts conviction of William Baird, later an abortion clinic owner, for exhibiting contraceptives and giving an unmarried girl a package of spermicide. Brennan wrote that:

> It is true in *Griswold* the right of privacy in question inhered in the marital relationship. Yet the married couple is not an independent entity with a mind and heart of its own, but an association of two individuals each with a separate intellectual and emotional makeup. If the right of privacy means anything, it is the right of the individual, married or single, to be free from unwarranted governmental intrusion into matters so fundamentally affecting a person as the decision whether to bear or beget a child.

Refusal to bear or carry a child already conceived, of course, meant abortion, as the Court would spell out only ten months later in *Roe v. Wade.*

What limits there might be to a so-called right of privacy that includes the right to kill a preborn child are hard to imagine. For example, in the brief of the Planned Parenthood Federation of America and their Massachusetts affiliate filed in *Eisenstadt v. Baird,* Harriet Pilpel and Nancy Wechsler argued that:

> In *Stanley vs. Georgia,* 394 U.S. 557 (1969), this Court, in holding that a state law that punished the "mere private possession of obscene matter" violated the First and Fourteenth Amendments, explicitly recognized as fundamental "the right to be free, except in very limited circumstances from unwarranted governmental intrusions into one's privacy" (394 U.S. at 564). The Court emphasized that the rights asserted in *Stanley* were the individual's "right to read or observe what he pleases—the right to satisfy his intellectual and emotional needs in the privacy of his own home".

An even more interesting application of the privacy right was the 1986 claim of homosexual activists arising out of a Georgia law prohibiting homosexual sodomy (*Bowers v. Hardwick,* 1065 S.Ct. 2841). Though ultimately rejected, the privacy right was raised there as including consensual sodomy and was supported by four of nine members of the Supreme Court.

It must be asked what limits, if any, privacy-right proponents are willing to accept. Does it include the "right" to use "recreational drugs" in one's home—if so, which ones? Does it include voluntary or possibly assisted suicide for those unable to kill themselves efficiently? Does it include consensual sadomaschism? Does it include the right to destroy a perfectly healthy bodily organ for personal monetary gain? (Recall that voluntary sterilization usually does just this, though for antifertility purposes.) Does it include consensual homosexual acts—if so, what is the age of consent? Does it include consensual heterosexual contraceptive intercourse by the unmarried—if so, why not abolish the statutory rape laws? Does it include the right of someone to withhold information about his health status, such as having AIDS or veneral disease, from a sexual associate? Does it include the right of physicians to withhold information from the sexual associates of AIDS-positive patients?

These "hard questions" have to be asked of constitutional right-to-privacy proponents. For too long they have had a free ride.

Appendix III

Planned Parenthood Abortion Workshop— Business Principles inside the Killing Center

A "health clinic" that kills 50% of its patients at the request of the other 50% reduces to absurdity the profession and practice of medicine. But in a permissive, hedonist, neglectful society, the fondness—indeed, the need for—euphemisms designates these killing centers as "family planning" clinics.

Planned Parenthood affiliates sell abortions to women through the eighteenth week from the last normal period by dilation and evacuation.[1] But selling abortions to women is, of course, a business, whether or not the abortion provider is a designated not-for-profit, tax-deductible charity such as Planned Parenthood. At a New York City Planned Parenthood abortion seminar showing how to set up additional killing centers (i.e., family planning clinics), newcomers were given presentations from operatives at Planned Parenthood's free-standing franchise operations.

Potential entrepreneurs were told that if they had a large clientele they would " . . . be taking in a large, large volume of cold, hard cash"—and that the money would have to be dealt with sensibly.[2] This, of course, meant efficiency of operation. Abortion could lower the costs of contraceptive services and keep the doors open and business coming seventy hours a week, not just thirty or forty, because fixed costs would be absorbed. Thus, instead of contraceptive services having to be used to pay the rent, electricity, etc., abortion would take up the slack.[3] But in order to achieve this happy economic condition, Planned Parenthood's staff suggested that the contraceptive caseload not exceed one-third of the total volume of customers. The rest could be referred elsewhere.[4] Other factors could affect clinic income, such as market fluctuations in the demand for abortion, and additional expenses could cause clinic income to fluctuate greatly, sub-

[1] *PPFA Medical Standards and Guidelines, Abortion Services in Planned Parenthood Affiliates,* pt 1, S&G, sec. 7-A, Abortion, December 15, 1977, 3.
[2] *Workbook of the First National Affiliate Workshop of Planning and Providing Abortion Services,* a conference held in September 1972, prepared by PPWP and PPNYC, Foreword by Susan Dickler, director, National Pregnancy and Abortion Services, Jerim Klaper, PPNYC, April 1973, "Digest of Presentation by Planned Parenthood Staff": NYC-7.
[3] Ibid., NYC-3.
[4] Ibid., NYC-11.

ject to the clinic's "visibility" and the arrangements "with the referral agencies".[5]

Costs could be kept down in several ways. For example, before the "doctor" kills his first fetus of the day, he scrubs for five minutes. Between slayings, only one minute is needed. "Cap, mask and shoe covers are optional."[6] Secondly, when PPNYC first opened its reproductive "choice" center (choices that terminate reproduction), sterile draping packs were used for each patient, as were sterile caps, gowns, masks, and shoe covers. However, it was then believed that "clean" techniques were needed and not "sterile" ones in order to satisfy Planned Parenthood's standards.[7]

Prospective abortion-shop owners were urged to undertake a feasibility study and market analysis: "What volume are you going to shoot for?"[8] Population-control investors were told that some initial capital plant investment was necessary for PPNYC to operate. But success in the child-killing business can bring its own problems. For example, because of the large patient volume at one PPNYC abortuary, the plumbing system became overloaded and had to be upgraded: "garbage accumulated in enormous quantities in the course of the day and its storage presented serious space problems." A heavy duty trash compactor was bought at a cost of $2,400.00 to solve the problem.[9]

Of course, advertising is absolutely essential to market outreach. PPNYC had the blessing of public officials who even did ads for them. A thirty-second TV spot, produced by PPNYC and aired during 1970, featured Shirle Mayer, M.D., assistant commissioner for Maternal and Child Health Services, New York City Health Services Administration. She was filmed at her desk saying:

> New York State law now permits abortion. The decision about having an abortion can be made only by the woman and the doctor who performs it. Abortions done under proper medical conditions are safe.... For information about abortion, call the Family Planning Information Service ... [FPIS phone number].[10]

Naturally, the Family Planning Information Service was run by PPNYC on behalf of New York City, whose public officials perhaps thought they

[5] Ibid., NYC-8.

[6] Ibid., Planned Parenthood of New York City, Inc., "Guidelines for Abortion Services", March 1973, A/G 16.

[7] Ibid., "Checklist of Equipment, Furnishings, Instruments, and Supplies for an Abortion Service", E-1.

[8] Ibid., NYC-6

[9] Ibid., "Checklist", E-8.

[10] Ibid., R/TV 1.

were lowering the welfare caseload.[11] Subway placards were also produced for targeted females in English and Spanish.[12]

And smart businessmen know that proper scheduling is essential to efficient workflow. Thus, counselors were told at the first phone interview that it must be decided whether to schedule the caller as a one-stop customer (pregnancy test, medical exam, and abortion) or a two-stop procedure (pregnancy test, medical exam, and abortion done later).[13]

Hassling abortion clients about not using birth control was explained as a tactless, unacceptable, and counterproductive customer-relations practice. One staffer suggested another reason for avoiding criticism for not using birth control or using it improperly " . . . in the long run, it's politically hazardous."[14]

Though it hardly needed to be mentioned at the seminar, it was dutifully pointed out that "[t]he cashier's desk is the last stop for the patient before she leaves the center."[15] Patients are urged, management suggested, to bring a certified check, traveler's checks, or money order. Medicaid patients were served if they presented their Medicaid cards.[16]

Planned Parenthood's Board and Public Affairs and other staff worked closely with New York City's Health Services Administration and the Department of Health to ensure that the abortion centers would run smoothly when they opened on July 1, 1970.[17] Assessing the liberating effect this new era of discretionary fetal killing had on Americans, Planned Parenthood's Alfred Moran and Marcia Lawrence said, "We believe New York's present abortion law, far from promoting indifference to life, is doing just the opposite".[18] Perhaps the reader has already guessed that the joint statement was designated "Abortion: An Appeal to Reason".

[11] Ibid., S/B 2.

[12] Ibid., S/B 1–2.

[13] Ibid., A/G 8.

[14] Ibid., NYC-4.

[15] Ibid., NYC-13.

[16] Planned Parenthood of New York City, Inc., *Guidelines*, A/G 7.

[17] Ibid., NYC-15.

[18] Alfred Moran and Marcia Lawrence, in consultation with staff of PPNYC, "Abortion: An Appeal to Reason", draft discussion paper, prepared January 1973, unpublished because of U.S. Supreme Court decision, AR-6.

Acknowledgments

The authors are indebted to many people for contributions to the completion of this book. To staff members at the Library of Congress for assistance in locating and using materials, particularly in the Margaret Sanger Collection. To Susan Boone, Curator, and Margaret Sly, Archivist for Records, Sophie Smith Collection, Smith College, Northampton, Mass., for assistance in locating materials and obtaining permissions for citation of materials from the Margaret Sanger and Planned Parenthood Federation of America papers at Smith. To Richard J. Wolfe, Curator of Rare Books and Manuscripts, Francis A. Countway Library of Medicine, Boston, Massachusetts, for assistance in locating materials and permission to cite materials in the Alan F. Guttmacher papers at the Countway Library. To Alexander C. Sanger and the Planned Parenthood Federation of America for permission to cite to and quote from materials in the Sophie Smith Collection.

We also express our appreciation to teachers, colleagues and friends who have taken care to provide comments, support, and suggestions in connection with the manuscript, and to countless others whose reading, collected materials, and collective wisdom have helped to shape this work and steer it to safe harbor. A special note of thanks to Sharon Latherow for assistance in preparing an early typescript of this book.

Our gratitude, above all, to our families, and our beloved wives, Cathy Marshall and Peggy Donovan, for their encouragement and patience in a project that spanned many years of moonlighting and day labor. Without your enduring faith, here as everywhere, "work in progress" might still describe these pages.

We dedicate this work to our Lord and Savior, Jesus Christ, who watches over His children always, when the wood is green as well as when it is dry.

Robert G. Marshall
Charles A. Donovan
July 29, 1991

Index

351